Praise for Alfred S. Regnery and
UPSTREAM:
THE ASCENDANCE OF AMERICAN CONSERVATISM

"Splendid. . . . Reading *Upstream* is like sailing through the Greek Islands on a luxurious private yacht—you don't want it to end. The uplifting story of American conservatism's rise to prominence is recounted in one smoothly written, meticulously researched book. . . . *Upstream* is bracing reading, a tonic for downcast conservatives who need to cast off old-man pessimism, reflect on conservatism's remarkable accomplishments of the last 50 years, and realize—borrowing from Barry Goldwater—that saying conservatism is out of date is like saying that the Ten Commandments and the Constitution are out of date."

—Human Events.com

"A vast *tour d'horizon* that . . . manages to collapse a huge number of insights and fresh information into a single, comprehensive volume."

—*The American Spectator*

"*Upstream*, in essence, is a Baedeker guide to the men and ideas behind conservatism."

—*The Washington Times*

"A finely wrought history of American conservatism. . . . Many fascinating and insightful vignettes. . . . *Upstream* reminds us that the advance of conservatism was a personal achievement of visionary men and women who, swimming against the tide, refused to accept the conventional wisdom that their principles were doomed to extinction. . . . A surprising tale, filled with improbable events and eccentric figures, and one faultlessly told in *Upstream*."

—Newcriterion.com

UPSTREAM

The Ascendance of American Conservatism

ALFRED S. REGNERY

THRESHOLD
EDITIONS

NEW YORK   LONDON   TORONTO   SYDNEY

THRESHOLD EDITIONS
A Division of Simon & Schuster, Inc.
1230 Avenue of the Americas
New York, NY 10020

First Threshold Editions trade paperback edition January 2009

THRESHOLD EDITIONS and colophon are trademarks of Simon & Schuster, Inc.

For information about special discounts for bulk purchases, please contact Simon & Schuster Special Sales at 1-800-456-6798 or business@simonandschuster.com.

Designed by Carla Jayne Little

Manufactured in the United States of America

10   9   8   7   6   5   4   3   2   1

ISBN-13: 978-1-4165-2288-1
ISBN-10:   1-4165-2288-3
ISBN-13: 978-1-4165-2289-8 (pbk)
ISBN-10:   1-4165-2289-1 (pbk)

To my father, Henry Regnery,
who was one of the founders

ACKNOWLEDGMENTS

Although I have been part of the conservative movement for most of my life, and although I have known many of the players, I found, as I began to write this book, that there was a great deal that I did not know. To educate myself I spoke with many people, all of whom were enormously helpful. I have many people to thank.

First and foremost, Trish Bozell, who edited many books for me when I ran Regnery Publishing, edited each chapter, provided many suggestions, and was an invaluable resource. I could not have written the book without her, and am greatly indebted to her. Bracy Bersnak, my researcher, was at my side constantly, dug out all sorts of little-known and hard-to-find information, and questioned me about facts, assertions, and conclusions constantly. I cannot thank him enough for his efforts and good counsel. Also particular thanks to my literary agent and good friend Alexander Hoyt, who was a constant source of encouragement and good cheer, and to Mary Matalin, who recognized the wisdom of what I had to say and convinced her colleagues at Simon & Schuster that they should be my publisher.

I did extensive interviews with many of the old players, and some of the new ones, in the movement. Among others, Judge Robert Bork, who knows the federal courts and the issues surrounding them as well as anybody, was very helpful, and I thank him profusely. Pat Buchanan served in both the Nixon and Reagan White Houses and ran a couple of his own campaigns, and was a great resource on questions of politics. Bill Buckley, who is as responsible as anybody for the subject matter of the book, deserves special thanks, not only for all he has done for conservatism, but for giving me a great deal of time and clarifying many issues for me. I discussed many ideas and issues with my old friend Angelo Codevilla, particularly concerning foreign and national security affairs. Thanks for your help, Angelo. Attorney Chuck Cooper, with whom I served in the Reagan Justice Department, gave me much sage advice about the courts, the law, and about the Roberts and Alito nominations, and what they will mean to the future of the Supreme Court. My good friend T. Kenneth Cribb, president of the Intercollegiate Studies Institute, read the manuscript, made many suggestions, and was on overall inspiration to me. Midge Decter, one of the original neocons, was helpful in explaining what motivated her side of the movement and how she moved from neocon to regular con. Lee Edwards, the unofficial historian of the movement and a stalwart at the Heritage Foundation, read the manuscript and offered many pointers and suggestions, as did both Stan Evans and John Fund; among the three of them, there are few things concerning the American right that they do not know, and I thank them heartily. I was privileged to have a long interview with the late Milton Friedman, one of the godfathers of free market economics, and a crucial ingredient in libertarian thinking. I also offer special thanks to former Speaker of the House Newt Gingrich, Judge Doug Ginsberg of the U.S. Court of Appeals, White House aide Tim Goeglein, former Energy Secretary Don Hodel, former Reagan OMB official Mike Horowitz, John von Kannon of the Heritage Foundation, and American Conservative Union president Dave Keene, all of whom went out of their way to be helpful and generously gave me the time I needed to extract wisdom from them. Paul Laxalt, my old boss in the Senate, provided many colorful and amusing stories about his great friend Ronald Reagan, for which I thank him. Leonard Leo, Gene Meyer, and David McIntosh from the Federalist Society were all enormously helpful explaining the great changes that have occurred in the law schools, the courts, and the legal profession. Former Attorney General Ed Meese, for whom I worked in the Reagan Administration, was a constant source of information and clarified many issues for me, for which I thank him. Congressman Mike Pence of Indiana, who is one of the conservative leaders in the House of Representatives, provided many insights into the current political situation. I thank him as well. I am grateful to Tony Perkins, President of the Family Research Council, who explained the intricacies of the Evangelical movement and its role in national politics. Dan Peterson, who formerly worked for the Center for Judicial Studies, was a great help discussing the earliest attempts to reform the courts. Steve Presser, professor of law at Northwestern, read and commented on Chapter 9, for which he deserves much gratitude. Ron Robinson of the Young America's Foundation was helpful, especially in discussing the contribution made by young conservatives. Bill Rusher, Phyllis Schlafly, Richard Viguerie, and Paul Weyrich all graciously gave me valuable time, advice, and anecdotes; all have been part of the conservative movement from the beginning; their help is much appreciated.

I want to thank Daryl Hart of the Intercollegiate Studies Institute, who helped me with Chapter 13, and John Miller of *National Review* for his help on Chapter 12. Father C. J. McCloskey, my favorite priest, and my godfather, Michael Novak, were both helpful in many regards, and encouraged me on many occasions, and I am grateful to both. My dear friend Audrey Garrett encouraged me at every turn, for which I offer many thanks. I also want to thank Anne Harrell, who transcribed hundreds of pages of interviews; Theresa Stonelake for many hours of tediously entering corrections into the manuscript; and the many, many others, too numerous to mention here, to whom I turned to for help or questions.

Writing books becomes consuming. When I published books, I agonized with many an author, but never realized just how consuming the writing process really was until I got deeply into this one. I neglected many things and many people in the process, particularly my late wife, Christina, and my children, George, Louise, Fred, and Charles. I thank them all for their patience and understanding.

CONTENTS

PREFACE

Not long after Ronald Reagan moved into the White House, in early 1981, David Keene, a well-connected and knowledge-able Washington conservative, received a call from Prescott Bush, the vice president's older brother, who was thinking of challenging Connecticut's liberal Republican senator, Lowell Weicker, in the 1982 Senate primary. Bush was looking for some political advice. "You know," Bush remarked, "we conservatives need to stick together."

"Press," Keene responded, "you're not a conservative, you've never been a conservative, and you never will be a conservative. You want advice on how to deal with Weicker, that's fine, but let's not delude ourselves by thinking you are something you are not." To which the vice president's brother said, "you don't understand, Dave. Ronald Reagan was elected president. We're all conservatives now."

Thirty years earlier, in 1952, when Prescott Bush, Sr., was elected to the Senate seat that his son was now eyeing, nobody claimed that "we're all conservatives now." In truth, few people would admit to being conservatives at all, and those who did were thought to have lost their minds.

The conventional wisdom in the days following World War II was, in a word, liberalism. Central planning and big government had ended the Great Depression and won the war, and with peace at hand, with its fascist enemies annihilated and its postwar economy booming, the United States dominated the world in almost every respect. The power brokers, the wise men, and most of the opinion-makers saw no reason why the growth of government and a planned economy should not continue, why liberal social policies should not be pursued. The allied countries had banded together after the war to form the United Nations, which would serve as the foundation for a new foreign policy. The Soviet Union, our great wartime ally did, to be sure, present some problems, but the United States could contain Communism within Soviet borders so as to cause few problems to the West.

But if liberalism was the conventional wisdom, many ordinary Americans were nevertheless conservatives, although few called themselves such. They had no organizations, they had no networks, they had no voice, and they had no power. The press, the intelligentsia, the publishing companies, the universities, and virtually all parts of the culture that disseminated ideas and beliefs were left of center and rarely aired anything but that which they believed. Conservative ideas, meanwhile—the principles on which the country had been founded, the principles which had built the United States into the most affluent and powerful country in the world—were considered revolutionary.

But then, out of the blue, during the 1940s and '50s, a few articulate and outspoken conservatives began to challenge the status quo. They were lonely writers, lecturers, and intellectuals—people like Friedrich Hayek, Russell Kirk, Whittaker Chambers, Ludwig von Mises, William F. Buckley, Jr., and James Burnham, among others—who bravely introduced a philosophy of individual liberty, free markets, limited government, traditional values, and anti-Communism. Little by little, these intrepid men published books, launched new magazines, and crisscrossed the country giving lectures. By 1964, when the Republicans nominated Barry Goldwater for president, the movement was no longer a debating society but a central part of the political culture. And by the time Ronald Reagan was elected to the presidency in 1980, conservatives had become a permanent part of the governing structure of the country as well.

As the movement grew, it became one of the dominant political yardsticks against which most of American politics was measured, and ultimately most Republican politicians latched onto the conservative label whether or not they were true believers. Even among Democrats, few of whom were right of center, "conservatism" determined the electibility of a candidate. By the time George W. Bush was elected in 2000, conservatives controlled the Republican Party, could count on a majority of federal judges of various shades of conservatism, had a substantial presence in every media sector, and had developed a vast array of public policy, activist, and grassroots organizations, among other assets.

As more people joined the movement—some of whom shared the ideas of the older generations, and some who did not—it acquired new groups and philosophies as well: Christian conservatives, more commonly known as the Christian Right, and the neoconservatives, to name only two. Although some of the newcomers' ideas meshed with the old, others clashed, and controversies flared. As time went on, it was no longer clear just who the "conservatives" were or exactly what they believed.

As with any political or philosophical movement, some things began to come undone as the movement matured. It might indeed be said, that the movement became a victim of its own success. At first it was made up of true believers—was there any other reason to join a movement with no clout at all? But as its strength grew, as it gained stature and popularity and more people joined, not often because they believed in its principles but because it was good politics, or just because it was the thing to do. And all too often, many did not understand the principles for which the movement stood. The word "conservative" became a label, and it applied to virtually everybody who wasn't a liberal.

As conservatives began to be elected—and by 1994, enough were to gain control of both houses of Congress and many state and local offices—they basked in the perks and the power. They convinced themselves that the most important thing they could do was to get reelected, and the best way to do so was to satisfy the voters by spending the taxpayers' money. Before long, Republicans, which most conservatives were, began to look no different than the Democrats they had replaced. As one wag put it, they got elected by calling Washington a cesspool, but after a couple of years on the job, they realized it was really a hot tub. The true conservatives, those who had elected them in the first place, assuming they would actually act like conservatives, did not like it at all.

Other politicians, who knew they needed to call themselves conservatives, wanted to fudge the idea by qualifying their conservatism. George W. Bush, who had few conservative instincts, announced during the 2000 primary season that if elected he would govern as a "compassionate conservative." Nobody ever quite knew what a compassionate conservative was, although as Bush worked his way through his first term and into his second, that there was more "compassion" than "conservative" in the term.

So the problem was not with the movement, it was with the politicians. A politician's job is vastly different from that of the ideologue or the philosopher. If elected officials cannot make compromises they can get nothing done. They soon learn that there are rarely enough votes to get just what they want, and that if they want to accomplish anything at all they need the votes of a good many people who may feel differently than they do. The ideologue, on the other hand, has nothing to lose but the argument, and so can remain true to his beliefs. His job is to perpetuate the ideas that he believes in, to hold politicians' feet to the fire, and to see that they deliver on their many promises.

Movements founded on ideas generally last for a long time. What will become of conservatism over the next years and decades? It is built on long and well-established ideas that have withstood time's ravages. But will those ideas be strong enough to make conservatism grow and flourish, or will it wither on the vine and once more give place to liberalism? Will it continue to have a major impact on American society, culture, and politics, or will America return to the post–World War II years absent the conservative movement? Will the ideas behind it—individual liberty, free markets, limited government, and a strong national defense—survive, or will they vanish and be replaced by ever bigger government, a managed economy, and the rest of liberalism's agenda? Those are the questions that an understanding of the history of the conservative movement will help to answer, and the questions that I try to answer in this book.

The conservative movement will have its ups and its downs, people will join it and others will leave. But those who built it over many years, and those who have adopted its ideas and philosophies, will remain. It is they, the true believers, who will continue pushing the ideas and philosophy that is conservatism's foundation forward, and who will keep it alive.

UPSTREAM

CHAPTER ONE

The Passing of a Conservative

Thirty-five years before he died, when he announced that he would seek the presidency, the scorn was almost universal. The wise men of Washington, joined by the media elite and the inhabitants of the colleges and universities, were condescending in their scorn. B-movie actor, they said. Amateur cowboy. Simple-minded fool. Amiable dunce. Besides, he was an unabashed conservative. Remember what happened to another conservative who had run for president, in 1964? This was a liberal country, and the presidency belonged to the liberals. No conservative could ever hope to get elected president, they said. Republicans in the White House were acceptable, from time to time, they said, as long as they were not too different from the Democrats. But conservatives did not belong there.

But today, Ronald Reagan is considered another Franklin Delano Roosevelt, a transforming president who changed politics, changed the country, changed everything. Ted Kennedy, the exhausted leftist icon who was expending whatever energy he still had to keep the old liberalism together and who had earlier called Reagan's foreign policy "unilateral, militaristic, reckless, and divisive" now joined the chorus. "On foreign policy he will be honored as the president who won the Cold War," said the senior senator from Massachusetts, "and his 'Mr. Gorbachev, tear down this wall' will be linked forever with President Kennedy's *'Ich bin ein Berliner.'*" [1]

They were all there, the wise men of Washington, the media elites, and the intellectuals, to pay tribute to a departed president who had not only succeeded in what he set out to do, but succeeded beyond anybody's wildest dreams. And he did so without abandoning his conservative principles. As he left the White House in January 1989, he had mentioned that he had come to Washington to change the country, and he left having changed the world.

First and foremost, the Soviet Union was gone. Out of business. Communism had been placed on the ash heap of history. And the economy? It had been nothing short of a disaster when this amateur cowboy entered the White House in 1981, and now was in the midst of the longest expansion in history. And the faith that the people had in the United States? When he was sworn in as president, fifty-two American diplomats had been held hostage by Iran for more than a year, utterly humiliating the United States. The hostages had been freed on the day he was sworn in, and by the time he left office, citizens' faith in the United States had never been higher.

And what were the critics saying now? Among presidential historians, the consensus was that Reagan was, along with Franklin Delano Roosevelt, the most important president of the twentieth century. James MacGregor Burns, noted historian and a liberal icon, said, "I put him at a relatively high level among all American presidents . . . even if you are a liberal like me, you have to take your hat off to a man who stuck to his conservatism and won."[2] Alonzo Hamby, a sympathetic student of American liberalism, wrote in 1997: "When passions cool after a generation or so, Ronald Reagan will be widely accepted by historians as a near-great chief executive. . . . He may not end up on Mt. Rushmore, but more than any other president since Truman, he will be a contender."[3]

Now that he was dead, they all came to pay their respects.

It was America's finest hour.

The week in which Americans bid farewell to their beloved fortieth president displayed the best of everything American. In his last trip, from the Pacific coast to the nation's capital and back to the Pacific coast, the week belonged to Ronald Reagan. But then, Ronald Reagan deserved nothing but the best from his fellow citizens.

Ronald Reagan was an American and a conservative, a pure, unapologetic conservative who had come to his beliefs by experience. In his younger years, he had been a liberal and a Democrat, but that had changed, little by little, as he saw his liberal principles put into practice, and fail. He recognized the values that conservatives held, and he read their books and their journals, tried out their principles in his speeches, and became a true believer.

Ronald Reagan was the conservative movement's president, but he was also America's president, one of America's great presidents, perhaps the greatest of the twentieth century. What he stood for and what he accomplished were more than conservatives could have ever wished for in a president, and put America back on track, after some difficult times.

The Reagan years had been both a conclusion and a beginning for conservatives. As we shall see, his administration was based on conservative principles that had been formulated over the previous thirty years, and thousands of conservatives had worked for years to elect a conservative president who would do more than pay lip service to conservative principles and then, after his election, implement liberal policies. For that reason it was a conclusion. It was a beginning because it meant that, for the first time, conservative principles could be turned into policy, and because conservative ideals could be articulated by a president, because the conservative movement would be able to move forward, after the administration was over, to expand and feel its influence grow for years to come. As we shall also see, that is exactly what happened as the movement, in the twenty-five years following Reagan's election in 1980, grew and gained influence previously unimagined by the Founders.

When Reagan was laid to rest, more than thirty years had elapsed since the last state funeral. For many Americans, a state funeral was a new experience.

When his body was brought to his library, on the misty shore of the Pacific Ocean, shortly after he died on June 6, 2004, more than one hundred thousand people came to pay their last respects to Ronald Reagan. They came carrying flowers, which they dropped at the base of a statue of their beloved president, dressed as a cowboy from his days in Hollywood. They brought little American flags, and they took pictures that would no doubt adorn mantels and pianos for years to come. "When I think of him," said one mourner, "I think of America. What is that saying—American like Mom and apple pie? He should be in that, too. Because he represented what this country is all about."[4]

Tremendous crowds, often waiting for eight or nine hours, came to the library in buses, to the top of a hill just outside Los Angeles, to pay tribute to him. "It has been really almost flawless, considering that we are bringing 100,000 people up to a mountaintop with almost no parking," said a volunteer press officer at the library.[5]

The next morning his body was taken to Point Magu Naval Air Station, twenty-five miles away and past tens of thousands who stood on the roadside, waving American flags, saluting the president they loved and already missed. An honor guard stood by, soldiers, sailors, marines, as the first of the day's three twenty-one-gun salutes was fired. Nancy Reagan, dressed in black, slowly climbed the long stairway, turned to wave, and disappeared into the huge air force plane that would bring Ronald Reagan, for the last time, to Washington.

Tens of thousands of his old friends and admirers lined the streets as the motorcade made its way slowly from Andrews Air Force Base, past Reagan National Airport, across the Memorial Bridge and past the Lincoln Memorial to Constitution Avenue. There, in direct sight of the White House, where Ronald Reagan and his dear Nancy had lived for eight years, the motorcade stopped. It was just six o'clock in the evening. Right on schedule.

A beautiful black standardbred named Sergeant York stood waiting, looking as if he were standing at attention, his saddle shining in the late-afternoon Washington summer sun. The saddle was empty; the leader would never ride again. The tradition of the riderless horse dated back to the time of Genghis Khan, when a horse was sacrificed in order to serve its master in the next life. The stirrups held a pair of well-worn and still-scuffed high brown riding boots. They faced backward, symbolizing a fallen warrior, a custom dating back to the funeral of Abraham Lincoln. They were Ronald Reagan's favorite boots. Nancy Reagan got out of the car to applause, and someone yelled, "God bless you, Mrs. Reagan!". The crowd cheered, and the greeter later explained to a reporter: "They put the red, white, and blue back in our flag. I know that sounds corny, but it's true."[6]

The honor guard represents America's best, and it looked it. Every crease was perfectly straight, every piece of brass perfectly shined, every shoe without a blemish. They removed the casket from the hearse and placed it on a caisson, originally built to carry a cannon. Six immaculate horses, perfectly trained and perfectly groomed, slowly began to pull the caisson, bearing its precious cargo, up Constitution Avenue toward the Capitol. Ronald Reagan had made the trip hundreds of times, but this would be the last. In all the others, never had tens of thousands of somber people lined the streets, paying their respects to their leader, never had the trips been the subject of such ritual, not even during his inaugurations. Twenty-one of America's finest jets roared overhead, one veering off to symbolize a missing man. Sergeant York, still without rider, walked slowly behind the caisson, the boots still facing backward. When the procession reached the west front of the Capitol, the place where Ronald Reagan had been sworn in as the fortieth president nearly a quarter century earlier, another twenty-one-gun salute sounded and six strong servicemen slowly carried the seven-hundred-pound casket up the ninety-nine steps to the Capitol. Each step was perfectly timed, perfectly coordinated.

The casket was placed in the Capitol Rotunda, perhaps the most ceremonial and dignified space in all of the United States. It rested on a pine bier constructed for the casket of Abraham Lincoln in 1865, and dignitaries and honored guests gathered to pay their respects. Nancy Reagan paused at the coffin, draped with an American flag, rested her hand on it as if she were smoothing out a wrinkle, and leaned over to kiss it gently. Before turning away she whispered a few words known only to her. Slowly she and the others left, leaving the president with only his honor guard standing at perfect attention.

Then the doors opened, and a stream of ordinary Americans filed in. Until the casket moved on to the National Cathedral two days later, they would continue to file past. Thousands upon thousands of people, who traveled thousands of miles or traveled a few blocks. They filed slowly through long lines, often waiting for four to six hours in unbearable heat, and finally through the marble corridors of the Capitol and into the Rotunda. Silently filing past the flag-draped casket, paying their last respects, each had a story to tell, a journey to recount, a reason for coming. Mostly, they loved Ronald Reagan, and just came to say good-bye.

On Thursday the world leaders, friends and adversaries, the people Reagan had known and dealt with as president, came to pay their respects to Nancy Reagan. She was at Blair House, the presidential guest house across Pennsylvania Avenue from the White House. First came Margaret Thatcher, now seventy-eight and in failing health. To call her relationship with Reagan special would be an understatement. Thatcher and Reagan shared the convictions of committed conservatives—free markets, economic decentralization, peace through strength, anti-Communism, and traditional values—and their convictions were at the heart of their leadership. Thatcher, who had been known as the Iron Lady, walked slowly now. She comforted Nancy Reagan, and in the leather-bound condolence book quoted from the parable of the talents from Matthew's Gospel: "Well done, thou good and faithful servant."

Next came Mikhail Gorbachev, now seventy-three, accompanied by the translator who had served him at five summits with Reagan. Gorbachev had never known quite what to expect from this actor and cowboy from California, but he had discovered that Reagan was no pushover. In their first meeting, in Geneva, on a cold and damp January day, Reagan gained the upper hand as he strode out to meet him without an overcoat, looking healthy and robust while Gorbachev huddled in a long, wool coat, a fur hat pulled down over his ears. Later, in words that resounded around the world, Reagan, speaking in view of the Berlin Wall, said, "Mr. Gorbachev, open this gate! Mr. Gorbachev, tear down this wall!" With the Soviet Union now gone, and with Eastern Europe now unchained and free, Mr. Gorbachev had come to wish Nancy Reagan well.

Another visitor was former Canadian prime minister Brian Mulroney, who was also a close friend of both Ronald and Nancy Reagan. He would recall, during his eulogy in the National Cathedral the next day, that once, as he and Reagan were standing together, their wives walking toward them, Reagan had looked at him and said, "You know, Brian, for a couple of Irishmen, we sure married up."[7]

The Capital City stopped that Friday, a national day of mourning. As the funeral procession made its way through central Washington and on to the National Cathedral, it passed hundreds of people who had come for a last glimpse, many huddled under umbrellas and rain parkas. Outside, a small group of protestors had staked out a position in sight of the cathedral, carrying signs that read "God Hates America" and "It's Fascism Again in Amerika." Another read "Reagan's Legacy = Feeding the Greedy, Not the Starving."

Inside, Ronald Reagan was eulogized, remembered, and praised.

Among the thirty-seven hundred invited guests sat each of the living ex–U.S. presidents, twenty-five heads of state, and eleven former heads of state; 180 ambassadors and foreign ministers, countless heads of large corporations, power brokers of every sort, journalists, and friends. For more than two hours of eloquent prayers, choruses, organ music, and testimonials, Ronald Reagan was mourned and remembered.

Margaret Thatcher, in a eulogy taped months earlier, when her voice began to fail, said, "He had firm principles and, I believe, right ones. He expounded them clearly. He acted upon them decisively." "Others saw limits to growth," Thatcher observed, but Reagan "transformed a stagnant economy into an engine of opportunity." And on Communism Thatcher said, "Others hoped for an uneasy cohabitation with the Soviet Union," but it was Ronald Reagan, she reminded the mourners, who had won the Cold War when it seemed lost to détente: "He sought to mend America's wounded spirit, to restore the strength of the free world and to free the slaves of Communism."

Thatcher continued: "He did not shrink from denouncing Moscow's 'evil empire.' But he realized that a man of goodwill might nonetheless emerge from within its dark corridors. . . . And when a man of goodwill did emerge from the ruins, President Reagan stepped forward to shake his hand and offer sincere cooperation."[8]

That man was, of course, Mikhail Gorbachev, who was seated nearby, as was Lech Walesa. One could not help but wonder what might have gone through their minds.

If the former prime minister hadn't made the point, President George W. Bush did:

> He acted to defend liberty wherever it was
> threatened. . . . When he saw evil camped across the
> horizon, he called that evil by its name. There were
> no doubters in the prisons and gulags where dissi-
> dents spread the news, tapping to each other in code
> what the American president had dared to say. There
> were no doubters in the shipyards and churches and
> secret labor meetings where brave men and women
> began to hear the creaking and rumbling of a col-
> lapsing empire. And there were no doubters among

those who swung hammers at the hated wall that the
first and hardest blow had been struck by President
Ronald Reagan.[9]

President Bush also spoke of Reagan's ideals, his grace, and his religious faith, and praised Reagan for his role as the leader of the modern conservative movement.

Former senator John Danforth, an Episcopal priest, officiated at the ceremony. He spoke of the Sermon on the Mount.

You are the light of the world. A city set on a hill
cannot be hid. It was his favorite theme, from his
first inaugural address to his final address from the
Oval Office. For him, America was the shining city
on a hill. . . . If ever we have known a child of light,
it was Ronald Reagan. He was aglow with it. He had
no dark side, no scary, hidden agenda. What you
saw, was what you got. And what you saw was that
sure sign of inner light, the twinkle in the eye. He
was not consumed by himself. He didn't need to be
president to be a complete person. The only thing he
really needed was to be with his wife.[10]

After all was done the cathedral's deep Bourdon bell rang forty times to mark Ronald Reagan's place in presidential history. The military pallbearers, in their best dress uniforms, slowly carried the casket to the great west door of the cathedral, where it would be taken back to Andrews Air Force Base and, for the last time, to the California coast so loved by Ronald Reagan, where he would find his final place of rest.

Ronald Reagan restored faith in America. He put the red, white, and blue back in the flag. He reaffirmed the validity and vitality of the American Dream. There were other accomplishments, to be sure, but that was his enduring claim to greatness and his greatest legacy.

When he was elected president in November 1980, the United States was in the depths of the worst economic recession since World War II. The financial state of the nation was measured by a misery index, and inflation, interest rates, and unemployment were in the double digits and at all-time highs. When he left, eight years later, the country was experiencing the greatest sustained economic expansion in the century. Reagan's fiscal policy, at first derisively called "Reaganomics," had as its centerpiece a massive tax cut, which Congress enacted in 1981. That tax cut was enormously successful, just as predicted by his conservative economists. It was conservative fiscal policy at its best.

When Reagan entered office in 1981 the Soviet Union was continuing its quest for world domination. He confronted the Soviet Union at every turn and did everything in his power to accelerate its fragmentation. In what has become known as the Reagan Doctrine, the United States supported anti-Communist insurgents, wherever they might be. President Reagan announced, early in his presidency, a massive buildup of U.S. forces and nuclear weapons and vowed to roll back the "Evil Empire," breaking the forty-year doctrine of "containment." Hundreds of thousands of Soviet troops were in Afghanistan. He sent over $2 billion in covert aid, sophisticated weapons, and covert advisors to help the Afghan freedom fighters resist the Soviet invaders. Soon after he left office, the Russian troops left Afghanistan, defeated and in disgrace. Within a year of his leaving Washington, Soviet Communism was beginning to crack, and soon thereafter it disintegrated. Not one shot had been fired.

He had presided over what became known as "the Reagan Revolution" and inspired a generation of conservatives who today hold countless elected offices and government jobs, and who dominate much of the Republican Party to this day. Political analyst Michael Barone has concluded that more Reagan Republicans won congressional seats in 1994 than when he was president.[11] In fact, "Reagan Republican" has become a term of art within the political world. Although a few "Roosevelt Democrats" may exist, no other twentieth-century president has been so honored.

Even Reagan's political adversaries—Democrats, liberals, former political opponents—could find few bad things to say about the departed president, and some even grudgingly praised him, something which, we will see, was inconceivable a few years earlier. The late Arthur M. Schlesinger, Jr., for example, the dean of American liberalism and one who had been consistently critical of every conservative idea and principle, said, "It is probably true that Reagan's intensification of the arms race . . . hastened the collapse of the Soviet economy. In a reversal that did him enormous credit, he . . . outdistanced his own national security bureaucracy in taking Mikhail Gorbachev seriously and in moving to end the Cold War."[12]

Yale Cold War historian John Lewis Gaddis, a consistent Reagan critic and a liberal, said:

> Historians are taking Reagan much more seriously. . . . There are very few who would still say what most were saying when he left office, which is that he was a cipher when it came to foreign policy. He was much more of a force than people gave him credit for at the time. . . . Consider the way things were when he came into office and the way things were when he left—totally different. The Berlin Wall came down less than a year after he left. The fact alone means we have to get over our preconceptions about this guy and acknowledge that something sub-stantive occurred.[13]

Ronald Reagan's success was the success of the ideas he believed in, and those ideas were the ideas of the conservative movement. They were ideas that had filled books and countless articles, and Reagan applied them to political problems. Peter J. Wallison, Reagan's White House counsel, said, in talking about the president's steadfast belief in principle, "The economy did not surge ahead because of one man's op-timism, and the Soviet Union did not collapse from force of personality. It was his ideas that ultimately account for his success. Reagan said he was not a great communicator, he said instead that he communicated great ideas."[14]

Ronald Reagan was a conservative first, and a Republican second. His administration was the realization of the dreams and the work of hundreds of thousands of conservatives who had labored for decades to turn their ideas into policy. Anti-Communism, traditional values, and free markets were his watchwords, were his campaign promises, and were the principles that his administration used as the foundation of its policies. It was the work of Russell Kirk, of William F. Buckley,

Jr., of Milton Friedman, of Friedrich Hayek and Ludwig von Mises, of James Burnham, Whittaker Chambers, Henry Regnery, Frank Meyer, and countless others. As President Bush said, in his eulogy of Ronald Reagan at the National Cathedral, "In the space of a few years, he took ideas and principles that were mainly found in journals and books, and turned them into a broad, hopeful movement ready to govern."[15]

CHAPTER TWO

It Wasn't Always That Way

Culturally, America was a conservative land in 1945. Values, manners, even the way politics was conducted were conservative. Politicians were generally polite to each other, respected each other's opinions, partly because they did not differ much on the issues, not as they would sixty years later. Today's permissiveness would have been considered 1945's scandal; and the social views of most voters would, by today's standard, have been considered conservative.

The United States has always been something of a schizophrenic place, and cultures and politics are often vastly at odds with each other. If the country was culturally conservative, its politics were far to the left. Among the elites and the power brokers, collectivism was held to be the wave of the future. At the close of World War II big government dominated the Western world. The United States came through the war relatively unscathed, re-emerging at the peak of its power in almost every way. It had finally overcome hard economic times—as difficult as any in its history. New social programs launched in the first years of the Roosevelt administration abounded, providing jobs and money to millions of people. The war, the greatest and most concentrated effort in the history of the United States, was the triumph of big government—of massive planning, construction, arms building, mobilization, and the rest. So in the view of most people, both the Great Depression and World War II had been won by big government.

The New Deal, spawned by a few professors, the FDR brain trust, had drawn hundreds of intellectuals and other professionals to Washington to institute the new programs, and tens of thousands more clerks and paper-pushers to do the work. The federal government had been nearly invisible to most Americans before the early 1930s, and, with the exception of the mailman and an occasional tax collector, Washington was a distant place referred to from time to time in the newspaper or during an Independence Day speech by a local congressman. But by 1945, the federal government was everywhere—it dominated the news, was omnipresent in the New Deal agencies, shaped the attitudes of veterans, and intruded into the daily lives and thoughts of the people.

Even more to the point, the intellectual climate of the country was overwhelmingly leftist. Free markets, laissez-faire economics, low taxes, limited government, private property, and deregulation were not popular concepts, and in fact were rarely even mentioned. Communism, the epitome of leftism, was considered idealistic and benign—after all, the Soviet Union had been our ally in defeating Nazi Germany, and Roosevelt had referred to Stalin as "Uncle Joe." The American Communist Party was commonly viewed as just another political party of sincere if somewhat muddled intellectuals.

Since much of conservatism is a reaction to liberalism, it is good to go back a generation or two and see just where liberalism gained its foothold in American political life. Teddy Roosevelt was the first progressive president, but his progressivism set the stage for much of what Woodrow Wilson would accomplish. Thus, a good place to start is the 1912 election and the man it made president.

Woodrow Wilson and his progressivism dominated American politics from the turn of the century until the late 1960s. Wilson was a Virginian, a Calvinist, an intellectual, and the forefather of contemporary liberalism. Elected as a liberal reformer, he could not have arrived in Washington at a better time to accomplish what he had in mind for the United States and the world. Teddy Roosevelt had preceded him with some reformist ideas and set the stage for passage of two constitutional amendments that would serve Wilson well, feeding the growth of government and liberalism. The Sixteenth Amendment, ratified in 1913, gave the federal government power to collect a personal and graduated income tax, allowing the federal government, for the first time, not only to raise large amounts of revenue with which to pay for the new programs Wilson and subsequent presidents had in store, but also to steer social policy through various income-redistribution schemes that would favor, or punish, one group of Americans over others, presaging a congressional tactic the liberals would use for the balance of the twentieth century.

The second constitutional amendment, the Seventeenth, provided for the direct election of U.S. senators. Until 1913, senators had been elected by the state legislatures, on the theory that sovereignty between the states and the federal government would be divided, and senators, dependent on their state legislatures for re-election, would "be vigilant in supporting their rights against infringement by the legislative or executive of the United States."[1] Founding Father Alexander Hamilton agreed; he believed that indirect election would be an absolute safeguard against federal tyranny. Even today, states' rights advocates hold that the direct election of senators was one of the most important nails pounded onto the coffin of federalism. In any case, Wilson was given a much freer hand to steer the federal government without interference from the states than ever before.

Wilson enacted social and economic changes and launched new programs, but more important, he initiated a whole new way of thinking about government. Government, in the eyes of most Americans dating back to the Founders, was to be limited and unintrusive. The Declaration of Independence and the Constitution were based on the premise that government was the great threat to freedom, and that the purpose of a constitution was to limit the power of government. This was of little concern to Woodrow Wilson, who would start transforming the federal government from a benign, small, and nearly invisible entity to the behemoth that it would be just thirty years later.

Wilson's administration was based on definite ideas—big government, scientific administration, social reform, and government power, to protect "the weak" against "the powerful." Wilson's philosophy of government changed America and ruled unchallenged until conservatism blossomed some forty years later. As he put it in his book *The State,* "Government does now whatever experience permits or times demand."[2] It was now the government's duty to manage economic competition and economic activity in the interests of the people. His attitude manifested itself in an array of innovative regulations and agencies, which became the model for liberal administrations for the rest of the century. The

Federal Reserve System, established in 1913, brought order to U.S. currency, managed credit, and was designed to head off economic crises, although it certainly did nothing to avert the Great Depression. The Federal Trade Commission was established to regulate the monopolistic practices of business and to protect consumers from various unscrupulous business practices, one of the first of many "independent" federal regulatory bodies composing what would later be known, derisively, as "the nanny state." The Federal Farm Loan Act created a system of cheap federally guaranteed loans to farmers, and the Adamson Act established the concept of federal wage-and-hour regulation through the eight-hour workday. But Wilson was not so liberal with civil rights; he was indifferent to the concerns of black Americans. He permitted segregation of the Post Office and Treasury, and generally made the federal bureaucracy less hospitable to blacks than it had been under Republican administrations.[3] Wilson's influence was felt in the domestic field for the balance of the twentieth century, as it was in American foreign policy, which was changed forever when the United States entered World War I in 1917. It was the end of American isolationism and the advent of what would become known as Wilsonianism. The entry of the United States into the European war, as described by British historian Paul Johnson, was "the primal tragedy of modern world civilization, the main reason why the twentieth century turned into such a disastrous epoch for mankind."[4] Wilson waged war relentlessly and ruthlessly. He threw everything he could into it; the cost was over ten times that of the Civil War, and over twice the total operating cost of the federal government since its founding in 1789. Vastly powerful bureaucracies were created, including the War Finance Corporation, which regulated private industry's participation in the war effort and manifested Wilson's commitment to corporatism—the notion that management, unions, and the government should together manipulate the capitalist system to the benefit of all three. Ignoring free-market economics, it became the favored business model among academics, leftist intellectuals, and liberal Republicans.[5]

Wilson's "peace" shaped the direction he thought the world should take: His foreign policy would be based on his own morality and ethics, armaments would be reduced to the lowest possible levels, and a League of Nations would enforce the peace. But he was too blind to see his vision for the utopian dream it was, and too inept in his attempts to implement it.

Wilson's principle of self-determination of peoples aroused hopes that could not be fulfilled. The dissolution of the Hapsburg Empire created a power vacuum in central Europe, laying the path for Hitler's conquest of the region. The breakup of the Ottoman Empire attracted European colonial expansion, which resulted in the rise of militant Islam.[6] Wilson's League of Nations, formed without American participation, provided liberals with an illusion of peace that it was impotent to maintain and facilitated the rise of Hitler and World War II; his war for democracy paved the way for totalitarianism; and his campaign for the self-determination of peoples contributed to the rise of virulent nationalism. And his promise to wage a war to end all wars bequeathed the world the bloodiest war in history.

Not the least of Woodrow Wilson's many questionable legacies were presidents Herbert Hoover and Franklin Roosevelt. Both worked in the Wilson administration, and both were arguably among its most Wilsonian members. Hoover was a registered Republican (unbeknownst to most) but had publicly supported the progressive Theodore Roosevelt in 1912 over the more conservative Republican William Howard Taft. Hoover was one of the most forceful of planners and adopted Wilson's ideas of a large, strong government and benevolent intervention in the economy. Hoover was not a socialist, but he was most assuredly no conservative, if being conservative means limiting the scope of government. Indeed, in the late twenties Hoover was "the darling of the progressives who still clustered about the figure of the fallen Wilson."[7] Admirers heralded him as "the Great Engineer." Calvin Coolidge later referred to him derisively as "the Wonderboy."

Hoover was aggressively recruited as the progressive candidate for president in 1920 by Franklin D. Roosevelt and others, but he was not interested. Roosevelt had been brought into the Wilson administration from the start as assistant secretary of the navy. When Wilson was asked by William Gibbs McAdoo, his confidant, campaign manager, and son-in-law, about tapping FDR for the job, Wilson thought "it was a capital idea." Roosevelt was thus anointed to continue along the path that his hero Wilson had laid out.[8] So when Hoover declined the mantle of Wilsonian progressivism, Roosevelt did, too, and justly so:

> Roosevelt in a very real sense [spent] seven years
> in Professor Wilson's school of public administra-
> tion . . . the origins of New Deal ideas go back to
> two main fountainheads—Wilson's New Freedom
> and Theodore Roosevelt's New Nationalism. The
> ideology and techniques of both men left a deep im-
> press on Franklin D. Roosevelt.[9]

FDR ran for vice president on the Democratic Party ticket in 1920 under James Cox. They went down to defeat, but FDR had established
himself as the heir of the Wilson legacy.

The GOP swept into office on Warren G. Harding's promise to return
American politics to the certainties of the pre–World War I years, to
normalcy, and, true to that promise, his administration repudiated the
foreign interventionism of Wilson, as well as its economic interventionism. Business boomed after Congress passed the Mellon Plan, named
after Treasury Secretary Andrew W. Mellon, which cut taxes and allowed
the United States to simultaneously pay down its public debt. When Harding died suddenly in 1923, he was succeeded by Vice President Calvin
Coolidge, known as "Cool Cal" because of his unassuming nature, social
reserve, and fondness for terse witticisms. Coolidge had been relatively
progressive as governor of Massachusetts, but believing in a limited federal government, he continued the laissez-faire policies of Harding.

When Coolidge declined to run for re-election in 1928, the field was
wide open to Hoover, who remained in his own right a popular figure.
Hoover had been chairman of the postwar U.S. Commission of Relief,
which he ran efficiently and effectively. Harding subsequently named
him secretary of commerce, where he gained the reputation of being
the most interventionist member of the Harding and Coolidge administrations. Hoover won the GOP nomination and easily beat New York
governor Al Smith, moving into the White House well in time for the
1929 stock market crash. As president, he continued the policies he had
advocated in both the Wilson and Coolidge administrations, and during
his one term as president, he started more public works projects than
had been commenced in the past thirty years combined. John Maynard Keynes, the final authority on planning and big government, found
Hoover's performance "thoroughly satisfactory."[10]

Hoover's interventionism reflected the trend of relying on the ability of the government to solve problems in America's culture and intellectual life. During the 1920s and 1930s, intellectuals had a greater voice than ever before in what was going on. Communications had greatly improved, the population was better educated and more interested in current affairs and the world. Public policy issues were treated in popular nonfiction books, by authors who were almost all noted liberals. Planning—centralized planning—was on the lips of intellectuals more prolifically than ever. Charles Beard, the country's leading and most popular historian, published a piece in *Harper's* magazine in December 1931 called "A Five Year Plan for America," in which he advocated centralized government planning of economic activity and the nationalization of public utilities.[11] Adolf Berle, later one of FDR's brain trusters, published with Gardner Means his wildly successful *Modern Corporations and Private Property*, which advocated, *inter alia,* a planned economy. *Business Week*, one of the most widely read business magazines, in June 1931 stated that "to plan or not to plan is no longer the question. The real question is: who is to do it?"[12] For most, the answer was "Government."

Hoover had been elected in large part because of his reputation as the consummate planner and administrator. But he could not plan and administrate the country out of the Depression. His interventionism, moreover, was abhorred by the business community, and after 1930 the Congress tried to rein him in. Hoover's fiscal irresponsibility arguably prolonged the Depression suffering by several years.[13] Though he got most of the blame for the Depression, if unfairly, Hoover gave Roosevelt a tremendous running start for the New Deal. Hoover had the novel assumption that it was the government's duty to ensure that no American who was willing to work should go hungry, and Roosevelt followed suit. He nevertheless campaigned against Hoover as running "the greatest spending Administration in peace times in all our history."[14] Ironically, all Roosevelt needed to get his growth of government under way was to continue what Hoover had started.

As unabashed liberal Walter Lippmann said in 1935, "The policy initiated by President Hoover in the autumn of 1929 was something utterly unprecedented in American history. The national government undertook to make the whole economic order operate prosperously . . . the

Roosevelt measures are a continuous evolution of the Hoover measures." [15] Rex Tugwell, one of FDR's resident intellectual assistants (and a Communist fellow traveler), admitted many years later, "When it was all over I once made a list of New Deal ventures begun during Hoover's years as secretary of commerce and then as president. I had to conclude that his policies were substantially correct. The New Deal owed much to what he had begun." [16] Roosevelt simply replaced the Great Administrator with a whole team of administrative experts, the brain trust. (After his presidency, Hoover became much more conservative, and by the time the conservative movement started to thrive he had become one of its most ardent supporters. He would be one of the original financial backers of *National Review*, often appeared at Young Americans for Freedom rallies, and was an active participant at conservative events. The Hoover Institution at Stanford, which Hoover founded, became one of his great causes, and became one of the preeminent conservative think tanks in the country.)

Roosevelt was highly admired by American intellectuals and academics for his antibusiness rants, his brain trust, and his wife; and even his critics, who were viewed as mindless know-nothings, brought the intelligentsia into his camp in droves. H. L. Mencken, the mordant critic from *The American Mercury* and not the least of those critics became almost hysterical on the subject of Roosevelt. "In my book," Mencken famously said, "that man was an unmitigated S.O.B. He was an S.O.B. in his public life and an S.O.B. in his private life. Any other questions?" [17]

As most of FDR's critics were portrayed as "the rich," or even worse, "economic royalists"—the business community, right-wingers—the common folk reacted by loving him even more, and by the time the 1936 election came along Roosevelt had put together the strongest political coalition of the century, and one that would serve Democrats in good stead for decades. Running against Kansas governor Alf Landon, he carried 62 percent of the popular vote and every state but Maine and Vermont. (How things would change in those New England states by the end of the century!) His coattails were so strong that the Democrats started 1937 with majorities of 334–89 in the House of Representatives and 76–16 in the Senate. [18] This enabled Roosevelt to begin building the American welfare state in earnest. His new programs included the

Social Security Administration (1935), which became far and away the largest welfare and benefits program in the country.

But where Hoover was something of a spendthrift, Roosevelt was prodigal. He spent billions on newly conceived public works projects, initiated every imaginable kind of regulatory agency, and started employment projects that ultimately employed nearly 9 million people. As an example, he pushed the Tennessee Valley Authority (TVA) through Congress, at tremendous cost, to tame the Tennessee River and provide cheap power to millions of impoverished southerners. It became a model for future adventures both at home and abroad. Such projects, together with his diplomatic recognition of the Soviet Union in 1933, were hailed by the left and the progressives for the remainder of the century. These programs earned plaudits from academia, intellectuals, and writers, and a corresponding increased consolidation of leftism among the educated class. When the Supreme Court struck down some of his programs, Roosevelt responded by threatening to pack the Court with new justices who would approve them. He was forced to back down, but the Court backed off, too, allowing future programs to be implemented.

COMMUNISM

Twelve years of the New Deal, World War II, and the wartime alliance with the Soviet Union with its accompanying blindness to the evils of Communism cemented leftism in the intellectual life of the country. Conservatives were considered at best hopelessly behind the times, at worst latent fascists or holdovers from the Gilded Age. And now the Great Depression seemed to have discredited the whole capitalist system. Before the Depression, left-wing bohemian intellectuals were absorbed in their carefree moral libertinism and aloof from practical politics. But they came to feel somehow responsible for the Depression, and so sought to make reparation for their earlier detachment through political activism.

Having already rejected orthodox religion, left-wing intellectuals thus turned to Communism for a systematic diagnosis and prescription for the ills of capitalism. Communism seemed to offer the moral seriousness they lacked. "A man does not become a Communist," wrote Whittaker Chambers in his classic *Witness,* "because he is attracted to Communism, but because he is driven to despair by the crisis of history through which the world is passing. . . . In the West, all intellectuals become Communists because they are seeking the answer to one of two problems: the problem of war or the problem of economic crises."[19] Rushing to an ideology that might assuage their troubled consciences blinded them to its moral evils and political realities, a blindness that involved them in a series of hypocrisies. Living in comfortable insulation from harsh economic truths, they nonetheless imagined that they understood others' experiences. While poverty in capitalist America was unnecessary, poverty in Communist Russia was an essential stage in the construction of a socialist utopia.[20] Although few joined the Communist Party USA, many became what were termed fellow travelers, and almost all found much to praise and little to criticize. Here was a new social order, a new economic order, and a new political order with answers to all of their anxieties about the world. Lincoln Steffens, the famous muckraking journalist, summarized the intellectuals' feelings about Lenin's new Russia in 1919 with his famous quip that he had seen the future, and it worked—this as millions in the U.S.S.R. were dying of starvation. *New York Times* Moscow correspondent Walter Duranty later wrote: "Stalin is giving the Russian people—the Russian masses, not Westernized landlords, industrialists, bankers, and intellectuals, but Russia's 150 million peasants and workers—what they really want, namely joint effort, communal effort."[21] In contrast with the despair of Depression-era America, the Soviet Union seemed filled with hope in the birth of a new age of freedom and equality.

Liberal intellectuals were fascinated with Communism because it represented the ultimate extension of their interest in the possibilities of government power. But since many liberals reproached themselves for lacking the nerve to join the movement, they were morally paralyzed when confronted with Communism at home and abroad; they lacked its instinct for the jugular. Then too, anti-Communism had been officially discredited during the war and our alliance with Stalin, and by 1945 had all but disappeared from the scene.

At first the Communist Party considered itself to be outside the American political system, and Communists looked upon FDR as a social fascist, i.e., a leader who hoped to stave off the revolution of the proletariat by adopting modest progressive reforms. But when Communists joined others on the left to combat fascism in Europe, they about-faced and embraced FDR and the New Deal. Now their strategy was to make Communism into "twentieth-century Americanism,"—i.e., the natural evolution of American ideals—and they successfully blurred the lines between Marxism and progressivism.[22] But a serious problem arose: The liberals in the universities, in journalism, and subsequently in the Truman administration naively bought this line, believing that the Communist Party was a normal part of the American political establishment rather than a direct subsidiary of the Soviet Union. After all, the Communist Party USA had sixty-three thousand members, ten thousand of whom were in the armed services. The party was publishing 2 million copies of books and pamphlets a year, and several newspapers; it had many schools, a strong foothold in the labor movement, and was actively involved in the Democratic Party in several states.[23]

In the fall of 1947, the CPUSA, emboldened by its cultural success, decided to follow Moscow's increasingly confrontational policy toward the West by creating a leftist third party and thus breaking up the two-party system. It persuaded Henry Wallace to run for the presidency as a Progressive in 1948. With support that was overwhelmingly, if not exclusively, Communist, Wallace won over a million votes in the 1948 election, finishing just behind the South's Strom Thurmond,[24] who ran on the States Rights Party ticket as an unreconstructed segregationist. The election showed the disparity between the cultural influence of the left and its electoral power. It also revealed the disenchantment of southern Democrats with their national party and their willingness to buck the party.

DEARTH OF CONSERVATIVES

When FDR died, World War II ground to a close, and the Truman presidency got under way in 1945, intellectual life in the United States was firmly liberal. George Nash, in his history of the conservative intellectual movement, says the United States was "a domestic superstate, a partially controlled economy, millions of conscripts under arms, and widespread fears of reversion to depression once demobilization set in. Further success for a philosophy of 'tax and tax, spend and spend, elect and elect.'"[25] The New Deal was an ongoing project.[26] Anything resembling conservatism was moribund. There had been scattered opposition to the rise of the left before the war. Irving Babbitt's New Humanists decried the spread of romanticism and the decline of higher education; a group of literary Southern Agrarians published a manifesto in defense of the passing Old South; and Albert Jay Nock called for an individualist remnant to wait out the age of collectivism. But these men hardly constituted a movement, and their views were not widely shared. Few public figures advocated such things as free markets, private property, limited government, self-reliance, laissez-faire, or even anti-Communism, and those who did were generally ostracized by the intelligentsia. The term "conservative" was rarely used, and it is probably safe to assume that few people really knew what it meant. Liberal dominance of the universities, the press—all the institutions of American life and culture—went almost unchallenged. But change was in the air, and the beginnings of a conservative movement would soon emerge.

CHAPTER THREE

Intellectual Underpinnings

By the mid-1940s, what passed for conservatism in some quarters was the defense of the New Deal. This, at any rate, was the substance of the "New Conservatism" called for by Peter Viereck and Clinton Rossiter.[1]

Viereck, a historian and Pulitzer Prize–winning poet who taught at Mount Holyoke College in Massachusetts, praised the heroes of European conservatism but embraced the New Deal as a reformist program that effectively staved off social revolution in the United States. His favorite contemporary politician was two-time Democratic presidential loser Adlai Stevenson. Rossiter, a political scientist at Cornell, held that America was essentially a progressive country, and any robust conservatism was alien to its soil. Though he thought its primary task was to serve as an advocate for the interests of American business, conservatism could not roll back the achievements of the New Deal, nor should it. Naturally, refusing to reject liberalism on principle, Viereck and Rossiter won applause from liberal critics and intellectuals. But their New Conservatism failed to attract politicians or gain a popular audience and was roundly dismissed by the few movement conservatives then on the scene.

But a few writers and thinkers were publishing books and articles, speaking across the country, and otherwise articulating critiques of liberalism and beginning to break into the press and the popular imagination.

The decade from 1945 to 1955 was the span when the intellectual foundation for the coming conservative movement was laid; a foundation that would serve as bedrock for the enduring movement. Ideas were its strength, and because people—both intellectuals and activists—were willing to stake their future on them, conservatism withstood the heavy onslaught of the left. Its principal advocates were not concerned with ideas only as an intellectual exercise or to better understand the world they were living in. They held practical ideas that challenged the status quo; they wanted to use their ideas to change the world. Although these conservatives did not think much of his theory of economics, they agreed with John Maynard Keynes, who said that "ideas are more powerful than is commonly understood. Indeed, the world is ruled by little else. . . . Sooner or later, it is ideas, not vested interests, which are dangerous for good or evil."[2] They lamented what had happened to the United States, and indeed to the rest of the world, during the first half of the twentieth century. They believed that cultural and political liberalism was at odds with American ideals at home and abroad, and saw that assaults on individual liberties, limited government, free markets, and Western culture ran counter to everything they believed in.

At least three, and in a sense, four different schools of thought began to emerge at more or less the same time, and although many of the people who were the first to make their voices heard had a similar way of thinking, they did not think of themselves as in the same camp, for they had little in common. Nor would they have ever imagined that they were forming what would become a movement of similar ideas. In fact, the three branches—libertarians or classical liberals, anti-Communists, and traditionalists—had considerable differences. The libertarians were largely concerned with individualism and individual freedom, believing that people should be allowed to follow their own pursuits, particularly in their financial and business enterprises, with as little interference as possible, and that capitalism or free enterprise was the only way to achieve liberty and economic growth. They were not concerned with religion and God or, particularly, with traditional values. In contrast with traditionalists and anti-Communists, many libertarians believed that a foreign policy that emphasized fear of Communism was a waste of valuable resources and a sure way to ensure the growth of government and higher taxes.

The traditionalists, for their part, were more interested in preserving what was left of Western civilization—the high culture, popular mores, and standards of conduct. Political problems, they held, were at root religious and moral problems. Legislation should be based on morality, and politicians should consider divine intent as manifest in natural law when making decisions. Although order was crucial to a civilized society, like libertarians the traditionalists believed in limited government and believed that private property and freedom were inseparable, and totalitarian government, in any form, was an abomination. As time went on and their arguments became refined, rather serious disagreements between libertarians and traditionalists arose, but they were ultimately resolved on a practical level.

The anti-Communists believed that the primary threat to the West and to Western civilization was the spread of Communism, as witness the Soviet Union and China, which exerted their influence around the world and attempted to subvert American culture and the American way of life internally. Communism represented everything abhorrent to Western values: It was tyrannical, repressive, socialistic, and atheistic. It used terror, deceit, and subversion for its ends and was determined to force its ideology on the rest of the world. The anti-Communists also believed that liberalism was a progenitor of Communism, and, because they shared the same substantive goals, was more often than not complicit in its spread.

A fourth camp, in a sense, were young conservative journalists, publishers, and activists who shared many of the beliefs of the other three intellectual schools, but as popularizers were willing to challenge liberals and liberalism in a more public setting. They recognized that a network of support through journalism, lectures, books, and debates was necessary to publicize the work of the intellectuals available to the public and thus to have an impact.

THE LIBERTARIANS

Two Austrian immigrants—Friedrich Hayek and Ludwig von Mises—were among the earliest and, as it turned out, most influential of the conservative intellectuals. Hayek, a naturalized British subject, had been born and educated in Vienna and in 1931 moved to Britain, where he joined the faculty at the London School of Economics. He studied in Vienna with Ludwig von Mises, published a number of academic treatises on economics, and became well known in economic circles as John Maynard Keynes's intellectual sparring partner. Keynes was then at Cambridge, and the most highly regarded economist internationally. Hayek challenged Keynes's new theory of macroeconomics—a challenge that few would dispute Hayek ultimately won.

Hayek published his little book *The Road to Serfdom* in 1944. A slight, unassuming, shy man, Hayek was always astounded that people would actually buy his books and heed what he said. When *The Road to Serfdom* was released in the United States, it was an instant success, and it eventually became one of those rare books that actually changed minds, and lots of them. According to E. J. Dionne, *Washington Post* columnist and no conservative:

> The publication of Friedrich A. Hayek's *The Road to Serfdom* in 1944 [is rightly seen] as the first shot in the intellectual battle that was to turn the tide in favor of conservatism.[3]

The Road to Serfdom taught that central planning and freedom were incompatible and that any entry onto the slippery slope of a planned, centralized economy would lead to collectivization and tyranny. Economic liberty was historically and logically a necessary prerequisite for political liberty. Hayek pointed to Nazi Germany and Communist Russia as paradigmatic examples of states where centralized economic planning led to full-blown totalitarianism. To strike at economic liberty, as modern liberals were doing, was to strike at the root of Western political liberty. Only in a society in which the rule of law was consistently applied, and in which rules of interaction were known to all and enabled all to plan personal economic activities, would freedom obtain, and thus allow the marketplace to function without interference. In other words, liberty and economic growth could thrive only in a society based on freedom of association and exchange according to the rule of law, and away from the control of centralized planners according to the whim of government. Democratic socialism, according to Hayek, was a contradiction in terms and could not exist, because it would require a technocratic elite to plan economic behavior on behalf of the people, eliminating private initiative and popular government. Instead, the primary goal of government in the economy should be to maintain competition. But Hayek did not advocate cold-hearted, pure capitalism without benefits to those in need. Minimum social security programs were fine as long as the laws were applied consistently and fairly, and as long as competition and private property were preserved and private initiative encouraged.[4]

The Road to Serfdom appeared in the United States in the fall of 1944, published by the University of Chicago Press. It was initially considered of minor importance, but within weeks it had achieved national prominence and was condensed in the *Reader's Digest,* and six hundred thousand copies were distributed by the Book-of-the-Month Club. The book remains in print to this day, having gone through nearly forty printings in the United States, and is available in over thirty foreign languages. Hayek, who made a coast-to-coast lecture tour, became an American academic celebrity. Several like-minded writers penned major reviews praising the book. Henry Hazlitt, who later became known as one of the United States' great free market apologists with his little book *Economics in One Lesson,* wrote in the *New York Times Book Review* that *The Road to Serfdom* was:

> One of the most important books of our generation. . . . It restates for our time the issue between liberty and authority with the power and rigor of reasoning with which John Stuart Mill stated the issue for his own generation in his great essay *On Liberty*. . . . It is an arresting call to all well-intentioned planners and socialists, to all those who are sincere democrats and liberals at heart to stop, look and listen.[5]

The planners and their acolytes were not so kind. That this articulate spokesman should stimulate such an overwhelming reaction alarmed them, and they responded accordingly. Reviewing *The Road to Serfdom* for the *American Political Science Review,* Carl J. Friedrich deplored Hayek's "ignorance of most relevant writings and experience in the field whereof he treats." He surmised that Hayek's ideal "free society" was "the bleak 1840s in England when Manchester exploitation reigned supreme, when the enterpriser was wholly free to practice his 'astuteness for ambushing the community's loose change.'"[6] In the *New Republic*, liberal economist Alvin Hansen dismissed Hayek's ideas as being out of touch with political realities. He averred that the Austrian's warning against the political ill effects of centralized economic planning was "not scholarship. It is seeing hobgoblins under every bed." And he concluded that "Hayek's book will not be long lived. There is no substance in it to make it live. But it will momentarily stir up a good deal of discussion, and this is all to the good."[7] Another reviewer thought that Hayek had conflated Nazism and Soviet collectivism, and, unselfconsciously reflecting the academic establishment's blindness to the evils of Communism, faulted him for not having "the grace, at the least, to acknowledge the very different manner in which the war itself has been conducted by the enemy and by our ally."[8]

But to those who agreed with Hayek, *The Road to Serfdom* gave a tremendous moral boost and opened the way for the free market movement that would play such an important role in the world over the coming half century.

Hayek's subsequent work suffered, at least in academic circles, for his having been branded a reactionary and Neanderthal. Mainly for this reason he left Britain and came to the University of Chicago, hardly at the time a safe harbor (although in time the economics department at Chicago would largely adopt Hayek's views). Hayek was awarded a chair at the Committee on Social Thought, which, though prestigious, was not the economics department where he belonged, and the chair was funded by the Volker Fund, a private foundation, rather than by the university.

Ludwig von Mises, Hayek's mentor from Vienna, emigrated to the United States in 1940 after becoming world famous as a bitter opponent of Nazism and socialism (both of which, according to Mises and Hayek, were cut from the same intellectual cloth). Mises worked for a time at the National Association of Manufacturers and finally settled at New York University, where he would remain until his retirement in 1969 at the age of eighty-eight. Mises took a less "humanitarian" view of economics than Hayek, believing that all the good things that government could guarantee could come about only at the expense of individual freedom and private property. Capitalism could not be diluted, he believed, and any attempt to do so would result in "statism," centralized planning, and the erosion of individual liberty. Mises's massive treatise *Human Action* was published by the Yale University Press in 1949, and although it received far less popular attention than Hayek's *Road to Serfdom* it was for libertarians (and conservatives) a capitalist manifesto.

Henry Hazlitt, in his column in *Newsweek*, had this to say: "*Human Action* is, in short, at once the most uncompromising and the most rigorously reasoned statement of the case for capitalism that has yet appeared."[9]

Economist Hans Sennholz, in a review in the *Freeman*, wrote: "*Human Action* is the legacy of a genius, left to us and to be passed on from generation to generation. . . . In the world of economic literature, *Human Action* now holds the position which Adam Smith's *Wealth of Nations* used to occupy."[10]

Mises and Hayek were the genesis of the revival of classical liberalism in America. They were joined later by Aaron Director, Milton Friedman, George Stigler, and James Buchanan, all of whom would be awarded Nobel Prizes in economics, and their collective influence was a crucial component in the growth of the conservative movement over the remainder of the twentieth century and into the twenty-first.

MONT PELERIN, SWITZERLAND, APRIL 1, 1947

The upshot of Hayek's tour promoting *The Road to Serfdom* was his decision to gather free-market advocates in April 1947 at the Hotel du Parc on the shores of Lake Geneva in Switzerland. The thirty-six participants came from the United States and Western Europe, and after several days of discussion, the Mont Pelerin Society was launched.

In his opening address, Hayek said he was "always surprised by the number of isolated men whom I found in different places, working on essentially the same problems and on very similar lines. Working in isolation in very small groups they are, however, constantly forced to defend the basic elements of their beliefs and rarely have opportunity for an interchange of opinion on the more technical problems which arise only if a certain common basis of conviction of ideals is present."[11]

At the meeting were, among others, von Mises, the dean of the Austrian school of economics; Wilhelm Roepke, a key player in the great German currency reform of 1948 and influential in the construction of the German *Witschaftswunder*; philosopher Karl Popper; Lionel Robbins from the London School of Economics; George Stigler, Aaron Director, and his brother-in-law Milton Friedman, all from the University of Chicago; American economist Henry Hazlitt; former editor of the *Washington Post* Felix Morley; and Leonard Read, F. A. "Baldy" Harper, and Orval Watts from the Foundation for Economic Education (FEE).[12]

Stigler, who went on to win the Nobel Prize for Economics, recalled in his book *The Memoirs of an Unregulated Economist,* "I had never met Hayek but my Chicago teachers certified my eligibility for the coming totalitarian firing squads. It showed my lack of inner conviction of the imminence of totalitarianism that the thought never entered my mind."

"It was a revealing first visit," Stigler wrote, "for the younger participants, including Milton Friedman and me. En route we were depressed as much by the austerity of the British economy as by their food (if an ersatz sausage is indeed food). We were instructed as well as embarrassed by the casualness of French life: We did not learn until we left France that we required food ration tickets. I concluded that the British obeyed all laws, the French none, and the Americans obeyed those laws that deserved obedience—in retrospect, something of a simplification. Indeed the black market was a boon to French economic life; it allowed prices to perform their functions."[13]

Milton Friedman recalled that there was a great deal of goodwill among the members at the first meeting, much of which came because many of the attendees had felt terribly alone, not realizing that other people thought as they did. The Americans, he said, were considerably more optimistic than the Europeans, simply because collectivism was less advanced there than in Europe.[14]

The Mont Pelerin Society's conference became a sort of rallying point for outnumbered troops, according to Friedman, and as it continued to assemble each year it became a sort of international "who's who" of free marketeers, classical liberals, and conservatives. Because it attracted scholars and writers from both sides of the Atlantic (and in later years from all over the world), it also served to give American participants a more cosmopolitan view of market ideas.

Topics discussed by members in the early years ranged from the nature of liberalism, to fiscal and financial policy, labor policy, and the European Common Market.[15] But by no means were all of the participants in accord in their beliefs or how they might be implemented. Mises, who became a fixture at society meetings, believed that the government had no role in redistributing income under any circumstances. But many of the other members, including Hayek, believed that government ought to alleviate poverty and to undertake certain modest social programs. According to Milton Friedman, after a spirited discussion on the topic, Mises stormed out of the room, calling the other members a bunch of socialists.[16]

The great value of Mont Pelerin, however, was that it became an integral part of the war of ideas. Although Hayek was an academic and a philosopher, he was also a realist who recognized that the relationships formed at its meetings could help free-market economists translate ideas into policy if they were properly cultivated. As one left-leaning magazine said about Hayek in an article about the Mont Pelerin Society:

> If the triumph of the New Right could be blamed on one person, that villain might be Austrian economist F. A. Hayek . . . Hayek was no mere academic scribbler or economist—he also was an activist who inspired and organized the modern political right's "war of ideas." Hayek pointed the way for the conservative think tank movement of today and incited the mainstream policy shift from Keynesian demand management to free-market supply-side economics.[17]

That may give Hayek a little too much credit, but certainly only a little.

In a sense, the Mont Pelerin Society is representative of the way the conservative movement grew over the years. One or two very able people with definite ideas wanted to see their ideas translated into policy. They raised the money to put on the first meeting from several wealthy individuals who shared the same principles, and called together leaders from various parts of the world who were also true believers. They drafted a statement of principles that spelled out what they believed, why, and what they wanted to do about it. The meeting was transformed into an organization, more money was contributed, more people were recruited as members and guests, and a lifelong network was born. The society focused on creating an international academy of classical liberals who would strive to win the intellectual battle against socialism by waging policy battles against it.

The influence of the Mont Pelerin Society is indeed impressive. It was partially responsible for the think tank movement, for one thing. Out of its meetings the Institute for Economic Affairs (IEA) in London was born, which in turn begat hundreds of other free-market policy institutes around the world.[18] Margaret Thatcher's program of privatization was drawn up at IEA, largely by Mont Pelerin members. Of the seventy-six economic advisors on Ronald Reagan's 1980 campaign staff, twenty-two were Mont Pelerin members.[19]

"Relatively speaking and perhaps even more important," Milton Friedman reflected, "in terms of practice, the U.S. at that time [1947] was still essentially a free-market society. Government was still very small. The whole history, from 1945 until 1980 in the United States, was one of practice going one way and opinion going the other. Practice went from smaller to larger government, opinion went from collectivism to greater interest in individualism and free markets. And that is why you have the political movement which enabled Ronald Reagan to get elected in 1980."[20]

Thus the society helped lay the intellectual foundations for the rise of politicians who implemented classical liberal policies throughout the world in the late 1970s and early 1980s in Europe and the United States, spreading to Latin America and post-Communist countries in the 1990s.

Mont Pelerin, September 1957

The Suvretta House is one of Switzerland's grand hotels. Some even consider it one of the grandest hotels in the world. Situated just outside St. Moritz, in the midst of snow-capped mountains and crystal-clear lakes, the hotel is a castlelike building connected to the village by a winding road. In the 1950s, trains were met by a coach with four white horses, taking guests on the mile-long drive along rushing streams to the elegant front door of the hotel, the site of the tenth anniversary meeting of the Mont Pelerin Society in September 1957. Most of the founding members were there, and several others, all interested in free-market economics, had been invited as special guests, including my father, at the invitation of Hayek. It would be my good fortune to be enrolled later in the month in a German boarding school for the year, and I was therefore traveling with my father. I was certainly the only fourteen-year-old boy from suburban Chicago at the Suvretta House, and I couldn't help wondering what in the world I was doing there.

Fortunately, my father did not make me sit through the meetings, so I walked up mountain passes and made friends with one of the hotel cooks, who took me trout fishing. If all of this was not sufficiently incongruous, after the meetings ended, my father and I were invited by Pierre Goodrich, an Indianapolis businessman and Mont Pelerin member who would later found the Liberty Fund, to travel in his rented 1954 Cadillac limousine through Switzerland and Austria. As I sat in the front seat of the limousine with the driver, listening to Mr. Goodrich and my father in the back, droning on about free markets and free trade, I recall thinking, looking out the window at rushing streams and pristine villages, that I would have preferred to be traveling on my bicycle.

THE ANTI-COMMUNISTS

While economic conservatives were organizing to resist creeping domestic socialism, anti-Communists organized to resist it abroad. Though it was forced to the margins of American political life during World War II, anti-Communism was not a new phenomenon in the United States. There is a proud history of staunch anti-Communism dating back to the early 1920s. This anti-Communism stretched across the spectrum from left to right, prominent within both the white and black communities, within the labor movement and management, and among Catholics, Protestants, and Jews. Indeed, any group targeted by American Communists quickly developed its own cadre of anti-Communists. At times this would be a defensive measure, often spearheaded by people who had been beguiled by Communism but had become disenchanted when they understood its methods and ultimate goals. Throughout the twentieth century, many of the most effective anti-Communists were former party members, fellow travelers, or undercover operatives.

In the years leading up to World War II, and even more during the war itself, Communists and fellow travelers were enormously successful in perpetrating the "brown smear," the idea that because the Soviet Union was our ally during the war, and because all of the West's resources were employed to defeat fascism, calling for anything short of a unified front against fascism was . . . fascist. As a consequence, anti-Communists were called disloyal to the war effort at best, and at worst fascists.

Conservative anti-Communists were nevertheless vocal in asserting, before the war ended, that Stalin intended to dominate Eastern Europe. Heavily Catholic Poland was a central issue, particularly among Catholic anti-Communists, whose warnings were echoed by Republicans in Congress, such as Senator Styles Bridges of New Hampshire and New York congressman Hamilton Fish. The Hearst newspapers, always critical of Roosevelt and staunchly anti-Communist, predicted that "Stalin would install in every country in Europe a Red Regime, which means more torture-chambers, concentration camps, massacres, atheism and continuous reign of terror."[21] The *New York Daily News* and the *Chicago Tribune* were similarly critical of the administration for conceding too much to Stalin while mapping out the postwar balance of power at the Yalta Conference.

And what did the left have to say about this criticism, so accurate as it turned out? William Randolph Hearst, owner of newspapers and radio stations, an outspoken anti-Communist and Roosevelt hater, became known as "Hitler's Helper" and "America's Number One Enemy."[22] Roosevelt himself came dangerously close to accusing his critics of treason when he said, "The war must not be impeded by a few bogus patriots who use the sacred freedom of the press to echo the sentiments of the propagandists in Tokyo and Berlin."[23]

When the clouds of war cleared in 1945 it became immediately apparent that Communism was not the benign democratic system depicted by Franklin Roosevelt and his entourage, and within months the Cold War began. Americans had believed, rightly at first, that the United States was the only world power of any consequence and that its influence would be predominant in the world. But almost immediately the Soviets reached out for more territory. As the war ended and Stalin enslaved Eastern Europe, contrary to the restraints included in the 1944 Yalta agreement, it became increasingly evident to policymakers that the negotiated peace was no peace at all. Soon mainland China was lost to Communism and then the Korean War broke out. The United States seemed to be losing power at every turn. Domestically, as the Rosenberg and Hiss spy cases came to dominate the news, Communists were revealed actually infiltrating the federal government to influence its policies, and not in the least in the best interests of the United States.

The beginning of the Cold War presented the Truman administration, still heavily populated with FDR holdovers, with something of a dilemma: how to construct a peaceful postwar order, preserve American interests overseas, and help our friends and allies expand their democratic and free-market systems, while not antagonizing our old friends in Moscow.

One answer came from George Kennan, a foreign service officer stationed in Moscow, later head of the State Department's Policy Planning Office, in his famous "long telegram" in February 1946. Kennan pointed out that the Soviets could not be trusted or bargained with because, pure and simple, they wanted to destroy us; permanent peaceful coexistence with the Soviets was impossible. The West must thus contain Communism's geographical expansion and restrict it to areas where it was already installed, and this should be done politically, economically, and diplomatically, but not militarily.[24] Containment, as it came to be called, was adopted by the Truman administration toward the Soviets and Red China. Liberal intellectuals, State Department hands, and foreign policy experts bought into Kennan's argument immediately, as it required no confrontation with Moscow while allowing them to talk the anti-Communist talk. Conservatives and true anti-Communists, on the other hand, viewed Kennan's approach as appeasement and therefore unworkable. Such an approach, they believed, was akin to Chamberlain's surrender to Hitler at Munich in 1938.[25]

The conservative answer to Kennan's containment policy was articulated in a series of books by James Burnham, a philosophy professor at New York University and sometime contributor to *Partisan Review.* Burnham had studied at Princeton and Oxford, worked in Detroit with

Communists in the trade union movement, and for a time in the thirties was the chief spokesman in left-wing intellectual circles for the Trosky-ite wing of the Communist Party. According to Marxist luminary Sidney Hook, Burnham was the party's most admired and "most distinguished intellectual figure."[26]

But Burnham came to believe that Communism would lead to bureaucratic dictatorship, rather than freedom for the masses. He became disillusioned with Trotsky's ideological rigidity and defense of the infamous Ribbentrop-Molotov Pact, in which Nazi Germany and the Soviet Union, bitter enemies, agreed to shake hands and divide Poland between them. In consequence, he broke with Communism, gradually migrating toward the right.

In 1947, Burnham wrote *The Struggle for the World*, in which he argued that a third world war, one against Communism, had started even before World War II ended. Burnham argued that international Communism, headquartered in Soviet Russia, was bent on world conquest and was therefore a threat to the cherished values of the free world, particularly those of the West. The struggle between Communism and the West, between slavery and freedom, was inescapably a struggle to the death. Its material weaknesses notwithstanding, the Soviet Union had the advantage of a focused foreign policy with definite goals, and the internationalist appeal of its doctrine. To counter this peril, Burnham believed, America must assume leadership of the non-Communist world, transforming itself into an empire if necessary, to ensure its influence. After consolidating its alliances, the United States should roll back Communist influence and control wherever it existed until it liberated the Soviet Union itself. Aggressive policies on Communism abroad should be complemented by aggressive policies against Communists at home. But Burnham doubted the resolve of the American people and its political elite, being young and naive, to carry out a consistent, successful anti-Communist foreign policy.[27]

Burnham's book received immediate attention, not least because it appeared a week after President Truman asked Congress for aid to prevent Greece and Turkey from falling under Communist domination. The *New York Times* reviewed it twice and interviewed Burnham, while the *Washington Post* devoted a long editorial to it entitled "Burnham vs. Kennan."[28]

In a tribute to Burnham in 2002, Roger Kimball of the *New Criterion* wrote that "he was fearless in opposing and exposing the totalitarian temptation. Which is to say that he was fearless in opposing and exposing the most corrosive, most addictive, most murderous ideology of our time."[29]

Burnham's influence among policymakers in the establishment was significant. He was called to Washington often to consult with the State and Defense departments and was a regular consultant to the CIA, through which he helped found the international Congress for Cultural Freedom, an important forum for left-of-center intellectuals agitating against Communism. He lectured at the Naval, National, and Air War colleges, as well as at the School for Advanced International Studies at Johns Hopkins in Washington.

Burnham also influenced conservatives profoundly throughout his lifetime. He is probably the single most influential philosophical architect of the conservative anti-Communist movement, which enlisted millions of foot soldiers before the fall of the Soviet Union forty years later. He joined Bill Buckley as a senior editor when *National Review* was founded in 1955, writing a regular column on defense and foreign policy called "The Third World War," a column that was read religiously by policymakers. Containment would continue to be the policy of the United States in one form or another for a generation, but never without a challenge from Burnham and his followers.

Many intellectuals were writing and debating U.S. foreign policy, providing the foundation for the growing anti-Communist movement; several of these were former Communists or fellow travelers—people like Louis Budenz, Whittaker Chambers, Frank Meyer, Will Herberg, and David Dallin. Their inside knowledge of Communism and their literary confessions and exposés of Communist tactics and atrocities became a conservative genre in the postwar years.

House Committee on Un-American Activities, Washington, August 3, 1948

Whittaker Chambers was not the first former Communist to testify before Congress about his experiences in the Communist Party, nor the first to accuse his former colleagues of complicity with Communism or even treason. But his testimony before the House Committee on Un-American Activities (HUAC) in the summer of 1948, accusing a high Roosevelt State Department official and Carnegie Endowment president, Alger Hiss, of having been an undercover agent of the Communist Party, set off one of the great dramas in American political history. The series of events unleashed by Chambers electrified the country, put the intellectual left permanently on the defensive about Communism, and gave a new sense of mission to the burgeoning right-wing anti-Communist movement. Even more, Whittaker Chambers planted the intellectual moorings for American conservatives that would last into the twenty-first century. More than the intrigue, more than the spy case, more than the vivid confrontation between the traitor and the patriot, the philosophical difference between East and West, between freedom and Communism, between God and godlessness, inspired the conservative movement.

Chambers was an unlikely witness. He was a senior editor of *Time* magazine, a favorite of editor Henry Luce. Born in Brooklyn in 1901, he studied at Columbia University, joined the Communist Party in 1924, and, as a journalist and translator for the party, became an undercover agent in the mid-1930s. He broke with the party in 1937 and reported his party activities to federal authorities shortly after the Hitler-Stalin Pact in 1939. His appearance was perennially disheveled; short and pudgy, with wrinkled clothes, he spoke in a monotone and, according to one committee member, "seemed an indifferent if not a reluctant witness."[30]

By contrast, Alger Hiss was a paradigmatic member of the American elite. From a prominent Baltimore family, he studied at Johns Hopkins and Harvard Law School, where he served on the law review. He clerked for Oliver Wendell Holmes on the U.S. Supreme Court and served in the Roosevelt administration in the early 1930s, culminating in his position as an assistant secretary at the State Department, in which capacity he accompanied FDR to the Yalta Conference at the end of World War II and presided at the San Francisco organizational meeting of the United Nations.

The House of Representatives' Committee on Un-American Activities was initially founded in 1938 to monitor Nazi collaborators in the

United States, but by 1948 it had become primarily interested in Communist infiltration of the U.S. government and the general threat of Communism. Democrats were not enthusiastic about such investigations, and the Truman administration planned to abolish the committee if the Democrats regained control of Congress in the 1948 elections. To increase its credibility the committee started holding hearings during the summer of 1948 to look into Communist infiltration of the federal government, calling as its first witness former Communist Elizabeth Bentley. She named names, including Lauchlin Currie, a former top aide to FDR, and Harry Dexter White, who had served in Roosevelt's Treasury Department and had been the chief architect of the World Bank. But Bentley was unable to produce corroborating evidence for the charges, leading the Truman administration to label her a liar.

HUAC then called Chambers to testify. After breaking with the party, Chambers had discussed his activities with Roosevelt assistant secretary of state Adolf Berle and repeated his story several times to FBI agents, but nothing had come of it. He had also, however, met with staff of HUAC, who were familiar with his story and thought that he might be able to substantiate Bentley's accusations. On August 3, he testified that he "had been a member of the Communist Party and a paid functionary of that party" before working for *Time*. He described the "apparatus to which I was attached" as an underground agent, known as the Ware Group, and named some of its members, including "Alger Hiss, who, as a member of the State Department, later organized . . . the United States side of the Yalta Conference." He went on to say that the Ware Group's function was "not primarily espionage," but "the Communist infiltration of the American government," adding that he had tried vainly to get both Hiss and Harry Dexter White to break with the party.[31]

Two days later Hiss appeared before the committee and denied that he was or had ever been a Communist, or that he had ever known or even seen Whittaker Chambers. Unlike Chambers, Hiss was an experienced and composed witness, and produced a long list of prominent character witnesses, including Supreme Court Justice Felix Frankfurter. Handsome and relaxed, he smiled often and appeared the very picture of credibility.

Chambers's accusation that Hiss had been a Communist was the lead story in the afternoon papers. By the time Hiss testified two days

later, the story had become national news, and the House of Representatives' Caucus Room was packed with reporters, curiosity seekers,
and supporters of Alger Hiss. Hiss's testimony was so convincing that
several committee members suggested dropping the entire embarrassing enterprise.

But a young congressman and committee member from California
named Richard Nixon, who had paid closer attention to Hiss's answers
and demeanor than his cohorts, was convinced Hiss was lying and
persuaded the committee to continue in order to determine whether
Chambers or Hiss had perjured himself. The committee then adjourned
to New York City and subpoenaed Chambers, who produced secret government documents that implicated both Hiss and himself in the Ware
Group and Communist espionage. In answer to a very specific question
by Nixon, Chambers provided information about his relationship with
Hiss that convinced the committee that Hiss had indeed known Chambers. It was the tip of the iceberg.

In a dramatic confrontation between Hiss and Chambers, Chambers
was asked, "Is this the man, Alger Hiss, who was also a member of the
Communist Party . . . ?" Chambers replied, "Positive identification."

Chambers waived his immunity, inviting Hiss to file suit, and appeared on *Meet the Press,* publicly repeating his accusation that Hiss had
been a member of the Communist underground, thus clearing the way
for Hiss's slander suit. But Hiss was in for bigger things in court than a
civil suit against Chambers: The U.S. attorney in New York eventually
indicted Hiss for perjury, as the statute of limitations for espionage had
run out. He was tried twice, the first case resulting in a hung jury, but
was finally convicted on January 26, 1950, of two counts of perjury: for
denying that he knew Chambers and for denying that he stole State
Department documents and handed them on to Chambers. Although
not convicted for being a spy, Hiss served five years in federal prison in
Danbury, Connecticut, and then spent the rest of his life denying that
he had ever been a Communist or a spy in order to protect the American
left, which had staked its credibility on his cause.[32]

For the remainder of his life, Hiss remained one of liberalism's icons
and Chambers one of its demons. The whispering, the profiles, the lectures, and the rest of the destructive campaign, the sort of campaign
that liberals execute so deftly, left Chambers looking like a psychopath,

a degenerate intellectual who had shown promise in his younger years, but had somehow gone bad; while Hiss, by contrast, was an upstanding citizen hounded by the "radical right."

In 1952, Chambers published his massive bestseller *Witness,* which was immediately acclaimed as one of the great autobiographies of the century. But it was much more than the life of a former Communist who testified before Congress: It portrayed the ultimate confrontation between good and evil, between freedom and oppression, between Western civilization and Communist barbarism. The Hiss-Chambers case was a watershed for conservatives in several ways, and Chambers remains a Cold War hero, among conservatives, for a variety of reasons.

First, the Hiss-Chambers case was a catalyst for the right-wing anti-Communist movement. It demonstrated to the world that the Soviets were infiltrating the U.S. government and stealing our secrets. Though the Hiss case was the most famous, several other high-profile cases involving domestic subversion made national headlines, such as the *Amerasia* and the Rosenberg cases. In the *Amerasia case*, State Department China experts were accused of passing top secret information to Chinese Communists, helping them to defeat their Nationalist opponent in the Chinese civil war. In the Rosenberg case, a civilian inspector at the Manhattan Project and his wife were convicted and subsequently executed for handing classified information on the American nuclear weapons program to the Soviets. But Hiss's conviction was the frosting on the cake, the one case that left virtually no doubt that Communism was an internal threat and that American Communists were committing treason in high places.

Second, the case put liberals on the defensive. Hiss was one of them, had gone to the right schools, held the right jobs, knew the right people, and held (they thought) the right views. As he was one of their own, liberals felt compelled to defend Hiss regardless of the evidence, and doing so damaged their credibility. Countless liberals fell into Hiss's trap and persistently denied his culpability. George McGovern, one-time presidential candidate, for example, wrote as recently as 1996 that "I have always believed that Hiss was a victim of the 'red scare' and of Nixon's political rapacity. It is a national outrage that this essentially decent and patriotic American went to prison as a consequence of the demagoguery of Nixon and the ignominious House Committee on Un-American Activities."[33] Upon Hiss's death, television's Peter Jennings lamented that Hiss "lost his livelihood and his marriage. He protested his innocence until the very end, and last year, we reported that the Russian President Boris Yeltsin said that KGB files supported Mr. Hiss's claim." (With the exception of CBS, the major news networks reported on Hiss without ever mentioning the famous Venona transcripts that unequivocally proved his guilt.[34]) Like the press, Anthony Lake, whom Bill Clinton nominated to be CIA director in 1997, claimed that the evidence against Hiss was "inconclusive," making Lake unfit in the eyes of many to serve as chief of the nation's intelligence service, and ultimately contributing to the withdrawal of his nomination.[35]

Conservative columnist Robert Novak observed after Hiss's death that there was a "deep-seated reluctance within the American liberal establishment to acknowledge that Hiss was a liar, spy, and traitor."[36] As George Will noted, "Clinging to their belief in martyrdom in order to preserve their belief in their 'progressive' virtue, [liberals] were drawn into an intellectual corruption that hastened the moral bankruptcy of the American left."[37]

For better or worse, the Hiss case launched the career of Richard Nixon. Nixon was a relatively unknown first-term congressman before the Hiss hearings, which catapulted him into the national spotlight and enabled him to win a California Senate seat in 1950. Nixon's handling of the case gave him enormous credibility with conservatives, building up capital and a reputation that he could later exploit to serve his own purposes.

In the preface to *Witness* in the form of a letter to his children, Chambers marvels at God's creation and elaborates on the confrontation America faced:

> Few men are so dull that they do not know that the
> crisis exists and that it threatens their lives at every
> point. It is popular to call it a social crisis. It is in fact
> a total crisis—religious, moral, intellectual, social,
> political, economic. It is popular to call it a crisis of
> the Western world. It is in fact a crisis of the whole
> world.[38]

Part of the task of conservatives, then, was to call their fellow men to recognize the dire threat that Communism posed to America and Western civilization and exhort them to struggle against decadence, futile though the struggle might be.

Finally, Chambers demonstrated clearly the philosophical connection between Communism and liberalism. As he explained, Communism was merely a more radical expression of liberalism: "When I took up my little sling and aimed at Communism, I also hit something else. What I hit was the forces of that great socialist revolution, which, in the name of liberalism . . . has been inching its ice cap over the nation for two decades. . . . It was the forces of that revolution that I struck at the point of its struggle for power."[39] This was also why all conservatives could agree to oppose Communism.

THE TRADITIONALISTS

Libertarians were conservative because they sought to defend economic liberty; anti-Communists were conservative because they opposed the greatest threat to liberty. But traditionalists were conservative because of their devotion to Western civilization itself; they were conservatives to the marrow of their bones. They believed that religious piety was the foundation of civilization. Traditionalists were troubled by the decline of high culture, the leveling of discriminating standards, and the corruption of popular mores, not least because these were the foundations of political life. But they needed an intellectual manifesto, explaining the tradition they were defending and making it relevant to the concerns of the postwar years. That manifesto was not long in coming.

SUMMER 1953: *The Conservative Mind*

By 1953, conservatives were beginning to be recognized as a growing political and intellectual force, and conservatism was gaining devotees and advocates in the political world, the media, and the universities. But criticism of liberalism, no matter how brilliant, was not enough. If the movement were to coalesce, it would need a definition of its beliefs. For although the term "conservative" was being increasingly heard, few people knew what it meant beyond restraining government growth and spending; fewer still knew its philosophical and historical foundations.

The Conservative Mind, by Russell Kirk, published in 1953, changed all that. Kirk, a thirty-five-year-old history instructor at Michigan State College (later Michigan State University), who was simultaneously pursuing a doctorate at St. Andrews in Scotland, was a shy but self-confident fellow, articulate despite his slight stutter, highly intelligent, and well educated. He had a mind that could assimilate a vast amount of material and present it in an understandable manner, and all in a superb style.[40] "To review conservative ideas, examine their validity for this perplexed age, is the purpose of this book," he told readers. The book was not, he went on:

> A history of conservative parties, but a prolonged essay in definition. What is the essence of British and American conservatism? What system of ideas, common to England and the United States, has sustained men of conservative instincts in their resistance against radical theories and social transformation ever since the French Revolution? . . . Conservatism is not a fixed and immutable body of dogma, and conservatives inherit from [Edmund] Burke a talent for re-expressing their convictions to fit the times. As a working premise, nevertheless, one can observe here that the essence of social conservatism is preservation of the ancient moral traditions of humanity.[41]

Kirk traced conservative thought from 1789 to the present—from John and John Quincy Adams, John C. Calhoun, Nathaniel Hawthorne, Orestes Brownson, Henry Adams, and Irving Babbitt in the United States; and from Sir Walter Scott, Samuel Taylor Coleridge, Benjamin Disraeli, and John Cardinal Newman in Britain, with great emphasis on the "founder" of true conservatism, Edmund Burke. *The Conservative Mind* expressed great faith in the beliefs of the American Founding Fathers, the Constitution, the Declaration of Independence, and the rule of law. The Constitution, embodying as it did the principle of limited government through checks and balances, was "the most successful conservative device in the history of the world."[42] The book also started from the premise that there is a supreme being in whose image man was created and to whom man is subservient. Tradition, Kirk believed, was the force that could control man's will and appetite; tradition was an unwritten law of conduct for society, the established order of civilization.

Kirk also dissected relentlessly every conceivable liberal panacea and error, and unmercifully ripped into every type of leftism—liberalism, collectivism, utilitarianism, positivism, atomistic individualism, leveling humanitarianism, pragmatism, socialism, and ideology.

The Conservative Mind made waves nationwide and was vastly important in solidifying conservatism into a movement. For the first time conservatives had a kind of historical manifesto, a book that defined who they were, what conservatism was, what and whose thinking it was based on, and what its consequences were. The writings of Edmund Burke appealed to conservatives for a number of reasons. First, Burke was the founder of conservatism in the English-speaking world; liberals who pointed out that there was no American tradition of conservatism could be refuted with the claim that Burkean traditionalists were heir to an Anglo-American conservative tradition. Next, Burke had been a lobbyist for American colonies in Parliament before the War of Independence, and not surprisingly, adopted a conciliatory posture toward them once the war began. He said it was a revolution prevented, not made, because it was waged to defend the inherited rights of the colonists and local self-government against the encroachments of a centralizing state. Finally, traditionalists looked to Burke as the penetrating critic of radical ideology and the French Revolution. Burkean traditionalists believed they carried on his struggle against radical ideology at home against liberalism, and they imitated his opposition to the French Revolution in their own opposition to the Bolshevik Revolution.

For an unknown author writing about an unpopular subject, Kirk received an astounding response. The *New York Times* review by Gordon Chalmers, president of Kenyon College, said Kirk was "as relentless as his enemies, Karl Marx and Harold Laski, considerably more temperate and scholarly, and in passages of this very readable book, brilliant and even eloquent."[43] Whittaker Chambers, the former editor of *Time* magazine's book review section, weighed in with the new editors on Kirk's behalf, telling them that *The Conservative Mind* was the most important book of the century; they responded by devoting the entire July 4 book section to it. "Kirk tells his story of the conservative stream with the warmth that belongs to it," *Time* enthused in its review essay. It suggested, with an appraisal "appropriately conservative in understatement," that the book "has an interest that is not mainly antiquarian."[44] Clinton Rossiter, soon to author a rival study of conservatism, hailed Kirk's effort as "one of the most valuable contributions to intellectual history of the past decade," whose "scholarship is manifestly of the highest order." In it, he said, "the so-called 'new conservatism' of the postwar period takes on new substance and meaning."[45]

Conservatism was suddenly intellectually respectable. Kirk presented conservatism as a plausible and reasonable alternative to liberalism, along with reasonable and plausible criticisms of liberalism. He demonstrated to conservatives that it was possible to remain an intellectual while still acting and thinking constructively about practical politics. Kirk followed *The Conservative Mind* with three books in quick succession, each of which applied his Burkean principles to practical matters: *A Program for Conservatives, Academic Freedom,* and *The American Cause.*[46] As Henry Regnery, Kirk's publisher, said, "Kirk gave an amorphous and scattered opposition to liberalism an identity."[47] His book appeared at just the right moment to unite prewar and postwar strands of conservatism.[48] George Nash observed forty years later that Kirk's book "stimulated the development of a self-conscious conservative intellectual movement in the early years of the Cold War. It is not too much to say that without this book we, the conservative intellectual community, would not exist today."[49]

Two other of the foremost traditionalists, Richard Weaver and Robert Nisbet, deserve attention. A shy, retiring man, Richard Weaver was a professor of English at the University of Chicago and expert in rhetoric. He was a popular professor and is still revered by conservative intellectuals. Weaver's most influential book, *Ideas Have Consequences,* published by the University of Chicago Press in 1948, became one of the major works that gave birth to the postwar conservative movement. Weaver argued that every culture must have its roots in what he called a metaphysical dream of reality, or enchanted view of the world. Western civilization's metaphysical dream of reality, rooted in medieval Christendom, had turned into the nightmarish twentieth century because of the triumph of William of Ockham's doctrine of nominalism. Nominalism rejected realism, teaching that there was no universal reality that the intellect perceives and that language reflects. Instead, the senses perceive reality, and the language we use to describe that reality is arbitrary. As Weaver put it: "The denial of universals carries with it the denial of everything transcending experience. The denial of everything transcending experience means inevitably . . . the denial of truth."[50] From this fatal philosophical error Weaver traced all the triviality of modern culture.

Western man could get a grip on reality again only by regaining his respect for truth in language and his respect for private property, which Weaver called "the last metaphysical right." Property is palpable and physical, demands responsibility and care, and requires man to protect it against those who would take it from him, especially the state.[51]

Weaver's cultural traditionalism and belief in political decentralization indicated that traditionalism and libertarianism could be reconciled, and made him a forerunner of the fusionism extolled by Frank Meyer. Meyer later wrote that *Ideas Have Consequences* helped him along his journey from Communism to conservatism, and he later called the book the "*fons et origo*" of the postwar conservative movement.[52]

Weaver translated his own ideas into practice, too. He taught in Chicago during the academic year, but returned to his native North Carolina during the summer to work with a horse-drawn plow on the family farm he had inherited. He lived his whole life as "a crusade to reestablish belief in transcendentals."[53] (Weaver always insisted on traveling by train from Chicago to North Carolina, a roundabout journey that took several days. My father, who knew him well, asked him once why he didn't simply fly, a three-hour trip. "You have to draw the line somewhere," responded Weaver.)

Another influential work criticizing the centralizing trends of twentieth-century life was written by Berkeley sociologist Robert Nisbet. In *The Quest for Community,* published by Oxford in 1953, Nisbet traced the development of modern ideas of state sovereignty, ideas that excluded any meaningful social role for nonstate institutions—what are now called "mediating institutions" in political life. From Bodin and Hobbes to Rousseau, the forerunner of contemporary totalitarianism, the trend of modern political thought had been to elevate the state to the status of the primary object of human loyalty. Church, family, and local community were denied any meaningful role in political life, because they rivaled the state for human loyalty. By deliberately reducing the role that these nonstate institutions played in the lives of individuals, the modern state deprived human beings of the social bonds necessary for the preservation of social order, and indeed, indispensable for the pursuit of human happiness. In replacing these tangible forms of community with an abstract, impersonal community of class, race, or nation, the modern state caused people to feel alienated, impoverishing their lives and fomenting social disintegration.[54]

Nisbet continued to be an influential force until his death in 1996. Wrote David Brooks, "Nisbet was a devastating critic of the politicization of everyday life, of the way family, friendship, and community have been suborned by the state. He anticipated, by nearly half a century, much of the current talk about family, neighborhood bonds, and reducing the size of government. And many of the answers he gave, starting with his 1953 book *The Quest for Community,* are more sophisticated and certainly more culturally learned than the ones we're stumbling upon today."[55]

New Haven, Connecticut, Fall 1951

It is interesting to speculate on the plans made by the administrators at Yale University during the early months of 1951 for the celebration of the 250th anniversary of the founding of the institution. Only two American universities were older, but Yale was the most prestigious. For a quarter of a millennium Yale had been at the peak of the American educational establishment in almost every way. Its alumni numbered presidents, senators, Supreme Court justices, heads of America's largest corporations and law firms, generals and admirals, and thousands of other prominent citizens among their ranks. A grand and very joyous party was surely in the works.

But there were rumors that a book was about to be published by one of Yale's most recent graduates, the former chairman of the *Yale Daily News,* the most prestigious undergraduate position, who had made his mark while a student and who, by most estimates, would soon make his mark in the world. The author had waited until after the manuscript had been accepted for publication formally to apprise the president, Mr. Griswold, of the forthcoming event. "We had crossed paths, never swords, several times while I was undergraduate chairman of the *Yale Daily News.* The conversation on the telephone was reserved, but not heated. He thanked me for the civility of a formal notification, told me he knew that I was at work on such a book, that he respected my right to make my views known. I was grateful that he did not ask to see a copy of the manuscript, as I knew there would be eternal wrangling on this point or the other." [56]

One wonders what sort of pangs passed through Mr. Griswold's stomach.

When *God and Man at Yale* did appear in October 1951 it caused a sensation. Young William F. Buckley, just twenty-five years old, had become a legend as a student. Veteran journalist John Chamberlain, in his preface noted, "Both undergraduates and professors seemed fascinated by Mr. Buckley. Some of them called him a 'black reactionary'; others said he was a true liberal in the old, traditional sense of the word. His editorials in the *Yale Daily News* were debated, reviled, and praised. Clearly he was someone. But the temper of the times being what they were, practically everyone I talked with thought young Mr. Buckley was fighting a losing fight. He was on the side of the 'past.'" [57]

Buckley's charges against Yale were not particularly complicated: (1) Yale, ostensibly a Christian institution, was undermining its students' faith by treating Christianity as one religious tradition equal in validity to others, and implicitly equally invalid; (2) in economics, Yale was promoting socialism and collectivism; (3) academic freedom was a hoax at Yale, there being a double standard that favored the left; and (4) to remedy the situation, the alumni should begin to direct the course of education at Yale through the board of trustees.

Within weeks after his book appeared, Buckley was a national phenomenon as well. On the day the book was released, the Yale Co-Op sold out its copies within an hour. Within a month it was on the *New York Times* bestseller list. The book was the subject of both enthusiastic and outraged reviews; it was debatable which sold more copies. *God and Man at Yale* sparked a firestorm of controversy not only at Yale, but in the entire liberal establishment. The *Saturday Review*, an influential literary magazine, published two reviews of the book, one favorable and one unfavorable. The favorable review, by Selden Rodman, hailed Buckley's challenge to "that brand of liberal materialism which, by making all values relative, honors none." Noting his disagreement with the author's first principles, Rodman nevertheless professed admiration for the "spirit and courage" of "his assault against . . . the dishonesty of those who pay lip service to one set of principles while teaching the youth, under a smokescreen of 'academic freedom,' other principles." Rodman's opposite number, Frank Ashburn, declared that the book "stands as one of the most forthright, implacable, typical and unscrupulously sincere examples of a return to authoritarianism that has appeared." He concluded by saying, "The book is one which has the glow and appeal of a fiery cross on a hillside at night. There will undoubtedly be robed figures who gather to it, but the hoods will not be academic. They will cover the face."[58]

To a great extent, the controversy arose from the fact that Buckley was an insider—he came from a prominent Connecticut family, he was the chairman of the *Yale Daily News*, a member of the exclusive Skull and Bones society. He was the sort of Yale graduate who should have gone on to the *New York Times* or one of the big New York publishing houses or the State Department or a university and become another of the many Yalies who joined the Establishment (he actually did join the CIA for a short stint in Mexico after he graduated, but quit within several months). What he did was a bit like reading another man's mail, or calling a gentleman a liar. Insiders were not, in the early 1950s, supposed to tell tales out of school.

The Yale administration went into overdrive to smooth over the controversy, which only made matters worse. In his Author's Preface, Buckley wrote, "I have some notion of the bitter opposition that this book will inspire. But I am through worrying about it." But it did not take long for him to recognize that he had been "naive beyond recognition":

> Much of what came was unexpected. I should have
> known better, of course, for I had seen the Appara-

tus go to work on other dissenters from the Liberal orthodoxy, and I respected the Apparatus and stood in awe of it.[59]

McGeorge Bundy, a Yale graduate and professor at Harvard, was commissioned by the *Atlantic Monthly* to review the book; Griswold gave his imprimatur to the review before it was published, and it subsequently became the official Yale response. Bundy described Buckley as "a twisted and ignorant young man" and the book as "dishonest in its use of facts, false in its theory."[60] He also attacked Buckley, as did many other critics and reviewers, as an ardent Catholic whose faith had motivated him to write the book. Yale chaplain and liberal activist William Sloane Coffin sniffed that Buckley should have gone to Fordham or some other suitably Catholic institution instead of Yale. There were charges that Buckley was a fascist—which would become a trope of liberal polemics against conservatives over the years—the *New Republic* saying, "It is astounding, on the assumption that Buckley is well-meaning, that he has not realized that the methods he proposes for his alma mater are precisely those employed in Italy, Germany, and Russia."[61]

If all of this was made to order for the publisher's publicity department, Buckley's response was even better. He left no stone unturned, using his sharp wit and pencil to skewer his attackers. In the *Atlantic,* Buckley refuted Bundy's claims point by point—at best, Bundy had not bothered to read his book at all, but at worst, he was "appallingly insincere." He noted the irony of Bundy's insinuating that he was a fascist, while upholding the belief that Yale should be governed by an "irresponsible, irreproachable . . . academic elite." He looked forward to congratulating Bundy on receiving from his alma mater the "privileged position of minor Court Hatchet-Man, which will undoubtedly be awarded him in recognition of natural talents and services rendered."[62]

To the as-yet-unborn conservative movement, the book was a godsend, and over time it would become a linchpin for several reasons. Perhaps most important, it launched the career of the man who would become the most famous, articulate, and outspoken of all conservatives over the next fifty years. Without Buckley the conservative movement, had it existed at all, would have taken on a far less sophisticated face, and would have been far less effective. As we shall see later on,

Buckley's prolific pen, his sharp tongue, and his charming wit would become the hallmark of the postwar conservative movement.

God and Man at Yale also opened the way for ardent, intelligent, and well-reasoned attacks on the liberal establishment. Viewed retrospectively, the violent reaction to it showed how concerned the liberals were about anything that questioned their monopoly on intellectual affairs, which gave conservatives a great moral boost.

Buckley had also exposed Yale's dirty little secret—that despite what it led generous donors, foundations, and alumni to believe about its curriculum, it (like other colleges and universities) was not handing down American values, Christianity, and the principles of free-market economics, but rather relativism, socialism, internationalism, and other liberal nostrums. Other colleges and universities were just as guilty as Yale, and the exposure of their guilt became a conservative preoccupation as the movement grew. Eventually a few institutions left the fold by teaching those permanent things that had gone out of fashion in Ivy League schools—older places like Hillsdale, Pepperdine, Grove City, and newer ones like the University of Dallas, Christendom, Liberty, Patrick Henry. Other books would appear—E. Merrill Root's *Collectivism on the Campus,* Felix Wittmer's *Conquest of the American Mind,* Russell Kirk's *Academic Freedom.* Of course conservatives in 1951 had no idea how far matters would deteriorate as the years wore on. But they had reason to be alarmed, for they knew that the principal source of the dominance of the left in intellectual life—journalism, think tanks, and entertainment—would be colleges and universities.

Buckley also aired the hypocrisy of the liberal concept of academic freedom. American colleges and universities, particularly the large, elite ones, remained the bastions of leftist power and ideology into the twenty-first century, dominated by liberal professors and administrations who hid behind the defense of "academic freedom."

Polemical attacks by conservatives on liberalism's failures in education would proliferate over the next half century, almost becoming an art form. To be sure, there were many attempts to mimic Buckley. This writer, a book publisher, must have seen no fewer than fifty manuscripts and book proposals that began, "This book picks up where *God and Man at Yale* left off." Most did not, and most did not get published. But Buckley's experience was paradigmatic for others who similarly encountered the hypocrisies of liberal academia; the new genre became a mainstay of conservative literature.

I vividly recall the first time I met Bill Buckley. It was probably shortly before *God and Man at Yale* was published, sometime in the spring or summer of 1951. I was eight, the second oldest of four children, and Mr. Buckley, as we were instructed to call him, was one of a constant stream of dinner and overnight guests whom my father brought home several nights a week. Many were authors or others who had dropped into his office, most realizing, from word of mouth, that there would be a home-cooked meal, a comfortable bed, and a friendly family merely for the asking. We lived just outside Chicago in a large, Victorian house with at least eight bedrooms—nobody ever was quite sure how many there were—and a gigantic dining room with a round table that comfortably seated twelve. Mr. Buckley, who was twenty-six, was charming, erudite, good-looking, probably had a few presents for the children, and was enormously entertaining.

Most of my father's guests were, to an eight-year-old, pretty boring. Russell Kirk told good ghost stories, but otherwise seemed to talk about religion and things I could not understand, smoked smelly cigars, and if he laughed at all, it was a sort of high-pitched nervous twitter that would send my siblings and me into gales of laughter. Richard Weaver never said much at all, as I recall, and was deathly afraid of cats, of which there were several in the household, and Mises spoke with such a thick German accent that what he said was virtually unintelligible. But Mr. Buckley told jokes, funny stories, seemed to have a wonderfully adventuresome spirit, and was just generally an all-around good guy.

And then there was the piano. My father was a cellist of considerable talent, my mother a pianist, and music was a great part of our family. All of the children had weekly music lessons, my brother and I violin, my sisters both piano, and Mozart, Bach, Haydn, and Beethoven were the order of the day. Brahms would be permitted on rare occasions, but the man had lived until close to the twentieth century, and in my parents' view was getting dangerously close to modernity. Pop music was strictly verboten, and was considered the root of a good bit of the evil in the world.

When Mr. Buckley sat down at the piano and proceeded to play a wonderfully jazzed-up version of "Three Blind Mice," my siblings and

I thought that we had died and gone to heaven. He started playing just a run-of-the-mill "Three Blind Mice," probably not much differently than any child would play it. But gradually the familiar tune morphed into jazz. I have no idea whether it was good jazz or bad jazz, but as far as we were concerned, it was just jazz, and that was good enough. What sheer nonsensical pleasure, what wonderful sounds and rhythms he created. He was immediately one of the family, at least as far as we were concerned.

My parents, on the other hand, were stunned. Here was my father's young, star author, the one who would put his company on the map (he did not know that yet, but it was probably already apparent that this could be a blockbuster), playing this forbidden tune. On their Steinway grand, no less, the piano that had recently been delivered from my father's childhood home. What were they to do?

Mr. Buckley was, of course, *the* favored guest from that day on.

CHAPTER FOUR

A Movement Takes Off

The considerable activity among conservative intellectuals in the 1950s had little or no immediate political impact. Dwight Eisenhower's election in 1952 was no boon to conservatives. To be sure, he broke the Democratic cycle started by Roosevelt twenty years earlier and was certain to be more conservative than Truman. But Eisenhower had beaten back Ohio Senator Robert Taft, a true hero to conservatives, to win the nomination.

Bob Taft was a *real* conservative and had given Ike a good run for his money in the primaries. Known as Mr. Republican, he was the son of President and Supreme Court Chief Justice William Howard Taft and had been in the Senate since 1937. During his political career he had moved to the right, becoming an outspoken critic of both FDR and Truman's domestic and foreign policies. A strong midwestern isolationist before World War II, he maintained his strong opposition to involvement in all foreign wars during the late 1940s, which raised many eyebrows, though less so as the Korean War dragged on. Taft was a strong American exceptionalist—he was convinced that the United States was based on certain noble ideas that placed this nation well above any other. Of these, individual liberty was the most important; he proclaimed early and often that the "principal purpose of the foreign policy of the United States is to maintain the liberty of our people." The three fundamental requirements to maintain such liberty, he believed, were an economic system based on free enterprise, a political system based on democracy, and national independence and sovereignty. All three, he feared, might be destroyed in a war, or even by extensive preparations for war.[1]

Taft worked hard in the 1952 primaries, visiting thirty-five states, making 550 speeches, traveling fifty thousand miles, and being seen by over 2 million people.[2] He went into the convention with a plurality of delegates, but in the end, with polls showing that Eisenhower, the former general and war hero, could beat *any* Democrat handily, Taft was outmatched. Taft was more popular than Eisenhower among party regulars, but Ike was more popular with the whole country. Added to Ike's popularity was the power of Eastern Establishment Republicans, who controlled the convention and wanted no part of the conservative Taft. After the convention Taft agreed to support Eisenhower in return for Ike's pledge to run not on a "me-too" Deweyite platform but on a platform Taft's supporters had drafted. True to his word, Eisenhower did run a conservative campaign, pledging to purge Communists from the government, the schools, the news media, and the labor movement. Unhesitatingly, he attributed the fall of China to Communism and the surrender of Eastern Europe to the Soviet Union to Communists and Communist sympathizers in Washington, accusing Washington bureaucrats of treason. As a result, Taft campaigned for him enthusiastically, as did Senator Joseph McCarthy.

Truman's presidency was in a shambles by the time the 1952 election came around, and the voters were ready for Eisenhower's message of less government, lower taxes, and an anti-Communist foreign policy. They gave Eisenhower and his promised conservative platform a resounding victory.

As the GOP nominee, Eisenhower was more conservative than Adlai Stevenson, his Democratic rival. But as conservatives would learn again and again over the next fifty years, being more conservative did not mean that an elected Republican would actually be a conservative no matter how his campaign promises, platforms, speeches, and the rest sounded. By the same token Ike was not a liberal. He believed in balanced budgets, spoke against the accelerated growth of government, and sounded like a good Cold Warrior. But he was much more of a conservative in the eyes of liberals than in those of conservatives, as any Republican president would have been in 1952, by which time liberals had grown accustomed to over twenty years of unadulterated leftism. Nixon, Eisenhower's vice president, was still well regarded by conservatives, largely for his handling of the Hiss case, and Eisenhower wanted him to reach out to the defeated Taft wing of the GOP. Eisenhower had no wish to deal with domestic Communism personally. He would charge Nixon with internal security, but as vice president, Nixon had little real influence over policy.

Internal security was a major issue for conservatives, who desperately wanted something done about the disastrous policy—or lack of policy—of the Truman administration. Fearing that any action would be perceived as a concession to Republican criticism, Truman had done nothing about internal security until he realized it would be a major issue in the 1948 campaign. And in truth, Eisenhower did little more, merely implementing a more stringent loyalty oath for government employees. Though he did not publicly criticize conservative anti-Communists like Joe McCarthy, he successfully tempered their power. Over the years, conservatives would be further disenchanted by Ike's failure to rein in federal spending, his mishandling of the Suez crisis, and his failure to intervene in the Hungarian uprising against Soviet domination in 1956.[3]

All this notwithstanding, Eisenhower's election demonstrated that FDR had not established an eternal Democratic coalition and that plenty of voters wanted somebody less liberal than Harry Truman. Taft, for his part, demonstrated that there were more than a few conservative voters, even if they were not supported by many pundits, intellectuals, or a recognized movement. Republicans on Capitol Hill were considerably more conservative on most issues than the Eisenhower administration; Taft, who was elected majority leader in 1953 when the Republicans took control of the Senate, commanded tremendous respect. But because there was no organized conservative movement, there was no way to mobilize popular support for conservative legislation. In spite of his having lost a bruising primary battle with Eisenhower, Taft worked well with the new president. As a sponsor of the Taft-Hartley Act, which restricted labor's power in collective bargaining, he was also a hero of the business community. But Taft died after a brief bout with cancer at the young age of sixty-three, in July 1953, leaving a tremendous leadership void. Taft's death left Eisenhower with only the Eastern Establishment moderates as his advisors, and he began to drift steadily to the left.[4]

Robert Taft had a long-lasting and positive effect on the conservative movement. As Barry Goldwater demonstrated when he was overwhelmingly defeated by Lyndon Johnson in 1964, losing campaigns can have their benefits. Numerous future conservative leaders cut their teeth trying to nominate Robert Taft in 1952, and what they learned served them in good stead in years to come. William J. Casey, for example, an active and enthusiastic Taft supporter, helped found *National Review,* became Ronald Reagan's campaign chairman in 1980, and served as director of Central Intelligence under him. Taft had Hollywood cachet, too—celebrity actors Adolphe Menjou, Gary Cooper, and John Wayne campaigned for him, as did novelist John Dos Passos.

Taft started the process of turning the Republican Party into a more unified conservative operation. Before the 1952 convention, he argued that the Republican Party needed to be won back from the Eastern Establishment liberals—the so-called Dewey wing of the party—to differentiate itself clearly from the Democrats. Doing so, he asserted, would bring millions of disenchanted Democrats and nonvoters into the party—exactly the project Barry Goldwater began in 1964 and Ronald Reagan completed in 1980. Taft also thought that doing so would make the Republican Party the political organization dedicated to ideas rather than electoral victory—something conservatives are still battling for.

Taft was the first postwar conservative political leader. Russell Kirk and James McClellan, in their classic book *The Political Principles of Robert A. Taft,* stated that "almost singlehandedly, Taft had strengthened and shaped the conservative strain in the American character, and had wakened many to the difficulties of the mass age . . . that healthful change must be in harmony with the historical experience of the nation."[5] Taft, they wrote, was one of the most accomplished members of Congress of the twentieth century and had left his mark for many years to come.

After Taft's death, William Knowland of California was elected to replace him as majority leader. A staunch defender of Nationalist China—his nickname was the "Senator from Taiwan"—he was an ardent anti-Communist who stood firm in his opposition to the Eisenhower administration's Asia policy. He was also a friend and ally of Joe McCarthy, who was then in the midst of his turbulent anti-Communist campaign. Knowland was a tough and stubborn conservative, but because of his vehement opposition to several of Ike's policies, he was effectively frozen from contact with the president, isolated, and thus virtually powerless. As a result, conservatives were without an effective political voice in Washington.[6]

THE PERIODICALS

By the early 1950s, from an intellectual and even an organizational standpoint, things were beginning to happen that would bind the various strands of conservative opinion into a movement. The diverse group of people who called themselves conservatives—the libertarians, anti-Communists, and traditionalists—began to coalesce and create a cohesive intellectual and political force, a process difficult at best. Conservatives were an odd group of intellectuals and politicos who would appear to have nothing in common, except for their hatred of Communism and FDR: libertarians or, as they called themselves, classical liberals, a few wealthy businessmen, some midwestern isolationists, traditionalist Catholics, a college professor here or there, and anti-Communists.

Little by little this unlikely group came together to form the conservative movement, but not without debates and discussions, intellectual confrontations, personal feuds, near bankruptcies, breaches of alliances, and many more difficulties. Those controversies, as well as the development of the fundamentals, would take place in the pages of periodicals and books published by, and for, the right.

Several small conservative journals, newspapers, and magazines turned out to have much more influence than appeared at the time. Two different incarnations of a little magazine called the *Freeman* emerged during the 1920s and 1930s, the first published for three or four years starting in 1920 by misanthrope individualist Albert Jay Nock; and the second, started in 1930, edited by Suzanne LaFollette, and including on its masthead Van Wyck Brooks, Eugene Lyons, Mark Van Doren, Frank Chodorov, and John Chamberlain. It also went under after only a year or so, again for lack of adequate financing, a plight of all opinion journals. In 1950 the *Freeman* was started up a third time, in yet another version, as a fortnightly—a small journal with limited circulation and, again, inadequate financing. Although it attracted many significant writers, it was never particularly prominent, and it certainly commanded little attention outside the circle of its readers. But its long-term impact was vastly disproportionate to its size. Edited by Henry Hazlitt and John Chamberlain, both journalists of considerable stature, it advocated free markets and deflated the overblown promises of what liberal statism could achieve.

Hazlitt was one of the great journalists of his era, a clear and decisive writer on economics who had held a variety of prominent positions, the last as an editorial writer for the *New York Times*. He was far more conservative than the *Times* management and the *Times* was much more conservative then than it later became. Hazlitt ultimately was too much for them. From the *Times*, he went to *Newsweek*, where he wrote the classic *Economics in One Lesson*, one of the best-selling economics books of all times, selling well over one million copies. The short and decisive book argued that government was only concerned with the consequences that were clearly visible and ignored those that were not, and that government intervention looked for short-term gain at the expense of long-term losses, with the result that wealth was likely to be destroyed by regulation, inflation, and taxation. It remains in print to this day because it brings the dismal science to life with vivid examples and clear prose.[7]

Freeman coeditor John Chamberlain, also a former *New York Times* writer, had written the introductions to both *God and Man at Yale* and *The Road to Serfdom*, as well as editorials for the *Wall Street Journal*, *Fortune*, and *Life*, and was a prominent and well-respected journalist in his own right. Even more than Hazlitt, Chamberlain used his stature to lend credibility to conservative causes.

In the grand scheme of things, the *Freeman* was tiny—by the end of its first year it had a circulation of fewer than twelve thousand. But to conservatives of the time and, as it turned out, of the future, it had as great an impact as anything else being published. It is hard to imagine, in a time when we are inundated with conservative magazines, books, and the rest, how lonely being a conservative was. A regularly published periodical, such as the *Freeman*, was a godsend, particularly as it contained articles by leading economists such as Mises and Hayek, senators (and conservative heroes) such as Harry Byrd and John Bricker, and literary figures such as John Dos Passos and Roscoe Pound. Not only did it remind its readers that they were not alone; it gave them much-needed ammunition for their battles.[8]

The left in 1950 had a magazine or journal for every taste, from the (Communist) *Daily Worker* and the *New Masses*, to the *Nation*, the *Reporter,* the *New Republic*, the *Progressive*, and down the line. The right had only the *Freeman*. But as would become evident many times over the ensuing fifty years, conservative publications such as the *Freeman* with limited budgets and small circulations would have a force far beyond their size.

The *Freeman* itself was riven over the race for the 1952 GOP presidential nomination, some of its staff ardent Taft supporters, while many board members backed Eisenhower. But, ultimately, the *Freeman*'s writers and ideas were far better than its finances. Although the *Freeman*'s financial problems seemed a supreme irony—a journal that preached the virtues of the the free market, competition, and sound money could not make a go of it in the marketplace—no journal of opinion could ever exist without the financial backing of wealthy donors and foundations. In 1954 it was bought out by the Foundation for Economic Education (FEE), which published it in a pocket-sized format as a monthly commentary on economic theory. As a result, it lost its rhetorical bite, its feistiness, and its strong opinions.[9]

The *Freeman* was not the only right-wing journal published in the early 1950s. *Human Events*, a weekly, had been founded in 1944 by Frank Hanighen, former isolationist, former foreign correspondent, and skilled Washington reporter; Felix Morley, at the time president of Haverford College and previously an editor of the *Washington Post*; and Henry Regnery, a Chicago businessman who would soon found the publishing company that would bear his name. *Human Events* was particularly critical of the foreign policy of the Truman administration and of the way the end of World War II was negotiated by Roosevelt, and was aggressively anti-Communist. Initially published as a weekly newsletter, it was distributed largely to small and medium-sized newspapers around the country, which were encouraged to republish its articles and editorials without attribution, giving it a far larger reach than its small circulation suggested. *Human Events* changed its course in the early 1950s, however, and started covering the Washington political scene from a decidedly conservative perspective, giving political activists around the country inside information and hard-hitting editorials. Over nearly sixty years, *Human Events* has been an essential component of the movement, covering conservative members of Congress, legislative activity, and other matters of interest to activists on the right.[10]

The *Freeman*'s short life was not for naught, however; it was a training ground for other conservative journals. With its demise, or as good as, it left a void. Into this void stepped William F. Buckley, Jr., and Willi Schlamm. Schlamm was an Austrian Jew, an expat anti-Communist and longtime employee of Henry Luce at Time-Life, with a stint at the *Freeman*. Along with Buckley, Schlamm was the motivating force behind the creation of *National Review*, and his vision and experience were indispensable. Realizing that divided ownership of the *Freeman* had been a chief reason for its breakup, there being no unified authority to resolve internal squabbling, Schlamm conceived the idea of having Buckley be the sole owner of the journal. But soon Schlamm's imperious nature drove him into bitter fights with his colleagues, forcing Buckley to fire him. However, Buckley's graceful diplomacy and sharp eyes were usually sufficient to reconcile bickering colleagues.

Buckley did not mince words when stating what he wanted to accomplish with *National Review*: "This magazine," he wrote in his prospectus, "will forthrightly oppose the prevailing trend of public opinion; its purpose, indeed, is to change the nation's intellectual and political climate." He spelled out what positions, on a wide range of policies, the magazine would take.[11] *National Review,* originally called *National Weekly*, would attack liberalism and attack it with gusto:

> This nation, we contend, is not yet ready for that decadent, lukewarm mood of indifference which permeates our Liberal press and, insofar as editorial convictions are concerned, makes most national journals indistinguishable from one another. *National Weekly* is committed to what was once called personal journalism—the manly presentation of deeply felt convictions. It loves controversy.[12]

Buckley was well enough known by 1955 to command the respect of the best and the brightest. He followed the success of *God and Man at Yale* with *McCarthy and His Enemies*, coauthored by L. Brent Bozell, which further consolidated his reputation as a leading conservative wit and intellect. And it was the best and the brightest whom Buckley brought in as editors and writers of editorials, news stories, and columns, to debate policy and issues among themselves and with others, and to bring the conservative branches into one unified force. To do so, Buckley would need editors from each group—traditionalists, libertarians, and anti-Communists.

Publisher William Rusher recalls that Buckley was a great recruiter, very deft in getting people who did not necessarily agree on much to work as a body. "Buckley brought us all together—Russell Kirk, Frank Meyer, and all sorts of libertarians and traditionalists, and anti-Communists just like myself and Chambers, who all had in common that the liberals were their great enemies but, very often, did not have much else in common and, indeed, regarded each other as rivals."[13]

Buckley had made it *National Review's* policy that anybody who joined the venture as a senior editor must already have an established reputation. No amateurs here. The initial senior editors were Willi Schlamm; James Burnham, ostracized by his former associates at the CIA and *Partisan Review* for his unflinching support of Joseph McCarthy; Willmoore Kendall, Buckley's mentor from Yale and one of the foremost political theorists of his generation; and Suzanne LaFollette, a veteran of the original *Freeman* and its postwar successor. Other editors were former Communist Frank Meyer; Buckley's Yale debate partner and brother-in-law L. Brent Bozell; Russell Kirk; best-selling novelist John Dos Passos; and former Communist Max Eastman. Shortly afterward, Whittaker Chambers joined as a senior editor and Rusher as publisher.

A principal part of *National Review's* purpose, according to Buckley, was to revitalize the conservative position and influence opinionmakers. The target audience were intellectuals, writers, and policymakers, not grassroots conservatives, although over the years these made up the bulk of Buckley's subscribers. From the first issue, the magazine was erudite, intellectually highbrow, and sophisticated, with Burnham as the enforcer of exacting standards. The writing was superb, the reasoning as good as the writing, and the topics diverse—from politics to American and European culture, conservative and anti-Communist philosophy, economics, and international affairs.

Conservatives were generally held in low esteem by the mainstream, a reflection of the constant drubbing given them by liberals. They were considered obtuse, Neanderthals, all-round second-rate. Many liberals could not believe that anybody in his right mind could think the things that conservatives thought; conservatism was considered some sort of disease, and conservatives probably mentally ill. When Barry Goldwater ran for president in 1964, *Fact* magazine, published by Ralph Ginzberg (convicted on a federal charge for printing and distributing pornography but then out of prison on bail), circulated a questionnaire to over twelve thousand psychiatrists asking whether Goldwater was psychologically fit to be president. In all, 1,189 reportedly responded that he was not. *Fact,* in its analysis of the poll, quoted psychiatrists who compared Goldwater with Hitler and Stalin, described him as "paranoid," "megalomaniacal," "unstable," "dangerous," and "a mass murderer at heart."[14] Malcolm Muggeridge, appearing on *Firing Line*, quipped that all he needed to know about Goldwater to back him was this finding by psychiatrists.

National Review, Buckley hoped, would change all this through its sophistication, sharp reasoning, and literary prowess. It would publish, with considerable style, the best that conservatism had to offer. When, inevitably, the left ridiculed it, Buckley countered with the debating skills he had honed with Bozell at Yale and outridiculed them.

The first issue included a "Publisher's Statement" written by Buckley (who was initially both editor and publisher), which, as publisher Rusher said, "flung down the gauntlet and practically dared his opponents to pick it up. It quite simply declared war on the liberals, who ran this country."[15]

But one should never underestimate the liberals' ill-bred capacity for nastiness; in the case of Buckley's new magazine, they rose to the bait, alternately turning their noses up in disdain and furiously denigrating *National Review* writers as reactionary idiots. Murray Kempton, a prominent liberal commentator, accused the magazine of being boring and trivial. Radical critic Dwight Macdonald called it dull, low-quality fare offered by obscure and eccentric "scrambled eggheads" for the "intellectually underprivileged," the "voice of the lumpen-bourgeoisie." Macdonald went on to say "Anxious, embittered, resentful they [*NR*'s editors] feel that the mainstream of American politics since 1933 has passed them by, as indeed it has, and they have the slightly paranoiac suspiciousness of an isolated minority group."[16]

Over the next fifty years, National Review was a bane to liberals and a godsend to conservatives. According to Jonathan Schoenwald in his book A Time for Choosing, "The most important development during this time was the creation of National Review in 1955 . . . the journal quickly became a theoretical and later a practical conservative switchboard, which plugged the famous and the ordinary into the same conversation. . . . [It] showed individual conservatives that they did not stand alone."[17] Schoenwald is correct, but National Review provided many more benefits over the years.

One of the benefits that did not exist was profits. NR was always short of cash and survived only because Buckley, one of the most popular members of the conservative movement, would send off a long letter each year to likely contributors, who dutifully sent back the needed funds. Bill Rusher said of the problem:

> A journal of opinion is not a commercial venture at all and therefore cannot be judged purely in terms of the survivability in a free market. It exists to expound a point of view and to persist in doing so whether or not that viewpoint is popular or commercially self-sustaining. In this respect it resembles a church, or a university, or a political party; and indeed, a journal of opinion partakes, to some degree, of the nature of all three.[18]

NR was a platform for the best conservative writers in the country. In issue after issue, Buckley, James Burnham, Whittaker Chambers, Russell Kirk, Willmoore Kendall, Frank Meyer, Brent Bozell, and others poured out stunning pieces on myriad topics, pieces that would otherwise probably never have been published, or would have been published in such scattershot ways as to have been ineffective.

Its offices gave hundreds of young writers an opportunity to learn how to reason and write—and so be heard. National Review alumni are scattered across the country as editors and writers. It was an inspiration to lonely conservatives across the country who realized, with each issue, that they were not alone. It helped many aspiring politicians sharpen their arguments and develop their platforms. Not the least of these was Ronald Reagan, who often said that he read every issue of *National Review* cover to cover. According to Bill Buckley, Reagan's positions on many issues were identical to those of *NR*, because they were *NR*'s. But that is not to say that the magazine was a propaganda organ for the GOP. Far from it. In fact, *National Review* declined even to endorse Dwight Eisenhower for re-election in 1956. It took it upon itself to declare various people or groups, which it felt were doing more harm than good, off the reservation, and barred them from its pages. It became the conscience of the conservative movement and remained so for a long, long time.

National Review pulled the three components of what would become the conservative movement into one cohesive unit. Traditionalists, anti-Communists, and libertarians complemented rather than contradicted each other; they formed the three legs of the stool that was necessary to a stable and cohesive political organization. Before they could become a movement, organized around practical policy positions, the traditionalists, libertarians, and anti-Communists needed to work out their philosophical differences and find common philosophical principles as bases for joint practical action. It was eventually up to *National Review* to fuse these different positions into a unified whole.[19]

In particular, this task fell to Frank Meyer. Meyer was a chain-smoking ex-Communist whose sleeping habits were known to most of the conservatives in the country. Bill Buckley recalled that "Frank had a rather beguiling habit of getting up at 3 o'clock in the afternoon and going to bed around 7 o'clock in the morning, which meant that half of the world was uniquely in his position for about 7 or 8 hours a day. So he was always on the phone talking to somebody, beefing them up, commenting."[20] He lived on a mountain in Woodstock, New York, where his home became an anti-Communist haven. From his Communist days, Meyer retained a zeal for political orthodoxy, and his regular column at *NR* was titled, appropriately, "Principles and Heresies."

As book review editor at *NR*, Meyer commissioned Whittaker Chambers to review Ayn Rand's popular 1957 novel *Atlas Shrugged*.

Rand was a Russian Jew who fled Communism and came to the United States with her family in the 1920s. In her novels, and later in more philosophical writings, she opposed anything that inhibited individual pursuit of personal fulfillment and defended freedom because it allowed individuals to practice "the virtue of selfishness." Rand's heroes, like John Galt in *Atlas Shrugged*, were Nietzschean *Übermenschen*, or supermen, who defied social conventions of all kinds and pursued happiness and greatness in spite of the restraints put on them by weak, lesser men and the ever-expanding state. Rand aroused in many a new appreciation for freedom, and inspired a devoted, even cultlike following. To this day, her novels continue to sell hundreds of thousands of copies per year. But some took a more jaundiced view.

Chambers was such a one. He found the novel lacking in literary merit and philosophically mirroring the Marxism it purported to reject in its ardent atheism, materialism, hedonism, and implicit belief in bureaucratic dictatorship. (Rand would have replaced the sign of the cross with the sign of the dollar.) Chambers pointed out that the rejection of God and the elevation of Promethean man in His place that he believed was at the root of Rand's philosophy and also the root of modern ills would set humanity down the path to totalitarianism. Indeed, in her dogmatism and self-righteous contempt for humanity, Rand seemed to be saying to most of her fellow men, "'To the gas chamber—go!'"[21] Stung by *NR*'s disapproval, Rand refused to attend any social gathering where Bill Buckley might be present.

The heresy that preoccupied Meyer from the mid-1950s on was the traditionalist belief that government was properly concerned with promoting virtue, which he thought could come only at the expense of freedom. Russell Kirk and Brent Bozell were the traditionalists most vehemently opposed to libertarianism. But Meyer faulted Kirk for relying too much on prudence and tradition at a time when conservatives needed to focus on first principles and break with the tradition of the New Deal.

Bozell argued in *NR* that libertarian claims that the expansion of government should always be resisted were prudent, but disagreed that the maximization of freedom should be the goal of politics. On the contrary, he believed that conservatives should work to make the political order conform to the transcendent moral order ordained by God, and that government ought to help make the people morally good. Making people morally good, of course, meant limiting freedom to do bad things, which the libertarian Meyer could not abide.[22]

Meyer called this willingness to use government to promote virtue "collectivism rebaptized," suggesting that it was infected by the same collectivist spirit that infected modern liberalism and Communism. In a series of articles and then in his 1964 book *In Defense of Freedom*, Meyer sought to reconcile freedom and virtue and unite conservative intellectuals in order to pursue effective political action. Conceding a point to the traditionalists, he admitted that nineteenth-century classical liberals were wrong to base their arguments for freedom on social utility; they should have based their argument on a metaphysical understanding of the human person as oriented toward freedom. But he insisted that, for their part, nineteenth-century conservatives, in their intemperate zeal to put down revolution, had neglected the just claims of freedom. It was the task of contemporary conservatives to put the claims of freedom and virtue, originally balanced in the Western tradition, back together. In opposition to Kirk and Bozell, Meyer contended that freedom did not undermine virtue, but was a necessary prerequisite for it. Though it was properly the ultimate goal of every man, Meyer thought that virtue was a personal duty, not a political issue, properly speaking. Virtue, he held, was not truly virtuous unless sought and attained free of external pressure, which he considered coercion. In this way, virtue and freedom were interrelated, and so were traditionalists and libertarians, because the American political system was designed to hold the two in balance, albeit a tense balance. Besides, as Meyer noted, "The position taken in this book is, I believe, an accurate representation, a crystallization on the theoretical level, of the empirical attitudes of the widespread and developing American conservative movement."[23]

This was what led Bozell to call Meyer's position "fusionist." Meyer and his followers didn't like the name, but it stuck. Philosophically pure traditionalists and philosophically pure libertarians considered fusionism an arbitrary combination of the two main wings of American conservatism, which to some extent it was. But as even the philosophical purists had to admit, it reflected the convictions of most ordinary American conservatives, and politically it worked.

THE INTERCOLLEGIATE SOCIETY OF INDIVIDUALISTS

Frank Chodorov liked to say that nobody stood to his right. The son of a poor Russian Jewish itinerant peddler, Chodorov was born on the Lower East Side of New York in 1887, and put himself through Columbia University. He taught school for a time until he became disgusted with the bureaucracy, held other odd jobs, and in the late 1930s revived the *Freeman* until he was fired for his independent writing style. In 1944 he launched a monthly newsletter which he named *analysis*. Chodorov called it "individualistic"—it advocated free markets, free trade, and the unrestricted employment of capital and labor. The state, wrote Chodorov, was the enemy, and bureaucrats and government beneficiaries were "a professional criminal class." *analysis* championed natural rights and the dignity of the individual and denounced "all forms of statism as human slavery." It struggled along for several years until 1951, when it merged with *Human Events*.[24] But in its brief lifespan, despite its small circulation and constant financial strictures, *analysis* had considerable impact. Inasmuch as it was about the only libertarian publication in the country, it became a must-read for young libertarians, who would pass copies around and quote from it. As was so typical in conservative circles, it was a struggling, one-horse operation most people had never heard of, and of those who had, all but a handful dismissed it as irrelevant. But *analysis* is still discussed sixty years later.

Chodorov believed that the institution most responsible for the growth of socialism in the early 1950s was the American academy. Thus the way to dislodge socialism was to foster individualism, as he called libertarianism, and conservatism, on college and university campuses. The Intercollegiate Socialist Society, organized in the early part of the century, had stimulated the growth of socialism, and therefore a similar organization on the right was needed. The ISS had never had many members, but those it did have—people like John Reed, Clarence Darrow, Walter Lippmann, Walter Reuther, Frances Perkins, Norman Thomas, and Jack London—had a huge influence on American politics and culture.[25]

Offering students a new paradigm—individualism—Chodorov believed, would bring about the ultimate demise of socialism. Training one bright student, who could go on to teach others, would be the most effective way of advancing the cause. And it was: Chodorov was a mentor of the young William F. Buckley, Jr. In 1950 Chodorov wrote a piece in *analysis,* subsequently republished in *Human Events,* entitled "For Our Children's Children," in which he shared his dream. The dream—an individualist version of ISS—might take up to fifty years to realize, Chodorov thought, but if that was what it would take, then so be it.

"We are not born with ideas," Chodorov wrote, "we learn them. If socialism has come to America because it was implanted in the minds of past generations, there is no reason for assuming that the contrary idea cannot be taught to a new generation." Being a writer, Chodorov expected his essay to inspire someone else to found a student group. So when a one-thousand-dollar check from J. Howard Pew—founder of the Sun Oil Company and benefactor of conservative causes—arrived in the mail, he sought the advice of his boss at *Human Events,* Frank Hanighen. Hanighen told him, "I have one rule. Never return a check."[26]

Chodorov decided to implement his idea. His new organization, called the Intercollegiate Society of Individualists, would distribute literature to students, promote campus chapters, conduct a lecture series and summer schools, and publish popular magazines and academic journals. (When the term "individualist" became a liability in the 1960s, associated with radicals on the left, the name was changed to the Intercollegiate Studies Institute.) It would seek out the best scholars to write for its publications and give conservative students a forum in which to articulate their right thinking.

Chodorov wrote that ISI's purpose would be "to teach individualism—economic, philosophical and spiritual—as a counter-agent to the collectivism to which the students are exposed. The presumption is that ideas have consequences: right action can only come from right ideas."[27] In 1956, the trustees adopted a mission statement that included:

> The . . . object of ISI shall be to promote among
> college students and the public generally, an under-
> standing of and appreciation for the Constitution of

the United States of America, the Bill of Rights, the
limitations of the power of Government, the voluntary society, the free-market economy and the liberty
of the world.[28]

Bill Buckley agreed to be the first president (on the condition that
he not have to do anything), a small staff was hired, and by early 1953
ISI was under way. Chodorov was not a tactician—he had no interest
in building a bureaucratic organization and believed that if a good idea
was around, bright students would find it. Which they did. Within the
first three years, ten thousand students had received over half a million
pieces of literature from ISI, all for free.

In their somewhat hysterical book *Danger on the Right,* Arnold Forster and Benjamin Epstein, both of the Anti-Defamation League of B'nai
B'rith, paid backhanded tribute to ISI's accomplishments after only ten
years of operation:

> The significance of ISI lies in the fact that in a de-
> cade it has spawned the cadres of what the Ameri-
> can Right seeks—an ideological movement that
> will wreak a counterrevolution on the political and
> economic front and eventually restore the America
> of 1928—or perhaps 1828. . . . Their energy, their
> dedication, and their talent for the written and the
> spoken word appear to overshadow anything that
> the more liberal youth on or off the campus can
> offer. . . . These young Rightists spawned in the last
> decade undoubtedly will make a substantial impact
> on American life.[29]

ISI took a long view of the work necessary to repair the foundations
of Western civilization and the American republic, which has been the
principal reason for its success. In its fifty-year history, ISI has been one
of the most influential conservative organizations and has stimulated the
minds of countless thousands of students and professors. Today it has a
staff of over sixty people and a budget of over $15 million per year and
publishes several magazines and journals. Its programs pepper college

campuses from Maine to California, it has its own book-publishing division, and it sponsors hundreds of lectures, seminars, and conferences each year. ISI's alumni includes significant conservative intellectuals and scholars, many journalists, and many more conservative professors, teaching from coast to coast. Many other projects have grown out of meetings set up by ISI, from periodicals like the *Individualist* at the University of Chicago to whole schools like Thomas Aquinas College in California.

Book Publishing

It is an old maxim in the book-publishing business that everything starts with a hardback book. Conservatism, fundamentally a movement based on ideas, proved the theory correct. Hayek, Mises, Buckley, Chambers, and Kirk ignited the conservative cause with books, and over the coming decades, books would be at the heart of the growth of the movement. Like the rest of the media in the years following World War II, book publishing, largely centered in New York City, was almost the exclusive preserve of liberals. There were, to be sure, a couple of small financially strapped publishers who published an occasional conservative book, but there was no house with an editor who actually sought conservative authors or promoted conservative books adequately. *The Road to Serfdom* was published by the University of Chicago Press; *The Conservative Mind* was accepted by Alfred A. Knopf and Company on the condition that it be cut to one-fourth its length.[30] Buckley probably thought that sending *God and Man at Yale* to one of the New York houses would get him committed.

Then there was my father. Henry Regnery was the original publisher of *Human Events* in 1944 and under the *Human Events* imprint published a series of pamphlets on foreign policy, free-market economics, and education. My father came from a wealthy Chicago textile family and worked in the family business for several years. But he was more of an intellectual than a businessman; he had studied at MIT, worked on a Ph.D. in economics at Harvard, and spent two years, from 1934 to 1936, studying at the University of Bonn during the early days of Hitler's power. When he returned to the United States he studied with and was deeply impressed by the legendary Joseph Schumpeter at Harvard. Schumpeter was part of the Austrian school of economics, but less of a libertarian than either Hayek or Mises. About Schumpeter, my father wrote:

> Whether he thought of himself as a conservative I have no idea, but he had the quality, which I think is an essential element of the true conservative, of being able to view the present in the long perspective of history, of seeing the present not as the end product or purpose of history, which I think is a typically liberal fallacy, but as a link connecting a long past with a limitless future.[31]

Regnery had a serendipitous combination of attributes: He understood the power of ideas; he was impressed by the reaction to some of his early publishing ventures; he was a conservative; and he had the financial resources to start, and maintain, a book-publishing business. He started his company in 1947, working from a small office above a drugstore in suburban Chicago. From the start, Regnery books addressed the major issues of what would become the conservative movement. One of the first was entitled *Blueprint for World Conquest*, edited by William Henry Chamberlain, a compilation of documents that set forth the international aims of Soviet Communism. The documents had never been published in the United States, and in fact were difficult to obtain. The book was published in 1947 to demonstrate, contrary to what the U.S. State Department and the liberal establishment believed, that Communism was not a benign alternative political system but an evil totalitarian ideology determined to dominate the world. It was the first of many anti-Communist books that Regnery would publish during the Cold War. Other books on a variety of subjects, especially history and culture, appeared over the next thirty years in rapid succession and helped to provide the intellectual background for the conservative movement. In the company's first catalogue, Regnery stated that his books would challenge the dominant current—he did not bother to point out that the dominant current was liberalism—in an intelligent and literate way. Which is exactly what he did.

Only occasionally were conservative books published by the large New York houses during this time. Although Whittaker Chambers's *Witness,* for example, was originally published by Random House, Regnery purchased the rights in the mid-1960s. But most authors, sooner or later gravitated to Chicago and the Henry Regnery Company.

The Grassroots

By the middle 1950s conservative intellectuals were beginning to make their mark through books, magazines, and journals. But an intellectual exercise is not a political movement, and in the case of conservatives, few intellectual leaders were interested in maintaining a strictly academic presence. Plenty of things were anathema to them, whether it be a bill in Congress, a foreign policy issue, or the appointment of another liberal to the Supreme Court. They wanted to see their ideas implemented. Being a Republican, be it noted, was no more synonymous with being conservative than it is now, but there were several solidly conservative House members and several in the Senate as well.

Which is not to say that there were not plenty of conservatives throughout the country who wanted the same things as the intellectuals. These people had supported Robert Taft in 1952, and would go on to support Barry Goldwater in his bid for the presidency in 1964. The movement was not a "top-down" enterprise. But aside from the reelection campaigns of a few conservative members of Congress, there was little organized political activity until 1960 when conservatives banded together to try to nominate Barry Goldwater for president. And as the movement expanded over the next decade, its ability to organize people at the grassroots level was one of its greatest assets.

Grassroots conservative activists, by and large, were "average" Americans who believed that their fundamental way of life was splintering before the onslaught of liberalism. A good many local organizations sprang up around the country, meeting regularly, hosting speakers, and discussing conservative ideas. Most of these had little or no contact with each other. One report written by a conservative in 1955 estimated that there were some 185 organizations and 135 publications "on our side" with "about 100 that have as their objective the fight against communism, socialism, internationalism, and one-worldism."[32] But as underdogs, they had the guilty pleasure of being rebels.

Of all the issues that concerned conservatives, Communism was considered the greatest and most immediate threat. By the mid-1950s, the Soviet Union was speeding along its international expansionist road and waging a pernicious propaganda war against the West. Conservatives viewed liberalism as a second cousin to Communism, and viewed the liberal elite who refused to confront the evils of Communism as traitors. Thus many middle-class Americans who had not been politically active devoted themselves to the anti-Communist cause. By the mid-1950s there were a number of right-wing organizations dedicated to fighting Communism—groups such as Dr. Frederick Schwarz's Christian Anti-Communism Crusade, the Christian Crusade run by the Reverend Billy James Hargis, the Life Line Foundation, and a few others. None had local chapters, but they published newsletters, sponsored speakers, and went on the radio. Over the years, groups arose, some responsible, others utterly irresponsible. None was able to build an effective organization with a nationwide appeal. That is, until 1958 and the appearance of the John Birch Society.

Founded by candy manufacturer Robert Welch, the John Birch Society became internationally known and subject to relentless criticism—by liberals, the mainstream press, and eventually many conservatives as well.[33] Welch, born in North Carolina in 1899, was a child prodigy who entered the University of North Carolina when he was twelve. At sixteen, he joined the U.S. Naval Academy, quitting after two years to attend Harvard Law School. But he then dropped out of Harvard to start a candy company in Cambridge. Eventually he teamed up with his brother, and after years of hard work, their company was successful. Welch also became an active member of the National Association of Manufacturers (NAM), where he served on the national board of directors and as a regional vice president. Becoming interested in politics, he ran unsuccessfully for the GOP nomination for lieutenant governor of Massachusetts in 1950 and became known as an outspoken conservative. Welch worked hard for Robert Taft in 1952, but when Eisenhower won the nomination, he was embittered and decided to dedicate his life to saving the country from liberalism and Communism.

Welch combined an ease of writing with considerable marketing skills and published several small books on conservative politics. In 1952, he distributed over two hundred thousand copies of a short book called *May God Forgive Us*, in which he traced the blunders and betrayals of the U.S. foreign policy in Asia that ultimately led to Communist victory in China. His mastery at organizing and marketing gave Welch ready access to conservative leaders in business and politics, access that he did not hesitate to use.

Welch eventually became completely obsessed with Communism, believing that it was infiltrating every aspect of American life and that the United States would likely be run by Communists during his lifetime—unless he stopped it. He set up a secret meeting of sympathetic business associates in Indianapolis in December 1958, where he lectured for two whole days on the nature of the crisis and concluded by asking those present to join him in founding the John Birch Society, named after an American missionary killed by Chinese Communists shortly after the end of World War II; ten of the eleven participants signed on. Welch's obsession with Communist conspiracies culminated in his book *The Politician,* which he initially wrote as a private letter and subsequently published. It alleged, among other things, that President Eisenhower was a conscious, lifelong agent of the international Communist conspiracy. The Birch Society took all the disparate problems of American politics, sorted them out, and provided JBS members with a comprehensive program that connected the dots in American life based on the theory that Communists were busily infiltrating every corner of American society, and offered them an alternative to ultimate Communist domination.

But as nutty as its views may have been, the John Birch Society was a model of efficient organization. Its members were asked to be active, not passive participants, and most of them complied. They were organized into local chapters, each with a chairman and overseen by paid coordinators. At the top was a national governing body of twenty or so men, who met once a month to set policy. The national organization published an array of literature, sent speakers around the country, managed hundreds of bookstores, suggested activities for the chapters, and raised money nationally. Its income in 1965 is reported to have been as high as $5 million, and it had somewhere between sixty thousand and one hundred thousand members. If it sounds as though the JBS was organized like a Communist cell, that is because it was.[34]

Birch Society chapters were spread from coast to coast and tended to be in small communities. The typical member was middle-aged, middle-class, white, college-educated, with a higher-than-average income, a churchgoer, usually Protestant, and probably a Republican.[35]

Birch Society members became involved in political campaigns and local school board elections and worked hard and effectively. Among their victorious politicians were Edgar Hiestand, James Utt, John Rousellot (later special assistant to President Reagan), and John Schmitz, all congressmen from California, Congressman Larry McDonald of Georgia, and Governor Evan Mecham of Arizona. In 1962, the JBS and its conservative fellow travelers withheld support from the California gubernatorial campaign of Richard Nixon, contributing significantly to his defeat. (This taught Nixon the important lesson that it was not possible to win without conservative support.)[36]

According to conservative activist Paul Weyrich, who attended Birch Society meetings but never joined, the leadership was often so ill-informed on issues that they got members working on causes that could not be won and that had little to do with real problems—"lots of esoteric discussion about things that were really irrelevant."[37]

During its heyday, the John Birch Society received an inordinate amount of attention from the press. The media portrayed it as a secretive fringe group, way outside the mainstream of American politics, and attempted to brush the entire right wing with the sometimes inane positions that the Birchers and Robert Welch took—positions vastly different from those generally taken by the conservative movement. President John F. Kennedy felt compelled to make a major speech about right-wing extremism in late 1961, talking about "fanatics who found treason everywhere," and urged Americans to reject such extremist politics. Although the Birch Society was not named, the press filled in the gap.

Eventually, many conservatives found Robert Welch's positions to be so incendiary as to be a real detriment to the movement. Russell Kirk wrote that Robert Welch "by silliness and injustice of utterance has become the kiss of death for any conservative enterprise." And in response to Welch's charges concerning Eisenhower, Kirk quipped that "Ike isn't a Communist. He is a golfer."[38] Congressman Walter Judd, one of the most respected conservative members of Congress, said in a speech that Mr. Welch's judgment was so flawed as to disqualify him from leadership of an effective anti-Communist movement. And Senator Barry Goldwater, who had constant brushes with the Birch Society, stated that Welch should resign from the organization, and should he refuse, the leadership should disband and reorganize under a different head.

The society eventually became too much for Bill Buckley at *National Review*, which increasingly viewed itself as the conscience of the conservative movement. In February 1962, *NR* launched the first of several attacks, which eventually effectively read Robert Welch, and subsequently the John Birch Society, out of the conservative movement. The first piece, an editorial written by Buckley and published on February 13, 1962, charged that Robert Welch "is damaging the cause of anticommunism," largely because "he persists in distorting reality and refuses to make the crucial moral and political distinction between an active pro-Communist and an ineffectually anticommunist Liberal." There were many fine members of the Birch Society, Buckley wrote, who were morally energetic, self-sacrificing, and dedicated anti-Communists, but they were not being well served by Welch.

Three years later, in August 1965, Buckley wrote three successive columns in which he expanded his criticism to the John Birch Society itself. How is it, Buckley asked, that the membership "tolerates the paranoid and unpatriotic drivel" of the leadership of the society, which found virtually everybody to the left of itself to be a conscious agent of the international Communist conspiracy? Buckley said he could only conclude that the majority of members sanctioned the irresponsible positions of the JBS and were thus contributing to the damage the group was doing to the conservative movement.

As he had foreseen, Buckley was heavily criticized for his editorials by people inside and outside the John Birch Society, although in the end few argued that he had not done the right thing. Looking back on his campaign, Buckley said:

> The Birch Society was doing a lot of damage to the
> hygiene of conservative thought on the matter of the
> Soviet Union. Someone said at the time that, if you
> call everyone a Communist, people might refuse to

> .notice even when there is a real Communist. I wrote
> very extensively on the Birch Society. I wrote all the
> editorials. I explained the position very carefully be-
> cause I knew *National Review* would be hurt by it,
> which we were for a while.[39]

Nevertheless, although the John Birch Society is today usually dismissed as a right-wing fringe group with little impact, it in fact played a
much greater part in the conservative movement than is generally held,
having organized the grassroots nationally as never before.

THE LECTURE CIRCUIT

Communications among right-wingers for fifteen years or so after World
War II were scattered and sporadic. There was no unified conservative
voice, and little commentary to reinforce the beliefs of conservatives at
the grassroots. Media editorializing came almost consistently from the
left, excepting a few papers like the *Chicago Tribune* and the *Wall Street
Journal*. So conservatives fell back on an old and trusted medium: lectures by prominent and knowledgeable people. Anti-Communists and
conservatives, traveling from one end of the country to the other, spoke
to social groups, business groups, civic organizations, college and university audiences—any place a crowd would gather. The speakers were
mainly leaders whose talks, usually followed by question and answer
sessions, were virtual tutorials on conservative truths and liberal er-
rors. These lectures not only helped formulate the policy positions that
would become the bedrock of modern conservatism, but stimulated the
development of the grassroots movement itself.

There were dozens of such speakers, journalists, retired military officers, authors, ex-Communists, active and retired politicians, and businessmen. A sampling gives an idea of the people involved.

Political scientist Raymond Moley, who organized Roosevelt's brain
trust and actually coined the phrase "the New Deal" before quitting the
Democratic Party in 1936 to become a conservative Republican, was
a popular speaker whose past made him particularly credible. Moley
believed that Democratic economic policies would replace the free-

market system with socialism and destroy the country in the process. He often spoke of the "new conservatism," which he defined as the preservation of human liberty. Moley was a popularizer who "tested, applied, and revised conservative ideology, and [was] surrounded by an array of intellectuals who kept [him] supplied with theories that could then be configured to sell to the mainstream public."[40]

Walter Judd was a respected congressman and a compelling public speaker. A medical doctor, he had been a missionary in China and a delegate to the World Health Assembly. Over the years, he earned many accolades, culminating in the federal government's highest civilian honor, the Medal of Freedom, which Ronald Reagan awarded him in 1981. Judd was an indefatigable public speaker: before the Japanese bombed Pearl Harbor, he gave fourteen hundred speeches in forty-six states warning against Japanese military expansion. During the 1950s, he spoke on topics as diverse as public affairs, China, foreign policy, and religion and ethics.

Former Notre Dame Law School dean Clarence Manion joined the national governing body of the John Birch Society and was a principal organizer of the draft-Goldwater movement in the late 1950s. He developed a popular radio show called the Manion Forum, which distributed thirty-minute radio commentaries to local radio stations until the late 1970s. Manion traveled about speaking on Communism, the law, and the Bricker Amendment, making over two hundred appearances in 1954 alone.

General Albert Wedemeyer, commander of the American forces in the China-Burma-India theater during World War II, had been, in effect, chief of staff to Chinese president Chiang Kai-shek, and was therefore an expert on the fall of China to Communism. Wedemeyer, a hero to many, was one of the most popular postwar conservative speakers, forcefully criticizing the Truman administration and the State Department's contribution to the fall of China. President Reagan awarded Wedemeyer the Medal of Freedom in 1985 for his resolute defense of liberty and his abiding sense of personal honor. "General Albert C. Wedemeyer," Reagan said, "has earned the thanks and the deep affection of all who struggle for the cause of human freedom."

Other popular speakers included Freda Utley, who as an idealistic young leftist had accompanied her Communist husband to Moscow in the 1930s to assist in the revolution. But she became disillusioned with Communism when her husband was taken away in the middle of the night by the NKVD, never to be seen again; she subsequently became a strong anti-Communist. She went on to become an expert on China and the Middle East and authored many books, including the best-selling *The China Story*, published in 1951, and *Will the Middle East Go West?* published in 1957. Utley made her living as an author and public speaker.[41] Especially worth mentioning are Russell Kirk and Bill Buckley, both of whom spoke for years, focusing on college campuses. Kirk enjoyed debating a liberal—often a local faculty member—on the merits of liberalism vs. conservatism or some similar topic and continuing to debate liberal students in the audience long after its formal conclusion. Buckley gave hundreds and hundreds of lectures for over fifty years, making him the most visible—and most vocal—apologist for conservatism for two generations. Kirk and Buckley traveled across the country debating foreign and domestic policy with evangelical zeal, smiting their opponents and winning converts.

All lectures were not, of course, to friendly, cuddly audiences. Buckley reports that "at the beginning, in the fifties and sixties, especially, college students, and of course faculty, were surprised, not to say aghast, at the heterodoxies they were hearing from the Right. But there was never (almost never) disruption."[42] As the sixties led into the seventies and the eighties, things changed, drastically. But more on that later.

Conservatives Find a Political Leader

Senator Robert Taft's death in 1953 left a large void in the conservative leadership. At first it appeared as if Joe McCarthy might fill that role, not for his leadership capabilities but because he was the most famous and outspoken anti-Communist. But he was censured by his fellow senators for his well-known excesses. McCarthy made no long-standing contribution to the conservative movement, except to liberals, in whose minds he was a demon—the anti-Communist they loved to hate. Conservatives were without a strong national leader between the death of Taft and the rise of Barry Goldwater in the late 1950s.

Soon after his election in 1952, Senator Barry Goldwater was recognized as somebody who might assume the mantle Taft had worn, and within three or four years he reluctantly did just that. Goldwater dropped out of the University of Arizona after a year to become president of his family's department store in Phoenix—Goldwater's—at age twenty-eight. When World War II broke out he volunteered for the Army Air Corps, flying in both the Atlantic and Pacific theaters and gaining a lifelong love of flying. He once wrote that flying an airplane "is the ultimate extension of individual freedom." After the war, he returned to Phoenix and became a respected young businessman, serving on the city council and helping organize the Arizona Air National Guard.

Goldwater, a true son of the West, had a close relationship with Arizona's several Indian tribes—he loved everything about his state. He was a plainspoken man, who always said what he thought—in many ways a classic "antipolitician," which endeared him to conservatives.

But Goldwater was also an able politician. He was Arizona's first Republican senator since Arizona became a state in 1912, beating powerful Democrat Ernest McFarland, the Senate minority leader and author of the GI Bill, in 1952. Coming from the Southwest, Goldwater represented a part of the country that became increasingly important to conservatives in the coming quarter century.

Not long after he was elected, Goldwater was named chairman of the Senate Republican Campaign Committee. His principal duty was to travel the country raising funds for Senate campaigns. Goldwater loved every minute of it, traveling from one end of his beloved country to another, getting to know people at each stop. His message was a harbinger of what the conservative movement would become as its three divisions coalesced in the late 1950s—he was an unshakeable anti-Communist, a strong free marketer, a firm advocate of the rule of law, and a believer in states' rights and a limited central government. He was disdainful of liberal Democrats and "modern" Republicans who hugged the middle of the road.

In the Senate, Goldwater was put on the Labor Committee and became a staunch advocate of right-to-work laws with an eagle eye for union corruption. Shortly after his arrival in January 1953, he joined sixty-two other senators in cosponsoring the Bricker Amendment, which proposed to amend the Constitution by making any foreign treaty in conflict with the Constitution invalid, and gave Congress the authority to regulate executive and other agreements with foreign powers. The Bricker Amendment was a favorite cause of conservatives, and responded to concerns that the UN Declaration of Human Rights, which four U.S. Supreme Court justices had cited in approving President Truman's authority to seize steel mills, could be used to impose rights not found in the Constitution through presidential fiat. The debate followed a classic pattern: Should more power go to the president, or to Congress? Secretary of State John Foster Dulles argued strenuously against the amendment, as did President Eisenhower. The amendment ultimately failed to get the necessary two-thirds majority in the Senate, but, as one of the most controversial issues in Congress in the 1950s it became a clear dividing line between conservatives and liberals.

Goldwater's reputation with conservatives was further boosted in the spring of 1957 when he put principle over partisan loyalty and publicly attacked the Eisenhower administration for its lack of fiscal responsibility. Ike had promised in his 1952 campaign to balance the budget and reduce federal expenditures to $60 billion by 1955—then went on to submit a 1957 budget of over $71 billion, a record for any peacetime year. In what would become a constant conservative theme, Goldwater charged that such excessive spending violated true Republican principles and reflected domination of the party by big-government liberals.

Goldwater was re-elected in 1958, again beating Ernest McFarland. Goldwater ran a tough campaign, making him one of a small number of prominent Republicans to be re-elected that year. Conservatives John Bricker, William Knowland, and William Jenner had either left the Senate or gone down to defeat in the midterm elections. When the Senate reconvened in 1959, Goldwater returned with a national reputation not only as a fine campaigner, but as one of the country's most outspoken and able conservative politicians. Clearly, Goldwater had filled the shoes that Robert Taft had left empty six years earlier. As the conservative cause moved away from being a movement restricted to ideas and criticism of the status quo and into political action, Barry Goldwater, as the right's standard bearer, would play a seismic role.

CHAPTER FIVE

Political Theory Becomes Real Politics

As the 1960 Republican convention approached, Americans—especially conservatives—were in a quandary. Eisenhower had been overwhelmingly re-elected four years earlier with the help of conservatives who had no place else to go. But now too many things were wrong. Americans had watched Soviet tanks roll into Budapest in October 1956 and were deaf to the cries for help from the Hungarian people as their courageous revolution was crushed. The next year the Soviet Union launched Sputnik, and Americans again watched helplessly the celebrations of anti-Americans around the world. Before the Eighty-sixth Congress was sworn in, in January, Fidel Castro had taken over Havana and started building his Communist paradise. Nikita Khrushchev, the U.S.S.R.'s new dictator—who a few years earlier announced that he would "bury" us, no doubt beneath the ash heap of history—was invited to visit in September and entertained by Eisenhower at the White House, while angry, frustrated young conservatives kept a silent vigil across the street in Lafayette Park. Khrushchev flew back to the United States the next fall and paid a visit to the United Nations, accompanied by a bevy of his cronies from Eastern Europe and his new friend Fidel, and infamously proceeded to bang his shoe on the desk during the General Assembly.

Nixon, considered by most to be the conservative candidate, arrived at the 1960 GOP convention in Chicago with the nomination pretty well sewed up. New York's liberal governor Nelson Rockefeller, who had indicated that he would accept a draft, backed out, leaving Nixon the nomination—or so it was believed. And so it was. But before the convention was over, Barry Goldwater would steal the show and emerge as the new force in American politics.

Goldwater had published his little 115-page book, *The Conscience of a Conservative,* earlier in 1960. It was ghostwritten by L. Brent Bozell, a senior editor at *National Review,* Bill Buckley's brother-in-law, and his coauthor of *McCarthy and his Enemies* (1954).[1] It translated the ideas of conservative intellectuals into something accessible to a more popular audience. Goldwater, in uncomplicated and clear prose, stated what conservatives believed and what their plan of action should be.

Goldwater concisely spelled out the conservative position on limited government, civil rights, government regulation, taxes and spending, the welfare state, education, and the Soviet menace. In doing so he brought the three conservative branches into a coordinated and seamless tract—a "fusion" of the three, which ended the three-way debate over reconciling conservative ideals and practical politics that had raged for fifteen years. As Goldwater said in his introduction, he wished "to bridge the gap between theory and practice." He took the ideas that established the roots of conservatism—economics, anti-Communism, limited government, and the Constitution—and explained how they could be applied to practical politics and government policy. The "challenge to conservatives today," he said, "is quite simply to demonstrate the bearing of a proven philosophy on the problems of our own time."[2]

The result was an astonishing success. *The Conscience of a Conservative* became, quite simply, the conservatives' new bible, the "underground book of the times," as Goldwater described it thirty years later. The first printing, a small hardback, was ten thousand copies, which the publisher sold to bookstores for one dollar each. Within a month, it ranked tenth on *Time* magazine's bestseller list, and two weeks later ranked fourteenth on the *New York Times*' list. By the time the 1960 election came along, just five months later, there were five hundred thousand copies in print. The *Wall Street Journal* reported that it was selling best in college bookstores, comparably to the perennial bestseller *The Catcher in the Rye.*[3] Eventually over four million copies would be printed; *The Conscience of a Conservative* became *the* political book of the century, probably with a greater impact than any political book since *The Communist Manifesto.* It is no exaggeration to say that *The Conscience of a Conservative* changed American conservatism from an abstract set of ideas into a practical political philosophy and, in the process, established Barry Goldwater as its most prominent spokesman, which he would remain until the emergence of Ronald Reagan. The book probably was also responsible for recruiting more people to the conservative cause than anything else. Typical was the impact it had on Paul Laxalt, who, in 1960, was practicing law in Carson City, Nevada. "One of my clients sent me a copy of *Conscience of a Conservative*," said Laxalt, "and, God, I found it absolutely fabulous. There wasn't anything around like that. And I just feasted on it." Laxalt thinks the distribution of the book "to young people like myself, a young lawyer who had run for office one time, before, was significant as hell. It was our Bible."[4] Laxalt, who was elected lieutenant governor of Nevada in 1962, was the first elected official to endorse Goldwater for the 1964 election.

During the last years of the Eisenhower administration conservatives tried to enlist Goldwater as a presidential candidate, an effort largely orchestrated by retired Notre Dame law school dean Clarence Manion, who engineered the publication and distribution of *Conscience*. Manion was on the John Birch Society Council, and close to society founder Robert Welch; behind the scenes, the Birch Society provided considerable support to the draft-Goldwater effort. Ronald Reagan later nominated Daniel Manion, Dean Clarence Manion's son, to the U.S. Court of Appeals for the Seventh Circuit in Chicago in 1986. After a bitter liberal-conservative fight on the floor of the Senate, Manion was confirmed by a vote of 48–46, but only after Vice President Bush was dispatched to Senator Goldwater's office. Goldwater had announced that he would vote against Manion, and his vote would have defeated the nomination. It turned out that the senator, beginning to show his age, was convinced that Manion's father had cheated him out of the royalties for *Conscience*, and Goldwater was prepared to see Manion's nomination go down in flames.

Others also agitated for the nomination of Goldwater. Toward the end of the 1960 preconvention season, a group of college students put together a Goldwater for vice president organization, hoping to pressure Nixon to put Goldwater on the ticket. The movement sprang up at a national college Republican meeting in Iowa in the spring, when the 435 delegates voted overwhelmingly to endorse Goldwater for vice president. Within weeks, Youth for Goldwater had chapters on over sixty campuses in thirty-two states with a headquarters in Washington, and had enlisted Marvin Liebman, a New York publicist, as its mentor.[5]

Manion, working independently of the students, was able to line up delegates committed to Goldwater for president from South Carolina, Mississippi, Arizona, and Louisiana, and organized Americans for Goldwater clubs in many cities across the country. Goldwater, who was criss-crossing the country speaking to enthusiastic Republican audiences, had virtually no interest in running for president or vice president, and moreover, was loudly critical of Nixon, who he said was drifting unacceptably far to the left; Goldwater resolved to do whatever possible to force him to the right. In a letter to a friend, Phoenix lawyer William Rehnquist, Goldwater made a statement that demonstrated his characteristic dedication to principle rather than political expediency. He wrote, "I would rather see the Republicans lose in 1960 fighting on principle, than I would care to see us win standing on grounds we know are wrong and on which we will ultimately destroy ourselves."[6]

Although he did not consider himself a candidate, Goldwater was still very much a presence at the convention, and the young conservatives who were there thought of him as their leader and mentor. His place in Republican politics was assured when, toward the end of the convention, in a move that conservatives would remember for forty years, Nixon flew secretly to New York City to meet with Governor Nelson Rockefeller, at Rockefeller's request, and acceded to his demands to liberalize the platform. Known as the "Compact of Fifth Avenue," the agreement between Nixon and Rockefeller swept through the convention like a cold wind and infuriated Goldwater. It was a reversal of the 1952 convention, when moderate Republican Eisenhower had to go to conservative Taft and incorporate his demands in the party platform. It fired a conflict between Goldwater and Rockefeller supporters that lasted for years.

Nixon had promised Goldwater that he would not meet with Rockefeller, who had been pushing for platform changes in return for his support of the ticket, until after the convention. Goldwater had met with Nixon the very morning of the Rockefeller meeting, during which there was not a murmur of Nixon's intentions. Thus Goldwater felt betrayed not only politically, but personally. Goldwater had scheduled a press conference the morning of the Nixon-Rockefeller announcement to release his delegates to Nixon. Instead, he blasted Nixon, charging that he had sold out to the GOP liberal establishment; it was immoral politics, he thundered, and self-defeating. If Rockefeller's demands were met, "It will live in history as the Munich of the Republican Party," said Goldwater, and assure defeat in November.[7] Nixon had shown, once and for all, that he was more interested in political compromise than in furthering the ideas of conservatism.

Goldwater's supporters at the 1960 convention may not have outnumbered Nixon's, but they were more vocal by far. Copies of the just-released *Conscience of a Conservative* were everywhere, being devoured by conservatives like red meat. Moreover, many Nixon delegates, uneasy with their candidate's shenanigans, found Goldwater increasingly attractive. But Goldwater did not want to run. In a meeting with the young leaders of the Goldwater for vice president effort, he all but begged: "Turn your group into a permanent organization of young conservatives. The man is not important. The principles you espouse are. Do this, and I shall support you in any way I can."[8]

After Nixon was nominated and the cheering stopped, Goldwater's name was placed in nomination by his fellow Arizonan, Congressman Paul Fannin, who called on Republicans to choose Goldwater as "the voice of conscience speaking for the conservatives of the nation"; he described Goldwater as the man who had challenged the imagination of America. Hearing Fannin speak of their favorite politician, hearing him praise Goldwater as the voice of conscience, and finally watching as Goldwater stood in front of them, his white hair shining in the bright lights, his dark-rimmed glasses prominent on his handsome rugged face, his chin jutting toward the microphone, sent shivers of pride down their spines. For the hundreds of conservatives in the convention hall, and the millions watching on television across the country, it was the moment they had dreamed about for years, particularly while withstanding the indignity and frustration of dealing with the liberal wing of their party, and the boredom while watching the passive Eisenhower years slip by as the Soviet Union expanded and became ever more belligerent. For most of the delegates, Goldwater was the only conservative they had ever known, and after the agony they had experienced with Rockefeller, then with Nixon, to have their man actually nominated was a thrill that they thought they would never experience.

When Goldwater finally rose to speak at the convention, his cheering supporters put on an eleven-minute demonstration of such exuberance as to astound even Goldwater. After they finally quieted down, Goldwater asked the chairman of the convention, against howls of protest from his supporters, to withdraw his name from nomination and asked his delegates to support Nixon and his vice-presidential nominee, Henry Cabot Lodge, Jr. But then, turning to his delegates, Goldwater admonished: "Let's grow up, conservatives. If we want to take this party back, and I think we can someday, let's get to work."[9]

The 1960 draft-Goldwater campaign was the first organized national conservative political effort since the war—the 1952 Taft campaign had been strictly within the confines of GOP politics, and Taft, even with more delegates, had willingly cooperated with Eisenhower to help him get the nomination and subsequently win the election. Although the people running the Goldwater effort were amateurs in every sense of the word, they came within striking distance of nominating their man for vice president. Had there been a conservative political operation of the class that would exist forty years later, Goldwater might easily have been the nominee. As it was, many conservatives cut their political teeth on the effort, and the campaign energized many people who had been frustrated during the Eisenhower years to put their heart and soul into a political campaign, with a principled and charismatic candidate.

The 1960 Goldwater effort launched American conservative politics. It is unlikely that Goldwater would have been able to get the nomination in 1964 had he not been nominated in 1960 and, as will be seen later, the 1964 nomination and campaign was of unparalleled importance to the movement, not only in terms of politics, but for the thousands of people Goldwater recruited, for the grassroots effort that developed, and continued, as a result of the campaign, for the solidification of many issues Goldwater so ably discussed, and for the way Goldwater was able to fuse the different issues that then made up the conservative movement.

The 1960 Goldwater effort also set the stage for the battle that was to come between the Eastern Establishment wing of the Republican Party and the midwestern-southern coalition. Conservatives knew all they needed to know about Nelson Rockefeller and his Republican Party, and they got a good taste of Richard Nixon. Only Goldwater was a true conservative, and only Goldwater remained true to his principles.

The draft-Goldwater movement was also a convergence of ideas and politics. *The Conscience of a Conservative* was a clear philosophical statement of what conservatives believed, a unique book in many ways, the likes of which did not exist on either side of the political spectrum. Goldwater admittedly was not an intellectual, but he offered a fusionist view of American conservatism that appealed to many Americans—the people Goldwater called "forgotten Americans," those without a viable political leader. In Goldwater they found a breath of fresh air, as demonstrated by the wild reaction to his speeches, his book, and the thought of his running for national office. Nixon played right into Goldwater supporters' hands by kowtowing to Rockefeller and picking Lodge as his running mate.

After Nixon and Lodge narrowly lost to Kennedy and Lyndon Johnson in November, the battle for the 1964 nomination, and for the soul of the party, was joined.

YOUNG AMERICANS FOR FREEDOM

The Goldwater for vice president students didn't wait until November to take Goldwater's admonition to heart and set off to create a new organization for young conservatives. Several of them had become acquainted through the National Student Committee for the Loyalty Oath, which supported the National Defense Education Act requiring recipients of federal aid to pledge allegiance to the Constitution and forswear membership in subversive organizations. Led by Doug Caddy, a student at Georgetown University, and David Franke, a student at George Washington University, the committee countered the efforts of liberal academic leaders and Senator John F. Kennedy to repeal the loyalty oath provision. (Ultimately, the oath was repealed by the Senate, but then condemned to a House committee, where it died). Many young conservatives formed friendships during this battle, gravitated to the Goldwater for vice president campaign, and ultimately founded the Young Americans for Freedom.[10]

In the first week of September 1960, less than two months after the convention ended, over one hundred young conservatives, representing forty-four colleges and universities, met at Great Elm, Bill Buckley's family home in Sharon, Connecticut. In two days, they created Young Americans for Freedom (YAF). After the usual parliamentary wrangling, the students adopted a statement of principles, known as the Sharon Statement, which embraced the conservative principles of the free society they believed the founders had upheld. In this manifesto, YAF echoed the same principles enunciated in *The Conscience of a Conservative*, albeit in fewer words.

YAF's first controversy was a significant one—whether to endorse Nixon in November. YAF's leaders reasoned that an endorsement from a new and small organization would do Nixon little if any good, but would do YAF harm by turning it into just one more partisan political movement. The second reason, of greater effect, was to set YAF apart from the Young Republicans *and* the Republican Party. YAF's function was not to be simply an arm of the GOP. It was to hold the party's feet to the fire, as conservatives would have to do time and again.

During its first months, YAF ignored Nixon and focused on ideological battles with the left, using the same tactics as the Communists and labor unions, which the left had all but copyrighted. One of the first such battles, in January 1961, was to confront a group of liberals seeking to abolish the House Committee on Un-American Activities, the congressional committee founded in the late 1930s to monitor the activities of foreign agents in America, which turned to investigating Communist influence after World War II. At a demonstration in front of the White House, leftist anti-HUAC pickets were met by YAF anti-Communists. For the first time in memory the left-wing pickets were outnumbered; the tables were turned. The left was beaten at its own game. More important, for the first time conservatives learned the public relations benefit of such activity—a mere handful of protesters could attract national press attention. The appropriation to fund HUAC passed the House by a vote of 412–6. Clearly the YAF group was more representative of public opinion than the leftist group. This small but public demonstration, according to one observer, saw the initiative in political propaganda pass from the youth of the left to the youth of the right.[11]

YAF flexed its young political muscles over the coming couple of years, holding rallies in New York City and Washington attended by thousands of people, with speakers such as Buckley, Goldwater, and Texas senator John Tower. YAF undertook a fund-raising campaign and quickly found willing donors. Within months, it had recruited nearly twenty-five thousand members, with chapters on over one hundred campuses in twenty-five states. The new recruits were bright, literate, and feisty enough to take on any left-wingers foolhardy enough to challenge them. Rick Perlstein, in his thorough but caustic book about Goldwater, *Before the Storm,* reports that YAFers "read twice as much as anyone else, the enemy's ideas and their own, delighting in dangling arguments, then slaughtering them in debate." Perlstein went on: "A flock of little Buckleys now tormented social scientists in colleges large and small."[12]

Even more important than its short-term battles, YAF was a breeding ground for future conservative leaders—congressmen, lawyers, activists, and writers. YAF bred "conservative cadres," which fanned out across the country, marrying the cause to their professional lives. If YAF later declined in significance, it was partly because of its success in creating a broader movement that took over and transformed the GOP.

GOLDWATER—1964

When Nixon lost in 1960, Goldwater's role as the conservative political spokesman was confirmed, and as far as conservatives were concerned, their Barry was the logical and only acceptable candidate for the 1964 nomination.

But Goldwater was, if anything, reluctant to get into the race. He loved the Senate, he loved Arizona, he loved his wife, and he hated being told what to do. He could not understand why he should give up his charmed life. He may have also sensed that his popularity, which was considerable, would change once he became a candidate for president. As many people have discovered, a politician can go a long way in Washington until he becomes a serious presidential candidate. At that precise moment the Washington press corps digs in, and reputations are often destroyed in no time. As long as he was just a senator from the Southwest, the darling of the conservative wing of the Republican Party, but no threat to the Eastern Liberal Republican Establishment, Goldwater would be treated as something of an anomaly, but with respect. During the spring and summer of 1961, *Time, Newsweek*, and *U.S. News & World Report* each published positive stories on Goldwater. *Newsweek* led off with a six-page piece calling Goldwater the "leading spokesman" for American conservatism and reporting that he was one of the most popular politicians among college students, one who exuded a charm that led one political enemy to say, "The trouble with the SOB is that even the people who hate him like him."[13]

Time, in a positive cover article in June, reported that Goldwater was one of the top two or three figures in the Republican Party, his office was inundated with invitations to speak, his book, *The Conscience of a Conservative*, had sold over seven hundred thousand copies, and his thrice-weekly newspaper column was syndicated in over hundred papers. Goldwater was so popular, according to *Time* because his message resonated so well with so many Republicans. "His message of smaller government," *Time* reported, was reinforced by Goldwater himself, who was "a tanned, trim (185 lbs) six footer with searching blue eyes behind his dark-rimmed glasses, and a thinning shock of silver hair . . . Goldwater has more than his share of political sex-appeal." The article concluded by saying that whether Goldwater ultimately became the party's conscience or its candidate, he would "have plenty to say about the tone and spirit of this party's platform, and even more to say about who will be standing on it."[14]

U.S. News & World Report, in August 1963, did a similarly positive profile of Goldwater, concluding that "next to President Kennedy, Mr. Goldwater has become the most publicized political figure in the nation," and opined that he should be able to bring 25 to 30 percent of all delegates to the 1964 convention with him, mostly from the South, the Midwest, and the West.[15]

Over the next couple of years, Goldwater's views became familiar to millions of Americans, as he became a fixture on national television, debating or being interviewed about the conservative philosophy of government, about politics in general, and about his criticism of the Kennedy administration. He also logged tens of thousands of miles traveling about the country on the speaking circuit, usually greeted by large crowds of admiring supporters, and generally receiving positive reviews of his speeches in the local press. In the month of June 1961 alone, he made twenty-three speeches outside of Washington. He appeared on hundreds of college and university campuses, at rallies sponsored by Young Americans for Freedom and the Young Republicans, and anywhere else a crowd would gather to hear his message. Lee Edwards, in his biography of Goldwater, says that "the media, like every other part of the liberal establishment, did not believe that Goldwater could win the nomination. Therefore, there was no real danger of his being able to implement his radical ideas."[16] But as Goldwater had himself predicted, the same magazines, newspapers, and television networks that treated him so well as he advocated his conservative philosophy in the early sixties changed their tune abruptly as the 1964 election approached with him at the head of the Republican ticket: Overnight, he became a warmonger, an extremist, and psychologically unfit to be president, among other accusations, although he had not changed his message in the slightest.

With the liberal Rockefeller wing of the party still dominant and controlling the nomination process, getting Goldwater onto the ticket would prove a monumental task. But Goldwater's backers, emboldened by their near success in 1960, were ready for a fight, and several groups sprang up to draft Goldwater for president.

William Rusher, publisher of *National Review*, and freshman Ohio Congressman John Ashbrook had gotten to know each other well in the Young Republicans—Ashbrook had been the YR national chairman several years earlier and was becoming a popular leader among conservatives. Both had files of correspondence from old YR friends and acquaintances, many of whom had become active in the senior party, and would, Rusher and Ashbrook believed, be thrilled to help draft Senator Goldwater. Enlisting the assistance of veteran Republican operative and former Cornell political science professor F. Clifton White, they invited a group of twenty-six old friends to meet in Chicago in October 1961 for what they described as a reunion, a meeting that was intended to set in motion the movement to nominate Goldwater in 1964 and ultimately take over the Republican Party. Nineteen of the twenty-six actually showed up at a seedy motel near O'Hare Airport that was reportedly best known for its hookers, while the fourth game of the World Series was being played. It was concluded that the group's goal would be to "re-establish the Republican Party as an effective conservative force in American politics." Drafting Goldwater, who still wanted nothing to do with the presidency, would follow in due course. Clif White subsequently met with Goldwater, assuring him that the group's purpose "was to turn the Republican Party into an effective conservative instrument," and that no effort would be made to draft Goldwater until after the 1962 congressional elections. Goldwater could not have been more pleased, gave the group his blessing, and offered to help in any way he could.

The group met again in December with a few more trusted friends, and White, the master strategist, laid out exactly how he planned to take over the party, precinct by precinct, county by county, and state by state. Enough money was raised to finance the group for the first couple of months, and White was hired to run it. He rented some office space across the street from Grand Central Terminal—his office number was Suite 3505—and set about putting the plan to work.

Over the next eighteen months, White put together the machinery to launch a draft movement that was unprecedented, given that Goldwater adamantly proclaimed he would not run; but each time he did, his mail increased, more local committees were formed, and more people signed on to help. Eventually, early in 1963, White felt that he had enough of a nod from Goldwater (which was, in fact, not much of a nod, but more a refusal to repudiate their efforts)[17] to publicly announce the formation of the Draft Goldwater Committee.

White and his friends may have been good organizers, but they knew organization would not be enough to win the nomination. Just getting past Rockefeller, who, it was widely assumed, would be the 1964 nominee, would be difficult: In a Gallup poll taken in early 1963, Republicans preferred Rockefeller over Goldwater by 49 to 17 percent.[18] But later that spring a newly divorced Rockefeller married his mistress, "Happy" Murphy, herself a divorcee with four children, which was a scandalous event for those times. In April, major confrontations arose in Birmingham, Alabama, between blacks led by Martin Luther King and local authorities over desegregation of lunch counters. Rockefeller was closely identified with the civil rights movement, and the atmosphere of racial discord took its toll on him with conservative voters: The May Gallup poll showed Goldwater running ahead of Rockefeller by a 35 to 30 percent margin. By October, according to U.S. News & World Report,

56 percent of Republicans in the House and Senate favored Goldwater versus 10 percent for Rockefeller. The numbers for state party officials were similar.[19]

Rockefeller took the offensive. He began to attack the "radical right" and Goldwater's participation in it, even announcing that if Goldwater were nominated, he would not support him unless Goldwater could prove he was not controlled by radical right-wingers. Goldwater fought back—he was never one to back away from a good fight on matters of principle—and his backers recognized gleefully that this was a battle royal between elite Eastern Establishment Republicans and the great coalition of southern, midwestern, and western conservatives who made up a majority of the party.

In the pages of *National Review* in February 1963 Bill Rusher had developed what he called the "Southern Strategy," which presumed that a conservative Republican with support in the Midwest and West could make inroads into the solidly Democratic South because of southerners' discomfort with the civil rights movement and thus eke out a presidential victory. In 1948 and 1956, southern Democrats had shown their willingness to buck their national party over segregation. The Kennedy administration played to this tune by proposing major civil rights legislation in June 1963 that would outlaw discrimination in public accommodations and employment. Shortly thereafter, Kennedy gave his blessings to Martin Luther King's March on Washington, which brought hundreds of thousands of demonstrators to the nation's capital with major, nationwide media attention. The Southern Strategy appeared to be working when an August 1963 Gallup poll showed Goldwater beating Kennedy in the South by double digits.[20] During the same period, a number of astute political analysts also predicted that Goldwater would give Kennedy a very good run for his money.

Everything changed, however, with the assassination of President Kennedy on November 22, 1963; it sealed the fate of Goldwater's campaign. Voters were unlikely to want three different presidents in one year's time. And without Kennedy, the perfect symbol of the Eastern Establishment, Goldwater lost his greatest asset. Lyndon Johnson was a master politician, a southerner, perceived to be more conservative than Kennedy, and he exploited public mourning to the fullest.

Goldwater knew he could not win, but he also knew he could not back out. He was the political leader of the conservative movement, and millions of conservatives relied on him to articulate what they believed. The "commitment, the bond I had made to so many conservatives and they to me was virtually unbreakable," he later said.[21] According to former campaign aide and biographer Lee Edwards, Goldwater "recognized that in running he assured conservatives of a strong, principled voice in the affairs of the nation. He knew he had no real chance of winning the election, but he hoped that by rallying conservatives, they would be able to take over the Republican Party and help get the country back on the right track."[22]

The fight for the 1964 nomination, largely fought between Rockefeller and Goldwater (Henry Cabot Lodge won the New Hampshire primary on a write-in, but he never went much further; Michigan governor George Romney also made a failed attempt) brought tens of thousands of conservatives into the world of politics. In every state that Goldwater entered, particularly those in the West, the South, and the Midwest, huge crowds of enthusiastic conservatives came out to see him, often organized by Young Americans for Freedom, the Young Republicans, or even the John Birch Society. These rallies served as recruiting centers for Goldwater supporters to join the conservative movement. In the California primary alone, Goldwater had 50,000 volunteers working in his campaign, many of whom had never been involved in politics before. On just one Saturday before the primary, 8,000 volunteers set out to canvass 600,000 homes, and by primary day had compiled a list of 300,000 Goldwater supporters.[23] Goldwater ultimately eked out a narrow victory over Rockefeller in the California primary—Rockefeller's new wife had a baby just before the vote, which sealed his fate, and Rockefeller dropped out of the race. William Scranton, governor of Pennsylvania and the epitome of the Eastern Republican Establishment, made a feeble effort to wrest the nomination from Goldwater, but it was too little too late.

The 1964 Republican convention may have been the largest conservative rally ever held, at least until that time. Delegates from every state, wild about Goldwater and releasing their frustration after years of liberal domination of their party, at last had their day. Goldwater was nominated on the first ballot to a demonstration rivaling any that had ever transpired in either party. His acceptance speech, the next evening, was vintage Goldwater, and laid out the principles on which he would run the fall campaign—essentially the same principles he had spelled out four years earlier in *The Conscience of a Conservative*. But one line of his speech would overshadow everything else, and haunt Goldwater throughout the campaign as his defense of fanaticism. "I would remind you," said Goldwater, "that extremism in the defense of liberty is not a vice! And let me remind you also that moderation in the pursuit of justice is no virtue!"[24]

Goldwater's nomination on that summer evening in San Francisco changed the conservative movement, changed the Republican Party, and changed American politics forever. The Eastern Republican Establishment, the wing of the party that had dominated it since the nomination of Wendell Willkie in 1940, had lost power to a new group of politicians, conservatives, who more than anything were driven by ideas: limited government, economic and political freedom, traditional values, and victory over Communism. These would be the issues on which Goldwater campaigned against an incumbent president whose policies, like those of his predecessor, were old, shopworn liberal Democratic policies, tried but untrue. And the campaign that had started with the Draft Goldwater Committee three years earlier and had attracted fifty thousand volunteers in California and countless more across the country would ultimately draw hundreds of thousands of conservative volunteers, change the way presidential campaigns were financed, and broadcast the conservative message to the country as only a presidential campaign can.

In the Goldwater campaign, the disparate grassroots and intellectual groups finally coalesced into a unified movement. William Baroody of the American Enterprise Institute had taken note of Goldwater in the late 1950s and cultivated him by inviting him for dinner to meet conservative intellectuals associated with AEI. His efforts paid off with a major role in the Goldwater campaign. Baroody assembled a team of first-rate thinkers to advise Goldwater on policy matters. One of those, Milton Friedman, who wrote speeches for Goldwater, had his ideas broadcast to millions of Americans who might otherwise never have heard them. No one could deny that conservative intellectuals had helped create the environment in which the Goldwater campaign was imaginable. Indeed, their role in bringing about the campaign was unprecedented and has been unmatched since.[25]

Goldwater and his campaign team recognized from the start that winning was simply not in the cards. Having been drafted against his will, Goldwater decided that if he had to run, he would do it his way. But Goldwater's indifference to victory gave him the freedom to run a campaign based on principle rather than political expedience, a campaign that could spell out broad philosophical concepts that would resound not only with conservatives, but with people who were disaffected by Lyndon Johnson's liberalism.

According to the *Washington Post*, Goldwater's "was the last of the free-form campaigns for the White House. There were no outsiders, no consultants in an inner circle reserved for friends and conservative believers."[26] He campaigned on conservative principles: He made it clear that he stood for federalism, smaller government, fiscal responsibility, and anti-Communism. Goldwater's message was largely about broad, general principles of conservatism rather than a discussion of issues that directly affected voters. It was politically ineffective, but it won people's hearts and minds.

Johnson, determined to win a personal mandate, gave no quarter to Goldwater. He put aide Bill Moyers in charge of a special committee that oversaw negative campaigning against Goldwater.[27] At every campaign stop, in every speech, and in every ad produced by his campaign, Johnson warned voters of the danger of extremism. He distorted Goldwater's voting record in the Senate, taking his remarks out of context and twisting them around every which way. He ordered the CIA to bug Goldwater's headquarters, and the FBI to bug his plane. The press, still controlled overwhelmingly by liberals, echoed and exaggerated Johnson's attacks. The Johnson campaign dwelt on two emotional and, as it turned out, particularly successful themes: one, that Goldwater was likely to start a nuclear war, and two, that he would end Social Security, widows' pensions, and "the dignity that comes with being able to take care of yourself without depending on your children. On November 3, vote for keeping Social Security."[28] But Johnson's most controversial ad, one that would be remembered as the apex of negative campaigning, showed a little girl standing in a field picking a daisy. An ominous voice in the background counts from ten down to zero, and suddenly the little girl disappears into the mushroom cloud of an atomic bomb. Johnson's voice then comes on saying, "These are the stakes—to make a world in which all of God's children can live, or to go into the dark. We must either love each other, or we must die." Another voice then said, "Vote for President Johnson on November 3. The stakes are too high for you to stay home."[29] It was a low blow, and a very effective one.

In the end, Goldwater got 38 percent of the vote against Johnson's 61 percent, carrying only six states—South Carolina, Mississippi, Georgia, Alabama, Louisiana, and his native Arizona—and was endorsed by only a handful of major newspapers.

The press piled onto the Goldwater loss, eager to declare conservatism a dead duck. "Barry Goldwater," said James Reston on the front page of the New York Times, "not only lost the presidential election yesterday, but the conservative cause as well." NBC News anchor Chet Huntley, also relishing the Goldwater defeat and the death of conservatism, claimed Goldwater voters were "segregationists, Johnson-phobes, desperate conservatives, and radical nuts."[30]

Yet as we look back forty years later, the benefits of the Goldwater campaign to the conservative movement are astounding. Ironically, it is probably no exaggeration to say that the Goldwater campaign, ending in a landslide for Lyndon Johnson, was the single most energizing event that the conservative movement experienced from 1945 to the present and started liberalism's slide into irrelevancy.

What were those benefits?

Presidential campaigns, like that of Rockefeller, usually hire people to do the telephoning, canvassing, literature drops, and the rest, and a handful of volunteers oversee them. It is estimated that at its peak five hundred thousand volunteers were actually working for Goldwater's election during the fall of 1964. As many as 3.9 million Americans may have worked for the campaign at some point, more than any political campaign in history.[31] For many, it was their first political experience, and served as a fiery baptism into the conservative movement, where they would remain for many years to come. I recall walking through the tunnel between the Senate Office Building and the Capitol with Barry Goldwater in 1979, when I was on the Senate staff, and commenting to him that I had gotten my start in conservative politics in his 1964 campaign. He responded that still, fifteen years later, nearly every day he met somebody who told him the same thing.

The Goldwater campaign started the process that enabled conservatives to get control of the Republican Party. Never before had a conservative been nominated. Among establishment Republicans it was presumed that the issues the party would consider in its campaigns would be the same issues the Democrats would consider, just carried out with different people and perhaps a little different style.

Not only did people donate their time to Goldwater in record numbers, but they donated their money, too. Until the 1964 campaign presidential elections were financed exclusively by large contributions from wealthy contributors, corporations, lobbyists, and other special-interest groups. In 1960, twenty-two thousand people had contributed $9.7 million to Kennedy's campaign and forty-four thousand people had contributed a total of $10.1 million to Nixon's.[32] LBJ's money largely came from labor unions and fat cats. But over *one million* middle-income people contributed to Goldwater's campaign. When the campaign was over, Goldwater had the names, addresses, and history of over five hundred thousand donors.[33] He showed that candidates could actually raise more money in small amounts from large numbers of people, and thereby gain financial independence from the GOP establishment.

Richard Viguerie, who had been involved in the campaign and had previously served as the first executive secretary of Young Americans for Freedom, realized the potential of tapping into the base of small Goldwater donors for future campaigns. In those days, campaigns were required to file lists of anyone who contributed more than fifty dollars with the clerk of the House of Representatives. Viguerie hired secretaries to go to the clerk's office and copy the names of Goldwater contributors on index cards. He then used the cards to set up a list marketing and direct mail company.[34] The Goldwater list would become the genesis of conservative direct-mail fund-raising that would raise tens of millions of dollars from millions of Americans over the coming years and finance a vast array of conservative organizations and candidates.

Direct-mail fund-raising became crucially important to the conservative movement and contributed directly to the movement's dynamic growth over the balance of the twentieth century. It has provided cash, on a consistent basis, to hundreds of conservative grassroots, lobbying, and advocacy groups, as well as to the think tanks that emerged in the 1980s and to candidates running for state and local offices and Congress. Equally important, direct mail provided a communications system to conservatives. Liberals had theirs: the daily papers, the national news magazines, television and radio networks—virtually all of the national media were controlled by liberals. Conservatives, at least until fairly recently, had no means of communication that would alert fellow conservatives about what they were doing or what they were running for. With the advent of direct-mail fund-raising, a line of communication was established directly into the homes and onto the desks of conservatives, informing them of issues, political campaigns, lobbying efforts, or whatever else the cause might be. If the donation response rate from a mass mailing was, say, 2 percent, the benefits of the other 98 percent were considerable as well, and were paid for by those who sent money. And as the lists grew from tens of thousands into millions of potential or actual donors, conservative political candidates, as well as newly founded organizations, had a ready source of funds, and a line of communication as well. As political commentator William Rusher notes, "The extensive interstate use of the U.S. mails as a principal avenue of political communication was founded squarely on the Goldwater contributor lists of 1964."[35]

The Goldwater campaign started the great shift of political power from the North and East to the South and West. Though LBJ was a southerner, he was beholden to the values of the Eastern Establishment and craved its acceptance. Goldwater was the first real westerner to be nominated by one of the major parties, and his campaign symbolized what would come to be recognized as the demographic shift that would transform American politics. Mississippi, Louisiana, Alabama, and South Carolina went for a Republican for the first time since Reconstruction, and Georgia for only the second time. Goldwater's southern coattails were also extensive. In Alabama, five out of eight House seats went Republican, eliminating over eighty years of Democratic seniority in one evening. Across the entire South, even in states like Virginia and Kentucky that Johnson narrowly won, Republicans were elected to state and local offices in record numbers. The shift from Democratic to Republican control had begun, and the South would lead the coalition that, together with the Midwest and the West, would elect Ronald Reagan in 1980 and take control of both houses of Congress fourteen years later.

Democrats, aided by the liberal press, early on hung the extremist mantle around Goldwater's neck, a mantle he was never able to shake. To be sure, there were plenty of "extremists" working and volunteering in his campaign. Many were John Birch Society members. Even Denison Kitchel, Goldwater's close friend from Phoenix and his campaign manager, had been a dues-paying member of the Birch Society until 1960; fortunately, the press did not learn of this until well after the campaign was over. Birchers had been involved in Goldwater's campaigns from the start. So when it became apparent that Goldwater could actually be a contender for the Republican nomination in 1964, the "extremists" signed on lock, stock, and barrel.[36] Since they often took initiatives on their own, the official campaign was forced to react to them.

The Birchers and other "extremists" were a mixed blessing to Goldwater. On the one hand, they provided many of the volunteers and an indeterminate amount of money. On the other, their reputation for extremism permeated the campaign and gave instant fodder to the anti-Goldwater press. But there was a hidden benefit. Republicans realized that if they were to win elections, they would need to neutralize the extremists but not offend them and so lose their votes. As we shall see, Republicans, largely through the efforts of Ronald Reagan, were able to do exactly that, thereby unifying the party as a responsible conservative force.

Republicans also learned that campaigning on broad conservative principles was not enough to win an election. There were simply not enough true-blue conservatives in the country who would vote for an unadulterated conservative message. Voters needed to know how a candidate's policies would affect *them*. They also learned the value of the negative campaign, which was used against Goldwater with extraordinary effectiveness. Republicans would have to respond in turn, and let the voters know that crime, Vietnam, black power, radical leftists, and other counterculterists were the Democrats' liabilities. Republicans also realized that the candidate himself had to have a certain tact. Goldwater's bluntness lacked grace, and came with a fierceness that enabled Lyndon Johnson to paint him as an unstable fanatic.

Perhaps the most enduring legacy of the Goldwater campaign was Ronald Reagan. Reagan was cochairman of the California Goldwater Committee and made several speeches for Goldwater during the 1964 campaign. Reagan was no stranger to conservatives; after his acting career wound down in the 1950s he had become the national spokesman for General Electric, and traveled the country making speeches supporting the free enterprise system. Near the end of the 1964 campaign, Reagan taped a speech supporting Goldwater, which he called "A Time for Choosing." After a certain amount of internal haggling, it was broadcast nationally and turned out to be about the single most effective half-hour speech of the entire campaign.

The speech was vintage Reagan; he started off announcing that he had spent most of his life as a Democrat, but had recently switched parties. Using anecdotes, humor, his good nature, and that little cock of the head, he urged the audience to vote for Goldwater. But he also sold the conservative message, as only he could do. It became known as "The Speech," and it launched Reagan's career.

The country had arrived at "a time for choosing" between big government and freedom, between totalitarianism and individual liberty. Reagan concluded with an admonition and an exhortation:

> You and I have a rendevous with destiny. We can preserve for our children this, the last best hope of man on earth, or we can sentence them to take the first step into a thousand years of darkness. If we fail, at least let our children and our children's children say of us we justified our brief moment here. We did all that could be done.
>
> We will keep in mind and remember that Barry Goldwater has faith in us. He has faith that you and I have the ability and the dignity and the right to make our own decisions and determine our own destiny.[37]

Reaction to the speech stunned even the believers. It captured their sense of urgency, their crusading zeal. The audience was asked to send money to pay for additional broadcasts of the speech; money came in by the truckload, and the speech was played repeatedly until the election.

Generally, after a losing presidential campaign wraps up, the bills are paid, things cleaned up, and the losing candidate's supporters and campaign staff go on to the next project, leaving little evidence that a campaign was ever run. But not so in 1964. Republicans may have been depressed about the awful showing their candidate made, but conservatives found a silver lining in the clouds of defeat. "Twenty-seven Million Americans Cannot be Wrong" became their watchword, as the newly minted young conservatives and recharged, middle-aged volunteers looked around for the next enterprise. They were not about to return to their former, nonpolitical lives—the Goldwater campaign had been like nothing they had ever experienced, and it was exhilarating. Pat Buchanan, himself a former Goldwater volunteer, wrote, "Like a first love, the Goldwater campaign was, for thousands of men and women now well into middle age, an experience that will never recede from memory, one on which we look back with pride and fond remembrance."[38]

THE AMERICAN CONSERVATIVE UNION

It did not take conservatives long to regroup. Just five days after the election, William F. Buckley, Jr., and Frank Meyer, both from *National Review*, Congressmen Don Bruce of Indiana and John Ashbrook of Ohio, and Bob Bauman, chairman of Young Americans for Freedom, met to determine the future. The upshot was the formation of the American Conservative Union (ACU), which was formally organized several weeks later at a meeting of forty-seven nationally prominent conservatives at the Statler Hilton Hotel in Washington. Of particular interest to the group was the sterling fact that 27 million people *had* voted for Goldwater—people who had seen through the distortions, deceits, and misrepresentations of LBJ's campaign. At least a portion of these needed to be organized into a strong political force to ensure that future campaigns could be waged more successfully. The ACU leaders were particularly concerned with the "pervasive influence of a single organization, Americans for Democratic Action," which was so powerful that even Lyndon Johnson dared not ignore it. The ADA was a small organization, ACU stated, "of liberals banded together to help other liberals achieve positions of power and influence in government, the press, radio and TV, and private foundations to work for a socialist America."[39] Why could not conservatives do the same thing?

The ACU stated that its goals would be essentially four: It would mobilize and consolidate the intellectual resources of the conservative movement; it would provide leadership to other, existing organizations, periodicals, and political leaders; it would attempt to influence public opinion toward conservative principles; and it would stimulate and direct citizen action for conservative causes, legislation, and political candidates. It proposed a budget of $250,000 (about $1.4 million in 2005 dollars), elected a board and officers, and elected Congressman John Ashbrook of Ohio as its first chairman. The organizers also adopted a statement of principles incorporating the ideas enunciated by Russell Kirk and the traditionalists, by Friedrich Hayek and the libertarians, and by James Burnham and Whittaker Chambers and the anti-Communists. The conservative movement was being fused into one cohesive body.

As one of its first orders of business, the organizing committee passed a resolution banning members of the John Birch Society from membership on the board of directors or the advisory assembly, and issued a statement that there was absolutely no relationship between the two organizations. It stated further that although the two organizations might agree that political and educational action was urgently needed to stem the collectivist tide, they disagreed on the extent to which an international conspiracy was responsible for the growth of Communism.

ACU was, in essence, the first conservative political action and lobbying organization, and would serve as the model for the hundreds of organizations formed over the next forty years. Still very much alive, it has weighed in over the years on hundreds of issues. It publishes an annual rating of each member of Congress to gauge their adherence to conservative principles, and hosts the annual Conservative Political Action Conference, which brings thousands of conservative activists from around the country to Washington, D.C., to hear from leaders of the movement, attend workshops, and network with each other.

That an organization based on the principles set forth by a losing candidate, founded just weeks after a landslide loss, should still be going forty years later is probably unique in American politics.

Two More Elections

Conservatives had learned a great deal from the Goldwater campaign, not the least of which was that they could actually run a conservative campaign and get a great many votes. As the results of the election were analyzed, it became apparent that the way people had voted in 1964 did not necessarily reflect a clean split between liberal and conservative attitudes—conservatives' enthusiasm for continuing to try to elect their own certainly remained high. This, on top of continuing news stories that talked of Goldwater's resounding defeat by Lyndon Johnson as an official end to conservatism, made active conservatives eager to prove otherwise. Two elections, one in 1965 and the other in 1966, raised the enthusiasm of conservatives for electoral politics to a new high.

BUCKLEY FOR MAYOR

New York Republican congressman John Lindsay was a pillar of the Rockefeller wing of the GOP. He represented the "Silk Stocking District," encompassing much of the Upper East Side of Manhattan. Lindsay, a six-foot-four Yale graduate, athletic, good-looking, waspish to his ivory teeth, had an 85 percent rating from the liberal Americans for Democratic Action, placing him farther to the left than many Democrats; in 1964 he had refused to support Goldwater. He was also the liberal Republicans' favorite candidate for the presidency. Hardly a news story about Lindsay could appear without defining him as the next likely Republican presidential nominee "The District's Pride—The Nation's Hope."[40] When veteran New York City Democratic mayor Robert Wagner decided to retire in 1965, Lindsay quickly announced that he would run for the job. New York's Liberal Party, which could often turn an election with its endorsement, immediately jumped onto Lindsay's train.

To the Conservative Party of New York, founded in 1962, a three-party mayoral race might be interesting. If the Liberal Party could support Republican Lindsay against the Democratic candidate, City Comptroller Abraham Beame, why couldn't the Conservative Party run its own candidate, splitting the vote three ways and offering a conservative alternative to the two liberals? And who should emerge as a candidate (reluctantly) willing to take on such an undertaking but . . . William F. Buckley, Jr.

Buckley had been featured in a *Time* magazine article in the summer of 1964, which generously credited *National Review* for goading Gold-water to run, thereby carrying out its original goal of changing the political face of the nation.[41] With such attention lavished on him, Buckley was becoming a fixture around New York and was better known among conservatives nationally than anyone other than Barry Goldwater. The conservative movement's most articulate and charming spokesman, running against the poster boy of liberal Republicanism for mayor of America's largest and most prominent city, would be sure to get national attention. It was particularly important because it gave Buckley a national bully pulpit from which to talk about conservative principles in a political campaign without worrying about whom he might offend—an echo of Goldwater's campaign two years earlier. At the outset of the campaign he vowed that he would not pander to ethnic, racial, or special interests, but state the issues as if he were not running for office, for he knew he could never win. In a typical Buckley retort to a reporter's question about what he would do if he actually did win, Buckley quipped, "Demand a recount."[42]

And what a set of problems New York City provided! Crime was rampant, the welfare state was thriving, racial tensions were at the boiling point, the infrastructure was decrepit, and the city had the highest unemployment rate in the country, with 250,000 people out of work. The budget was out of control though real estate taxes had doubled over the past ten years, and the city would have a deficit of $256 million for 1965. If that weren't enough, the subways were so rampant with crime that many citizens were afraid to use them, the schools were a mess, and the middle class was leaving the city in droves (more than one million middle-class citizens had left the city in the past ten years, and who could blame them?) Even the city's water system, which used water piped from upstate New York, was such a shambles that water was being rationed. Asked what he would do about it, Buckley said, "Let them drink wine."[43] What made it all worse was the fact that the U.S. economy was in very good shape in 1965, with GNP up 8 percent and unemployment at a very respectable 4.5 percent nationwide.

With his charm and wit, Buckley was able to make the case for conservative ideals and principles in a way that Barry Goldwater could not. The city's worst problems were largely due to race—the black and Puerto Rican underclass. No politician would dare confront these issues, but Buckley did, often citing studies done by liberals that were, for the first time, looking at such issues, studies like *Beyond the Melting Pot,* by Daniel Patrick Moynihan and Nathan Glazer, on American ethnicity. Interestingly, Moynihan and Glazer were among the first liberals to emerge as neoconservatives. Buckley challenged the way the city dealt with poverty and welfare, suggesting that drug addicts should be quarantined and the city should look into the feasibility of moving chronic welfare cases out of New York. The stage was a national one because the national press could not resist Buckley's good humor and outrageous arguments. *New York Times* columnist James Reston, who had declared conservatism dead the day after the 1964 election, less than a year later said of Buckley:

> He is symbolic of the new generation of Republican
> conservatives—more intelligent, more sophisticated
> than the Goldwater generation, and in New York
> much more effective with the voters. What happens
> in New York will undoubtedly have considerable ef-
> fect in the Republican Party all over the country.[44]

If Buckley did well, Reston continued, "Other conservatives in other states will undoubtedly be encouraged to put up conservative candidates, and this is bound to hurt the Republican Party all over the nation."[45]

The Buckley campaign reinvigorated conservatives after the Goldwater drubbing by LBJ and gave impetus to something Goldwater had started, which would become, by 1980, one of conservative politicians' greatest weapons: Buckley got Democratic, as well as Republican, votes. These Democrats were white, working class, socially conservative, churchgoing; the kind that would vote for George Wallace in 1968 and became known in 1980 as "Reagan Democrats." Although Lindsay ultimately won with 45 percent of the vote, to Beame's 41 percent, Buckley won 13 percent and over 340,000 votes. In the process, Buckley made major strides for the movement and inflicted sufficient damage to Lindsay that the mayor's office was the end of the line for him. Said the *New York Times* in October 2005, in a long piece recounting the importance of Buckley's race:

> Buckley's bid for office was an important chapter in
> one of the crucial events in modern political history,
> the transformation of the consensus politics of the
> peak cold-war years of the 1950s and early '60s, its
> agenda set by liberals, into the more polarized poli-
> tics of our era, ruled by conservatives.[46]

The Democratic Party did not like the fact that the New York mayor's race had provided a referendum on the Great Society, and that William F. Buckley, Jr., *the* conservative icon, got 13 percent of the vote in the most liberal city in the country. The edifice of the party's grand coalition, in place from the days of FDR's New Deal, was developing wide cracks.

Unlike the Goldwater campaign, which many conservatives were convinced would be won, few were disappointed when Buckley lost; most were thrilled that he had run at all and done as well as he did. Ultimately the mayor's campaign was not about getting elected but about advancing the conservative cause. Conservative columnist George Crocker, in the *San Francisco Examiner,* summed it up well when he said conservatism was not a momentary phenomenon that would crumble when elections were lost:

> There is a misconception in many minds that con-
> servatives "learned their lesson" in 1964 and will
> henceforth only put up liberal candidates. To think
> of this is to have a shallow opinion of representa-
> tive government. Conservatism is not just a political
> technique, to be tossed overboard when an election
> is lost. It is something deep and indestructible. It is
> a philosophy.[47]

The Buckley campaign was about ideas, but also about practical politics—about running a spoiler candidate in what would otherwise have been a clearly decided two-way race in order to show liberal Republicans that conservative voters were not only independent, but might field winning third-party candidates. In this respect, it was a distinct move forward for the conservative movement; the Buckley candidacy advanced the movement one more step by opening the door another notch for the great political realignment that would gather momentum over the next several years. The lessons learned were not lost on the Buckley family: Two years later Buckley's brother Jim ran as the Conservative Party candidate for senator from New York and won a similar percentage of the vote. Then in 1970 he ran again in a three-way race and was elected with 37 percent of the vote.

Conservatives now needed a campaign of national proportions that was winnable, in which the candidate's personality would make his conservative philosophy more compelling. Within months after Buckley had left the New York City hustings and returned to *National Review*, conservatives had what they needed: the winnable race for the governorship of California, and the candidate who could win, and who had just the personality needed.

REAGAN FOR GOVERNOR

By 1966, Democratic governor Pat Brown had served eight years in Sacramento, and his popularity was on the downswing. He was a classic tax and spend liberal who believed that government could solve all the world's problems, and as a result had driven California into severe deficits. He then promised a tax increase to pay for the deficits after he was re-elected. Like New York City, California was faced with difficult problems—a population that had doubled since 1945, increasing pollution, overdevelopment, overcrowded schools, huge state expenses, and crime. California also had its share of racial problems, exemplified by riots in the Watts section of Los Angeles in August 1965, which resulted in thirty-four deaths, over one thousand injuries, and the total destruction of the central business district of Watts. Its student unrest or, to define it more accurately, militancy, exemplified by riots at the University of California at Berkeley in December 1964, resulted in the arrest of nearly eight hundred students. And it also had labor unrest, such as César Chavez's strike against grape growers and the consequent national grape boycott.

When first approached in 1965 by a group of Los Angeles millionaires about running for governor, Ronald Reagan laughed, but when people kept pestering him he drove across the state for six months canvassing voters until he was finally convinced that he had a good chance of winning. In January 1966, just two months after Bill Buckley had received 13 percent of the vote in New York City, and just fourteen months after Barry Goldwater had carried only six states against Lyndon Johnson, Reagan announced that he would run for governor of California.

Republicans had dominated California politics for years, at least until William Knowland, the Senate majority leader, decided in 1958 that being governor offered a better route to the White House than the Senate. But then Pat Brown, California's attorney general, trounced Knowland. Brown was re-elected in 1962, beating Richard Nixon, whom Californians believed thought of Sacramento only as a good jumping-off spot for another bid for the White House. The disarray of the California GOP was compounded by the vicious primary contest between Goldwater and Rockefeller in 1964, when the conservative and liberal wings of the party tore each other to pieces, after which many of Rockefeller's supporters deserted Goldwater in the general election.[48]

By 1965 Democrats outnumbered Republicans in California, and no proven Republican candidate emerged to challenge Brown in his bid for a third term. As Reagan analyzed the situation, he thought that with a well-run, well-financed campaign, he would have a good shot at winning. For one thing, Goldwater had done considerably better in California than he had nationally, even while running a lousy campaign. Participating in a series in *National Review* looking at the 1964 Goldwater loss, Reagan wrote: "All of the landslide majority did not vote against the conservative philosophy, they voted against a false image our Liberal opponent successfully mounted. Indeed, it was a double-faced image. Not only did they portray us as advancing a kind of radical departure from the status quo, but they took for themselves a posture of comfortable conservatism." Reagan concluded that "we represent the forgotten American—that simple soul who goes to work, bucks for a raise, takes out insurance, pays for his kids' schooling, contributes to his church and charity and knows that there just 'ain't no such thing as a free lunch.'"[49]

Reagan also carefully studied the results of the 1964 California Senate race, in which his friend, fellow actor, and conservative Republican "song and dance man" George Murphy had beaten liberal Democrat

Pierre Salinger, JFK's former press secretary. While Johnson carried California by over one million votes in 1964, in the same election Murphy beat Salinger by 3 percent. Reagan concluded that it was Goldwater, not conservatism, that had been rejected by California voters; thus a conservative actor, running a good campaign, could get elected.

Holmes Tuttle, a successful Los Angeles businessman and old friend of Reagan's, put together a group of wealthy backers who agreed to raise the money Reagan would need, and Tuttle arranged to hire the crack campaign consultant team of Stuart Spencer and Bill Roberts. They had managed Nelson Rockefeller's 1964 primary battle against Goldwater, and had won thirty-four out of forty congressional races for Republican candidates.[50] Reagan's campaign was a well-oiled machine, and Spencer-Roberts added a degree of professionalism that Goldwater never achieved. Reagan ran on conservative issues and attacked Brown as an ineffective governor. He was careful not to offend working-class Democrats with antiunion rhetoric, as he believed he could get some share of the labor vote. Reagan easily won the June primary, beating San Francisco mayor George Christopher with 65 percent of the vote. California's moderate and liberal Republicans were sufficiently impressed by the magnitude of Reagan's victory and the charm of his personality that they fell in behind him instead of sitting out the election, as they had in 1964.

In the general election, Democrat Brown did what every other Reagan opponent would do in subsequent elections: He underestimated him. Brown thought of Reagan as a know-nothing actor, a right-wing Goldwater clone, and could not imagine that Californians, who had already elected him twice, would fail to re-elect him for a third term. Brown derided Reagan as an actor in his speeches, and even ran ads equating Reagan with actor and Lincoln assassin John Wilkes Booth. Californians, who knew a lot about actors, were not impressed, so Brown changed tack and went after Reagan for being a right-wing extremist. He harped on the extremist theme and enlisted other Democrats, including state controller and future senator Alan Cranston, to flag the issue across the state. The chairman of the state Democratic Party even published a twenty-nine-page document entitled "Ronald Reagan, Extremist Collaborator—An Exposé," which portrayed Reagan as a "front man who collaborated directly with a score of top leaders of the super-secret John Birch Society and used his acting skill and TV charm to soft-sell the doctrines of radical rightists who condemn Social Security and other social advances as Communist-inspired."[51] Cranston, whose extremism on the left made Reagan look like a piker on the right, issued a second "white paper" associating Reagan with the Birch Society and anti-Semitism.

Reagan took the smears in stride, to the consternation of the Brown campaign, and campaigned instead on real issues. The extremist issue had been brewing since Reagan was first mentioned as a candidate—since it had hurt Goldwater, the Democrats were convinced it would hurt Reagan. In response to a question about the John Birch Society, Reagan said, "They're buying my philosophy, I'm not buying theirs."[52]

By early October, a month before the general election, Democrats realized that the charge of extremism was not sticking. So they started to attack Reagan's character, which proved equally ineffective. Reagan ran consistently ahead in the polls and was elected with a majority of one million votes, almost the same margin Johnson had achieved against Goldwater two years earlier. Reagan carried many Democratic working-class precincts and rural and suburban areas that were heavily Democratic. He ran well in Mexican-American neighborhoods and brought most of the Republican ticket with him, including Alan Cranston's opponent, an unknown first-time candidate. Pat Brown's son Jerry was the only statewide Democrat to win in the 1966 election. (He would subsequently be elected governor in 1974, earning the nickname "Governor Moonbeam.") In sum, Reagan received nearly one-third of the Democratic vote.[53]

While Brown had attacked Reagan as an extremist, a dumb and mindless actor, and a dolt, Reagan had run on particular issues—taxes, crime, education, the size of government, and other bread-and-butter issues that affected the way Californians lived. By doing so, Reagan avoided Goldwater's mistake of campaigning too broadly on general principles. Reagan also was the first candidate to begin to pull together the conservative coalition that would become such a dominant force in American politics over the next thirty-five years. Especially important was the addition of what became known as "Reagan Democrats," the people who had been a significant portion of the grand Democratic coalition put together by FDR in 1932 and who would ultimately elect

Ronald Reagan president in 1980 and re-elect him, in a landslide, in 1984. These were the conservative working-class Democrats, many of them union members. They were anti-Communists, mostly churchgoers who believed in strong families, many were second-generation Americans, and there were lots of them. Even local labor union leaders, one of the mainstays of Democratic politics, voted for Reagan in significant numbers, according to studies done after the election by Democrats.[54] Reagan, a former New Deal Democrat himself, knew how these people thought and he knew how to talk to them and how to appeal to them.

That Reagan should have beaten an old-line Democrat in a state where Democrats outnumbered Republicans by a large margin, just two years after Lyndon Johnson's landslide victory, suggested that a sea change might be under way in American politics.

The death of extremism as a political issue in this highly visible campaign was a turning point. Jonathan Schoenwald, in his study of American conservatism, says:

> Cutting off the millstone of extremism from around their necks amounted to nothing less than a turning point for conservative Republicans; now they could unite around an individual rather than an ideology and allow for the possibility of support from their liberal brethren. . . . Casting off extremism also permitted moderate and liberal Republicans to view conservatives as more reliable and less predictable, which opened the door for a broader coalition in support of a candidate who represented a belief system in which all factions could find value.[55]

Although Reagan's victory in California gave conservatives hope for the future, the 1960s provided few other bright spots for the right.

CHAPTER SIX

The Worst of Times

The period between Ronald Reagan's election as governor of California in 1966 and his 1976 campaign for the GOP presidential nomination was at once crucial and devastating to American conservatism.

Lyndon Johnson's Great Society was going full tilt—creating new agencies, departments, social programs—and spending money with the zest of another New Deal. Democrats in 1964 had gained their largest margins, in both Congress and the statehouses, in almost three decades, riding on LBJ's coattails. Though Republicans regained a substantial number of seats in 1966, they remained in the minority. For their part, the federal courts, bulging with liberal judges (and overseen by Chief Justice Earl Warren) were reshaping the political landscape with decisions on civil rights, crime, reapportionment, prayer in the schools, school busing, obscenity, and abortion. The big media were dominated by liberals with hardly a conservative murmur. As the 1960s wore on, militant black radicals, demanding a larger piece of the economic and cultural pie, began their own riots in Detroit, Newark, Washington, and other cities resulting in millions of dollars of damage and hundreds of people injured and killed. In addition, illegal drug use was gaining a foothold, and the breakdown of the family structure, particularly among minorities, was burgeoning. Crime in the major cities was another major problem, doubling from 188.7 to 398.5 per 10,000 people between 1960 and 1970.[1] The universities were being radicalized by leftist students who, if not in complete control, thought that they were. The liberals who ran the universities were impotent to stop them because they shared the same fundamental principles as their radical students and, in any case, often felt uncomfortable exercising authority. The Vietnam

War was raging, soldiers were coming home by the thousands in body bags, and the United States faced a humiliating defeat at the hands of Communism. With the Brezhnev Doctrine—once a Communist state, always a Communist state—the Soviet Union remained as bellicose and expansionist as ever, not hesitating to smash the freedom fighters of their satellite Czechoslovakia in 1968. Richard Nixon was elected partly because he was perceived to be a conservative, but arguably ruled as the most socialist president of the century, ultimately resigning in disgrace. Liberals were in charge; conservatives were on the defensive.

Or so it seemed. For beneath the surface much was happening with the growing conservative movement that may have appeared insignificant at the time, but was in the end of great import.

Ronald Reagan, elected over a liberal incumbent in a landslide, became the chief executive of the largest and most visible state in the country. Two years later, in 1968, Vice President Hubert Humphrey, former head of Americans for Democratic Action and a liberal icon, was narrowly defeated by Nixon. The old Democratic coalition of blue-collar workers, blacks, and southerners was quickly coming unglued as the Democrats were becoming more radical and more powerful. Flexing their muscle through riots and altercations within the Democratic Party, the left-wingers had driven millions of Democrats into the GOP. The right-wing extremists who had so damaged Barry Goldwater in 1964 had effectively left the party, but quiet wars were being waged between Goldwater conservatives and the liberal establishment.

The next several years saw the emergence of both the New Right, which later merged into the religious right, and the neoconservatives, mainly liberal Jewish intellectuals, providing new allies against liberalism. At the same time, conservatives began to develop institutions that would help carry them into power.

But the single most important precursor of the turn to conservatism was the success, radicalization, and breaking up of American liberalism.

LBJ's "GREAT SOCIETY" AND THE ZENITH OF LIBERALISM

The 1960s was a period of triumph that fires the liberal imagination to this day. With dynamic leaders and unchecked power, liberals transformed the politics and culture of the country, combining John F. Kennedy's suave image with Lyndon Johnson's political savvy.

When he ran for president in 1960, Kennedy needed a southerner on the ticket. Johnson, the Senate majority leader and the most powerful Democrat in the country, was more interested in power than policy, and willing to say and do just about anything to gain it. Over his congressional career, which included twelve years in the House of Representatives and another twelve in the Senate, the uncouth, arm-twisting Johnson had voted for and against segregation, for and against the loyalty oath for student recipients of federal loans, for and against social welfare programs, had been an anti-Communist and an anti-anti-Communist, and had taken both sides on nearly every other issue that came along, earning the disdain of Washington liberals for his cynicism and personal vulgarity. But no price was too great to win the presidency for either man. Johnson was puzzled by Kennedy's popularity and reciprocated his disdain. He told historian Doris Kearns that Kennedy "never said a word of importance in the Senate and never did a thing. It was the goddamnest thing . . . his growing hold on the American people was a mystery to me."[2] When Kennedy was assassinated in November 1963 and Johnson ascended to the presidency, the liberals were initially appalled. But Johnson turned out to be a more dedicated liberal than Kennedy, and much more effective.

Johnson cannily presented his legislative agenda as a continuation of the Kennedy legacy. He viewed the upheaval over civil rights as an ideal opportunity for him to play a role in history. The skill he had honed in the Senate at balancing the demands of his conservative Texas constituents with those of Washington's professional politicians helped him become one of most productive legislators in U.S. history. From almost his first day in the Oval Office, he resumed the agenda of the New Deal, but on an even more ambitious scale.

In May 1964, in his commencement address at the University of Michigan, Johnson laid out his vision for America: "In your time we have the opportunity to move not only towards the rich society and the powerful society, but upward to the Great Society." The Great Society, he explained, would bring an end to poverty and racial injustice, and would create a life where "the city of man serves not only the needs of the body and the demands of commerce, but the desire for beauty and the hunger for community."[3] Vast new government programs were the benchmark of his campaign against Barry Goldwater, and after winning 61 percent of the presidential vote in 1964 and overwhelming majorities in both houses of Congress, he could claim the popular mandate to launch his massive agenda.

During 1965 Johnson submitted sixty-three legislative proposals to Congress, which over the next few years churned out more progressive legislation and spent more federal money than in any period in history. New programs and departments sprang up—Medicare, aid to education, rent supplements, federal scholarships for higher education, the Legal Services Corporation, the Office of Equal Opportunity, and a host of other programs and government agencies that splatter the Washington bureaucratic landscape to this day.

Not only were the War on Poverty and the Great Society a total repudiation of limited government, but they were big government at its most extravagant. The Johnson programs redefined the welfare state, wrote James Piereson:

> From a package of programs through which Americans lent assistance to the poor, the sick, and the disabled to a system through which certain new groups could command government support as a matter of right and as compensation for past injustices. Society was cast as the guilty party, the recipients as its aggrieved victims. This sleight-of-hand in turn made it difficult for government to require the beneficiaries of its aid to adapt their behavior to the standards of middle-class life.[4]

The premise behind the War on Poverty was vintage liberalism—poverty resulted from inadequacies in the way society, particularly the marketplace, worked. The only way to remedy poverty and injustice was to redistribute the national income from rich to poor. Whereas conservatives accepted inequality as natural and human suffering as a consequence of original sin, liberals believed that since man was naturally good, if he did commit a wrong or failed, the fault must lie with society. People were not poor because they had failed but because they were victims of the rich, or were discriminated against, or were otherwise, somehow, oppressed by society. It was up to the government to rectify these social injustices for the benefit of groups defined as underprivileged. The "defined groups" were represented by the liberal elite, the real beneficiaries. Welfare was no longer a matter of simply helping people who were down and out, but a matter of redistributing the wealth. The War on Poverty turned theories of social policy into reality, and an ugly reality at that. According to historian Sanford Unger, "Critics would denounce the War on Poverty as a feeding trough for the white middle-class. But the jobs, the salaries, the benefits would spill over onto those upwardly mobile hustlers and strivers who waited in the ghettos for the first hint of encouragement and opportunity to appear."[5]

Criticism of the War on Poverty from the right became a favorite pastime. Ronald Reagan turned it into an art form, using the fifty-thousand-dollar welfare queen as the poster child of the Great Society. Columnists Thomas Sowell and Walter Williams delighted in pointing out the abuse that was rampant in LBJ's schemes; Sowell found that "a lot of anti-poverty money is going to people who are not poor. There are whole classes of people who live off the poor—or rather, off the vast sums of money that are poured out from the public treasury and private philanthropy, in hopes of helping the poor." He even published a poem about it.

Effectively, Great Society programs bound their beneficiaries to the Democratic Party, creating a permanent shadow government of so-called poverty pimps, both inside and outside the government, who administered the programs and kept the grant money flowing from every nook and cranny of Washington. Republican senator Everett Dirksen of Illinois, always one to turn a fitting phrase, called one Great Society program, the Office of Economic Opportunity, the "greatest boondoggle since bread and circuses in the days of the ancient Roman Empire, before the republic fell."[7]

It did not take long to realize that the War on Poverty was not going to eliminate any social problems, something conservatives had predicted all along. But the programs were not simply unsuccessful; many social critics, citing the law of unintended consequences, correctly predicted that the programs would actually make things worse. As the Great Society programs extended into the future, these welfare schemes created a whole class of dependent poor people with all of the attendant problems that have since emerged—the breakdown of families and the consequent spread of crime, drug abuse, and squalor.

These political transformations wrought by liberalism in the 1960s may have been its high-water mark, but they also fertilized the sprouting seeds of conservatism.

First, the trend toward an imperial presidency that culminated in Lyndon Johnson's use of executive power renewed the argument, made first by the framers and subsequently by a long line of believers in constitutional government, for the balance of power between Congress and the executive. Conservatives responded to the expansion of executive power with a flurry of literary activity, including James Kilpatrick's *The Sovereign States*, which was a ringing defense of federalism; Felix Morley's *Freedom and Federalism,* in which the former editor of the *Washington Post* placed federalism in its historical context and made the case for the preservation of constitutional government as a safeguard from the growth of socialism. James Burnham's *Congress and the American Tradition* argued that the survival of political liberty depended on Congress, which Burnham believed was failing to exercise the authority the Founders had given it, allowing the executive branch to wield too much power.[8]

Second, as seen earlier, the Great Society's assault on the U.S. Constitution eventually spawned an active conservative legal counterforce. Before LBJ, welfare, education, legal services, housing, and many other services were provided, if at all, by the states. Such services had been thought of as assistance, or aid, but under the Great Society, they became innate rights. As such, they were protected by federal courts, leading to massive litigation, litigation that was often funded by the government.

Third, the Great Society had a distinct impact on budgets and taxation. Not only were Johnson's new programs extravagant, they were entitlements—money was committed for as long as the program continued, leaving Congress with no control over spending. In 1966, these entitlements made up 30 percent of the federal budget, and discretionary spending 63 percent; forty years later, in fiscal year 2006, entitlements accounted for 64 percent of the budget and discretionary spending 27 percent.[9] Congress thus deprived itself of authority on budgetary matters, inasmuch as a large portion of each budget was committed before committee hearings and budget negotiations even began. During Johnson's presidency, for the first time in history, the federal government spent more on welfare than on defense (even though the Vietnam War was raging), and it became the norm to pay for it with deficit financing. Deficits grew every year that LBJ was in the White House, and as entitlement programs expanded, the annual deficit ballooned from over $3 billion in 1966 to $53 billion in 1975.[10] It has continued to expand by leaps and bounds ever since.

Thus, under Lyndon Johnson, liberalism reached its greatest triumph. But the fruits of that triumph contained the seeds of its own destruction. But conservatives, smarting from the defeat of 1964, were not positioned to take advantage of this. Instead, that opportunity was seized by Richard Nixon.

RICHARD NIXON

After his narrow defeat by JFK in 1960, Nixon returned to California to run for governor against Pat Brown in 1962 and was once again defeated. In his concession speech, he famously remarked, "This is my last press conference; you won't have Dick Nixon to kick around anymore," and *Time* magazine agreed: "Barring a miracle, Richard Nixon can never hope to be elected to any political office again."[11] But if Nixon was consistent in anything, he was consistent in tenaciously pursuing his own ambitions, and sitting on the sidelines was not one of them. It was probably no miracle, but Nixon's comeback was stunning. According to Jonathan Aitken, his biographer, "He prepared himself for his comeback with the discipline of a former heavyweight champion returning to the ring. . . . It was a period when he discovered new strengths within himself, as an individual and as a politician, without which he could not have won the presidency."[12] He turned down lucrative offers to become president of corporations such as Pepsi Cola International and Chrysler, instead moving to New York to join a Wall Street law firm.[13] Nixon considered Wall Street the best place to rebuild his political career; he would be in touch with the foreign policy establishment, surrounded by big corporate deals and big money, and with access to the national press when needed. Nixon bumped into Bill Buckley on the street one day soon after his arrival in New York and said, "This is where the action is—not with those peasants back in California."[14]

Nixon had campaigned for Barry Goldwater in 1964, but found conservatives distasteful, partly because he saw them as a threat to his own political future, but also because he was a compromising, middle-of-the road sort of Republican. As the 1966 congressional elections approached, Nixon saw an opportunity to help many of the Republicans defeated in the 1964 landslide return to power—and help himself back into the limelight. In attacking the increasingly vulnerable Lyndon Johnson, he thought he could mend the wounds separating liberal and conservative party leaders. When Nixon's law partners helped him raise over one hundred thousand dollars for GOP candidates, he hired a young aide named Patrick J. Buchanan and hit the campaign trail. Recalled Buchanan, "He got a propeller-driven plane and we went all over the country. He hit something like sixty-six congressional districts in thirty-five states. He predicted what would happen, and his predictions were almost all right on."[15] The Republicans captured forty-seven House seats, three Senate seats, eight governorships, and 540 seats in state legislatures. Nixon, recognized at last as a Republican hero, was the new leader of the opposition and well positioned to seek the GOP presidential nomination in 1968.

As 1968 drew near, Nixon gathered considerable conservative support. Even though he did not think much of Goldwater's conservatism, Nixon stayed in close contact with the Arizona senator, who, thankful for Nixon's help in 1964, loyally pledged his unqualified support in 1968. Nixon later said that his decision to campaign for Goldwater was the single most important step on his return to power during the so-called wilderness years.[16] But this premature display of loyalty forfeited any leverage Goldwater and conservatives might have had over Nixon. Nixon also had the backing of Senator Strom Thurmond of South Carolina, who had switched parties in 1964 to support Goldwater and was now the most powerful Republican in the South. Others followed, arguing that Nixon was "conservative enough" and, anyhow, the only GOP candidate who could win. Besides, next to the other two possibilities, liberal governors Nelson Rockefeller of New York and George Romney of Michigan, Nixon seemed relatively conservative. But many other conservatives, including most of the draft-Goldwater movement, distrusted Nixon and kept looking for a true conservative believer. As Nixon aide Pat Buchanan said, "Nixon was a fellow traveler of the American Right. He considered conservatives 'they,' not 'us.' 'They' were our allies, but they were not 'us.'"[17]

As was his way, Nixon left no stone unturned in seeking the GOP nomination. He had a "liberal desk" run by Ray Price to deal with the liberals, and a "conservative desk" manned by Pat Buchanan. He knew he needed movement conservatives to win, a lesson he had learned the hard way in California in 1962, and proceeded to hold off-the-record meetings with prominent conservatives to woo support for his candidacy. He also enlisted the help of a number of conservative policy analysts who developed issue papers and stayed in touch with conservatism's growing grassroots organizations.

Nixon, as part of a general effort to build up his support among conservatives, arranged a meeting with Bill Buckley and Bill Rusher of *National Review* in January 1967 in hopes of cultivating *NR* support. Nixon asked Buckley whether he thought California's governor Reagan would be a contender for the nomination, to which Buckley responded that it was "preposterous even to consider Reagan as an alternative. . . . He is an ex-actor who has been in office now for less than a month."[18] Buckley had known Reagan personally since 1960 but, according to Rusher, expected Nixon to get the nomination and was completely comfortable with such an expectation. Buckley, in his own mind, had resolved the sticky problem of Nixon vs. Reagan by advising friends that, as an immutable proposition in the natural law, "No actor can possibly be qualified for the presidency." When, years later, he was asked what had become of his dictum, Buckley simply responded, "I've changed my mind."[19]

Rusher, unmoved by Nixon's courting, argued against an endorsement from *National Review*. But Nixon used the Buckley connection to great advantage, appearing on *Firing Line* and receiving a long profile in *National Review*.

Nixon announced his candidacy in February, and won ten out of the first eleven primaries; Rockefeller beat him only in Massachusetts.

Romney, after blaming his previous support for the war in Vietnam on his having been brainwashed by the U.S. military while on a trip there (Eugene McCarthy quipped that a quick rinse would have been enough), dropped out of the race two weeks before the New Hampshire primary. Reagan assured Nixon that he would not run, though spontaneous support arose for him in the West and the South, where many Republicans were still wary of Nixon. Despite the relative weakness of both Rockefeller and Reagan, Nixon was concerned that if he did not get the nomination on the first ballot, a pincer movement by Reagan and Rockefeller could erode his strength so that one of them, most likely Reagan, would walk away with the prize.

After Ronald Reagan was sworn in as governor of California in January 1967 he immediately assumed a national status, and by 1968 was the most charismatic Republican speaker and the party's best fundraiser, attracting enthusiastic crowds wherever he went. He told his friend Holmes Tuttle during the 1968 primaries that "it was important for him to 'enunciate [his] principles' and pull the Republican party in a conservative direction."[20]

Reagan recognized that he had a future beyond Sacramento, but also believed that running for president in 1968 was premature. During the early months of 1968 he was asked about his presidential plans constantly, and became, in biographer Lou Cannon's words, "an avowed noncandidate."[21] But conservatives remained steadfast in their loyalty to him, and Reagan was their favorite-on candidate until the eve of the convention, when he threw his hat into the ring, hoping he might get past the first ballot. But Reagan's first instinct had been right; it was too soon. Nixon was easily nominated by a placid convention in sunny Miami.

VIETNAM

Kennedy had left Johnson a growing number of problems that Johnson could not ignore, not the least of which was the escalating war in Vietnam—the war that ultimately caused Johnson not to run for a second term and defined his failed presidency. In the 1964 campaign, Barry Goldwater said that he would either escalate the war in Vietnam and win a decisive military victory, or get out, and most conservatives agreed. Campaigning against Goldwater, Johnson portrayed himself as the peace candidate, accusing Goldwater of being a warmonger because he advocated bombing North Vietnam as a means of winning the war. Just like Wilson in 1916 and FDR in 1940, Johnson promised not to send "your boys into any foreign wars." And like his predecessors, he did just the opposite—shortly after his election Johnson started to expand the war by bombing North Vietnam as Goldwater had proposed.

Vietnam was the liberals' war. Democrats controlled both houses of Congress for the entire Vietnam era; the same Democrats who funded the Great Society funded military intervention in Vietnam. The media establishment also backed the intervention, the strongest among them being the *Washington Post* and the *New York Times*, the two most powerful liberal papers in the country. (Both eventually abandoned Johnson and advocated withdrawal, the *Times* in early 1966, and the *Post* during the summer of 1967.)

That liberalism was bound up with the Vietnam War was not lost on the antiwar movement. Carl Oglesby, president of the far-left Students for a Democratic Society (SDS), told a march on Washington in November 1965:

> The original commitment in Vietnam was made by President Truman, a mainstream liberal. It was seconded by President Eisenhower, a moderate liberal. It was intensified by the late President Kennedy, a flaming liberal. Think of the men who now engineer that war—those who study the maps, give the commands, push the buttons, and tally the dead: Bundy, McNamara, Rusk, Lodge, Goldberg, the President himself. They are not moral monsters. They are all honorable men. They are all liberals.[22]

While liberals were generally enthusiastic about Vietnam, conservatives found themselves in something of a quandary. For the most part they believed in fighting Communism abroad and believed that the North Vietnamese invasion of South Vietnam threatened all of Southeast Asia. But fighting any wars where it was unclear what vital national interest was at stake was not consistent with traditional conservative foreign policy. Moreover, few conservatives liked the way the Kennedy and Johnson administrations conducted the war, few believed that committing half a million U.S. troops to a ground war in Asia was anything but foolish, and nobody liked the no-win strategy of trying to get the best negotiated settlement possible. Most conservatives agreed with Barry Goldwater that "we had two clear choices: Either win the war in a relatively short time, say within a year, or pull out all our troops and come home."[23] But many conservatives supported the war because they viewed it as part of the larger fight against Communism.

Looking back, it may surprise many that liberals, not conservatives, were primarily in favor of intervention. As Norman Podhoretz, longtime editor of *Commentary* and one of the clearest thinkers on the Vietnam question, explains, liberals were still living in the Wilsonian tradition of reshaping the world according to their ideals:

> It is important to realize that the people—mostly liberals—who favored an emphasis on the political aspect of the struggle against Communism tended, if anything, to be more interventionist in their proposals than the military-minded cold warriors. What the military-minded generally favored was sending arms to non-Communist regimes, and letting them tend to their own defense. But the politically-minded, who believed that Communism thrived on institutions of social injustice, wanted to force these regimes into adopting reforms which would in their judgment deprive Communism of its breeding ground: and they were only too willing to tell other countries exactly how to organize their political and economic institutions to this particular end.[24]

Vietnam and the Great Society were part, really, of the same enterprise: If poverty could be eliminated in the United States, it could be eliminated abroad. Johnson believed that if Communism triumphed, or if he faltered, the political fallout would put the domestic programs so dear to his heart in jeopardy. Since failure to succeed abroad would lead to failure at home, Johnson could not and would not admit defeat.[25]

The Johnson administration had deceived the people about Vietnam from the very beginning, publicly denying its intention to escalate the war during the 1964 campaign, then using the Tonkin Gulf incident to justify it. As the early supporters of the war abandoned the cause, Johnson escalated his prevarications; he distorted facts, misrepresented casualties, and lied outright about the chances of winning the war. The war lost its moral legitimacy, going along its bloody way only because its leaders could accept neither defeat nor victory.

Many years later I came to know Gene McCarthy, who had mellowed and returned to his Catholic roots. Before entering politics, McCarthy had been a professor of sociology, and was well versed in the thought of St. Thomas Aquinas. He was a liberal, but an honest one, with a high regard for the truth. McCarthy was also a liberal icon, because he had challenged LBJ in 1968 and run as the Democratic peace candidate. Liberals worshiped Gene McCarthy. He had a weekend house near mine in the Blue Ridge Mountains of Virginia and would often hitch a ride with me in my pickup truck through the thick Washington traffic on Friday afternoons, during which we would have long discussions about politics, theology, and many other things. I turned to him one day—it was July, about one hundred degrees outside, and we were stopped dead in traffic—and asked him why he had staked his career on Vietnam. "Why were you willing to be *the* member of Congress who would become the leader of the opposition to LBJ's war?" McCarthy said it was quite simply because nobody in the administration would tell him the truth. "We would bring McNamara up to the Senate for a hearing, and he lied about everything," he said. "I would go over to the State Department to talk to Dean Rusk, and he lied. We would have meetings at the White House with Johnson, and he made Rusk and McNamara sound like pikers." (McCarthy had known Johnson well, both in the House and the Senate). In the end, said McCarthy, he thought he had no other choice.

Liberalism reached its political zenith with Johnson's Great Society, but in overextending itself to Vietnam, liberalism lost its balance and came crashing down to earth. Vietnam sent a fissure through the heart of the American left that never healed; until Vietnam liberals were relatively unified and spoke mainly with one voice. A few Marxists and radicals hovered around, but liberals generally were patriotic Americans who loved their country. Many remained loyal to Johnson throughout the war, in order to support his domestic programs. John Kenneth Galbraith expressed the opinion of many liberals when he said, "Our gains under the Johnson administration on civil rights outweigh our losses on behalf of [South Vietnam's] Marshal Ky."[26]

But to other liberals, those frustrated by domestic social problems like racism and poverty, American intervention in Vietnam seemed the epitome of hubris—how could we tell other countries how to conduct their business when we conducted our own so poorly? It seemed that America, instead of defending freedom abroad, was exporting its own ills, and causing much bloodshed in the process. This critique of liberal America captured the imagination of many young radicals and converted many mature liberals to its cause. Many, like the intellectuals around the *New York Review of Books* and in the elite universities, developed a visceral hatred for the United States and the principles on which it was founded. Bill Bennett, who would later become Reagan's secretary of education and a prominent conservative spokesman, tells of being attracted to the anti-Vietnam left while an undergraduate at Harvard—at least until he realized that the antiwar crowd hated America and everything about it. "I may have disliked the war," said Bennett, "but I did not hate my country."[27]

These new radicals were not so much antiwar as anti-American, championing the cause of North Vietnam and underprivileged groups as though supporting their struggles made them more authentic. These "radical chic" protestors gave themselves the heady experience of revolution without having to risk a penny or a drop of blood.[28] Eventually, the antiwar movement became synonymous with a counterculture. Casual drug use, promiscuity, long hair, and all the trappings of hippie life became the norm.

As the popular antiwar movement became more vocal it degenerated into contempt for every sort of authority. Leftist activists began shouting obscenities at anybody who disagreed with them, drowning out school administrators, representatives of the Johnson administration, military speakers, and conservatives. They provoked conflicts with the authorities to gain the ready attention of a fawning media. At Columbia University in the spring of 1968, Students for a Democratic Society (SDS) took over administration buildings for several days not so much to air their stated grievances, but to undermine "the system," and the Columbia administration caved in, setting a pattern for others. Later that summer the SDS, led by the radical Weathermen, marched in Chicago in the "Days of Rage," but this time they were met by the police and beaten back. But even before Chicago, the New Left had begun to come apart. Black nationalists, Indian nationalists, Hispanic activists, feminists, and homosexual liberationists competed for victim status, joining the chorus of oppressed minorities. Their competition for privileged victim status, their celebration of individual autonomy, and their zeal for grabbing headlines left them with little to unify them. Once they added division over tactics to divisions over ideology, they lost all coherence as a movement.

The only effective opposition to the New Left came from conservatives. The antics of the left appalled many previously uncommitted students and drove them into groups like the College Republicans and Young Americans for Freedom, both of which were actively involved in combating the antiwar movement. YAF, with the help of a number of other bipartisan student groups, organized rallies on campuses and a demonstration in Washington in November 1965. In 1966, the College Republicans helped organize a bipartisan group called the National Student Committee for the Defense of Vietnam, which collected a half million student signatures on three hundred college campuses supporting American troops and presented them to Vice President Hubert Humphrey.[29] While the radical SDS was occupying administrative buildings at Columbia, the conservative Majority Coalition launched a counter-protest, even trying to blockade the buildings to starve out the radicals.

Though much attention has been given to the effect the sixties cultural revolution and Vietnam had on the left, the consequences for the conservative movement were profound. Eager to take on the radicals, conservatives honed their debate and organizational skills and met their hostile contemporaries head-on. While the New Left splintered into myriad different groups competing for privileged victim status, conservatives, though with their own internal divisions, continued to be active as one force into the next decade. SDS broke apart, but YAF forged ahead. Young leftists began their Long March through the educational institutions of America, but suffered long-term electoral defeat. Young conservatives stayed active in politics, leaving their rivals behind.[30]

1968

While Reagan supporters were disappointed that he had not been nominated in 1968, most rallied behind Richard Nixon. They recognized that the travails of liberalism—student protests, black power riots, huge expenditures for wars against poverty—would drive socially conservative Democrats into the Republican Party.

Lyndon Johnson was defeated by the leftist culture, the attitudes and ideas that had emanated from the universities and the left-wing intellectuals, and which became the center of attention in the media. Ultimately, the war ended in 1975 with the surrender of South Vietnam, by which time virtually everybody, regardless of their politics and regardless of how supportive they had been initially, had concluded that we never should have intervened in the first place.

Johnson was challenged in the 1968 primaries by New York senator Robert Kennedy, and by Minnesota senator Eugene McCarthy, one of the most outspoken critics of the war in Congress and a darling of students. McCarthy opened the floodgates of opposition within the Democratic Party and forced LBJ to step down as the presumptive nominee in favor of Vice President Hubert Humphrey.

When leftist protesters started rioting in the streets of Chicago, during the Democratic National Convention in August before a worldwide television audience, hurling obscenities and filth, the Democratic Party leadership was deeply embarrassed. "The world is watching," chanted the grungy protesters, and indeed it was: As Chicago police fought and arrested thousands of protesters the country cheered. The disorder at the Democratic convention widened the rift between liberals and the party's working-class voters, a rift that never completely healed. When Connecticut senator Abraham Ribicoff, placing George McGovern's name in nomination, blasted the "Gestapo tactics" of the Chicago police department, Mayor Richard Daley, the most powerful Democratic mayor in the country, interrupted Ribicoff, screaming, "Fuck you, you Jew son of a bitch, you lousy motherfucker, go home." An unbelievable seventy-four thousand letters were sent to Mayor Daley, 94 percent of which supported him.[31]

The radicalization of so many Democrats drove the traditional base of southerners, blue-collar workers, Catholics, union members, farmers, and other socially conservative Democrats—those later known as "Reagan Democrats"—out of the Democratic sway and into the Republican embrace. The old Roosevelt Democratic coalition was replaced by government employees and dependents, racial minorities, and hubristic intellectuals, making it much less stable. It also meant that the Democratic Party would become philosophically split, left and right, which made it much more difficult to satisfy its disparate constituencies.

Nixon's campaign happily capitalized on this internecine fighting and the leftward drift of the Democrats. But George Wallace was also a factor, particularly among urban working-class Democrats in the North and, of course, southern Democrats. The remainder of the party was still divided between the McCarthy antiwar supporters on the left and the more moderate Humphrey Democrats. Nixon promised to unite the country at home and bring "peace with honor" to Vietnam, undermining Humphrey's arguments for continuing the administration's policies there—arguments that Humphrey in any case felt uncomfortable making. Nixon came across as the peace candidate with a secret plan to end the war.

Hubert Humphrey returned to the Senate in 1970, after he lost to Nixon, and was re-elected in 1976, but died early in 1978 after a bout with cancer. One day, in the summer of 1977, he asked Paul Laxalt, the conservative Republican senator from Nevada, to come to his office, where he told him that he no longer believed that liberalism was what the country needed, but that he agreed with most of what Laxalt said. He was too old and too sick, he told Laxalt, to explain why or to express his newly found beliefs.[32]

Domestically, Nixon campaigned like a conservative. Until 1968, law and order had been almost exclusively a state and local issue, but Nixon perceived that the undermining of public authority by liberals could be turned into votes for himself. In a piece in the *Reader's Digest* in 1967,

Nixon had written, "In a few short years, America has become among the most lawless and violent nations in the history of free people" because liberal court decisions—i.e., Democrats—"were weakening the peace forces against the criminal forces."[33] Nixon's rhetoric broke open the gates of criticism of the federal courts, which would, over the next thirty years, grow to dominate American politics.

In speech after speech, Nixon promised that he would secure the borders of the country against the pestilence of narcotics, appoint judges who were tough on crime, and develop federal programs to support local law enforcement agencies to fight street crime. Nixon's chief speech-writer on the issue was Patrick J. Buchanan, then thirty-one and recently an editorial writer at the *St. Louis Globe Democrat*. One Nixon ad, run hundreds of times across the country, showed a nervous woman walking down the street on a dark, wet night while an announcer stated: "Crimes of violence in the United States have almost doubled in recent years . . . today a violent crime is committed every sixty seconds . . . a robbery every two and a half minutes . . . a mugging every six minutes . . . a murder every forty-three minutes . . . and it will get worse unless we take the offensive." The commercial ended: "This time vote like your whole world depended on it."[34]

The law and order theme resonated with conservatives and won Nixon many votes. It also established the right as pro–law enforcement and the left as anticop. Congress established, at Nixon's request, the Law Enforcement Assistance Administration (LEAA), which provided hundreds of millions of dollars to state and local governments for law enforcement. Other legislation brought crimes that were traditionally state and local offenses into federal courts, giving federal prosecutors unprecedented power. The downside, as far as conservatives were concerned, was a vast increase in the power of the federal government—power that might not be used just against ordinary street criminals. Law and order was also a politically effective issue in that it linked the fear of street crime with the public's disgust with social disorder. Conservatives gained many new recruits as they fought against leftist student demonstrators, black radicals, and antiwar protesters who did not hesitate to use violence on people and damage private property. Working- and middle-class Americans saw little distinction between the demonstrators and common criminals.

Nixon's law-and-order speeches struck a chord with conservatives in the 1968 campaign and in the early years of his administration. Such distrust as still existed was further allayed when Nixon chose Maryland governor Spiro Agnew as his running mate. Agnew was tough on crime and urban disorder, but also had a strong civil rights record. Nixon aide Stephen Hess summarized it: "If you put all the conflicting Republican elements into a computer, and programmed it to produce a vice president who would do least harm to party unity, the tape would be punched SPIRO T. AGNEW."[35]

Agnew became Nixon's strong right arm, blasting student disorder, race riots, pointy-headed liberals, and the antiwar demonstrators, all to the delight of conservatives. He took no prisoners:

> The criminal left belongs not in a dormitory but in a penitentiary. The criminal left is not a problem to be solved by the department of philosophy or the department of English; it is a problem for the Department of Justice. Black or white, the criminal left is interested in power. It is not interested in promoting the renewal and reforms that make democracy work; it is interested in promoting those collisions and conflicts that tear democracy apart.[36]

Agnew also became the GOP's best fundraiser, traveling across the country speaking to conservative audiences. By mid-1970 he was receiving 250 speaking invitations a week, and with Pat Buchanan and William Safire as his speechwriters, he attacked leftists, student radicals, and the media in a ringing and quotable style that became the envy of politicians everywhere. "In the United States today," Agnew told a 1970 audience in San Diego, in one of his most memorable lines, "we have more than our share of the nattering nabobs of negativism." Liberals were "pusillanimous pussyfooters" and "vicars of vacillation" and the press "the hopeless, hysterical hypochondriacs of history."[37]

Nixon avoided mistakes Goldwater had made in 1964, most particularly by remaining closer to the political center, but he borrowed heavily from the successful aspects of the Goldwater campaign. He took in large sums from many small donors through direct mail and enlisted the help of the conservative grassroots organizations to take on nuts-and-bolts campaign duties.

Nixon, running a flawless campaign and taking full advantage of the self-destruction of the Democrats, eked out a victory over Humphrey in 1968, to the relief of conservatives. But their relief would not last for long; Nixon the conservative became Nixon the moderate as soon as he entered the White House.

REGULATION

Following a large and widely publicized oil spill off the coast of Santa Barbara in January 1969, liberals and the nascent environmental movement called for the enactment of strict environmental laws to punish polluters, and for the development of an environmental movement similar to the civil rights movement. Nixon, seeing a political opportunity, decided to outflank the liberals, particularly Senator Edmund Muskie of Maine, Humphrey's running mate in 1968 and chairman of the Senate Public Works Committee, which had jurisdiction over environmental issues. Nixon and Muskie began a bidding war for the most stringent bill, in the course of which the administration introduced thirty-six different environmental laws. Congress rejected most of them, but Nixon was not about to be outdone, so when Congress balked at establishing a cabinet environmental department, Nixon created the Environmental Protection Agency by executive order. He brought together various parts of other agencies and gave it broad regulatory power—broader power, in fact, than a cabinet-level department, because the EPA was an independent administrative agency and could issue regulations on its own authority.

Nixon's environmental efforts had a far-reaching impact. Until then, federal regulations were designed to create a fair playing field for business and consumers, and individual regulatory agencies had jurisdiction over single industries—the securities industry, the electric power industry, the railroads, and so on. But EPA could regulate all industries and have vast impact on the economy through its own regulatory power, without regard to the acts of Congress or the goals of a particular administration.

Nixon created the Consumer Product Safety Commission and the Occupational Safety and Health Administration, further burdening businesses with an array of new regulations; both legislated through bureaucratic fiat rather than through the democratic process and federalized many activities that had previously been regulated by state and local governments. According to historian Steven Hayward, Nixon's regulatory revolution was his most profound legacy, creating a vast centralization and expansion of government power, reaching to the most remote recesses of private enterprise, and becoming nearly three-quarters of the federal regulatory apparatus.[38]

WAGE AND PRICE CONTROLS

When Nixon was inaugurated in January 1969, inflation was running at nearly 5 percent per year, and within a year, unemployment was approaching 6 percent and economic growth had stalled—a condition that came to be known as "stagflation." Nixon responded to Democratic criticism of his handling of the economy in January 1971 by submitting a federal budget calling for large spending increases across the board, expecting it to result in an $11 billion deficit. He believed he could simply buy his way out of his economic problems. In an interview with ABC News after the budget was submitted, Nixon explained, "We're all Keynesians now."[39]

By August 1971 things had so worsened that foreign governments began to make a run on the dollar in fear that the United States would devalue its currency. Nixon responded with an executive order putting a 10 percent tariff on all imports, allowing the value of the dollar to float in international markets, compounding the blunder by imposing a ninety-day wage and price freeze. Despite the warnings of economist Milton Friedman and others, Nixon adopted wage and price controls, fully realizing that they would hurt the economy, but freely admitting that short-term political gain trumped long-term economic considerations: "Whenever political considerations are not present" said Nixon, "we can afford to look at things purely from an economic standpoint. But that will not be often."[40] George Shultz, who was secretary of the treasury and chairman of Nixon's Council on Economic Policy, asked his old friend Milton Friedman what he should do, knowing of Friedman's complete disdain for wage and price controls. The only honorable thing, Friedman told Shultz, would be to resign. But Shultz stayed.[41]

CHINA

Nixon's greatest diplomatic victory was his trip to China. But at the time it sent conservatives up the wall. Until Nixon's visit, China was closed to the West. The U.S. had no diplomatic mission there and the Chinese had none in Washington. Since "Red" China was viewed as an archenemy of Western democracy, there was no trade and little travel. Instead, we had warm relations with Taiwan, which had been established by General Chiang Kai-shek's Nationalists after mainland China fell to the Communists in 1949. Preserving our alliance with Taiwan and keeping Red China out of the United Nations had been a popular conservative cause ever since, State Department objections notwithstanding. Mainland China, for its part, would accept entry into the UN only on the condition that Taiwan be expelled. But since Taiwan held a permanent seat on the UN's Security Council and had the backing of the United States, it successfully vetoed every attempt to let Red China in.

Throughout his career, Nixon had been a staunch defender of Taiwan. But in 1971 he secretly dispatched Henry Kissinger to Peking to pave the way for formal relations with Red China, and in February 1972, Nixon himself made the trip to Peking and broke bread with Mao Tse-Tung, to the fanfare of the journalists in tow. Although he tried to gloss over the Taiwan friendship, the stark reality was that American pledges to Nationalist China had been broken. Conservatives were livid, and any affection the conservative movement had left for Nixon dissipated at his landing in Peking. William F. Buckley accompanied him as one of the eighty journalists on the trip, seventy-nine of whom filed stories hailing Nixon as the diplomat of the century. On the contrary, Buckley wrote:

> We have lost irretrievably any remaining sense of
> moral mission in the world. Mr. Nixon's appetite for

> a summit conference in Peking transformed the af-
> fair from a meeting of diplomatic technicians con-
> cerned to examine and illuminate areas of common
> interest, into a pageant of moral togetherness of
> which Mr. Nixon managed to give the impression
> that he was consorting with Marian Anderson, Billy
> Graham and Albert Schweitzer.[42]

As Nixon left China, he signed the "Shanghai Communiqué" affirm-
ing Peking's claim over Taiwan—the final stab in the back—stating that
there is only one China, of which Taiwan is part, and that all U.S. military forces would be withdrawn from the island. Conservatives would
never forgive Nixon for what they considered a betrayal, even though
Nixon promised that our defense treaty with Taiwan would remain in
force when he returned to Washington.

APPOINTMENTS

The Nixon administration was almost entirely devoid of movement conservatives. Virtually all of the cabinet and subcabinet officers, as well as
aides and advisors to the president, were establishment moderate Republicans. About the only exceptions were speechwriter Pat Buchanan,
press aide Lyn Nofziger, Howard Phillips, who headed the Office of
Economic Opportunity, and Tom Charles Huston, former head of Young
Americans for Freedom, a White House aide. "There was a group of us
called the Committee of Six," recalled Pat Buchanan. "The trouble with
the Committee of Six was, people kept getting fired from it."[43] Few were
ever replaced.

Nixon had railed against Chief Justice Earl Warren in his campaigns
and pledged to appoint only judges and Supreme Court justices who
were "strict constructionists," who would undo Warren's handiwork.
But his judicial appointments were mostly well-connected mainstream
Republican lawyers chosen for reasons other than judicial philosophy,
and who continued the leftward trend of the federal courts. In reality, although he talked about returning the courts to constitutionalism
and was one of the first lawyers to occupy the White House in years,

Nixon had no judicial philosophy, no idea of what he wanted his judges to be. Of his four nominees to the high court—Warren Burger, Harry Blackmun, Lewis Powell, and William Rehnquist—only Rehnquist, an old Goldwater friend, turned out to be a conservative. The other three continued, to a great extent, the work of Nixon's nemesis Earl Warren.

THE 1972 CAMPAIGN

Within eighteen months of his inauguration, conservatives began to mutter about dumping Nixon and finding a conservative candidate for 1972. The American Conservative Union led the charge against Nixon's welfare policies and found in a poll that 66 percent of Republicans disapproved of him; similar numbers of Republicans found fault with his national security efforts, particularly his promotion of the Strategic Arms Limitation Treaty, which they viewed as far too soft on the Soviets.

In August 1971, weighed down by increasing disappointment with Nixon, *National Review* brought together a coalition of conservatives to "suspend" support of Nixon's administration. Known as the "Manhattan Twelve," they drew up a document called, simply, "A Declaration," which appeared in most of the conservative journals and papers around the country.[44] This declaration, signed by the editors of *National Review* and *Human Events*, the head of the American Conservative Union, the New York Conservative Party, and Young Americans for Freedom warned Nixon that conservative support was far from automatic. Conservatives had hoped, it stated, that Nixon's election in 1968 would make substantial headway in reorienting the country's policies in a more conservative direction. Instead they had to swallow "excessive taxation and inordinate welfarism." But the most severe criticism was reserved for Nixon's foreign policy: He had waffled in opposing Soviet moves in the Middle East and German chancellor Willy Brandt's "Ostpolitik," he had made overtures to Communist China while receiving nothing in return, and he had done little to correct the deteriorating military standing of the United States. The disaffected conservatives were not (as yet) searching for a challenger to Nixon in 1972, the document said, but they would keep their options open over the coming months.

Others soon joined the anti-Nixon ranks. *Human Events* reported that "an increasing number of conservatives are beginning to think the unthinkable: that a Nixon defeat in 1972 might not be so catastrophic after all. These conservatives reason that it would be better to have a liberal administration, with all the consequences that it might bring, than to permit Richard Nixon to destroy the Republican Party as a vehicle for conservatism.[45] *Human Events* predicted that the Nixon administration would set conservatism back by at least as many years as Nixon served, if not more. *National Review*'s feisty publisher Bill Rusher, who had been a chief ringleader behind Goldwater's nomination in 1964, drafted a thirty-page memorandum, distributed to conservatives across the country, setting forth reasons the right should dump Nixon. The conservative movement, he asserted, would be better off with a Democrat in the White House, someone who could "be vigorously opposed by a hungry, articulate and thoroughly conservative Republican party." It was widely held that Nixon's elections had been bad for conservatives, who had a bare toehold in the administration. It was time to end it.[46]

John Ashbrook, a conservative congressman from Ohio, thought so, too, and at the end of 1971 announced that he would oppose Nixon for the nomination. Ashbrook's conservative credentials were impeccable: chairman of the Young Republicans, one of the founders of the American Conservative Union, a founder of the draft-Goldwater movement in 1963, and highly regarded as a legislator. Telling his followers that "the net result of [the Nixon] administration may be to frustrate for years to come the emergence of the conservative majority," Ashbrook ran on a campaign slogan of "No Left Turn." After receiving less than 10 percent of the vote in several primaries, he withdrew and reluctantly supported Nixon.[47]

But there was one problem, a large one. Reagan, Goldwater, Senator John Tower of Texas, and Strom Thurmond continued to support Nixon, leaving the conservative opposition with no political leaders to turn to . . . and Nixon with the conviction that the conservatives had little political clout.

In the end, the Democrats solved the problem in 1972 by nominating George McGovern, whose campaign themes largely echoed the thinking of the New Left. After his failed bid for the nomination in 1968, McGovern led fellow Democrats in implementing a series of changes in the way delegates were chosen, with the result that convention delegates were apportioned to minorities, women, and the young in numbers proportional to their percentage of the state's population. The effect was to shift power away from white southern Democrats, local party bosses, and labor unions, and toward New Left activists. The reforms rewarded states that consistently went for Democratic presidential nominees—by definition the country's most liberal states—with bonus delegates, tilting the nomination process still further to the left. As a result, the Democratic Party's nomination process rarely reflected the larger party constituency, with a lasting, long-term impact on the party. Were it not for the post-1968 convention reforms, McGovern might not have been nominated in 1972, nor many liberal candidates since that time.[48]

Nixon lost little sleep over *National Review*'s opposition. Conservatives were so horrified by the McGoverniks that they turned back to Nixon, and the "dump Nixon" effort was little more than a shot in the dark. But as the 1970s and 1980s progressed, this sort of campaign was exactly what conservatives would perfect, enabling them to have great impact on policy issues and political appointments.

Although conservatives had threatened to abandon Nixon, having nowhere else to go in 1972, they lethargically helped him win one of the largest electoral landslides in years. The Democrats were in complete disarray, having largely been taken over by special-interest groups. There were no fewer than fifteen potential presidential candidates during the primary season, ranging from segregationist George Wallace and national security hawk Henry "Scoop" Jackson on the right to Teddy Kennedy and George McGovern on the left. Wallace was shot while campaigning in the Maryland primary, and though he survived, he was unable to continue. Kennedy dropped out after the 1969 Chappaquiddick scandal, and the rest faded away until only McGovern was left.

Given the almost obsessive hostility of the press toward Nixon, along with the student protests and the general disdain that the Eastern Establishment held for him, the Democrats convinced themselves that Nixon was in trouble and that anybody could beat him. McGovern was the result. A docile and gentle fellow, he maintained a certain moderation in the Congress, but drifted away to the left as his primary campaign progressed. He absorbed every leftist and antiwar kook who happened along into his organization, and by election day was so far out as to embarrass even liberals. He proposed a thousand-dollar federal grant to every man, woman, and child in the country, which he coupled with a populist attack on the wealthy. McGovern promised to bring all troops home from Vietnam within ninety days of his election, withdraw all troops from Asia and many from Europe, and cut the defense budget by 37 percent, spending the savings on social programs. He said that the threat of Communism was no longer real: "I don't like Communism, but I don't think we have any great obligation to save the world from it." McGovern's signature theme, unveiled in his acceptance speech at the Democratic convention, was "Come home, America." As if that were not enough, he equated the mass murderer Ho Chi Minh with George Washington and remarked that "Watergate is the kind of thing you expect under a person like Hitler."[49]

Nixon once again ran as a conservative. Unabashedly, he campaigned against centralized power and for limited government, against a strong executive, and for returning power to state and local government. His watchwords were less regulation, lower taxes, and a "new patriotism."

Nixon won in a landslide with 61 percent of the popular vote (just shy of LBJ's margin over Goldwater in 1964), losing only Massachusetts and the District of Columbia. He received the votes of 37 percent of registered Democrats and 51 percent of union members, and in the South he won eight out of every nine white votes. McGovern got only 29.1 percent of the popular vote—the lowest percentage of any major-party candidate in the history of presidential elections. It was not that people liked Nixon—nobody ever liked Nixon—but that they were appalled by McGovern. The 1972 election was a total repudiation of leftism.

Strangely, Nixon had no coattails—he wanted the landslide for himself, so the Republicans in Congress were on their own. Republicans did pick up twelve seats in the House, leaving them still in the minority, but lost two Senate seats and did poorly in state races as well, holding only nineteen governorships as opposed to thirty-one in 1968. Nixon's campaign organization was almost totally divorced from the Republican

National Committee (he set up, instead, the famous Committee to Re-Elect the President, known colloquially as "CREEP"), and even Bob Dole, then chairman of the RNC, was unable to get an appointment with Nixon during the entire campaign.

Nixon, with a mandate for himself, planned in his second term to govern without the help of either his cabinet or Congress, neither of which he trusted. In doing so, he alienated many members of Congress who otherwise might have supported him when Watergate loomed.

The liberal media, whose disdain for Nixon only increased with his huge victory, were aghast. According to British historian Paul Johnson, Nixon's success "not only humiliated the media liberals but actually frightened them. . . . The aim was to use the power of the press and TV to reverse the electoral verdict of 1972 which was felt to be, in some metaphorical sense, illegitimate" (a foreshadow of Bush/Gore). According to many in the press, there had to be a bloodletting. They needed to make sure that nobody ever behaved like Richard Nixon again.[50]

To the conservative movement, the second Nixon term was a political opportunity lost. The huge mandate against McGovern, along with a conservative platform and campaign—even the initial steps Nixon took in the second term—led conservatives to believe that maybe, just maybe, Goldwater, Thurmond, and Reagan had been right to support Nixon. In his first budget after his re-election, Nixon proposed eliminating over one hundred federal programs.

National Review applauded Nixon's embrace of the silent majority's principles, but warned of the liberal response: "Nixon must realize that any attempt to move as he proposed to do will inflame the other constituency. The people at OEO and HUD, assorted poverty bureaucrats, the education lobby, the counter-Pentagon over at HEW, the liberal press and its allies, will put on the heat. They will burn up the phone wires and flood the corridors of Congress."[51]

Nixon put the brakes on federal spending almost immediately, and by early 1973 he had exercised the president's power to impound funds for over one hundred federal programs, as promised. Impoundment, a rarely invoked presidential power, allowed the president to refuse to spend money that Congress had already appropriated. Nixon made no bones about the fact that he intended to use the power much more broadly than legal interpretations found constitutional. "I have nailed my colors to the mast on this issue: the political winds can blow where they may," Nixon proclaimed, promising more if Congress did not bend to his will.[52] As *National Review* had predicted, the liberal roof blew. Each program had a constituency of recipients, and a constituency of members of Congress responsible for these sacred programs—the pork needed to get them re-elected.

That Nixon had few friends in Congress became apparent as the Watergate scandal unfolded. The story, tattered through repetition, battered Nixon and the Republican Party, and put the conservative movement back by years. After Nixon finally resigned in August 1974, Jerry Ford ascended to the presidency and appointed Nelson Rockefeller, the conservatives' old nemesis, vice president. This was a bitter pill for conservatives to swallow after supporting Nixon in 1968 and 1972 over their better judgment. From a political standpoint, the devastating aftermath of Watergate was best demonstrated by the 1974 off-year congressional elections; the Republicans lost forty-three seats, leaving Democrats with a 291–144 majority, and four Senate seats, giving Democrats a 62–38 majority.

Not only was the new Congress more Democratic, it was also more liberal. The "Watergate babies," as the newly elected members were known, reflected the counterculture, the antiwar mentality, and the anti-Nixon, Watergate-reformist attitude that would change the entire tone of Congress. The *Democratic Review*, published by the Democratic National Committee, estimated that the 1974 freshman class was more than twice as liberal as the Democrats they had replaced, and when a *Washington Post* survey asked incoming Democrats, "What nation, if any, do you consider a threat to world peace?" the largest group, 27 percent, answered the United States, and only 20 percent the Soviet Union.[53]

Conservatives had risked their credibility to support Nixon in 1968, and although many bitterly opposed his nomination, it was largely conservatives, led by Barry Goldwater, who assured him his place on the ticket. By the time Nixon resigned the presidency, he had broken virtually every promise he had made and left a legacy of liberal policies and initiatives almost unmatched by Republican or

Democrat in the twentieth century. Reflecting on the Nixon years, Pat Buchanan, one of Nixon's closest aides, said, "Looking back on the budget, economic and social policies of the Republican years, it would not be unfair to conclude that the political verdict of 1968 had brought reaffirmation, rather than repudiation, of Great Society liberalism . . . Johnson laid the foundation of the first floor, and we built the skyscraper." [54]

CHAPTER SEVEN

The Neocons, the New Right, and the Grassroots

NEOCONSERVATIVES

As the collapse of liberal hegemony in American political life became apparent, many people switched their allegiances. Others simply realized that their previous philosophical assumptions had been mistaken, and drifted to the right. But one small group of intellectuals who joined the conservative cause proved to be particularly important to the future of the movement. Their former comrades on the left called them, derisively, "neoconservatives," and the moniker stuck. These neoconservatives caused considerable suspicion within the traditional conservative ranks, and continue to do so to this day.

Neoconservatism, never a movement per se, has been described as a persuasion. There is in fact no clear definition of it, for its adherents disagree on a good many things, and the boundaries have always been fluid. What is called neoconservatism in 2008 has little to do with its original inception. Today's neocons are largely journalists, think-tank residents, scholars, and government officials who advocate an interventionist foreign policy, strongly support the invasion and democratization of Iraq, and uphold "big-government conservatism." As self-described "big-government conservative" journalist Fred Barnes put it: "They simply believe in using what would normally be seen as liberal means—activist government—for conservative ends. And they're willing to spend more and increase the size of government in the process."[1]

But first a look at the original neoconservatives.

The radicalization of the left may have excited student revolutionaries, and their demonstrations may have added spice to their college careers, but the rioting students disrupted the serene and staid world of academia. As the bulwark of Western culture—the universities, the arts, literature, and the media—became more radicalized, the anti-Communist liberals became disenchanted with their colleagues and their surroundings. The counterculture, black power, sexual revolution, student protests, and the emerging hatred for America were bad enough, but worse was the reaction of many of their liberal colleagues or, more accurately, the lack of reaction. As vocal obscenities and attacks on civil order went unanswered by the liberal establishment, a small group of anti-Communist liberals found themselves drawn to the right. Those who were Jewish—and many were—were moreover shaken by the emerging anti-Semitism on the left. Black radicals, Arab revolutionary organizations, and the Soviet Union, all anti-Semitic, were either lionized or at the least defended by the leftist radicals.

In response to the Berkeley free speech movement and the occupation of the university presidents' offices at Columbia, Cornell, Harvard, and a good many other colleges and universities, the neoconservatives mounted a spirited and sophisticated defense of the social order, "a defense that, to its great shame, the mainstream liberal community found itself unable or unwilling to provide."[2]

Many of the neoconservatives had met at the City College of New York during the 1930s. From discussing the finer points of Marxism, these intellectuals conceived of politics as something that should be instructed by theory and learned to use the sophisticated application of theory as a form of political combat.[3] According to Irving Kristol, ideas were their stock in trade: "What rules the world is ideas, because ideas define the way reality is perceived."[4]

The early neoconservatives were, indeed, men of ideas, and they were adept at making their ideas known. They wrote books and articles, gave speeches, debated widely, and became distinguished academics. Two journals—*Commentary*, which was founded in 1945 and published by the American Jewish Committee, and the *Public Interest*, founded in

1965 by Irving Kristol and Daniel Bell—became the mainstay of neo-conservative thought, the pages where the ideas that defined them took shape. Until 1959, when Norman Podhoretz became its editor, *Commentary* focused on pro-Israel and anti-Soviet articles, as well as issues of interest to the Jewish intellectual community; after 1959, future neo-conservative writers mainly took over.

Many neoconservatives, initially, were almost exclusively interested in domestic social policy. Vietnam and other foreign policy issues were secondary. According to Kristol, speaking about *Public Interest:*

> We made one easy editorial decision at the outset: no discussion of foreign policy or foreign affairs. Vietnam was arousing a storm of controversy at the time, and we knew that our group had a wide spectrum of opinion on the issue. We did not want any of the space in our modest-sized quarterly to be swallowed up by Vietnam. The simplest solution was to ban foreign affairs and foreign policy from our pages.[5]

They recognized the economic and social costs of Johnson's War on Poverty's social engineering programs, but unlike traditional conservatives, they were not as interested in dismantling the welfare state as in making it work. Nevertheless, their arguments generally outraged the left and delighted the right.

One of the first of the intellectuals to take on the question of liberal social policy was a young Harvard sociologist named Daniel Patrick Moynihan. Moynihan emerged from the shadows during 1965 as a researcher in LBJ's Labor Department when he wrote a report on black family stability, pointing out that illegitimacy in the black family was escalating (it was then at 25 percent) and that the deterioration of the family in the black community would undermine urban tranquility. Shortly after leaving the Labor Department Moynihan wrote an article for *Commentary* in which he claimed that the "conceptual difficulties" of the War on Poverty "were a result of the work of intellectuals" who had gathered in Washington in the Kennedy administration and wished to radicalize American society. The poverty programs that these intellectuals had designed had deliberately left out traditional assistance for the poor in lieu of community action programs. As a result, the poor became yet more disgruntled, which led to urban violence.[6] Nixon hired Moynihan after the 1968 election to head his Urban Affairs Council, intended as the domestic equivalent of the National Security Council, through which Nixon thought he could generate original thinking on domestic policy issues. Economist Herb Stein remarked that "Moynihan was Nixon's soaring kite reaching out for the liberal chic Eastern establishment, whose respect Nixon did not have but wanted."[7]

Moynihan would become one of the most outspoken neoconservatives, writing and speaking on liberalism, the deterioration of order and tradition, and social policy. He served as ambassador to the UN under Gerald Ford and, in 1976, he was elected to the United States Senate from New York, beating Conservative incumbent Jim Buckley. But then, to the chagrin of his old neoconservative friends, he abandoned his nascent conservatism and settled in as a liberal stalwart. "He was one of us until he got elected," said Midge Decter, wife of Norman Podhoretz, "and then he broke our hearts."[8]

Edward Banfield, a Harvard political scientist, published *The Unheavenly City* in 1970, a best-selling critique of urban planning. It pointed out that social programs designed to help the poor often did more harm than good, benefiting the affluent instead. Banfield recognized the existence of an urban "underclass," describing the "lower-class culture" as people who were so "present-oriented" that they lived mainly for immediate gratification and impulsive adventure. The result, not easily reversed, was an urban landscape littered with drug use, fatherless families, and random crime.[9] Being unable to refute Banfield, liberals attacked him, viciously. But *The Unheavenly City* has stood the test of time, and now books agreeing with many of its conclusions on race, crime, and welfare are warmly received, "often by the same people who had denounced Banfield's book twenty years earlier."[10]

For the first time, conservatives could bolster their critiques of liberal policies by citing case studies by respected academics, which brought establishment cachet to the conservative cause. According to Bill Buckley, the neoconservatives brought to the disposal of the conservative movement an entire intellectual and totally new apparatus:

People like Irving Kristol and Norman Podhoretz had done a lifetime of reading and of intellectual exercises and when they put this formal training at the disposal of the conservative cause, it enormously influenced the weight of what we said. . . . The neoconservatives lent us a discipline that we weren't born with, in the matter of arranging arguments, absorbing social data, acting on them, bringing non-ideological skepticism, empirical skepticism to some of the major enterprises of the liberals. And that stayed with us.[11]

Buckley knew from experience how effective these arguments could be. In his campaign for mayor of New York City, he cited Moynihan and Nathan Glazer on the social pathology of liberal social programs—to the chagrin of rival John Lindsay and the *New York Times*. "The *Times* and the rest of the establishment press," according to neoconservative Ben Wattenberg, "never took conservatives seriously until Kristol, Podhoretz, Moynihan and the rest came along. They could not ignore them and, to a certain extent, they put a respectable face on the conservative movement."[12] An added benefit, as far as credibility was concerned, was that the early neoconservatives were all Democrats. "All of us had voted for Lyndon Johnson in 1964," said Nathan Glazer in the last issue of the *Public Interest,* in spring 2005, "for Hubert Humphrey in 1968, and I would hazard that most of the original stalwarts of the *Public Interest*, editors and regular contributors, continued to vote for Democratic presidential candidates all the way to the present."[13]

If conservatives found the arguments of the neoconservatives useful, there was little if any reciprocity. Kristol, probably more sympathetic to conservatives than most of the others, found Buckley charming and likable, but thought *National Review* "too strident," insufficiently "analytical and intellectual," and he rejected its "hostility to the New Deal and its enthusiasm for Jeffersonian individualism."[14] He thought *NR* was "simpleminded in its anti-statism in general and its contempt for all social reform in particular." While increasingly doubtful of governmental solutions to problems, neocons were not hostile to government itself, nor to government programs like Social Security.[15] The neocons, said

Kristol, sought to reshape the welfare state along more modern lines, to attach to it what he considered the *conservative* predispositions of the American people.

In neoconservative critic and historian Murray Friedman's view, the early neocons, many of whom were from immigrant backgrounds, associated conservatism with country clubs, the Republican Party, and big business—"a sort of 'goyische' fraternity," as he put it, "and with the ideological posturing of right-wing fanatics." By contrast, the neoconservatives thought of themselves as dissenting liberals, "children of the depression," as Midge Decter declared, who retained a measure of loyalty to the spirit of the New Deal.[16] If the neoconservatives had little patience for the conservatives, some conservatives felt even less kindly toward the neocons, even if they found their arguments interesting. In the early 1970s Irving Kristol showed up at a Philadelphia Society meeting in Chicago to debate Milton Friedman on federal housing policy. During the debate, Kristol declared, while pointing out that Washington was doing a terrible job of running the program, that he was no longer a neocon, but a full-fledged conservative. Most of the audience was impressed. But not Frank Meyer, who was busily uniting conservatives under the banner of "fusionism," and was the undisputed conscience of the movement. Meyer jumped up onto his chair, interrupted Kristol's presentation, and, pointing an accusing finger at him, said, "You, sir, are no conservative. You are nothing but a goddamned Tory Socialist," and stormed out of the room.[17] Nevertheless, Meyer and other conservatives knew that whereas they might not need to be soul brothers, they needed each other.

Until McGovern, many Democrats had not differed markedly from Republicans in their attitudes toward Communism and national security. But George McGovern's nomination as the Democratic standard-bearer in 1972 marked the end of anti-Communism in the Democratic Party—and the beginning of the neoconservatives' formal desertion to Republicanism.

But to these Democrats, the Republicans did not offer much of an alternative. Nixon was finishing his first term in 1972 and, despite his anti-Communist reputation, had accelerated détente and had allowed the Soviets to extend their global reach, as well as allowing America's strength to deteriorate. The United States was not winning the Cold War, and anti-Communist Democrats were concerned because, according to one critic, the Soviet Union "had captured the commanding heights of the culture and represented a serious threat to Americans, to Western freedom, and, not least important, to Jews and Israel."[18] And thus a group of the nascent neoconservatives turned to Democratic senator Henry "Scoop" Jackson of Washington State, one of the most hawkish Democratic members of either house of Congress and one of the most strident Cold Warriors of either party.

Jackson was pro-defense, anti-Communist, advocated nuclear superiority over the Soviets, and was one of the last prominent anti-Communist liberal politicians. Following a minor role in the 1972 presidential primaries, Jackson formed a close alliance with Podhoretz, Moynihan, Jeane Kirkpatrick, and other neoconservatives, establishing the basis for his more serious effort of 1976. When Jimmy Carter was elected instead, neoconservative opposition to his administration, particularly its appeasement of the Soviet Union, was centered in Jackson's Senate office. It became a veritable training ground for young anti-Communist Democrats, many of whom subsequently joined the Reagan and both Bush administrations, becoming the nucleus of the second generation of the neoconservative "persuasion."

After McGovern's nomination and subsequent shellacking by Nixon in 1972, several neoconservatives, at the urging of former Yale Law School dean Eugene V. Debs Rostow, formed the Committee for the Present Danger. Rostow, a tough-minded liberal anti-Communist, had served in the State Department during the Johnson administration, and was one of the architects of the Vietnam War.[19] The CPD became a meeting place for Republican and Democratic Cold Warriors. It was a diverse group Washington insiders—Jim Schlesinger and Paul Nitze, Nixon confidant David Packard of computer manufacturer Hewlett-Packard, novelist Saul Bellow, second-generation neocon Paul Wolfowitz, former defense secretary Donald Rumsfeld, and former California governor Ronald Reagan were all members, as were most of the original neoconservatives. The group advocated nuclear superiority over the Soviet Union and supported the building of strategic weapons, including the B-1 bomber. The CPD was a typical neoconservative enterprise—its members were well connected and influential, especially in the foreign policy arena, and they appeared frequently in prominent journals and magazines. But as lifelong Democrats, even with the embarrassments of George McGovern and Jimmy Carter, they were reluctant to break ranks and join the party that had attracted such ridicule for as long as they could remember. One courageous soul was needed to break ranks.

The logjam was broken one late winter day in 1980, when Carter invited a contingent from the Committee for a Democratic Majority, a group of neoconservatives and other moderate Democrats, to the White House to see if he could solicit their support in his upcoming re-election bid. When Carter was offered less support than he thought his due, he stalked out of the meeting. Midge Decter, who was in the meeting, recalls that "one of our number that day was Jeane Kirkpatrick. As we left the White House we were approached by the group of television reporters who seem to hang out on the White House lawn every day waiting for something to happen, and—as it would turn out for all of us, fatefully—she faced the cameras and announced that she was going to support Ronald Reagan.[20]

Carter was never popular with the CPD members. Decter reported her husband, Norman, as saying, "Carter was the third U.S. President he'd met and the first one that he felt that, if you made one false move, you'd be taken out to the Rose Garden and shot. He'd get these little red spots on his cheeks when he was annoyed with us. He'd leave the room and send Mondale in to be nice."[21]

Over forty CPD members joined the Reagan transition team in 1980 and helped formulate much of Reagan's foreign policy. Reagan, a former Democrat himself, felt comfortable with the hard-line neoconservatives, who shared his views on Communism and the Soviet Union, even though they were not necessarily soulmates on his domestic policies. Several neocons joined the top ranks of the Reagan administration, including Jeane Kirkpatrick as UN ambassador and Bill Bennett as chairman of the National Endowment for the Humanities and later secretary of education; both were Democrats when they joined the Reagan team, but subsequently became Republicans.

Bennett's choice as head of the NEH proved to be a bitter pill for the old right, and a cause of enduring resentment. Traditional conservative Mel Bradford, professor of English at the University of Dallas and a native Texan who viewed Abraham Lincoln as the father of big and intrusive government, was the favored candidate of conservative intellectuals, who made a concerted effort to get him nominated. Bradford was as close to a Southern Agrarian as anybody in the old right. But Bennett was backed by the neoconservatives, who went to bat for him with all the fervor they could muster. In the process, they all but destroyed Bradford's reputation and caused a rift with the old right that still exists. In a letter to me in 2006, a member of one of the NEH's committees at the time, and a certified member of the old right, wrote that the neoconservatives "used the usual Marxist tactic of labeling an opponent a Fascist, and in the case of Bradford, a Southerner, accusing him of being soft on slavery, and other forms of vilification, until the senators who had said that they would support him dropped him in favor of Bennett, whose credentials were far inferior, but who was made to appear a conservative when he most decidedly was not."[22]

But in most regards, conservatives welcomed Bennett, Kirkpatrick, and the rest of the neoconservatives with open arms, as established intellectuals who could add a new dimension to their battles with the left. "The conservative movement as a whole," wrote *National Review*'s John Miller, "adapted to the neoconservatives and even absorbed them, in the grand tradition of the 'fusionism' that Frank Meyer and others had espoused in the 1960s as they confronted philosophical differences between conservatives and libertarians. Like metals that combine to forge a stronger alloy, the mixture of older conservatives who had supported Barry Goldwater and new ones who were joining the Reagan bandwagon both broadened the movement and made it better able to govern in the 1980s and beyond."[23]

Neoconservative numbers have always been, and remain, small—traditional conservatives have often played a parlor game trying to name more than thirty of them; in his book *The Neoconservative Vision*, Mark Gerson lists thirty-nine, perhaps an all-time high. Most are prominent scholars who have written for the *Public Interest* and *Commentary*—including Podhoretz and Kristol, Daniel Bell, Nathan Glazer, Seymour Martin Lipset, Aaron Wildavsky, Jeane Kirkpatrick, Paul Wolfowitz, Ben Wattenberg, and a handful of others. But neoconservative thinkers and writers also had close ties with journals such as the *American Scholar, Foreign Policy*, the *New Criterion, Encounter*, and the *New Leader*, and more recently have regularly appeared in such mainstream publications as *TV Guide, Reader's Digest, Fortune, Business Week*, and *U.S. News & World Report*.[24]

Although the neoconservatives have provided traditional conserva-tives with potent arguments dealing with a handful of domestic social policies, they do not share many traditional conservative concerns. They have virtually no interest in limited government, wanting instead to make big government more efficient and thus efficacious. When Reagan budget director David Stockman wrote in his 1985 book *The Triumph of Politics* that the Reagan revolution would rescind the welfare state, Irving Kristol attacked the notion bitterly in the *Wall Street Journal*, scolding Stockman for his simple-mindedness. The proper task of a conservative administration, wrote Kristol, was to prune the overgrowth of an essen-tially sound form of government.[25] More recently, Kristol wrote:

> [Neoconservatives'] 20th-century heroes tend to be TR, FDR, and Ronald Reagan. Such Republican and conservative worthies as Calvin Coolidge, Her-bert Hoover, Dwight Eisenhower and Barry Gold-water are politely overlooked. . . . Neocons . . . are impatient with the Hayekian notion that we are "on the road to serfdom." . . . Neocons feel at home in today's America to a degree that more traditional conservatives do not. Though they find much to be critical about, they tend to seek intellectual guid-ance in the democratic wisdom of Tocqueville, rath-er than in the Tory nostalgia of, say, Russell Kirk.[26]

By that standard, was Frank Meyer correct? Are neoconservatives re-ally conservative? According to pundit Robert Novak, "Neocons are more neo than they are con." Many movement conservatives would agree, pointing again to their comfort with big government. *National Review* editor Rich Lowry complains that "in practice . . . strong-government conservatism has mostly been a rationalization for lazy and politically expedient accretions to government."[27] Still others are not so charitable, believing that the neocons subverted the conservative movement from within and are responsible for most of its woes. Former Nixon and Rea-gan White House aide Pat Buchanan, after running for president him-self in 1992, 1996, and 2000, has turned criticism of neoconservatives into an art form; his position is perhaps best set forth in the title of his

2004 book *Where the Right Went Wrong: How Neoconservatives Sub-verted the Reagan Revolution and Hijacked the Bush Presidency.*[28]

Neoconservatives have not made their mark through electoral politics. Other than Daniel Patrick Moynihan of New York and Henry "Scoop" Jackson of Washington state, both Democrats, few neoconservatives have been elected to anything. Whereas Moynihan spoke and wrote like a neoconservative, but acted like a liberal, voting in the Senate along almost straight Democratic Party lines, Jackson was the perfect neocon, a liberal on most domestic issues and a hard-liner on foreign policy, particularly as it pertained to Communism. Nevertheless, in the eyes of some neocons, their influence on politics, while not felt directly at the ballot box, was profound. In a reflective piece in the *Weekly Standard* in 2003, Irving Kristol wrote, "The historical task and political purpose of neoconservatism would seem to be this: to convert the Republican party, and American conservatism in general, against their respective wills, into a new kind of conservative politics suitable to governing a modern democracy."[29] This was written long after Ronald Reagan had governed successfully for eight years. Few movement conservatives would agree with Kristol.

By the mid-1990s the original neocons, most prominently Irving Kristol and Norman Podhoretz, were still writing their books and articles critical of the Clinton administration. At the same time, William Kristol, son of Irving and Gertrude Himmelfarb, rose as a young conservative star as staff director to Vice President Dan Quayle, and later by leading resistance to Bill Clinton's health care reform. Said Richard Viguerie:

> I never thought of Bill Kristol so much as a neocon as just a good conservative. It was he, in my opinion, who gets the lion's share of the credit for deep-sixing Hillary-care. Gingrich and Dole were talking in the press about this as a terrible idea, but one whose time had come. There would be a fax from Kristol four or five times a week, giving marching orders for the day. I hosted a breakfast for him one morning to introduce him to some of the other conservatives. I don't recall the split coming until some time after that, after he started the *Weekly Standard.*[30]

After the 1994 elections, William Kristol, along with other neocons and with media mogul Rupert Murdoch's money, founded the *Weekly Standard*, through which a younger generation kept the neoconservative flame burning. Their influence seemed all but expended by the late 1990s, especially after the *Standard* backed John McCain against George W. Bush for president in 2001.

But then 9/11 erupted—and neoconservatives returned to prominence. Those around the *Standard* had consistently warned of the rising danger of terrorism and called for the toppling of Saddam Hussein throughout the 1990s. Thus when the Bush administration was forced to confront these threats, neoconservatives in the media and in government—Bill Kristol, Paul Wolfowitz, Richard Perle, et al.—made a case that the president and his national security team found compelling. Neoconservatives had not only a new lease on life, but renewed vigor, staking a claim to be the new champions of American foreign policy. When the United States invaded Iraq in 2003 and as the war wore on without resolution, rivals of neoconservatives on the right and the left gave vent to their frustrations by blaming the war on a neoconservative "conspiracy." But neoconservatives could fairly claim that the Bush administration's policies could hardly have been drawn straight from the pages of the *Weekly Standard*, with its abundant criticism of occupation policies.

THE NEW RIGHT, THE RELIGIOUS RIGHT

Dispirited liberal anti-Communists and New York intellectuals were not the only ones offended by the excesses of the McGovernites and the hard left. A vast group of evangelical Christians, mostly in the South and the Midwest, had, during the period following World War II, remained content with their small-town life and had little to do with politics or with national or international affairs. Life was generally peaceful and controversies were local. Drugs were somebody else's problem, abortions unknown. The Vietnam War was a legitimate battle against Communism, and service to one's country was considered a patriotic duty: If sons and fathers came home wounded or in body bags, it was all part of the Lord's plan. Protests? Not in those communities.

At the same time, conservative activists in Washington and across the country were beginning to realize that thinking and talking about conservative policies was not enough. They had tasted deeply of politics in the 1964 Goldwater campaign, rejoiced in Reagan's wins in California in 1966 and 1970, and now wanted to get a foothold in Congress and the state capitals. But conservatives were not winning anything—the left was. And as the left won battle after battle, conservatives began to learn how the left used pressure to influence members of Congress and the executive branch to get what it wanted. To make a difference, these conservative activists, soon known as the "New Right," would need to recruit more foot soldiers, and to reform the way things were being done politically. Paul Weyrich, who became one of the right's principal strategists and organizers, tells of attending a meeting in the early 1970s of conservative congressional staffers gathered to discuss how to defeat a piece of pernicious liberal legislation. As the discussion wore on, Weyrich raised his hand and asked who was doing the head count. "And they said, what? What do you mean head count?" Weyrich responded, "Who's for us, who's against us, and who's undecided?" "What difference does that make?" he was asked. "Because," responded Weyrich, "we're about to have a vote, and if we don't know where the votes are, we're going to lose." "But," somebody objected, "it's much more important that we debate the philosophical points here." To Weyrich, that said it all, and he decided to do something about it.[31]

About the same time, Weyrich attended another meeting. What he discovered would make all the difference:

> In 1969, right after Nixon's election, there was fear on the left that Nixon was going to propose a rollback of civil rights, which would exempt rooming houses with up to eight people from the civil rights laws. The traitor Leon Panetta, who was working for Nixon at the time, came and told a civil rights coalition what they were planning. So, my senator got an invitation to attend this strategy meeting of the civil rights coalition and he couldn't go and I said, do you mind if I go? He said sure, if they'll let you in. So, I went there, just sat in the back, nobody asked me

who I was, anything, and there, before my eyes, was revealed the tactics of the left. I had seen the manifestation of it, but I had never understood the operational end of it. The meeting was run by an aide to Democratic Senator Birch Bayh, who had with him an aide to Mac Mathias, a brand-new elected Republican senator from Maryland. They had put together a bill, which both senators were going to cosponsor, that would prohibit the rollback. The meeting was to work on that bill. So, National Committee for an Effective Congress, a liberal pro–civil rights group, said we'll write senators and say we're going to double rate the bills, so they'd get two black eyes if they vote against it. There was a guy from Brookings who said we've got a study coming up on discrimination on housing but it won't be ready for another six months, but we can get a sort of preprint done, a preview. There was the ACLU who said they would sue, in order to frame the issue. That was the first time in my life I had heard of a lawsuit being filed for other than an honest purpose. Representatives from the Methodist church were there, who said they would supply lobbyists to go from senator to senator. There were several black groups who wanted to have demonstrations across the country and Bayh's guy said, you do that and you're going to provoke a backlash. You have your demonstrations here in Washington and there'll be no problem with that, you'll be safe here. But if you go out there, stirring up trouble, you're going to lose us votes. So they reluctantly agreed to just hold the demonstrations here. And columnist Carl Rowan was there. He had just left the Johnson administration and was doing a column for the *Post* and said that, if they would give him the timing, he would get them together with the editorial board of the *Post* and he would certainly write columns on it himself. And I'm probably for-

getting one or two groups, but the point is the whole
panoply of the left was there, from nonprofit groups
to political action committees, lobbyists in between
And they concocted a strategy to beat back the bill.
Nixon never proposed the actual rollback.[32]

Concerned that nobody on the right, or within the Republican Party,
was doing anything but talk, a group of a dozen or so conservatives started
meeting regularly to discuss how to organize the right to be as effective as
the left. Many of these blossoming activists had cut their teeth in Young
Americans for Freedom, the College Republicans, and other youth groups
during the 1960s. If such tactics worked for college students, why not in
Washington?

Richard Viguerie said:

> What we began to do was to reverse engineer the
> left, just like the Japanese reverse engineered Amer-
> ican products. At first Japanese products were shod-
> dy, but over time, they got to be as good as ours, or
> better. We did the same thing.[33]

They would sit around Viguerie's dinner table and discuss what the
left had, and create the same thing. Foundations, political action committees, special-interest groups, pressure groups, lobbying groups, and
whatever else they could think of were formed, all using the latest technology available and usually raising the money they needed by direct
mail. "We were going to save the world by sundown, every day. That is
how we thought," said Viguerie.[34]

If any one incident set off the Washington-based political activists, it
was the new president's, Gerald Ford's, choice of Nelson Rockefeller as
his vice president in 1974. Rockefeller, whom the right had been battling
since 1960, "was the very symbol of everything we conservatives had
always opposed," said Richard Viguerie, and Gerald Ford "revealed the
true colors of so-called 'moderate Republicanism' by choosing him."[35]
"The Rockefeller nomination catalyzed us," said Paul Weyrich. "People
were furious. We had Goldwater, we had Reagan out in California. And
he picks Rockefeller?"[36] Sitting around Viguerie's kitchen table, conser-

vatives attempted to devise a strategy to derail the appointment, and the New Right was born.

But the Rockefeller choice was much more Machiavellian than most people realized at the time. George Bush was the vice president most establishment Republicans were pushing on Gerald Ford. But behind-the-scenes conservatives realized the danger of choosing Bush over Rockefeller. Said Pat Buchanan, "If Rockefeller is the VP and something happened to Ford, Rockefeller could handle the country for a year, but Reagan could beat him for the nomination in 1980 and we'd have a chance of taking the party back. But if Bush were the VP, he would be the heir apparent, and would be a shoo-in for the 1980 nomination." So Buchanan checked around with some of his conservative friends, and wrote a memo to Ford telling him that Rockefeller would be acceptable to the conservative movement. "Sure enough, Ford picked Rocky and after that, all the right-wingers started screaming about it. The whole idea was to put a stick of dynamite under the right wing, and that is exactly what it did. The right was dead, and it sure came alive in a hurry."[37]

The so-called New Right was not new at all, of course. Its leaders had been active in conservative politics since at least as far back as the Goldwater campaign. Fighting for conservative causes on virtually every front, they had become sophisticated political operatives, each expert in his own area. By the late 1970s, Viguerie had developed a potent direct-mail fund-raising company with mailing lists of millions of conservative donors and the ability to raise hundreds of thousands of dollars seemingly at will. Paul Weyrich helped found the Heritage Foundation, and then launched the Committee for the Survival of a Free Congress, which supported conservative candidates in congressional elections and provided policy papers to members of Congress. Howard Phillips, formerly president of the student government at Harvard and a founder of YAF, later headed Nixon's Office of Economic Opportunity, only to resign in protest over the president's failed promise to veto expansion of the welfare state. Subsequently, to mobilize conservative grassroots activists, he formed the Conservative Caucus, which by 1980 had an extensive network of state and local chapters and an annual budget of $3 million. Terry Dolan formed the National Conservative Political Action Committee (NCPAC), through which he pumped money, which Viguerie helped him raise, directly into political campaigns and, indirectly, launched media attacks on liberal candidates. Dolan targeted liberal congressmen and contributed to the defeat of six liberal senators in 1978 and 1980, forging the way for the GOP to take control of the Senate. The four men and their organizations proved to be a powerful political coalition.[38]

The New Right leaders knew from experience that they could influence congressional elections nationwide and bring enough pressure to bear on the Republican Party to turn it to the right. Unlike the members of the now Old Right, they were not particularly concerned with the nuances of political philosophy or free-market economics. Being more practically oriented, they recognized that a great many Americans, particularly in the South, West, and Middle West, were socially conservative but political inactive, and that mobilizing them could bring a mass base and renewed strength to right-wing politics.

What issues were they were concerned about? Anti-Communism, for one. After America's withdrawal from Vietnam and the fall of Saigon, conservatives felt impelled to dig in their heels against the Soviet Union. As the Nixon-Ford administration, with its accelerated policy of détente, wound down in 1976, conservatives wanted a more aggressive foreign policy, one that would protect the vital interests of the United States. The ensuing plaintive and pliable Carter administration provided plenty of ammunition for the New Right. Carter blithely announced plans to give the Panama Canal to volatile Panama (a scheme first hatched, several years earlier, by Henry Kissinger), infuriating conservatives. The New Right led the way in opposing the Panama Canal treaty, which ultimately passed, but the campaign against it swelled its ranks.

Although the New Right did worry about taxes, excessive regulation, and the expansion of the federal government, its greatest ire was reserved for the "social issues"—pornography, homosexuality, feminism, abortion, and prayer in the schools—problems that concerned millions of middle-class Americans and allowed these New Right leaders to form an alliance with evangelical Christians.

The evangelicals were largely outside the political realm from the 1920s until the 1970s—which is not to say that no preachers or other Christian spokesmen were outspokenly political. The Reverend Carl McIntyre, Billy James Hargis, Bob Jones, and Catholic bishop Fulton Sheen were a few of the Christian voices that filled the airwaves as far back as the 1930s. But they were voices in the wilderness, preachers with an audience but no organization, little money, and no way—and perhaps no wish—to mobilize their people for political action.

The evangelicals were socially conservative and politically inactive, and there were lots of them. Not necessarily fundamentalists, evangelicals believe that the Bible is the inspired, inerrant word of God. Unlike mainline Protestants, they had little in the way of an institutional hierarchy or theological tradition, but placed great emphasis on dramatic conversion of the heart to Christ. In 1976 a Gallup poll found that about a third of all Americans, or about 50 million adults, claimed to have undergone a born-again conversion.[39] They did not have a definite set of political principles, but tended to vote for candidates attuned to their religious beliefs; in 1976 more than one-half of all evangelicals voted for Carter, who wore his religious beliefs conspicuously on his sleeve. By 1980, however, disillusioned by Carter, they voted for Reagan by a margin of roughly two to one.[40]

The cultural and political revolution of the 1960s and 1970s, engineered by the Supreme Court, catapulted the evangelicals into conservative politics. Abortion, feminism, pornography, sexual deviancy, the banning of school prayer, and the breakdown of the family made it apparent that Christian values were everywhere under attack. The liberal elites had accomplished their agenda through judicial fiat, and now faced an unexpected backlash from the people.[41] As political commentator Kevin Phillips pointed out, "The world of Manhattan, Harvard and Beverly Hills was being exported to Calhoun County, Alabama, and Calhoun County did not like it."[42]

And then there was abortion. If liberals cheered the 1973 Supreme Court decision of *Roe* v. *Wade* for its policy implications, they came to rue its political aftereffects, as that decision, more than any other, eventually became the *cause célèbre* of the Christian right.

Abortion was of insignificant political importance in 1973; about the only organized opposition came from the Catholic Church. Mainstream Protestants may have been uncomfortable about it, but not enough to speak out, and evangelical Christians at the time were largely ambivalent on the issue. As far as they were concerned, abortion did not affect them—few probably knew anybody who had ever had one. In his autobiography, the late Jerry Falwell commented that "after *Roe* was

decided, leaders of the Catholic Church spoke courageously in opposition to the Court's decision, but the voices of my Protestant Christian
brothers and sisters, especially the voices of fundamentalist leaders,
remained silent."[43] Harold O. J. Brown, a prominent evangelical theologian and ethicist and an editor at *Christianity Today*, suggested that
anti-Catholic bias may have played a part. "A lot of Protestants reacted
almost automatically 'If the Catholics are for it, we should be against it.'
That proved to be a very unwise position, but it took a while to realize
that. The fact that Catholics were out front caused many Protestants to
keep a low profile."[44]

Brown wrote editorials in *Christianity Today* arguing that "abortion
affects what you think human beings are, and what you think they are
worth, and what you think should become of them,"[45] but failed to
generate much attention. Eventually he enlisted the help of C. Everett Koop, a pediatric surgeon whom Reagan would subsequently name
surgeon general, Billy Graham, and, in 1977, evangelical theologian
Francis Schaeffer. This culminated in a film, produced by Schaeffer's
son Franky, called *Whatever Happened to the Human Race?*, and a companion book that offered a biblical basis for opposing abortion. It argued
that abortion is both cause and result of the loss of appreciation for the
sanctity of human life, and that the long-term consequences would be
infanticide and euthanasia, that is, a culture of death. Koop and Schaeffer traveled across the country showing the film in Protestant churches.
As a result, Koop maintains, conservative Christians "began to associate
the need for tying their faith to social action."[46] The power of Schaeffer's
arguments were also evident in Pat Robertson's emergence as a leader
of the religious right. He welcomed Schaeffer to his nightly television
show, *The 700 Club*, and turned the missionary's analysis of the West's
decline into part of his own rationale for starting the Christian Coalition in 1986 and making a bid in 1988 for the Republican presidential
nomination.

Before *Roe*, abortion had been banned in most states with large
evangelical populations, and many fundamentalist Christians were not
immediately aware of *Roe*'s implications. But as the mainline Protestant
churches increasingly cheered the decision, evangelicals increasingly
opposed it. In doing so, they came face-to-face with other political issues that made them realize that they could no longer live their apoliti-

cal, sheltered lives if their culture was to survive. Liberalism meant to change their world. Evangelicals would not go quietly.

Evangelicals may not have been happy with the leftward trend of the culture, but they needed a push to get them involved politically. That push came when the leaders of the New Right and evangelicals began to mingle and to listen to each other's concerns. The New Right needed foot soldiers, and the evangelicals needed to protect their culture. Their last reluctance dissolved with the question of whether their children could pray in school. Beginning with the Supreme Court's 1963 decision banning organized prayer and Bible reading in the public schools, school prayer became *the* defining issue to evangelicals, and put them on the road to what would become known as the Christian right.

The Supreme Court's declaration that school prayer was unconstitutional, on top of the decline of educational standards, the rise of sex education, and, in some cases, busing and affirmative action, catapulted parents and pastors into founding thousands of small, private Christian schools. As long as they declared a policy of nondiscrimination, the IRS allowed such schools to receive tax-deductible contributions.[47] But in 1978 the Carter administration tightened the reins and proposed regulations requiring private schools to prove that they were *actively* trying to integrate . . . or lose their tax-exempt status. Parents and pastors were outraged, arguing that if churches could operate as tax-exempt organizations, why not church-run schools? Carter's commissioner of internal revenue received so many letters of protest, 126,000, along with some threats, that he sought Secret Service protection. Richard Viguerie called the IRS controversy "the spark that ignited the religious right's involvement in real politics."[48]

The New Right leaders traveled around the country visiting evangelical leaders, urging them to get involved, to *do* something *political* to protect their beliefs. Then, in the fall of 1979, Weyrich traveled to Dallas, Texas, to speak at a rally organized by evangelical preacher James Robison, who had been thrown off a talk radio station in Fort Worth for preaching against homosexuality. Over twelve thousand people packed the Dallas Auditorium to hear speeches by a parade of evangelical preachers. When the rally was over, the leaders asked Weyrich what their next step should be. "You need to take a poll," said Weyrich, "a national poll to determine whether or not your constituency will tolerate your being active in politics." Asked how much it would cost, Weyrich guessed thirty thousand dollars, took up a collection, and paid a pollster to survey evangelicals and fundamentalists about whether they wanted their pastors to get involved in public policy organizations to help preserve their way of life. "The result," said Weyrich, "was overwhelming. They wanted the pastors involved in politics."[49] The New Right had found its foot soldiers.

But let's jump back a few years and take a look at one of the people who would lead the evangelicals into conservative politics.

From the shadows of relative anonymity in the early 1970s came a Baptist preacher from Lynchburg, Virginia, who came to have a profound impact on the Christian right and the growth of the grassroots conservative movement. Jerry Falwell was a jolly, good-natured fellow, with a puckish sense of humor; as an undergraduate at Baptist Bible College, he once flooded a dorm room with a garden hose.[50] In the 1950s and 1960s, Falwell was a vocal opponent of ministers' involvement in politics, but that changed with Roe v. Wade. Falwell was one of the first evangelicals to recognize the implications of Roe, but also recognized that it could be used to political advantage. When liberal Protestants applauded Roe, and adopted a wide range of liberal positions, Falwell realized that all political issues were connected. The particular problem of abortion was linked to a broad decline in public morality and patriotism. And because morality was necessary if people were to enjoy political liberty, virtue and republican government were related. Thus Falwell set about to promote them both: First he began preaching against abortion; then during the 1976 bicentennial celebrations he organized rallies to promote patriotism.

In October, candidate Carter, supported by many evangelicals, appeared in a much-publicized interview in Playboy magazine, which led Falwell to criticize Carter on his national television program. Shortly after he went off the air Falwell received a telephone call from Carter's special assistant, Jody Powell, who demanded, in no uncertain terms, that he "back off." Quite undaunted, Falwell saw the incident as his baptism by fire into national politics.[51]

Falwell's Thomas Road Baptist Church in Lynchburg, Virginia, had one of the largest congregations in the country. Falwell also had a widely broadcast television show, was becoming a visible national Christian leader, and wanted to translate this into political influence.

Shortly before Weyrich orchestrated the poll of evangelicals, he, Phillips, and several other New Right activists had met with Falwell in his office in Lynchburg to discuss the possibility of combining the emerging bloc of evangelical Christians with the growing grassroots conservative movement. Viguerie, who was not at the meeting but was much involved, and Weyrich were Catholics, and thought that if enough pressure could be put on Republicans to take a firm stand against abortion, it would draw antiabortion Democratic Catholics into the Republican Party. This would make the party more socially conservative. What better group to bring that pressure on the Republicans than the evangelical Christians? And thus was born the Moral Majority, which set out to organize evangelicals at the grassroots into a politically active organization that focused on social issues.

Christian conservatives, Catholic and Protestant, realized they had more in common with each other than with their secular liberal neighbors. They might remain theologically sectarian, but they became politically ecumenical. The Moral Majority's makeup included Baptists and Catholics, Mormons and Jews, believers and unbelievers, any and all who upheld the principles that Falwell had laid out: "pro-life, pro–traditional family, pro-moral, and pro-American."[52]

Many of the Moral Majority's early leaders were Baptist ministers with large congregations and their own broadcast organizations. Having been through local political skirmishes over prayer in schools and pornography, they had political and media savvy. Falwell was a successful "televangelist"; by 1980, his *Old Time Gospel Hour* radio program reached four million homes every week.

The Moral Majority was not the first political organization of evangelicals, but it was soon the largest: Within three years, it had chapters in all fifty states, trained one hundred thousand pastors, priests, and rabbis and several million volunteers, published a newsletter reaching nearly 850,000 homes, broadcast a daily commentary by Falwell to over three hundred radio stations, and had an operating budget of over $10 million raised from a mailing list of over two million people.[53]

As impressive as the numbers were, a better measure of the effectiveness of the Moral Majority may be garnered from the virulent attacks it drew, and from all sides. Liberals could hardly be contained. Falwell was accused of book burning and bigotry of every sort; Southern

Poverty Law Center president Julian Bond and People for the American Way founder Norman Lear compared Falwell to the Ku Klux Klan and labeled him a neo-Nazi. Senator George McGovern warned, "I personally regard him as a menace to the American political process." Many older conservatives were also uncomfortable with the explicit religiosity of the Christian right. Barry Goldwater, blunt as ever, suggested that "it is every American's patriotic duty to kick Jerry Falwell in the ass."[54]

Falwell responded with good-natured pugnacity: "Liberals have been imposing morality on us for the last fifty years. Is there anything wrong with fighting back?" He also became skilled at disarming opponents with his warmth and charm.[55]

Most important, the Moral Majority introduced the evangelical Christian community to right-wing activist politics in an organized way. Thousands of pastors, previously apolitical, now hit the national scene with their great oratorical and organizational skills, and soon millions of churchgoers became aware that they could make a difference. Which they promptly did.

Falwell's ambitious political agenda brought immediate results. The Moral Majority registered somewhere between two and three million evangelicals to vote in the 1980 congressional and presidential campaigns, while their state chapters got involved in local fights against gay rights ordinances, limitless abortion, and pornography.[56]

The 1980 election was the first major political campaign in which the Christian right actively played a role. White fundamentalists accounted for two-thirds of Reagan's margin of victory over Jimmy Carter and played a significant part in defeating several Democratic members of Congress, notably liberal stalwarts George McGovern, Birch Bayh, and Frank Church, placing the Senate in Republican hands for the first time in a quarter century.

Evangelicals may not have been part of the Reagan campaign apparatus at the higher levels, but Reagan was well aware of their value and assured them of his appreciation. The Religious Roundtable, an organization of conservative televangelists, organized a meeting in Dallas that coincided with the 1980 Republican convention and was attended by some fifteen thousand people. Reagan made an appearance and stole the show, telling the group, "I know you cannot endorse me, but I want you to know that I endorse you." He assured the audience that, if he were elected, federal interference with religious broadcasting would stop along with IRS harassment of religious schools. But, Reagan warned, "If you do not speak your mind and cast your ballots, then who will speak and work for the ideals we cherish? Who will vote to protect the American family . . . ?"[57]

During the 1980s, the Reagan years, the Christian right flourished. Organizations such as Focus on the Family, the Religious Roundtable, and Concerned Women for America attracted hundreds of thousands of members and raised millions of dollars. Several evangelicals held cabinet or subcabinet positions in the Reagan administration, notably Reagan's first secretary of the interior, James Watt, the most controversial member of the administration. But the religious right by no means set the agenda: Whereas Reagan paid lip service to the right-to-life issue, abortion remained legal; and although he said he favored prayer in the schools, it remained illegal. In part, this reflected a generational gap, for Reagan's priorities were shaped not by the contemporary Christian right, but by the broader postwar conservative movement. He remained focused on the issues he grew up with: Communism and the growth of government. Social issues came to the fore only after he had reached political maturity. Keep in mind, too, that whatever Reagan's preferences, the issues had been abducted by the federal courts. Its usefulness apparently exhausted, the Moral Majority folded up shop in the mid-1980s, but not the Christian right; it changed horses, continuing to grow in effectiveness, if not in size. Many like-minded organizations sprang up to finish what Moral Majority had left undone.

One was the Christian Coalition, founded in 1989 by televangelist Pat Robertson of the Christian Broadcasting Network. By the end of the 1980s, the Christian right had the most formidable and sophisticated radio and television operation in the country after ABC, CBS, and NBC, and in 1990 Robertson's CBN was the largest noncommercial broadcast network in the world, with cable networks in over forty countries. Its total revenues exceeded $150 million, much of which came from the Family Channel, a for-profit and publicly held company that was sold to Fox Kids Worldwide in 1997 for $1.9 billion. Robertson's flagship program, *The 700 Club*, reached over 19 percent of all U.S. television households in 1985, and had a daily audience estimated at more than two million adults.[58] Christian broadcasting's power came from its ability to put Christian political commentators in direct touch with millions of viewers and voters.

The son of a U.S. senator from Virginia, a Yale Law School graduate, and a Baptist minister, Robertson founded the Christian Coalition after a failed run for the Republican presidential nomination in 1988—failed, yet successful in a way. Although never taken seriously as a candidate, Robertson won hundreds of thousands of votes in the primaries—he finished a surprising second in the Iowa caucuses—and received a large amount of attention from the secular media.

Like Falwell, Robertson drove the left crazy. His often quirky behavior added fuel to their fire, often embarrassing even his supporters. A famous example was a film that showed Robertson praying for the diversion of Hurricane Gloria from his CBN facilities in Virginia Beach. "Storm, we command you to turn north and then go east. Your winds shall die down and you shall go harmlessly into the ocean in the name of Jesus."[59] When the storm obeyed, Robertson told the *New York Times* that it was "extremely important because I felt, interestingly enough, that if I couldn't move a hurricane, I could hardly move a nation." Then there was his forthright rhetoric: "There is no such thing as separation of church and state in the Constitution. It is a lie of the Left and we are not going to take it anymore."[60] A more recent example was his call in 2005 for the United States to "take out" Venezuelan dictator Hugo Chavez.

In 1989, Robertson transferred his campaign apparatus, along with many of his supporters, to the Christian Coalition, which was designed to coordinate the activities of local conservative Christian groups on state and local issues. Within a few years, the Christian Coalition had gained control of the Republican Party machinery in several states, and wielded substantial influence in more than half of the state parties. Evangelicals were so appalled by the presidency of Bill Clinton that the Christian Coalition's ranks swelled; membership doubled in 1993, giving it over one million donors and activists, who were indispensable to the Republican landslide in the 1994 midterm elections.[61] Former College Republican activist Ralph Reed worked closely with Robertson and used his activist skills to become the architect of much of this growth. All this notwithstanding, the coalition has slowly shrunk since the mid-1990s.

Dr. James Dobson, a child psychologist by training and evangelical leader, broke into the public arena with his 1970 book *Dare to Discipline*. Taking a traditional approach to corporal punishment for children, it was embraced by Christians as a corrective to postwar liberal nostrums. By the late 1970s, Dobson had become so popular as a writer and speaker that he left his teaching job at the University of Southern California to engage in his ministry full-time. He founded Focus on the Family in 1977 and produced a radio program that reached millions of listeners each week. When Colorado voters sought to overturn local gay rights ordinances by a popular amendment, Dobson's support was crucial to its success (though it was subsequently struck down by the U.S. Supreme Court). Dobson was also vital in the foundation of the Family Research Council, a profamily Christian think tank in Washington, D.C. Perhaps because he keeps his distance from Washington, Dobson is less pragmatic than Robertson, more willing to criticize the GOP, and totally unconcerned about offending the mass media.

INFLUENCE ON THE MOVEMENT

Tens of millions of potential voters can have considerable influence on politics, whether or not they vote en bloc. In spite of the dominance of elitist cultural liberalism, the Christian right has kept its moral principles alive in public debate, even though successes have been elusive: abortion is still legal, prayer in the schools is still illegal, the gay rights movement is still gaining ground, pornography is still available everywhere to all ages. But Christian conservatives keep fighting, because they are not motivated by political ambition but by religious conviction. "The fact that you have fought evil and lost," said former energy secretary and evangelical leader Don Hodel, "does not give you the right to stop fighting evil. Where did God say, give me your best effort for five or ten years and I'll set you loose. If we lose, we will try one more time, and another and another."[62] Tony Perkins, head of the Family Research Council, believes most evangelicals "do not come to politics because they want to be political players, they come to make a difference and they operate out of their faith. . . . We have to stick to what is right, and work for victory."[63]

For their conservative allies, the fact that evangelicals are uncompromising in what they believe has another benefit: They don't compromise on other things either. "Evangelicals," according to Tony Perkins, "are fiscally conservative. They don't like a lot of government, and they don't want a lot of government. . . . Our principles are non-negotiable, and we stick by our word. So an elected evangelical has a much greater chance of having a voting record that is conservative fiscally and socially, as opposed to a fiscal conservative who will often negotiate his fiscal conservatism away."[64]

The Christian right has the best communications system of any group of voters in the country—its own television and radio networks websites, and magazines—with thousands of pastors ready to dive into political matters, and an unparalleled network of political activists. More important, because of its political force, politicians court its vote, from the president on down to state legislators and city councilmen. It has provided an indispensable mass base for the conservative movement, without which electoral victory would be unthinkable. It helped make the GOP the majority party in the United States for more than a decade.

Although evangelicals rallied to George W. Bush for the GOP presidential nomination over John McCain in 2000, their lukewarm support in the general election cost Bush the popular vote. Bush's assiduous efforts to win their hearts over the next four years paid off in his strong showing in 2004: Nearly 80 percent of white evangelicals—nearly a third of his support and his largest voting bloc—voted for him in 2004.

As different as they are, the neoconservatives and the religious right have some surprising parallels. Both emerged at roughly the same time, and both developed in reaction to what each considered the leftward drift of their parties—neoconservatives to the radicalization of the Democratic Party, and the religious right to the failure of both parties to address the issues they felt were important. Neither has been particularly concerned with the virtues of limited government. Neoconservatives believe that government should benefit the underprivileged as long as it does so efficiently. Members of the religious right are more suspicious of government than the neocons, but generally believe that government should be used to enforce basic standards of public morality and to achieve certain limited goals, such as supporting the traditional family through tax policy.

The neoconservatives and the religious right are ideological movements, with strong, sometimes uncompromising opinions. They believe that Israel should be supported at any cost, and that Islam is the great threat to Western civilization. The great difference is that the neoconservatives are a mere handful of people with creative ideas and intellectual curiosity, and the religious right represents millions of people with what Midge Decter describes as one very big idea—perhaps the biggest idea of all.[65] But the ideas that motivate evangelicals, according to Don Hodel, "are tremendous motivating ideas, the whole idea of the value of life is a very important philosophical idea."[66]

PHYLLIS SCHLAFLY AND THE RISE OF THE GRASSROOTS

Perhaps the most effective grassroots mobilizer in the history of the right has been Phyllis Schlafly, a petite housewife from St. Louis, mother of six, devout Catholic, Harvard graduate, and lawyer. She published a conservative, anti-Communist newsletter from her kitchen table for years, which turned into the *Phyllis Schlafly Report*. It is probably inaccurate to categorize Phyllis Schlafly herself as a Christian conservative, but she exemplifies a traditional movement conservative who has taken up some of the Christian right's ideas and favorite causes. Well informed on many policy issues, from foreign affairs to the power of the federal courts, Schlafly has also grasped grassroots politics, and she has been a delegate to every Republican national convention since 1952. In 1958, Schlafly and her husband, Fred, a St. Louis lawyer, determined to form a joint Catholic-Protestant anti-Communist organization, but when they approached Protestant Dr. Fred Schwarz of the Christian Anti-Communist Crusade, he turned them down, aware of his supporters' anti-Catholicism. Changing directions, the Schlaflys formed the Cardinal Mindszenty Foundation, named after the Hungarian cardinal who was imprisoned and tortured by the Communists. It organized small groups to educate Roman Catholics about the threat of international Communism, and by 1962 had established a network of over three thousand groups in forty-eight states. It also organized seminars, attended by thousands of people, on the history of Communism, its tactics, its techniques, and its horrors, with popular lecturers such as Clarence Manion, Raymond Moley, and General Albert Wedemeyer.[67]

But Schlafly always kept one foot in Republican Party organizations. As president of the Illinois Federation of Republican Women, an organization of over fifty thousand, and as vice chairman of the National Federation, she supported Goldwater in 1960 and 1964. Her most visible contribution to the 1964 campaign was a little book, *A Choice, Not an Echo*, a take-no-prisoners account of how eastern liberals dominated the Republican Party and disgorged "me-too" Republican candidates, warmed-over Democrats who could not and should not be elected. Over three million copies were sold or given away door-to-door by the Goldwater campaign, and the book was instrumental in delivering the crucial California primary to the senator from Arizona.[68]

Liberal Republican women, shaken by Schlafly's success, engineered her defeat in the race for chairman of the National Federation of Republican Women in 1967. But that race helped her to consolidate her national network of conservative women, whom she soon rallied to fight the Equal Rights Amendment.[69]

The ERA had been kicking around Congress since the 1920s, with supporters from all sides of the political spectrum, but it was not passed by Congress until 1972, and then by overwhelming margins—only fifteen votes against it in the House and eight in the Senate. Within a year it was ratified by thirty states, and only eight more were needed for it to become part of the Constitution. On the surface it sounded innocuous enough, stating simply: "Equality of rights under the law shall not be denied or abridged by the United States or by any State on account of sex. The Congress shall have the power to enforce, by appropriate legislation, the provisions of this article." Most Republicans supported it,[70] just as it had slipped by women of sound views without raising an eyebrow.

Until Phyllis Schlafly noticed it, that is. The suddenness of *Roe* v. *Wade*, handed down not long after passage of the ERA through Congress, helped Schlafly alert people to the menace of this seemingly innocuous document. The cultural revolution of the sixties had caught most Americans unawares, but also alerted them to the federal government's attempts to implement left-wing social reform in the name of freedom and equality.

In her newsletter, Schlafly set out the case against the ERA; by the time the battle was over, its circulation had grown to nearly forty thousand—not bad for a mailer that got its start in the kitchen. Passage of the amendment, she argued, would force women to live in a world where there were presumably no differences between men and women, at any time or any place, leaving women far less well off then before. The family, said Schlafly, "is the basic unit of society, which is ingrained in the laws and customs of our Judeo-Christian civilization [and] is the greatest single achievement in the history of women's rights." Passage of the ERA, she continued, would deprive women of the privileges they had, abolish their right to child support and alimony if divorced—of their very security—and even subject them to the draft, which would become one of the most potent arguments against it. "The 'women libbers,'" wrote Schlafly, "spoke of equal pay for equal work to sugarcoat an agenda that was fundamentally anti-family, anti-children, and pro-abortion . . . . [W]omen libbers view the home as a prison, and the wife and mother as a slave."[71] Schlafly also argued that the ERA was a way for feminists to push abortion on demand and homosexual rights into the Constitution; once having done so, the liberal federal courts would interpret the amendment as broadly as possible, and who could tell what the results might be? But since most Republican members of Congress, as well as the Nixon and Ford administrations, favored the ERA, Schlafly reached out to the churches for recruits to help women fight the good fight:

> I called a demonstration at the Illinois capital in, I think, May of '75, and prayed for a thousand people to come, and they came. And a lot of them came on church buses. Most of these people had never been to Springfield, didn't know where Springfield was, and didn't know anything about anything, but they came. And it was a stunning thing that happened. And we kept having these events and they came out of all the churches. We had Catholics, Protestants, we had some Chicago rabbis who were very helpful, the Orthodox Jews. And I included the Mormons in the group, although that was hard for some people to swallow. Anyway, it was a real ecumenical movement.[72]

The backbone of Schlafly's organization was made up of evangelical Christian women who had not previously been involved in politics,
but now felt threatened by the strident feminist ideology. According to
Schlafly biographer Donald Critchlow, "These women brought an evangelical enthusiasm that energized the entire anti-ERA movement and
impressed state legislators with their commitment to stop ERA from
being ratified."[73] Studies done at the time showed that 98 percent of
these women were church members, while only 31 to 48 percent supported the amendment.[74]

Schlafly's primary opponent was the increasingly radical National
Organization for Women. To put it baldly, Schlafly and her legions of
Christian ladies, or "Eagles," as she called them, drove them up the wall.
The feminists resorted to a policy of shrill ad hominem attacks, which
did them more harm than good. As Critchlow points out, "The bitter antagonism that emerged in the ERA fight reflected a politics-is-personal
style that emerged in the 1970s and the fact that the ERA fight went
to the heart of deeply philosophical issues over the meaning of life and
lifestyle in America."[75] In one famous confrontation in 1973 at Illinois
State University, the late feminist extraordinaire Betty Friedan shrieked
at Schlafly, "I consider you a traitor to your sex, an Aunt Tom . . . I'd
like to burn you at the stake."[76] Such hysteria reinforced the growing
conviction that the ERA was merely part of the radical feminist agenda,
another whip to lash traditional women into conformity.

But try as they might, the feminists could not stop Schlafly. She got
enormous media attention and became a folk hero to her supporters.
She became a regular on daytime television shows such as the Phil Do-
nahue and Mike Douglas shows, she had a five-year contract with CBS
radio starting in 1975 as a regular commentator, and as of 1977, *Good
Housekeeping*'s reader poll regularly listed her as one of the ten most
admired women in the world.[77]

When Schlafly entered the battle in July 1972 most people assumed
the ERA would easily pass. By 1977, five more states, thirty-five in all,
had ratified it (though several states later rescinded their ratification).
Shortly before the period for ratification expired, Congress, backed into
a corner, was forced to approve an extension for three more years. But
when the original deadline passed in 1979, Schlafly did not hesitate to
declare victory: "It was the end of the seven years and I held a big event

at the Shoreham Hotel and proclaimed that ERA was dead. . . . You should realize that, in 1979, the conservatives had never had a victory and it was just stunning to them."[78]

After Nixon resigned in 1974, Gerald Ford threw full White House support behind the ERA in order to position himself as a centrist. For his pains, after barely turning back a challenge from Ronald Reagan for the GOP presidential nomination in 1976, Ford, with scant support from either the burgeoning Christian right or Phyllis Schlafly's legion of right-wing ladies, went down to defeat at the hands of Jimmy Carter. When Reagan won the nomination in 1980, his platform expressly opposed ERA, helping draw anti-ERA activists into the GOP. The congressional extension was later ruled unconstitutional, but the question was moot—Schlafly had defeated the ERA.

Schlafly's battle against the ERA was critical to the resurgence of the conservative movement, of the Republican Party, and of the move of the GOP to the right. When Nixon resigned in 1974, only 18 percent of voters identified themselves as Republicans. But six years later, in 1980, the Republican Party was viewed by many voters as the party of the regular American middle-class citizen, of the little guy, rather than the party of Wall Street, big business, and the country club set. "The catalyst for this transformation," according to social critic and Schlafly biographer Donald Critchlow, "was found in the grassroots reaction against feminism, legalized abortion, ERA, and the ban on prayer in school."[79] Feminist Sylvia Ann Hewlett, writing after the ERA was defeated, summed it up as tidily as Phyllis Schlafly could have done herself: "It is sobering to realize that the ERA was defeated," wrote Hewlett, "not by Barry Goldwater, Jerry Falwell, or combination of male chauvinist pigs, but by women who were alienated from a feminist movement the values of which seemed elitist and disconnected from the lives of ordinary people."[80]

As the ERA fight was winding down, Schlafly transferred the STOP ERA machinery to a newly formed organization called the Eagle Forum, which today boasts eighty-five thousand members across the country. A classic grassroots political organization, it is considered the front-line bastion in the resistance to feminism. According to Schlafly, about 80 percent of its members are evangelical Christian women who promote a pro-family agenda in the Republican Party and Congress.

The ERA fight was extremely important to the growth of the Christian right and the conservative movement. Inasmuch as it was fought in the state capitals, it taught these newly roused women that battles were to be fought, and won, on the state and local level. It showed that religious conservatives with important theological differences and historical enmity could cooperate to combat the burgeoning religion of secular liberalism. And it aroused ordinary Americans to resist the cultural revolution. Not least, the ERA battle helped banish the liberal Republican establishment into the wilderness.

Phyllis Schlafly taught conservatives, for the first time, that they could fight city hall and win. Liberals operated by the Brezhnev doctrine: If Congress passed something, started a new program, created a new agency, it could never be rescinded. But Schlafly balked. As the bell was about to ring, at the last minute, she jumped into the fray and stopped the ERA dead in its tracks. "It was an incredible victory," said Paul Weyrich, "because it was not only important for the issue itself, but it taught conservatives that, ha, you don't have to accept what the liberals tell you about something. Go in there and fight it out yourself, and you can win."[81]

CHAPTER EIGHT

The Bargain of a Lifetime

In the beginning, in the early days of the post–World War II period, when conservatism consisted of a few lonely intellectuals who warned that the trend toward the left, that the slide to socialism and appeasement of Communism, was a sure ticket to hell, finding the money to pay for the defense of Western civilization was, if not impossible, a great struggle. Those few who did contribute were chiefly concerned about the rising tide of socialism, the decline of economic freedom, and the burgeoning welfare state. A primary ground for their concern was Hayek's *Road to Serfdom*, published in 1944. Nevertheless, conservative causes drew little money, not more than $2 or $3 million per year in the mid-1960s, as compared to, say, the $300 million the Ford Foundation was giving left-wing causes at the same time.[1] Still, those little sums helped develop many of the ideas that became the foundation of the conservative movement. Without them, many conservative intellectuals would never have found jobs at prestigious universities where they could propagate their ideas, nor the time to research and write books. After one million copies of Hayek's book were in print and he was virtually a household name, the University of Chicago did agree to give him a chair, but only on condition that somebody else pay for it. One individual, a businessman from Kansas City named William Volker, stepped forward. When Bill Buckley decided to launch *National Review* in 1955 and set out to raise $450,000 (about $3 million in 2006 dollars), he struggled for months, visiting potential donor after potential donor, before he succeeded. And it was not as if Buckley was unknown—he had already authored two best-selling books, one of which was among the most-talked-about books of the year.

Fifty years later, by the time the conservative movement had changed not only the country, but the world, those early donors had gotten the bargain of a lifetime.

In the early days, conservatives were really revolutionaries; those who joined the cause did so because they believed fervently in what they were doing and were willing to work for a pittance, or for nothing, to further their ideals. Donors, for the most part, took the same approach; only a handful of wealthy people were willing to go out on a limb and risk the disdain, and even jeers, not only of the uninitiated but of friends and colleagues.

A great myth prevails that various Texas oil tycoons greased the right wing with millions of dollars, that conservatives were always rolling in money, that the groups had vast secret sums stashed away in foreign banks. There *were* right-wing Texas oil tycoons, and some of their money *may* have gone to the fringe right-wing groups, but not to the conservative movement. According to former *National Review* publisher Bill Rusher, not one nickel toward the founding or maintenance of that magazine ever came from the proverbial rich Texas oil families.

My father, Henry, used to tell an amusing story about Texas oil tycoon H. L. Hunt, who, in the 1950s, was a right-winger, allegedly the richest man in America, and one of the people rumored to have financed the movement. Hunt, who, incidentally, had bigamous marriages (and was the figure around whom the TV smash hit *Dallas* was made), threw money around like water, and always, always turned requests for money from conservatives into what people could do for him. Hunt called my father one day in the late 1950s, told him he had written a political novel spelling out how the country could be saved (giving citizens varying degrees of political clout, and votes, depending on their wealth), and that he wanted my father to publish it. He would send a plane to Chicago, Hunt said, to fly my father to Dallas so he could cut the deal. My father dutifully arrived at Hunt's house, which he described as Texas colonial—a huge place patterned after Mount Vernon, but about four times the size, all in the gaudiest taste, situated on hundreds, or perhaps thousands, of acres of Texas grassland. Hunt met him at the door, took him into the living room, handed him a manuscript, and said he would return in a couple of hours. As my father started to read, he noticed Hunt through the window, riding back and forth across the distant grassland on a tractor, plowing. When he returned, he asked my father what he thought of the book. "Unpublishable," said my father. "It does not meet our standards, and besides there would be no market for it."

"How much money would you need," Hunt asked, "to make it worth your while to publish my book?" "Mr. Hunt," my father replied, "you don't have enough money to get me to publish your book." Hunt subsequently self-published the book under the title *Alpaca*. The *Texas Monthly* described it as surely the oddest of all Texas political novels and reported that "the thin book sold for 50 cents a copy and, thanks to cheap paper and even cheaper glue, fell apart in the reader's hands. At one author's signing, two of Hunt's daughters helped promote sales by singing a version of a popular ditty of the era: 'How much is that book in the window? The one that my daddy wrote.'"[2] But back to the real world . . .

Resources were so scarce in the early days that virtually every conservative organization operated on a shoestring budget, when not near bankruptcy. The entire revenue of the Intercollegiate Studies Institute (ISI) in 1960 was $45,000; by 1969 it was $350,000:[3] Young Americans for Freedom, a year after it was founded in 1960, had a deficit of $20,000; by its tenth anniversary in 1970, its budget was $414,000.[4] That same year, five years after it was founded, the American Conservative Union had a budget of less than $200,000; by 1970, it was raising about twice that. The few magazines and journals that existed operated at a loss (a trademark of opinion journals) and were able to continue only with the help of a few kind souls.

Wealthy people usually like to be lost in the middle, not stand out, and above all put their money into safe and respectable investments. The "country club Republican" denotes a well-to-do businessman who adheres to the old adage that "to get along, go along."

So, too, for philanthropy. Most American foundations have a pattern of gifts to well-respected universities, mainline Protestant churches, dog pounds, environmental groups, symphony orchestras, and hospitals, but few to organizations agitating for dramatic political change.

"There are certain wealthy people," according to John von Kannon, vice president and treasurer at the Heritage Foundation, "who will say to themselves, 'I am willing to be unpopular at the country club and stand up for what I believe.' These people could be very comfortable getting on corporate boards and being feted by the liberals. But something in them tells them to be rebels—it is people like Dick Scaife, Henry Salvatori, Roger Milliken, and others. It is the equivalent of the Virginians saying 'I may lose my plantation, but I have to fight the king.'"[5]

Like those discussed earlier—the intellectuals and journalists, disenchanted leftists and Communists, publishers and writers who were willing to risk all—a handful of wealthy conservatives ventured their careers, social status, and even their family harmony to fight for their beliefs.

Like the intellectuals they supported, most of the early conservative donors were men of ideas, men who participated in the development of the movement and became intellectual partners in the enterprise. In doing so, they helped transform the conservative movement from a group of disconnected and obscure intellectuals into a political and policy movement that would transform American politics.

Other donors recognized that the free enterprise system that had enabled them to become wealthy was threatened, and they responded, not to protect their wealth, but to preserve a system that they believed would best serve their country and their fellow men.

A few of the early financiers of the conservative movement exemplify them all.

WILLIAM VOLKER

A German immigrant, Volker settled in Kansas City in the 1870s and started a wholesale business that distributed dry goods and household supplies throughout the West. His firm prospered from the outset, largely because of hard work: Volker worked eighteen-hour days, traveled incessantly, and hired bright and industrious people. He was shrewd, frugal, a man of high standards. By 1906, he was a millionaire, explaining his good fortune simply by saying, "Providence has been good to me." Unchanged by success, he continued to "ride the street cars and eat a sandwich at his desk and run errands for himself."[6] His lifelong zeal for good works—providing money and leadership for a long list of charitable and civic endeavors—included the creation of one of the first profit-sharing plans organized by an American business, and by 1947, Volker's eight hundred employees owned 70 percent of the stock in the business. He served on the Kansas City School Board for many years and maintained a farm for the rehabilitation of prisoners; in all, he gave over a third of his income to charity each year. Withal, he was a very modest man who spurned recognition for his good works. At his death in 1947, most of his wealth went to the Volker Fund, with assets of over $15 million (about $130 million in today's dollars). Volker's nephew, Harold Luhnow, was designated trustee.[7]

Luhnow had been greatly impressed by Hayek's *Road to Serfdom* and started using the Volker Fund's resources to finance free-market activities and libertarian scholarships. He recognized that the struggle for economic freedom was a battle of ideas, and that it was the intellectuals, the journalists, the writers, and the filmmakers who would change the collectivist culture. Among his early projects, he financed the first meeting of the Mont Pelerin Society in 1947 and subsidized chairs for Hayek at the University of Chicago and Ludwig von Mises at New York University. Luhnow also subsidized Aaron Director, an economist at the University of Chicago who happened to be Milton Friedman's brother-in-law. In addition, Luhnow facilitated meetings of libertarian economists to share ideas and establish friendships. Milton Friedman's classic *Capitalism and Freedom* and Hayek's *Constitution of Liberty* both evolved from such meetings, as did the Law and Economics school (see Chapter 9), and the Public Choice school, which gave rise to the school voucher movement.[8]

The Volker Fund also helped finance study for young people, thereby developing a cadre of well-educated scholars who would live their lives teaching, writing, and lecturing on free-market economics. The Volker impact continues to this day. Volker closed its doors in 1965 and much of its remaining resources, about $6 million, went to organizations such as the Hoover Institution at Stanford University, making up a significant part of Hoover's endowment, and the Intercollegiate Studies Institute.[9]

"The Volker Fund played a very positive role in the development of free-market economics," according to Milton Friedman. "They made the Mont Pelerin meeting possible, they made Hayek's stay at Chicago possible, they financed summer sessions and lectures. You cannot underestimate their influence."[10]

HENRY REGNERY

My father was not a conventional conservative financier who donated to the cause by financing think tanks and conservative organizations. He took the unique and indispensable role of devoting his life and fortune to publishing seminal conservative books. After graduating from MIT in 1931 he spent two years studying in Germany at the University of Bonn, returning to Harvard to work on a Ph.D. in economics with Josef Schumpeter. While in Germany, he saw firsthand how the Nazis seized control and used government power to smother freedom and destroy the common good. During World War II he worked in the family business, a large and profitable Chicago textile-finishing firm, but by the war's close, decided that he was much more interested in preserving Western civilization than in selling textiles. The postwar settlement convinced him that Communism was the primary threat to the West, and that free markets were essential to political freedom.

The Joanna Western Mills Company, which my grandfather had started and built into one of the largest textile finishers in the country, offered my father a comfortable and secure life. (Interestingly, my grandfather went to work for William Volker in 1892 in Kansas City and came to Chicago in about 1900 to oversee a small windowshade facility, which he ultimately bought and built into a substantially larger firm than the Volker Company. He and Volker remained partners of some sort and very close friends.) My father was well educated and socially prominent, and his life could have been typical of second-generation businessmen who enjoyed all the perks of upper-class American life. But ideas were far more important to him than making money, and he felt strongly enough about the welfare of the West to devote his fortune to publishing conservative books, which he believed would provide the best ammunition in the war of ideas against socialism. He was a lonely figure on the publishing landscape of those years.

My father never expected to make money publishing books, and he was right. No records exist to show how much he spent, but my guess is that, between 1947 and the late 1960s, he sank $2 to $3 million into the enterprise ($12 to $15 million in today's dollars). He often struggled to keep both home and the small publishing firm afloat (and no doubt he as often wished he had taken H. L. Hunt up on his offer). The market for conservative books was small, and investors were few. I recall his going to visit J. Howard Pew on several occasions, always to return disappointed. (Pew, who headed the Sun Oil Company, was a staunch conservative who contributed to ISI and Grove City College, his alma mater, and many other conservative causes. Unhappily, his millions went into the Pew Family Trust, now a large funder of the left.)

My father's correspondence is replete with pleas to various possible donors for money to help underwrite some particular book. Some of his pleas were successful, others were not, but somehow the books were published. Many of the seminal books of the conservative movement were published by the Henry Regnery Company and are still in print; they articulated the core principles of the movement. Certain titles, such as *God and Man at Yale* and *The Conservative Mind*, were even profitable. But the company operated at a loss and had to be subsidized by my father or go under. In the late 1970s, after selling the Henry Regnery Company to my brother-in-law, my father, who had kept the rights to many of the old conservative titles, started a new company under the banner of Regnery Gateway, which he also financed. I became its head in 1986, and by the late 1990s it had become the most successful conservative publishing house in the country.

Harry Earhart

"Our basic role is to influence ideas," said former Earhart president David Kennedy, "and often this can only be accomplished over the long term."[11] In business since 1929, Earhart is one of the oldest conservative foundations and has seen the success of its long-term efforts as have few others. Among other projects, Earhart finds talented students, through a network of friendly professors, who are given fellowships to study economics, philosophy, history, and related topics. Its success is most easily measured by that of its fellows: Of the thirty-five Nobel Prize winners in economics since the prize was established in 1969, nine have been Earhart fellows, including F. A. Hayek, Milton Friedman, George Stigler, James Buchanan, Ronald Coase, and Gary Becker. Other Earhart fellows include Allan Bloom, author of *Closing the American Mind*, economist Lord Peter Bauer, who was given a peerage for his influential work criticizing state-led development policies, and former Librarian of Congress and Pulitzer Prize–winning author Daniel Boorstin.[12] Earhart has supported conservative institutions such as the Atlas Economic Research Foundation, the Intercollegiate Studies Institute, and think tanks including the American Enterprise Institute and the Hoover Institution at Stanford University.

Harry Earhart was born in 1870 in rural Armstrong County, Pennsylvania, the son of a storekeeper. With only an eighth-grade education, he started a number of businesses, eventually manufacturing lubricating oil in Detroit, and, in 1912, he formed the White Star Refining Company, selling petroleum products throughout the Midwest. The company was sold in 1930 to the Vacuum Oil Company, which eventually became part of what is now Mobil Oil.

Harry Earhart set up the foundation in 1929 and appointed his children trustees. But by 1949, dissatisfied with their lack of interest in the world of ideas, he asked them to resign and named an outside board of men who shared his views on free markets and limited government. He later brought in suitable family members to a second board, which appoints the trustees to the first board, ensuring that the foundation remain true to his vision—a highly unusual arrangement, but a successful one. Earhart died in 1954, but never has the board of his foundation wavered from his free-market and conservative views.

And how different it is from hundreds of other foundations. Many of the large liberal foundations are now run by boards of trustees (sometimes family members, sometimes not) who totally disregard the intentions of the founder. The Ford, MacArthur, Pew, and Carnegie foundations, four of the most left-leaning in the country, were all formed by businessmen who made their fortunes in the free market and would be appalled at the misuse of their money.

Most of Earhart's money supported individual scholars, graduate students, and researchers—of 305 Earhart grants made in 2000, 78 percent went to individuals. But many conservative organizations have been Earhart beneficiaries as well, although most were involved in intellectual and scholarly pursuits. Earhart, unlike some other founda-tions, never concentrated its grants on a particular side of conservatism but supported scholarship in various areas—economic freedom, anti-Communism, and traditional "old right" conservatism. It was one of the early funders of the Mont Pelerin Society, but also underwrote the work of Leo Strauss and supported the publication of the collected works of Eric Voegelin. In the 1970s the Earhart board recognized that Western culture and the ideas of liberty were being threatened by the nihilism of the left and decided that the foundation should support scholarships in history, philosophy, and literature.[13]

The Earhart board decided to spend down the assets and close the foundation's doors by the end of 2015. It had been giving grants, as re-cently as 2004, of some $3 million to $4 million; at the time, its remaining assets were about $45 million. In the big scheme of things, these grants have purchased a tremendous quantity of wisdom and good works.

HENRY SALVATORI

Henry Salvatori arrived from Italy at the age of six, in the very first days of the twentieth century, and instantly became a loyal and patriotic American. His family settled on a farm in New Jersey, and as Salvatori remembered later, "Those early days on the farm served to shape my character, basic nature and even my philosophical outlook." He went to the University of Pennsylvania, in Philadelphia, where he studied electrical engineering. After receiving a master's degree from Columbia, he decided to see the "Wild West" and took a job with an oil-exploration company in Oklahoma. Working fifteen-hour days, he learned to use seismology to find oil and before long, during the depths of the De-pression, had started his own company. With nine thousand dollars in capital at a time when the unemployment rate was nearly 25 percent, Salvatori started off in a one-room office in Los Angeles with one truck. He used his geophysical skills to help small oil companies find oil, and within a year had ten crews working in five states across the West. Com-petition was fierce, but Salvatori knew the industry and proved to be an exceptional businessman; he eventually landed a contract with Stan-dard Oil of Indiana, and by 1936 his company was second only to the one he had left several years earlier. Ever the innovator, Salvatori was one of the first to explore for oil offshore, and by 1955 his company was the world's largest offshore seismic contractor.[14]

As an employer, Salvatori was as innovative as anybody in California; in 1951 he started a profit-sharing plan which made his employees virtual partners with him at no cost to themselves, and in 1954 offered his nine hundred employees a leave of absence during which they could pursue other job opportunities while keeping all their benefits, a step that even *Fortune* magazine applauded.

By the mid-1950s Salvatori was a confirmed political conservative. "During the 1950s," Salvatori explained, "the radical left policies that had prevailed since the early 1930s had begun to prove ineffective and dangerous, resulting in the election of Eisenhower. But during his eight years in office the philosophy of the radical left still dominated academia and especially the news media, reasserting itself with the election of Kennedy."[15]

Salvatori was one of the early financial backers of *National Review*. He was also an early donor to the Intercollegiate Studies Institute, ultimately providing ISI with over $2 million. In 1964 Salvatori went to work for Barry Goldwater as the chairman of his campaign in California. Goldwater's defeat did not bother Salvatori in the least; he immediately understood that Goldwater had started a conservative revival and determined to help make that revival thrive.[16]

Wanting to devote most of his time to politics, Salvatori sold his business to Litton Industries in 1960, which made him one of the wealthiest men in California, enabling him to devote his fertile talents to the conservative cause. In October 1964 he convinced Goldwater to allow actor Ronald Reagan to make a nationally broadcast speech in support, then proceeded to raise the money to pay for it, contributing most of it himself. "A Time for Choosing" launched Reagan's political career and resulted in more contributions to Goldwater's campaign than any other political speech in the history of television.[17] Two years later Salvatori was instrumental in recruiting Reagan to run for governor. Salvatori and his fellow California businessmen promised Reagan two things if he chose to run: They would raise the money, and they would accept no favor, no office, no appointment in return. It was a winning combination, and it was vintage Salvatori.

But Salvatori was also a political realist, and as much as he admired Ronald Reagan, Salvatori thought he was unelectable in 1976 and supported Gerald Ford. But by 1980 he was once again deep in the Reagan fold, and a charter member of Reagan's "kitchen cabinet," supporting him, raising money, and advising his campaign.

Until his death in 1997, Henry Salvatori was one of the right's most generous supporters, giving away most of his vast fortune to conservative causes and candidates. He never failed to tell anybody how indebted he was to his adopted country. He was forever promoting the American founders, the Constitution, and free markets. "He took the fruits of a lifetime's work," wrote Bill Buckley, "and put them at the disposal of men and women of a younger generation, charging only that they pursue the ideals he so eloquently served since the day when at age six he got off the boat from Italy, and began a lifetime of productive work, leaving signs of his personal grace everywhere he lived and worked."[18]

RICHARD MELLON SCAIFE

According to the *Washington Post*, "[Richard Mellon] Scaife's biggest contribution has been to help fund the creation of the modern conservative movement in America . . . Scaife's philanthropy has had a disproportionate impact on the rise of the right."[19] If there is one conservative donor who drives liberals crazy, it is Dick Scaife, not only because he is one of the largest donors, if not the largest donor, to conservative causes, but also because the liberals can't figure out what motivates him. Perhaps, too, because Scaife, by effectively helping to build conservatism, has accelerated the decline of the left. If any conservative donor has paid the price for his generosity in the liberal media, it is Richard Mellon Scaife. His jealous protection of his privacy feeds their hunger for conspiracy theories. Scaife is invariably referred to as a "radical right-winger," a "right-wing extremist," the "archconservative godfather" behind "the vast right-wing conspiracy," or, because of his desire to remain anonymous, as "reclusive."

Richard Mellon Scaife was born in Pittsburgh in 1932, the grandnephew of former treasury secretary Andrew Mellon; his mother was

one of the principal heirs to the Mellon banking, oil, and aluminum fortune and, until her death in 1965, controlled several of the Mellon family foundations. Her primary interests were population control and the
arts, but when Dick Scaife took over management of the foundations in
1973, much of the money—and there was lots of it—started going to
the conservative movement. Since then, the organizations and causes
receiving major support from Scaife read like a Who's Who of American conservatism. After supporting Goldwater in 1964, Scaife came to
the conclusion that if conservatives were ever going to come to power,
they would need a body of ideas and policies that could compete with
liberalism. The war of ideas, in other words, caught the imagination of
this multimillionaire, and Dick Scaife, being Dick Scaife, decided to get
into the good fight.

According to an aide, Scaife "saw what the Democrats were doing
and decided to do the mirror image, but do it better. In those days you
had the American Civil Liberties Union, the government-supported legal corporations, a strong Democratic Party with strong labor support,
the Brookings Institution, the *New York Times* and *Washington Post*,
and all these other people on the Left—and nobody on the Right. The
idea was to correct that imbalance, and the first idea was to copy what
works."[20]

Scaife and his assistants recognized the effectiveness of the left. The
dogmas espoused by Americans for Democratic Action, the Brookings
Institution, the ACLU, and a host of other liberal groups reigned unchallenged. Even a cursory review of the Johnson administration, not to
mention the Nixon administration, reflected policies that had been developed in liberal think tanks, in academic institutions, and by left-wing
public interest lawyers. It was high time the right followed suit, and to
conservatives, Scaife was a godsend. Scaife was one of the earliest contributors to the Heritage Foundation, which would become the largest
and most powerful conservative think tank in the country, and Scaife's
favorite conservative institution. Scaife assembled a staff of highly competent men who became active participants in conservative circles in
Washington and New York; Richard Larry and Dan McMichael, his two
principal assistants at the foundation office in Pittsburgh, were among
the most trusted outside advisors to many of the policy and activist organizations and think tanks.

Overall, Scaife has poured over $25 million into Heritage; has generously funded the Hoover Institution at Stanford University, established years earlier by Herbert Hoover, but more recently a haven for conservative scholars and writers; and assisted the American Enterprise Institute, a venerable Washington-based think tank. Scaife continues to finance causes dear to his heart. In 2004, his foundations gave over $15 million to conservative ventures.

Scaife was insistently anonymous in his philanthropy, to the extent of stipulating anonymity as a condition of his giving. This anonymity lasted until the Clinton years, when he became the principal funder of *The American Spectator*'s campaign to expose President Clinton's peccadilloes and indiscretions—a campaign that led to Clinton's impeachment, but also opened Scaife up to huge media attention. He is no longer anonymous, but Dick Scaife continues to be one of the movement's principal funders even to this day.

Roger Milliken

Roger Milliken, head of the great textile company that bears his name, has been one of the conservative movement's most generous donors. But Milliken hasn't always been happy with the results of his largesse, and his contributions, particularly since the 1990s, have often raised the eyebrows of some of those whom he earlier supported. But at ninety years of age, and as one of the very early backers of conservative causes, Milliken may have seen more of the fruits of the millions of dollars he has provided to conservatives over the years than any other donor. "He has a history of picking winners," said the *New Republic* in January 2000, "candidates, journals, and think tanks that shaped American politics."[22]

Every law student who has read the 1965 Supreme Court case of *Textile Workers Union* v. *Darlington Manufacturing Co.* knows that Roger Milliken can be tenacious, and that he stands up stoutly for what he believes. After a concerted battle, employees at one of his cotton mills voted to unionize. In response, he shut down the plant and sold the equipment; after a twenty-five-year court battle, Milliken was ordered to pay $5 million in back wages (although by that time nearly a fourth of the employees had died).[23] The company remains nonunion to this day, and the eleven thousand employees are treated as well as, if not better than, those of the competition. Although Milliken is tough with his charitable contributions as he is with business, he has a broad understanding of the conservative movement and the ideals that are its foundation, and rarely imposes ideological restrictions on his donees. But not always. As one of the original founders of the Heritage Foundation, Milliken provided an annual six-figure contribution to the think tank. But when Heritage became, in Milliken's eyes, too friendly to Asian industrial interests, he cut it off. Says John von Kannon, Heritage's chief fundraiser, "He went from two hundred thousand dollars a year to zero." But eventually he rejoined the Heritage fold, even though Heritage did not change its views on trade.[24] He also had no hesitation in supporting Democrats over conservative Republican politicians when he felt they were not sufficiently true to the cause, or supported things Milliken opposed.

Milliken was one of the earliest conservative donors, and has remained, throughout his long life, one of the largest. He was an early and active member of the John Birch Society, was the largest contributor to the founding of *National Review*—Milliken was a Yale graduate and was thrilled with the release of Buckley's *God and Man at Yale*—and enthusiastically joined the effort to nominate Goldwater in 1960. When Nixon was nominated instead, Milliken was one of the first to help organize the 1964 draft-Goldwater campaign, and remained one of his largest benefactors. Former South Carolina governor Jim Edwards states flatly that "Roger was responsible for getting Goldwater the nomination in 1964."[25]

Milliken and Co. was started by Milliken's grandfather in 1865; Roger took the helm in 1947, and continues to run the $3.9 billion corporation—one of the largest privately held corporations in the country. The company, headquartered in Spartanburg, South Carolina, manufactures and sells a broad range of textile and chemical products, with plants scattered around the world. Roger Milliken has received countless awards and commendations for his style of management and for the innovation demonstrated by his company, which is the owner of over two thousand patents.

Milliken was instrumental in convincing South Carolina Senator

Strom Thurmond to switch from the Democratic to the Republican Party in 1964, which released the Republican tidal wave that swept through the South. When Nixon ran for re-election in 1972, Milliken, according to the *Washington Post*, personally delivered $363,000 in cash and checks to Nixon's campaign director hours before a new law requiring public disclosure of such donations went into effect.[26]

Milliken, in the 1980s, became a fierce opponent of free trade, largely because of the damage that was being done to the textile industry by cheap imports from Asia. He has supported protectionism ever since. "A fatal flaw of the current idea of 'globalization,'" says Milliken, is "the lack of recognition that subsidized global production creates a strong incentive to create overproduction that outstrips global demand."[27] Such an imbalance threatens economic stability, he believes, and the paramount place enjoyed by the United States in the world marketplace.

Few conservatives agree. Milliken nevertheless continues to back conservative causes. After Nixon, he generously supported Reagan in 1976 and 1980, and was an ardent backer of Newt Gingrich's takeover of the House of Representatives in 1994. All three abandoned Milliken on trade issues, yet he continued to support them.

Milken later supported Pat Buchanan, who was one conservative who sang Milliken's song on trade. Milliken was Buchanan's largest benefactor during both of his presidential campaigns, and provided much of the money to establish and fund American Cause, Buchanan's political organization.

According to Pat Buchanan, Milliken is the "ideal American capitalist, a capitalist who believes he's got an unwritten social contract with his workers and obligations and duties that go up and down. He personifies the idea of an entrepreneur and a businessman and a great patriot."[28]

Other early conservative donors include Joseph Coors, the late president of the Colorado brewery that bears his name, who put up much of the original money to fund the Heritage Foundation; Indiana lawyer and investor Pierre Goodrich, whose money, over $100 million, established the Liberty Fund; Sir Antony Fisher, who funded the Institute for Economic Affairs in London and numerous other free-market think tanks, including the Atlas Foundation; Wall Street financier and former ambassador Shelby Collum Davis; and Charles Koch, president of Koch Industries.

Although many individual donors and foundations became prominent during and after the Reagan years, two stand out. For without them, the conservative movement would have a much different face. These are the now defunct John M. Olin Foundation and the very much alive Lynde and Harry Bradley Foundation.

The John M. Olin Foundation

The Olin Foundation provided over $450 million to conservative causes from 1982 to 2005, when it closed its doors. Its contribution to the cause of freedom must have exceeded the wildest dreams of John M. Olin (who died in 1982).

For the first several years of its existence the Olin Foundation was a rather typical rich man's charity, giving to hospitals, universities, the Episcopal Church, and, yes, conservation organizations. Olin made a personal contribution to Phyllis Schlafly's 1952 congressional campaign, because she ran from his home district, but he did not involve the foundation in politics.[29] Then in 1969, armed radical students seized control of the student union at Cornell University, Olin's alma mater and the recipient of a considerable piece of his charitable giving, and the administration and faculty ingloriously caved in. Several prominent conservative professors, including Walter Berns, Allan Bloom, and Thomas Sowell, resigned their positions at Cornell in disgust. Olin was appalled, and decided to use his fortune to further the principles of freedom and the free enterprise economy that had enabled his company to prosper.[30] He told the New York Times in 1977 that his greatest ambition was "to see free enterprise re-established in this country. Business and the public must be awakened to the creeping stranglehold that socialism has gained here since World War II."[31] He turned the John M. Olin Foundation into "a venture capital fund for the conservative movement."[32]

Olin grew up in St. Louis, where he made a considerable fortune as head of the Olin Corporation, started by his father, which manufactured guns, ammunition, chemicals, skis, and other products. Although he was a Republican, he was not, at least until the Cornell debacle, particularly conservative—certainly no philosophical conservative. But he saw that the system that had enabled him to build a large and thriving business was under attack and that without the support of people like himself that system would not survive. And he had the foresight and good fortune to hire an able and perceptive staff for his foundation—men who understood the essential needs of the conservative movement. Most important, his staff realized that political action, by itself, was useless without also "fighting a battle for men's minds." Executive Director Frank O'Connell put it this way: "Because our aim is the propagation of ideas, our successes will be measured by the degree to which our efforts increase the dissemination and understanding of those ideas."[33]

Olin made a point of funding only the brightest scholars and the most prestigious institutions, and was not interested in conservatives who were "preaching to the choir"—Olin wanted to change minds. Nor was he afraid of long-term projects. Typical was the John M. Olin Faculty Fellowships program, which helped promising conservative scholars gain tenure, by allowing them to take a year off from teaching to write books and journal articles with which to burnish their credentials. Between 1985 and 2005 over one hundred "countercultural" scholars received $8 million through the program, many winning tenure at prestigious universities.

Olin also funded a number of institutes within universities that had specific areas of study and research. Among the most significant were those in law and economics, a discipline which began at the University of Chicago in the 1950s, teaching that legal rules, procedures, and cases should be analyzed on the basis of their economic consequences as well as the dispensation of justice. The Olin centers at Yale, Harvard, Stanford, and George Mason University are but four of the institutes that helped to make law and economics a major force in American law schools, in the courts, and in the legal system itself. Olin's foundation spent some $68 million on this project alone. It has left an indelible stamp on the movement.[34]

THE LYNDE AND HARRY BRADLEY FOUNDATION

Lynde Bradley was an electrical engineer who, at the turn of the century, designed an efficient governor to control the speed of electric motors. With a one-thousand-dollar investment from a friend, Dr. Stanton Allen, he started the Allen-Bradley Company. Joined in short order by his brother Harry, their Milwaukee company thrived and the Bradley brothers became among Milwaukee's most prominent citizens. Lynde died in 1941, leaving his share of Allen-Bradley to a small foundation to do good works for the city of Milwaukee.

Harry was an early supporter of Robert Taft's presidential campaign in 1952, an early Goldwater supporter, one of the original backers of *National Review*, an ardent anti-Communist, and an unapologetic member of the John Birch Society. One day in 1959, he discovered that his New York bankers were sponsoring a lunch for the ambassador from the Soviet Union, whereupon he "declared that nobody should break bread with 'Soviet murderers' and promptly closed the company's account."[35] Harry died in 1965, but Allen-Bradley continued to thrive until Rockwell International bought the company in 1985 for $1.65 billion. The Lynde and Harry Bradley Foundation, which had assets of $14 million before the sale, was suddenly worth nearly $300 million, making it one of the twenty largest foundations in the country.

Bradley would be the largest conservative foundation if it could remain true to the intent of the Bradley brothers. Two trustees— William H. Brady, a Milwaukee businessman and solid right-winger, and Andrew "Tiny" Rader, an Allen-Bradley executive and chairman of the Bradley board—knew that the Ford Foundation, the Carnegie Endowment, and a number of other large foundations had been taken over by liberals, and wanted no repeat at Bradley. "The principles Harry [Bradley] believed in," said Rader, "gave us the strongest economy, the highest living standard, and the greatest individual freedom in the world. We felt it was our task to do everything we could to preserve those principles."[36]

Heritage Foundation development director John von Kannon recalls that after Allen-Bradley was sold to Rockwell, "I got a phone call from Bill Brady, saying I am on the board of this new foundation. We want to make sure that what happened at Ford doesn't happen to us. I knew you when you were publisher of the *American Spectator*. Can you introduce me to the other conservative foundations? So we had a meeting with Dick Larry of the Scaife Foundation and Jack Brauntuch of the JM

Foundation and two or three others. They decided to hire Mike Joyce from Olin, who knew the conservative landscape and knew how to run a large foundation. It made all the difference, and helped Bradley become a major player in conservative philanthropy."[37]

The Bradley board provided funds to major universities, including Harvard and the University of Chicago, to employ tenured professors who would have long-term impact on the conservative movement. When Michael Joyce and his staff spread the word that Bradley wanted to help, the money started to flow to hundreds of conservative organizations and undertakings. By 1990, Bradley was giving away $25 million, nearly 60 percent of which went to the right; by 2000, annual grants totaled $45 million.

A good percentage of Bradley grants have remained in Wisconsin. Several of the board seats were reserved for Wisconsinites, the others for national conservative leaders such as former Colorado senator Bill Armstrong, former Delaware governor Pierre du Pont, and *National Review* chairman Thomas "Dusty" Rhodes.

Although much of the "Wisconsin" money has gone to cultural institutions such as the Milwaukee Art Museum and the symphony, Bradley has also used Wisconsin as a laboratory for policy reforms, including school choice and welfare reform, that have gained national recognition. A closer look shows how a relatively small amount of money, well directed, can have a huge impact.

Welfare is one of the liberals' signature programs, and at the heart of their concept of constituent politics—the idea that the recipients of government largesse should feel that they have an ownership stake in the program and should remain beholden to the government and those who keep the money flowing. But in hard fact, welfare became a culture of dependency, creating more problems than it solved, many of which were visible just miles from Bradley's office in downtown Milwaukee. High crime rates, juvenile delinquency and truancy, out-of-control illegitimacy, dysfunctional families, malnutrition, and unlivable housing were but a few of the most visible problems. Conservatives had been critical of the system for years, and by the mid-1980s a few were offering solutions along with the criticism. Charles Murray, for one, in 1984 published *Losing Ground*, a book that challenged the conventional view of the welfare state. The book touched off massive controversy between liberals, who hated what Murray had to say, and conservatives, who loved it; Bradley was Murray's principal supporter.

The Bradley Foundation funded projects to refine Murray's arguments and translate them into policy recommendations and, through its Bradley Scholars program at the Heritage Foundation, gave a two-year fellowship to University of Texas professor Marvin Olasky, whose work on welfare was published as *The Tragedy of American Compassion* in 1992. Olasky found that volunteerism and Judeo-Christian morality were missing in the welfare system, and believed that properly channeled, they could transform welfare from a heartless and counterproductive system into something that would actually help the poor to become independent and productive.

Bradley was close to Tommy Thompson, the conservative governor of Wisconsin who would become George W. Bush's secretary of health and human services in 2001, and who shared Murray and Olasky's views on welfare. Wisconsin's liberal welfare policy, in Thompson's view, was ripe for reform. Bradley was only too happy to help, and supported Thompson's initiative, including over $2 million to the Hudson Institute to develop an entirely new welfare plan for the state.

Wisconsin subsequently adopted Thompson's plan, which became the model of welfare reform for the rest of the country: Welfare rolls were reduced by nearly 90 percent. By 1996, when Congress passed and Bill Clinton signed massive welfare reforms, Wisconsin's plan was held up as the successful forerunner. With grants totaling less than $5 million, the Bradley Foundation had uprooted a program that was embedded deep in the liberal culture, first at the state level, and then at the national.[38]

According to Milwaukee author John Gurda, if there is a single lesson in everything the Bradley Foundation does, it is that "freedom is a difficult discipline, imposing on its adherents an obligation to nurture, in belief and in practice, the principles that give a free society its particular vibrancy."[39]

CONSERVATIVE AND LIBERAL FINANCES

The right has never had the sort of money available to the left. During the early years of the movement, from 1945 into the mid-1970s, no more than about a dozen foundations were willing to give money to conservative causes, and most of those were small, family charitable organizations. In addition, there were only a few hundred "high-dollar" conservative donors who between them contributed $3 million or so yearly to movement causes.[40]

The liberals, on the other hand, have been virtually swimming in money for years. The five largest conservative foundations' *total assets* are less than the money the five largest left-leaning foundations give away *in a year*. The large mainstream foundations—Ford, Rockefeller, Carnegie, and a few others—were giving away hundreds of millions of dollars to support every sort of liberal scheme in the 1960s and 1970s. These liberal foundations are largely wedded to the view that social progress is achieved through government action, expert knowledge, and scientific research, and by international organizations that bring world peace and prosperity. The activities of the liberal Ford Foundation in the 1970s are a good example. Founded in 1936 by Henry and Edsel Ford, the Ford Foundation has consistently supported "progressive" causes, including various pro-abortion groups, international organizations stressing "world peace," and legal assistance clinics and other groups that advocate activism on the part of welfare recipients and beneficiaries of other federal programs. Henry Ford II, who was the last member of the family to serve on the board, resigned in protest in 1976 because of the foundation's leftward direction. In his letter of resignation, Ford made no secret of his distaste for what the foundation started by his grandfather and father was doing: "In effect," he wrote, "the foundation is a creature of capitalism, a statement that, I'm sure, would be shocking to many professional staff people in the field of philanthropy. It is hard to discern recognition of this fact in anything the foundation does. It is even more difficult to find an understanding of this in many of the institutions, particularly the universities, that are the beneficiaries of the foundation's grant programs."[41]

McGeorge Bundy, who served as LBJ's national security advisor and was an architect of the Vietnam War, became head of the Ford Foundation in 1965 and instituted a major shift in the way the large foundations did business, which became known as "advocacy philanthropy." Ford and the other big foundations set out to use government programs to mobilize liberal interest groups. Their support has continued unabated. (To provide a yardstick, the Ford Foundation gave away about $300 million a year during the 1960s, and over $500 million in 2005.)[42] These constituents in turn lobbied Congress and the regulatory bodies that implemented the programs and brought lawsuits seeking broader interpretation of the laws—all in order to push the envelope way to the left of the wishes of Congress and state legislatures. This included the expansion of welfare, legal services for the poor, feminist goals, affirmative action, and expansion of civil rights laws, abortion rights, environmental activism, and nuclear disarmament. With huge grants, groups such as the Environmental Defense Fund, the Women's Law Forum, and the Mexican American Legal Defense and Education Fund were created. Ford, Carnegie, MacArthur, and other mainstream foundations invented the now-familiar liberal phenomenon of self-appointed, well-financed advocacy groups promoting complaints against the taxpayers and seeking expanded benefits or compensation on behalf of their constituents. The left, and the Democratic Party itself, became a conglomeration of interest groups on the government dole, always seeking to increase their share of the pie. And they helped to transform the welfare state from a New Deal system of aiding the underprivileged into the Great Society of entitlements and a permanent underclass.

But as always, there were unintended results, not only in negative social effects of liberal policies, but in the conservative response liberal donors aroused. Liberal excesses spurred conservative donors to underwrite new organizations to promote limited government alternatives to the liberals' schemes. Foundations like Olin, Smith Richardson, Bradley, and Scaife allotted yet more grant money to intellectual pursuits. Says James Pierseon, former president of the Olin Foundation:

> These funders were more self-consciously conservative than libertarian. While sympathetic to the writings of Hayek and the ideals of classical liberalism, they adopted a broader intellectual framework encompassing fields beyond economics: preeminently religion, foreign policy, and the traditional humanities. In contrast to Hayek and his followers, they

were also prepared to engage the world of politics
and policy and to wage the war of ideas in a direct
and aggressive style.[43]

During the 1980s and 1990s some of the conservative foundation
leaders were impressed with the arguments and positions of the neoconservatives, many of whom were affiliated with the elite universities
as well as being professional writers published in the leading journals.
At times, even liberals found their arguments compelling. Soon neoconservative journals such as *Commentary*, the *New Criterion*, and the
National Interest got a sympathetic hearing in the conservative foundation world. But the foundations were also interested in the new think
tanks, free-market research centers, and the ever-growing list of activist
conservative organizations. As Piereson points out, when Ronald Reagan was elected in 1980, only a handful of organizations were doing
conservative research and policy analysis. By 2000, there were literally
hundreds.

All in all, the grants made by the Olin, Bradley, and Scaife foundations, among other conservative foundations, were only a drop in the
bucket compared to what "mainstream" and "progressive" foundations
were pouring into the left. In 2002, the twelve largest foundations in
the country had combined assets of $109 billion and gave away over
$6 billion, $136 million of which was spent on public policy initiatives.
Not one of those foundations is conservative, and virtually none of their
grants went to conservative groups. The twelve largest conservative
foundations, on the other hand, had combined assets in 2002 of $1.7
billion, gave grants totaling about $85 million, including $29 million to
conservative public policy initiatives.[44]

Comparing, again in 2002, the twelve largest "progressive" or liberal
foundations to the twelve largest conservative foundations, we find a
similar imbalance between the right and the left: The twelve largest
progressive foundations have combined assets of $11 billion against
combined assets of $1.7 billion for the conservative, and spending by
the progressive foundations was $38 million, versus $29 million by the
conservatives.[45] This is in addition to what the mainline foundations
spend on liberal causes; virtually none of the mainline foundations, on
the other hand, support conservatives. In other words, the liberal think

tanks and policy institutes were spending nearly six times the conservative expenditures in 2002.

The good news is that conservatives use their money much more effectively, which at least partially explains why, though the money available to the left has been vastly disproportionate to that to the right, conservatives are winning the war of ideas. Not only are their ideas better, but conservatives have figured out how to get more bang for their buck. According to a study done at the Stanford University School of Business:

> [The conservatives] are succeeding by aggressively promoting their ideas. By contrast, liberal and mainstream foundations back policy research that is of interest to liberals. But these funders remain reluctant to make explicit financial commitments to the war of ideas, and they do relatively little to support the marketing of liberal ideas. . . . The advantage lies in how the money is spent. Conservatives have found ways to package and market their ideas in more compelling ways.[46]

Some on the left are willing to admit this. The leftist magazine the *Nation* had this to say in 1995:

> The money that [conservative] foundations spend on ideas may be paltry next to the ocean of special-interest money that pumps through the US political system, but by strategically leveraging their resources, conservative foundations have engineered the rise of a right-wing intelligentsia that has come to wield enormous influence in national policy debates.[47]

So not only do liberals misuse taxpayer dollars through the government spending they promote; they are wasteful and inept with their own money.

Liberals are forever obsessing about how conservatives raise and spend money. Their activists are fond of portraying themselves as poor and the right as having bottomless coffers. Countless investigations, studies, and websites follow the flow of funds to conservative organizations and identify the funders. At best, they sniff something sinister; at worst, they smell a vast conspiracy. In a 2004 report, a self-appointed watchdog of conservative foundations published an extensive study on conservative funding called *Axis of Ideology: Conservative Foundations and Public Policy*.[48] The study, elaborately produced, concluded that "conservative foundations have been instrumental in shaping the public policy debate around a variety of issues, including, but not limited to, school choice, welfare reform, decentralization of government, the privatization of social security, and pro-family and marriage programs."[49] Conservatives, the study also concluded, have had greater impact with their foundation money than liberals.

People for the American Way, a prominent left-wing group, published a report in 1996 called *Buying a Movement: Right-Wing Foundations and American Politics*, which unearthed a vast conspiracy between conservative donors and recipients. "Right-wing foundations," the report concluded darkly, "have developed a truly comprehensive funding strategy, providing grants to a broad range of groups, each promoting right-wing positions to their specific audiences." The report went on to unveil the news that conservative foundation "largesse" had kept "alive in the public debate a variety of policy ideas long ago discredited or discarded by the mainstream. . . . The success of the right-wing efforts are seen at every level of government, as a vast armada of foundation-funded right-wing organizations has both fed and capitalized on the current swing to the right in Congress and in the state legislatures."[50]

DIRECT MAIL

Although the foundations and the large donors have been crucial to the movement, its lifeblood came from direct mail.

Marvin Liebman was one of the first conservative impresarios. Trained in public relations, he put his organizational genius to work for conservative causes in the 1950s. A former Communist himself, anti-Communism was his passion. In the 1950s he had an office on Madison Avenue in New York, was known to everybody, always had a good story to tell, and could form a new organization in a matter of hours. Bill Buckley described him as "a one-man public-relations industry directed exclusively to the promotion of conservative and anti-Communist activities, who attracted his many friends by his humor, his intense loyalty, and his delight with his life and times."[51] The formation of Young Americans for Freedom in 1960 was largely Liebman's idea (it initially operated out of his office), as was the American Conservative Union in 1964. But his anchor organization remained the Committee of One Million (Against the Admission of Communist China to the United Nations), an organization that successfully kept the Chinese out of the UN until sabotaged by Richard Nixon.

Liebman raised money by running full-page ads in such papers as the *New York Times*, the *Herald Tribune*, and the *Los Angeles Times* asking people to send a check to help pay for the next ad. He then recorded the names on three-by-five cards, and from time to time would send letters asking for more.

In the summer of 1961, while serving his two-week National Guard stint at an army base in Illinois, young Richard Viguerie answered a help-wanted ad in *National Review* for a fundraiser for the newly formed Young Americans for Freedom in New York. A very green Louisiana boy, Viguerie arrived at Grand Central Station early on a Saturday morning and walked through deserted streets to the *National Review* office on East Thirty-fifth Street, where he was to meet Bill Rusher. "My bags were heavy and I was tired and wished I could take a rest," recalls Viguerie, "but signs along the street said *No Stopping or Standing*, and I just had to keep walking." Viguerie had a sinking feeling in his stomach when he found the building door locked. And then a voice behind him boomed, "Mr. Viguerie, I presume?" As he turned around Bill Rusher, nattily dressed and sporting a bowler hat, as usual, greeted him warmly.

Viguerie sufficiently impressed Rusher to be escorted to meet Liebman, who was in charge of raising money for YAF. Liebman, explained Viguerie, "showed me his mail room, where he kept maybe tens of thousands of donors' names on three-by-five index cards, who had given one hundred dollars, and how often, and that type of thing. I was like a duck that was two or three years old and had never seen water, but I knew what to do. I said, where has this thing been all my life?"[52] After six months of raising money for YAF Viguerie was made its executive director, where he stayed until 1965, when he left to set up his own company.

At about the same time, Liebman departed New York for London to produce plays and sold Viguerie his mailing list of some fifty thousand names. Viguerie bought a couple of other lists, giving him a total of one hundred thousand or so potential donors.

The plan worked beyond Viguerie's wildest dreams, and before long he was a venture capitalist for the budding conservative movement. He assumed all the risk, producing a mailing for a client using his own mailing list and paying for it out of his own pocket. If enough money came back, Viguerie was paid; if not, he absorbed the loss. Because he had the names, Viguerie could go to a political candidate or somebody interested in a bill before Congress and offer, for free, to raise all the money needed.

Direct mail has raised countless millions of dollars for the conservative movement since the early 1960s. It has been responsible for the election of a large number of conservative politicians, for funding hundreds of grassroots organizations, and in the process has educated millions upon millions of people on conservative issues. According to Viguerie, "Direct mail is the second largest form of advertising in the country. When I send out these millions of letters, I am raising much-needed money for a conservative cause. I am also identifying who the activists are by asking them to fill out a survey, a petition, or to send a postcard to some senator, and to bypass the monopoly of Walter Cronkite and the gatekeepers out there and go right into people's homes. So that is what built the conservative movement in the '60s and the '70s.[53]

"But equally important, we are going right into people's homes with a message, educating people on conservative principles."[54] In the years before an alternative conservative media existed, direct mail enabled conservatives to do an end run around the mainstream liberal media and win voters to their side.

The ability to raise money through direct mail could make or break a political campaign. Early in his primary campaign against Gerald Ford in 1976, Ronald Reagan ran out of money. But he scraped together ninety thousand dollars and bought a half-hour's air time on NBC; he sat on a corner of a desk in the studio and gave his great twenty-five-minute stump speech denouncing the Panama Canal Treaty, chastising Henry Kissinger, and criticizing those responsible for détente with the Soviets. During his last five minutes, Reagan made a plea for money. He raised, in those five minutes, over $1 million. But much more important, he also garnered nearly one hundred thousand new names and addresses of conservative donors. The result? Without those names, Ronald Reagan likely would never have been president of the United States. By the time the 1980 campaign got under way Reagan had built a mailing list of over a quarter of a million donors.[55] In a sense, those quarter of a million people *were* the conservative movement, and Reagan could contact them in the wink of an eye. He could raise the money needed, and communicate directly with his most loyal supporters at the same time. No other candidate had anything remotely resembling such a base.

Reagan had learned, of course, from Barry Goldwater. Many of Reagan's supporters were the same people who had sent little checks to Goldwater. In 1964, Goldwater's campaign had felt the first great impact of direct mail. Until then, most money for Republican presidential candidates had come from wealthy contributors and large corporations, usually in large checks. The Republican National Committee had twenty-five thousand or so donors on its lists who could be counted on to pony up when needed and who, as a result, called the shots. But Goldwater was not a traditional top-down Republican, but a true man of the grassroots. As the campaign got under way, his fundraisers realized that the big Republican money would not be available to him, so they turned to his grassroots base. The results were nothing short of spectacular: over five hundred thousand people sent in checks[56]—checks for five, ten, twenty-five, and occasionally fifty or a hundred dollars arrived at the Goldwater headquarters by the mailbag full. When the campaign was finished, campaign financing had changed forever.

But so had something else. He who pays the piper calls the tune, and no longer could the fat cats have that honor. Control of the nominating process had suddenly shifted to the grassroots, which meant to the people, the conservatives. No other factor was as important in purging the liberal Eastern Establishment from the Republican Party than direct-mail fund-raising. From 1964 on, the little people, which meant the conservatives, would have their say in the nominating process, in the way the Republican National Committee was run, and ultimately in who would control the party.

It is the same donors—the individual, committed conservatives around the country—who finance the Christian right. According to former secretary of energy Don Hodel, who served as the chief operations officer of both the Christian Coalition and Focus on the Family, virtually all of the money—and it is a great deal of money—comes through the mail.[57] "Who would have ever heard Jerry Falwell's voice outside of Lynchburg, Virginia," asked Richard Viguerie, "without direct mail?"[58]

Direct mail is crucially important to conservative organizations. Individual donors still make up the bulk of the money given to conservative causes, and during and after the Reagan years, there was a vast increase in both the number of such donors and the amount they gave. In recent years the Heritage Foundation, the largest conservative think tank, reported that over twice as much of its money came from individuals as from foundations, 59 percent to 27 percent. And small, direct-mail donors often become large donors. According to Heritage's John von Kannon, 60 percent of the checks for over ten thousand dollars come from people who started as small direct-mail donors. "We had a donor whose first gift was twenty-five dollars," said von Kannon. "Three years ago, he wrote a check for $10 million."[59]

I myself was involved in something that serves as a good example of the power of direct-mail fund-raising and the response of conservative donors to a good cause. During the spring of 1992, while serving as president of Regnery Publishing, I was approached by Sergeant Stacey Koon, the Los Angeles police officer who had been in charge of the arrest of Rodney King. Koon and three of his colleagues had been acquitted of widely publicized charges of excessive use of force in the arrest, whereupon the most serious race riot since the 1960s engulfed Los Angeles. The results were staggering: fifty-five people killed, over two thousand injured, hundreds of millions of dollars of property damaged, and a lingering legacy of hatred and injustice. Koon, who had swiftly become the most notorious and hated cop in the country, wrote a book about his experiences and sent it to me. After careful and extended research, including a lengthy visit with Koon and his family in Los Angeles, I decided to publish it.

Previously, President George Bush, running hard for re-election against Bill Clinton, had announced that he had ordered the Justice Department to see if there was sufficient evidence to file federal civil rights charges against Koon and his fellow officers.

The more I learned about the case, and the better I got to know

Koon and his family, the more I realized that a real travesty of justice was being committed. I was convinced not only that Koon was innocent (as the jury in Simi Valley had found), but that the federal government had no business getting involved. The policemen had had their day in court and did not need another go-round, but the worst sort of politics was being played, and the usual grandstanders and self-righteous civil rights agitators were eager to stir up trouble, no matter how trumped-up the charges. Koon was facing the full force of federal prosecutors and the FBI, who had been as much as told by the president to get a conviction, whatever the cost; without the means to present a vigorous defense, Koon was likely to go to prison.

So I called Bruce Eberle, an old friend in the direct-mail business, told him what I thought, and asked him to try to raise money for Koon's defense. Eberle and I drafted a letter appealing for funds and ran it past Koon and Ira Saltzman, his Los Angles lawyer. Bruce thereupon assembled a list of fifty thousand known conservative donors, which he offered to mail at no risk to us. Any money that came back would pay for the mailing costs first, Bruce explained, and the rest would go to Koon's defense. The first mailing brought in well over fifty thousand dollars, and thirty thousand dollars went right to Koon.

We continued to mail under the auspices of the Stacey Koon Defense Fund, using Koon's new book, *Presumed Guilty*, as a premium, and money arrived by the bagful.[60] In August, Koon and his fellow officers were indicted by a federal grand jury; in April 1993, Koon and one of the other officers were convicted and the other two acquitted. In August, Koon was sentenced to thirty months in a federal prison. His expenses, by this time, were huge, but we were able to pay them in full.

Over the next three years, we raised enough money to pay all of Koon's legal expenses. The majority of liberals, cop-haters, and a gaggle of congressional Democrats, most loudly Maxine Waters, objected to what they thought was an insufficient sentence, and the Clinton Justice Department, only too happy to oblige, appealed the sentence on those grounds. The circuit court of appeals agreed with them, so I hired my friend Ted Olson, with whom I had worked closely in the Reagan Justice Department, and who would subsequently defend George W. Bush's defeat of Al Gore, to take the case to the U.S. Supreme Court. The Court agreed to hear the case, and reversed the circuit court in a

9–0 ruling, holding that the thirty-month sentence was reasonable, and *Koon* v. *United States* became the established case interpreting federal sentencing guidelines.[61] In the meantime, we raised enough money to support Koon's wife and five children for the duration of his incarceration, defended him in a civil case brought by Rodney King (we won hands down), and had money left over for his children's education. Altogether, we sent tens of millions of pieces of mail and raised over $4 million from over sixty thousand people, after expenses. It is fair to say that we educated millions of people on the merits of the case and on questions of justice generally with the mail (we also distributed over fifty thousand copies of Koon's book).

Without direct mail, and without the mailing lists that had been compiled over the previous thirty years, there would have been no money raised for Sergeant Koon, his case would have been without defense and subject to the full force of the Department of Justice, and a fair hearing would likely have not happened. As it was, justice was done.

CHAPTER NINE

The Law, the Courts, and the Constitution

The United States Constitution, Russell Kirk claimed, has been the most successful conservative device in the history of the world.[1] The Constitution establishes the basis of what American conservatives believe government should do—establish federalism, protect states' rights and religious freedom, establish an effective criminal justice system and representative government, and above all, protect citizens against unbridled government power. According to Kirk, "The application and enforcement of the Constitution converted that document, initially a species of compromise between two powerful factions in the States, into the sword of Federalism."[2] Writing in *National Review*, Frank Meyer outlined the conservative understanding of the Constitution as "restriction of government to its proper functions: within government, tension and balance between local and central power; within the Federal Government, tension and balance between the coordinate branches."[3]

Starting in the early 1950s, several liberal Supreme Court justices, in large part, rewrote the American Constitution in such a way as to make it virtually unrecognizable and, in so doing, polarized the left and the right more than any other single force in the country.

The essence of the Constitution is quite simple: it establishes the federal government in its three branches and enumerates the powers of each. It establishes the separation of powers among the three branches of government, and sets forth the concept of federalism. The first ten amendments—the Bill of Rights—establish the idea of limited government by protecting people against unbridled government power; the Tenth Amendment itself specifies clearly that all power not specifically reserved to the federal government belongs to the states and the citizenry. It is unfortunately accurate to say that liberals are ready to distort the Constitution in order to expand the power of the federal government over individuals and take on activities properly reserved for the states. Conservatives find the Constitution just fine the way it is. Asked what he would have added to the Constitution if he were to have found himself at the Constitutional Convention in Philadelphia in 1787, Supreme Court Justice Clarence Thomas answered, "Don't make stuff up that is not already in here."[4]

More important, conservatives believe, to a greater extent than liberals, in process, convention, and structure as the sources of civil society and social order. To liberals, politics reigns supreme, short-term gains are more important than the long term, and traditions and long-established structures are expendable. It is no accident that few liberals believe in originalism (which we will discuss in due course). "What is conservatism?" asked Abraham Lincoln in his famed Cooper Union Address. "Is it not the adherence to the old and tried against the new and untried?"

Not so long ago the federal courts were considered the least corruptible branch of the government, the branch that protected what many felt made America unique: the rule of law, limited government, property rights, individual rights, and religious liberty.

Conservatives consider the framers of the Constitution the first conservatives. The American Revolution was a necessary antecedent to the adoption of the Constitution; it was not an innovating upheaval but a (conservative) restoration of colonial prerogatives or, as Edmund Burke described it, "a revolution not made, but prevented."[5] The king and the British Parliament had inflicted injustices on the colonies— exorbitant tax rates, unreasonable regulations—which flew in the face of the colonists' concept of liberty and spurred them to rise up to protect and preserve the traditional freedoms of British subjects. George Washington, John Adams, Alexander Hamilton, James Madison, and James Monroe are true American heroes and the intellectual godfathers of the American conservative movement. To them, limited government, states' rights, and the protection of private property were crucial to maintaining liberty, the cornerstones of the sort of civil society they foresaw.

The Federalist Papers, written by Hamilton, Madison, and John Jay as newspaper articles to explain the purpose and meaning of the Constitution, became, in a sense, the founding documents of American conservatism. Federalism, one of the conservative movement's guiding lights, provided, the *Federalist* authors believed, the best way of providing a safeguard against tyranny.

For nearly 150 years, the Constitution remained the unquestioned authority for American conservatives, and indeed, for most Americans of whatever persuasion. But after World War II, conservatives saw a new threat to constitutional order, i.e., FDR's radical attacks on the structure of American politics which initiated a form of democratic socialism totally foreign to the American republic.[6] As Frank Meyer pointed out, FDR had profoundly altered the political system by seizing for the presidency vast power from Congress, shackling the individual, and sapping the power of the states.[7] Conservatives were appalled at Roosevelt's court-packing plan to expand the size of the Supreme Court to fifteen judges in order to give him a majority, which they viewed as an outright assault on the constitutional order. They were equally appalled at his explanation for doing so: "We have," Roosevelt argued, "reached the point as a Nation where we must take action to save the Constitution from the Court and the Court from itself."[8] The Roosevelt Supreme Court may not have been as tumultuous as what was to follow in the 1950s and 1960s, but it certainly laid the groundwork. According to University of Chicago law professor and libertarian Richard Epstein, "The New Deal Court . . . indicated both expansive federal powers and limited protection of individual rights of liberty and property against both federal and state regulation. The transformation represents the defining moment in modern American constitutional law—the Court's shift toward the big government model that continues to dominate today."[9]

Though the Supreme Court acquiesced to FDR's demands by standing by tamely as he restructured the federal government, conservatives had a generally high opinion of the federal courts, particularly the Supreme Court. In his book *The American Cause*, published in 1957, Russell Kirk wrote:

> In popular respect, the Supreme Court stands even
> higher than the Congress and the President. . . . No
> other judicial body in all the world is so powerful

and so reverenced as is the Supreme Court of the
United States. For Americans feel that the Supreme
Court, whether or not they agree with its particular
decisions at a particular time, in the long run shelters and represents the American principle of liberty
under law and the American principle of a government of laws, not of men.[10]

Barry Goldwater, in *The Conscience of a Conservative*, called the
Constitution "a system of restraints against the natural tendency of government to expand in the direction of absolutism."[11] It was intended,
said Goldwater, not to establish a democracy but to "frustrate a tyranny
of the masses and self-seeking demagogues." The Constitution should
be strictly construed, he wrote, and noted that nothing in it sanctioned
federal intrusion into such matters as agriculture and education. According to Felix Morley, former president of Haverford College and one
of the founders of *Human Events*, American conservatism was simply
"Constitutionalism, in a strict rather than pliable interpretation."[12]

By Eisenhower's election in 1952, all nine Supreme Court justices
had been appointed by either FDR or his successor, Harry Truman,
and the Court generally reflected the politics and philosophy of the
Democratic Party. Ironically, Eisenhower's first Supreme Court appointment, Chief Justice Earl Warren, in September 1953, drove the
American system sharply to the left. Warren was a powerful and influential justice; after John Marshall, he was the most influential chief
justice in history. The "Warren Court," which extended several years
beyond the retirement of Warren in 1969, drastically altered the balance of power among the three branches of the federal government
and changed the concept of federalism established over the preceding
century and a half. These changes, together with the subject matter
of the cases decided by the Warren Court, had a huge impact on the
conservative movement.

But first let me add a word about the circumstances surrounding the
new chief justice's appointment. Earl Warren was the popular Republican governor of California, first elected in 1942. He began his public
career in 1925 as an assistant prosecutor in the Alameda County District Attorney's Office in Oakland—the same office, the same position,

in which, several years later, Edwin Meese III would serve. Warren was elected California attorney general in 1938, and was involved in one of the most controversial activities of his public career—the relocation and incarceration during World War II of Japanese-Americans living on the West Coast. Japan was perceived as an enemy of the United States as early as 1940, and the West Coast Japanese as part of that threat. Attorney General Warren believed that the Japanese people in California were a threat to law-abiding citizens, not unlike the threat posed by organized crime figures or Communists. California was, in Warren's view, a paradise for law-abiding natives, and he was prepared to protect its citizenry from foreign enemies on domestic soil.[13]

As attorney general, after Pearl Harbor, Warren declared that "the Japanese situation as it exists in this state today may well be the Achilles' heel of the entire civilian defense effort."[14] He strongly advocated relocation, which he believed could only be accomplished by the army and by force.[15]

Warren, however, opposed internment for Germans and Italians, because "they were no different from anybody else."[16] In a word, Warren was a practicing provincial, xenophobic racist. One of his biographers noted that "Warren has never publicly expressed regret or admitted error for his part of the Japanese evacuation."[17] Interestingly, FBI director J. Edgar Hoover, hated by liberals, opposed internment, telling Roosevelt that there was little if any evidence that Americans of Japanese origin were a security threat.

Warren was elected governor of California in 1942. Although he was a Republican, he has often been described as part of the California progressive movement, a liberal who believed that government should undertake an affirmative role in solving problems. He later wrote in his memoirs that he was a Republican only because California "was an overwhelmingly Republican State."[18]

Warren ran reluctantly as Tom Dewey's vice-presidential running mate in 1948 (Dewey referred to him as "that dumb Swede") and was an on-again off-again candidate for president in 1952; he arrived at the 1952 convention in Philadelphia, where Eisenhower narrowly beat Ohio senator Robert Taft, with too little support to win the nomination, but enough to twist arms. Some accounts claim that Eisenhower cut a deal with Warren to the effect that if Warren could deliver the California delegation and Ike were subsequently elected, Warren would get the first open seat on the Supreme Court.

Then in September 1953, Chief Justice Fred Vinson, appointed by Truman in 1946, died suddenly of a heart attack, just eight months after Eisenhower took office, and some say that Warren was on the phone within hours calling in his chit. Eisenhower, who had probably forgotten all about the deal, reportedly told Warren that he had not meant the chief justice's seat, and Warren would have to wait. No deal, said Warren, you said the first opening and this is the first opening. Ike gave in and appointed Warren by a recess appointment shortly after Vinson's funeral. Warren was subsequently confirmed in March 1954.[19]

But Warren had never been a judge, and Eisenhower had no way of knowing how he would rule; the appointment was nothing more than a shot in the dark. Party loyalty was about the only gauge that presidents had in determining how judges would rule on cases until well into the 1980s. But that story anon.

Warren's nearly sixteen-year tenure as chief justice of the Supreme Court, from October 1953 until June 1969, lurched the country sharply to the left and would ultimately spawn a revival in conservative legal circles that would become one of the most vibrant and intellectually provocative efforts on the right. Earl Warren, William Brennan, Hugo Black, and William O. Douglas, probably more than any other liberals, provided American conservatism with badly needed stimulus. Conservatives often object to being called reactionaries, but in the case of the United States Supreme Court, their reaction helped to build the movement.

The Warren Court polarized the left and the right on several fronts. First was its impact on the substance of the cases it was deciding—desegregating the schools, banning prayer and Bible reading in the schools, reapportioning the state legislatures and the House of Representatives, forcing the states to reorder laws concerning voting rights, rewriting state criminal justice laws, abolishing all state laws limiting abortion, and ordering states and the federal government to institute plans of affirmative action, to name a few. Earl Warren and his colleagues launched what would become known as the "culture wars," which catapulted the "social conservative" movement into becoming one of its most powerful factions. The Warren Court brought notoriety to the Court, thrusting the judiciary into the very center of the battle between liberals and conservatives, and in so doing, toppling the courts from the most respected to the most derided branch of government. In short, the Warren Court arbitrarily *arrogated* power from the congressional and the executive branches to itself. The Constitution had been twisted beyond recognition.

Conservatives also viewed what the Warren Court was doing as antidemocratic and elitist. Judges who substituted their own vision for that of the American people and their representatives in government took on the role of rulers who were convinced that their view was far superior to that of the common man. Their judicial opinions, as far as conservatives were concerned, demonstrated a distrust of the American electorate, a distrust of local officials such as school board members, police officers, governors, and even jurors.

Conservatives agreed with Justice Hugo Black, who, in a bitter dissent in the case of *Tinker* v. *Des Moines Independent Community School District*, argued that local officials should be permitted to determine the extent to which freedom of expression should be allowed in their public schools. The *Tinker* case overturned a school rule banning the wearing of black armbands to protest the Vietnam War, saying such protests were protected by the First Amendment. Local school officials, Black contended, knew better than federal judges how to run their schools.[20]

The Constitution fashioned the federal courts to be the least intrusive branch of government. For 150 years or so, they had conformed to Hamilton's assurance in *Federalist* 78 that the judiciary would be the least dangerous of the three branches of government. The courts had in large part acted as a brake on the other branches of the government until the middle 1950s, the exception being the Court's use of the commerce clause of the Fourteenth Amendment during the Roosevelt administration, which was cited repeatedly to justify expansive New Deal programs.[21]

But that all changed. The Warren Court took what had begun during FDR's tenure and expanded it exponentially, so that virtually every constitutional case it decided transferred power from the states to the federal government, and almost always enhanced and enlarged the power of the federal courts.

Conservatives were outraged. *National Review* and *Human Events*, along with conservative columnists and editorial writers, let out blasts of protest with each of the Warren Court's expansive decisions. In 1966, Brent Bozell, who had left *National Review* to found the Catholic magazine *Triumph*, published *The Warren Revolution*, which provided the historical, philosophical, and political foundation to understand the hammer blows being dealt the legal system and the Constitution. Bozell, with a law degree from Yale, analyzed case by case what the Warren Court was up to, explaining along the way the various parts of the Constitution that were at stake. More important, Bozell used history and logic to refute, one by one, the arguments made by the academic and intellectual apologists for the liberalization of the law, for the first time including a historical analysis of judicial review.[22]

Earl Warren, as chief justice, was the front man on the Supreme Court. But he was not the most liberal nor the real architect of the liberalism fomented by the Court. That honor went to Eisenhower's third appointment, William J. Brennan, a Democratic state supreme court judge from New Jersey.

The 1956 election was approaching when Associate Justice Sherman Minton announced that he would retire, allowing Eisenhower to get some political benefit for his re-election bid. He wanted a Catholic from the Northeast, and a sitting judge, but more important, a "judicial conservative" who would decide cases according to the law rather than his personal preference, balancing Warren. His first choice was John A. Danaher from Connecticut, who had served in the Senate from 1939 until 1945, and whom Eisenhower had appointed to the U.S. Court of Appeals. But Danaher was a conservative and had been a close ally and staunch supporter of Robert A. Taft. Moreover, the New York liberal Republicans were desperate to stop Danaher, who, they knew, would try to return the Court to its constitutional place. They urged their man in the Eisenhower administration, Herbert Brownell, the attorney general, to do everything in his power to stop Danaher. Brownell had to come up with an alternative quickly and, arriving early at a meeting of the American Bar Association to give a speech, listened as a member of the New Jersey Supreme Court spoke to the assembled lawyers about court reform. Brownell was impressed with what the fellow had to say, and inquiring about him was told his name was William J. Brennan, that he was a well-regarded judge, a moderate Democrat of Irish extraction, and seemed to have all of the qualifications Eisenhower was looking for. Brownell hurried back to the White House to tell Eisenhower that he had found the perfect candidate; the fact that Brennan was a Democrat only made him more appealing, as Ike wanted to demonstrate that his administration was bipartisan. After Brennan was offered the job, Eisenhower got a call from his old friend Arthur Vanderbilt, chief judge of the New Jersey Supreme Court, a Republican, who wanted to know why Ike was appointing a liberal Democrat to the high court. No liberal, Ike replied, and referred Vanderbilt to the speech Brennan had delivered before the ABA. After a long pause, Vanderbilt told Eisenhower that Brennan had not written the speech, he had; Vanderbilt had sent Brennan to deliver it in his place, as he had laryngitis.[23] Brennan was subsequently confirmed by the Senate with only one opposing vote, that of fellow Irish Catholic Joe McCarthy of Wisconsin.[24]

Brennan never sought the limelight and was largely overlooked by the public. In a piece that I coauthored in 1984 with Stephen Markman, now a member of the Michigan Supreme Court, and published in *National Review*, we concluded that:

> An examination of Brennan's opinions, and his influence upon the opinions of his colleagues, suggests that there is no individual in this country, on or off the Court, who has had a more profound and sustained impact upon public policy in the United States for the past 27 years. Perhaps more than anyone else, Justice Brennan is responsible for the current dominance of the Supreme Court within our constitutional system, and for the transformation of the federal judiciary from its traditional status as a body that interpreted the laws into a "super legislature" where the judges' own policy choices become supreme law.[25]

Brennan, according to Edward V. Heck, professor of political science at San Diego State University, "even more than the Chief Justice . . . deserves to be remembered as the cutting edge of Warren Court liberalism."[26] It was Brennan who provided the intellectual horsepower during the early part of the Warren Court, and in the process, the Court adopted his liberal agenda for the country. Brennan had no qualms about substituting his own liberalism for the law, nor about finding a remedy, whether or not it existed in the Constitution or the law, for every wrong that offended him.

Not long after Eisenhower retired in 1961, he was asked if he had made any mistakes as president. "Yes, two," Ike responded, "and they are both sitting on the Supreme Court."[27]

Desegregating the Schools

When Warren joined the Supreme Court in late September 1953, the Court was mired in debate over the thorny issue of school segregation. *Brown v. Board of Education*, one of five cases consolidated by the Court for purposes of argument, involved the question of whether the separate but equal doctrine, established in 1896 in the notorious case of *Plessy v. Ferguson*, should be reversed, permitting the Court to find that segregation in the schools violated the equal protection clause of the Fourteenth Amendment. The *Brown* cases had been argued some months before Chief Justice Vinson died, and the Court was badly split: four members thought that *Plessy* should be reversed. Three, including Chief Justice Vinson, thought it should be retained, and two, Felix Frankfurter and Robert Jackson, did not like segregation but could not find adequate grounds to overturn the *Plessy* case.[28] Initially, Frankfurter did not think he could rule that segregation in the states was unconstitutional, and said he could not accept a broad rule that "it's unconstitutional to treat a Negro differently than a white."[29] But soon he began to change his mind and was frustrated that a majority could not be cobbled together, believing that a case as important as one desegregating the schools should come from a united court. When he heard that Vinson had died, he commented caustically, "This is the first indication that I have ever had that there is a God."[30]

After Warren had taken his seat on the Court and the case was reargued, he applied his considerable personal and political skills to persuade his eight colleagues to vote to end school desegregation. It was his first case, and arguably his most notorious; his ability to pull together a unanimous majority established him as a formidable leader.

Warren's opinion in the *Brown* case was not based on the law, or constitutional doctrine, reasoning, or precedent. It was based on social science, on Warren's notion of the importance of education and the effects of racial prejudice. As University of Virginia law professor G. Edward White says in his biography of Earl Warren:

> The *Brown* decision was a classic manifestation of mid-twentieth-century liberal theory in its effort, through the affirmation of principles such as equality of opportunity, to fuse the idea of affirmative, paternalistic governmental action with the idea of protection for civil liberties. *Brown* also marked the origins of Earl Warren's stance as a liberal judge.[31]

In respect to the *Plessy* case, which had caused a great deal of agonizing, Warren's solution was simply to overturn it with a sentence or two, ruling that since *Plessy* involved segregation in railroad cars, it had nothing to do with education, and, ergo, was not an issue. Justice Robert Jackson's clerk at the time was a young lawyer named William Rehnquist, who prepared a memo called "A Random Thought on the Segregation Cases," which unambiguously stated that "*Plessy vs. Ferguson* was right and should be reaffirmed."[32]

The Supreme Court later ordered that integration of public schools proceed "with all deliberate speed" and, in one of the few such instances in history, several states in the South announced they were not going to comply and adopted a plan referred to as "massive resistance." Even President Eisenhower, for political reasons, declined to support the *Brown* decision, telling reporters it would make no difference one way or the other. "It is difficult through law and through force to change a man's heart," he explained.[33]

Brown may not have been the first shot by the Supreme Court across the conservative movement's bow, but it was among the loudest, despite the distasteful subject matter of the case. "An overwhelming majority of the people in the South," wrote James Jackson Kilpatrick, editor of the Richmond, Virginia, *News Leader*, "believe in the prudence and wisdom of essential race segregation in the Southern States. They feel an excellent case can be made for utilizing the powers of their states to protect, as far as may be possible, the integrity of the white and Negro races."[34] But most conservatives outside the South, and many southerners as well, cared little about the merits of integration versus segregation of the public schools, and *Brown* did raise two issues that, for conservatives, were much more important: First was the question of federalism and the Supreme Court's willingness to alter the balance of power between the federal government and the states. Conservatives believed that if the Court could abolish a power exercised by a few states, a precedent was created that allowed all powers exercised by all states to be abolished as well. The second question was: what were the Supreme Court and the federal courts in general doing in this dispute in the first place? The courts were not the legislature, were accountable to no one, and had no means of measuring how people from whom all power was supposed to derive felt about an issue. Deciding disputes between litigants was one thing. But legislating from the bench was another, and contrary to the Constitution. According to Kilpatrick, "The Supreme Court undertook to accomplish by judicial fiat what the Tenth Amendment declares can be accomplished by the Constitution alone: The court undertook to prohibit the States from exercising a power they had reserved to themselves."[35] The law was supposed to be permanent. Changes of the nature now being administered by nine unelected men had always come about slowly and deliberately through decisions made by the legislature, which took into account the attitudes of the people. What the Supreme Court did in *Brown* shattered, once and for all, the sense of permanence and set the pattern for future innovations. To conservatives, the loss was overwhelming.

The Warren Court and Anti-Communism—Red Monday

Monday, June 17, 1957, was not a good day for conservatives, particularly those concerned about Communism. On that day the Warren Court handed down four cases, all dealing with subversives and Communists; the combined result drastically altered the approach by government in its fight against subversion. Conservatives had a double-pronged objection: First was the substance of the cases—the ability of the government to fight Communist subversives. Second was the Court's propensity to step into areas in which it had no business—all to protect the rights of a small group of "victims" against the best interests of the country.

June 17 became known among conservatives as "Red Monday," a takeoff on "Black Monday," May 27, 1935, when the Court had gutted the New Deal legislative program.

The Warren Court had largely gutted America's domestic security program put together by Congress as the Soviet threat increased. It was a combination of civil and criminal sanctions against Communists, former Communists, and fellow travelers, and included congressional investigations, loyalty investigations by government agencies, mainly the Justice Department, and loyalty oaths required of public employees. During the 1956 term, the Court ruled against the government in twelve separate cases involving Communists, leaving the government's domestic security program in shambles. By the end of the term, four cases remained involving Communists, and the Court handed down all of them on that one day in June 1957.

The first, *Watkins* v. *United States*, involved testimony before the House Un-American Activities Committee (HUAC) by John Watkins, a suspected Communist who had been held in contempt for refusing to divulge the names of fellow party members. Earl Warren concluded that Watkins's conviction was invalid under the due process clause of the Fifth Amendment, and that HUAC had too much power, having "been allowed, in essence, to define its own authority." Moreover, said the chief justice, such investigations could "lead to ruthless exposure of private lives in order to gather data that is [sic] neither desired by Congress nor useful to it."[36] Congress, in other words, did not have the power to conduct unlimited inquiries unrelated to a congressional function.

The second case, *Yates* v. *United States*, threw out the convictions of fourteen alleged Communists prosecuted under the Smith Act, which made it a crime to advocate violent overthrow of the United States government, and in the third, *Sweezy* v. *New Hampshire*, the Court reversed the contempt conviction of a professor for refusing to answer questions by the New Hampshire attorney general about his past political activities. Said Warren, "Mere orthodoxy or dissent from the prevailing mores is not to be condemned: The absence of such voices would be a symptom of grave illness." Warren went on to say that the rights of political expression and academic freedom were virtually absolute, and that he could "not now conceive of any circumstance wherein a state interest would justify infringement of rights in these fields."[37]

The last of the Red Monday cases reversed the conviction of John Stewart Service, a former State Department employee and "China hand" who had been fired by Secretary of State Dean Acheson in 1951 for disloyalty to the United States. Service, notorious for his activity on behalf of Communist China, had been named by Joe McCarthy as one of the State Department employees responsible for the loss of China to the Communists.

Conservatives did not stand idly by. *National Review* was livid:

> The Supreme Court struts on in its drive to subvert American political institutions. Of the three decisions last week, the boldest, the most impudent, and the most anarchical was that calling for the reversal of the contempt citation against John Watkins. The meaning of that decision is stupefying, for it sets up the Supreme Court as arbiter of the intentions of Congress.

And on the role the Supreme Court was assuming, *National Review* went on:

> [The Supreme Court] is sitting no longer as a judicial bench but as the nation's supreme legislature, unmaking *and making* the nation's laws, often in arrogant disregard of the explicit words and recorded intentions of the constitutionally designated legislative body.[38]

The charge would dominate conservatives' criticism of the Supreme Court for the next fifty years.[39]

U.S. News & World Report, conservatives' favorite newsweekly at the time, was shocked and disgusted, both at the Court's abuse of its own power and at its broadening the rights of individuals, while limiting the power of the states and Congress.[40] Even more troubling was the fact that the Warren Court had made it much more difficult to prosecute Communists and subversives at a time when the rapacity of the Soviet Union for conquest was apparent to all.

Americans felt particularly threatened by Communism in 1957—the Hungarian Revolution had occurred just a year before and most Americans were still appalled at American inability to support the courageous freedom fighters, who were felled brutally by Soviet tanks. (Sputnik would go up four months later, reminding Americans that the Soviet Union was a very tough competitor for what they had thought was their dominant position in the world.) It was not long before Robert Welch added Warren to the John Birch Society's list of "active and conscious members" of the international Communist conspiracy, with a grassroots movement to impeach Warren riding on its heels, complete with bumper stickers, rallies, and fundraisers held across the country.

Congress reacted as well. A spate of legislation was introduced to limit the power of the federal courts, such as the proposal by Senator Russell Long of Louisiana to amend the Constitution to require a reconfirmation of all justices every twelve years.[41] But it was all sound and fury, and signified nothing. The upshot of the "Red Monday" cases was to provide the right-wing anti-Communist movement with one of its most potent arguments—that control of subversives by the federal government was ineffective. If many conservatives cared little about school segregation, they cared a great deal about Communist subversion.

REAPPORTIONMENT—ONE MAN, ONE VOTE

Until 1962, the state legislatures determined questions concerning congressional and legislative apportionment and redistricting. Apportionment was a political question, and the federal courts had no jurisdiction in such cases. Earl Warren, William O. Douglas, and William Brennan were eager to find areas to reform; their chance arose when cases involving the makeup of the state legislatures reached the high court's docket. Legislative districts were divided according to factors such as size, wealth, and population, which usually failed to reflect the growth of urban and suburban areas and the decline of populations in rural areas, often resulting in dramatic differences in representation. In 1960 in California, for example, Los Angeles County had one state Senate seat for its 6 million people, while the three smallest counties in the state, with a combined population of seventeen thousand, shared one seat (a discrepancy of which a certain former California governor was well aware). Why, Earl Warren wondered, should we not do the same for equality of representation as we did for equality in the schools? So in 1962, in *Baker v. Carr*, a case challenging the apportionment of Tennessee state legislative districts, and several other cases following on its heels, the Supreme Court proclaimed its own power over such political issues and declared that state legislative districts that were not equally populated violated the Equal Protection Clause of the Fourteenth Amendment. Needless to say, no two districts were equal, which meant that over the next several years the Supreme Court ordered the redrawing of virtually every legislative district in the country that did not meet the newly developed constitutional standard of "one man, one vote."[42] In 1964, the Court expanded its reach by asserting jurisdiction over congressional districts, too, even though the Constitution, in Article I Section 4, specifically gave that authority directly to state legislatures.

The reapportionment cases were considered by Earl Warren to be the most significant of his tenure on the Supreme Court.[43] In his mind, they were essential to freeing government from the influence of special interests, and were consistent with his concept of justice—that "every major social ill in this country can find its cure in some constitutional principle." But conservatives saw the reapportionment cases as an interpretation of the Constitution that was "neither faithful to its literal text nor consistent with the context in which it had been framed."[44] The Court had blatantly disregarded the clear and indisputable mandate of U.S. tradition, which was strict constructionism, according to Brent Bozell, and sought to "impose the ideology of equality on the American political system, notwithstanding the clear purposes of the architects of the system and irrespective even of the wishes of the people who now live under it."[45]

Conservatives were in virtually unanimous agreement with Justice Harlan, who, in his dissent, wrote that "the decision shunted aside history and judicial restraint and violated the separation of powers between legislatures and Courts," placing "basic aspects of state political systems under the pervasive overlordship of the federal judiciary."[46] He correctly predicted that the decision would be followed by a flood of partisan litigation over the makeup of political bodies. As with many of the other Warren Court cases, it was not that conservatives were concerned about the makeup of the state legislatures—the reapportionment cases largely transferred power from rural areas to the cities—but that the Court's willingness to hear such cases in the first place was an intrusion into the doctrine of federalism and states' rights. Former Nevada governor Paul Laxalt (later a senator and Ronald Reagan's best friend in Washington) expressed the opinion of most conservatives in smaller states: "I know it sure concerned the hell out of me, reapportionment did, because it meant the rural parts of the state lost their voice. We functioned as every other state did, very well with Las Vegas having one senator and Virginia City having one senator. We liked that."[47]

Conservatives in Congress reacted strongly; Illinois Senator Everett Dirksen, a Republican, proposed a constitutional amendment to override the case and allow the states to apportion legislatures as they wished. He came close to getting the necessary petitions from two-thirds of the state legislatures to require Congress to call a constitutional convention to consider the amendment, but as the legislatures themselves were reapportioned in early 1970s, the effort fizzled. The newly reapportioned legislatures, after all, were not interested in returning to the old system.

Felix Frankfurter, in his dissent in *Baker* v. *Carr* in 1962, a landmark decision of Brennan's career, warned that "there is not under our Constitution a judicial remedy for every political mischief. In a democratic society like ours, relief must come through and around popular consensus that sears the conscience of the people's representatives."[48] But to Warren, the result was all that really mattered.

PRAYER IN THE SCHOOLS AND THE ESTABLISHMENT CLAUSE

Until *Roe* v. *Wade*, the 1973 abortion case, no set of decisions by the Supreme Court was more upsetting to conservatives than those reinterpreting the establishment of the religion clause of the First Amendment.

228   ALFRED S. REGNERY

The establishment clause simply says, "Congress shall make no law respecting an establishment of religion, or prohibiting the free exercise thereof." Many schools, both public and private, traditionally started off the day with a prayer or a reading from the Bible. But, starting in 1962, the Warren Court declared that prayer and Bible-reading in public schools constituted state endorsement of religion, thereby violating the First Amendment. "Nothing," according to critic William Martin, "generated more lasting resentment against the Supreme Court and stirred more concern among conservative Christians."[49]

The Court had addressed the establishment clause before Warren's appointment, when it banned a program of religious education in public schools in 1947, holding that schools could not be used for the dissemination of religious doctrines. In the same year, in *Everson v. the Board of Education of Ewing Township, New Jersey*, the Court laid the groundwork for what would become its interpretation of the establishment clause against any religious practices in public life. Hugo Black infamously wrote for the majority:

> The "establishment of religion" clause of the First Amendment means at least this: Neither a state nor the Federal Government can set up a church. Neither can pass laws which aid one religion, aid all religions, or prefer one religion over another. . . . No tax in any amount, large or small, can be levied to support any religious activities or institutions, whatever they may be called, or whatever form they may adopt to teach or practice religion. . . . In the words of Thomas Jefferson, the clause against establishment of religion by law was intended to erect a "wall of separation between church and State."[50]

But prayer and Bible-reading were considered outside the scope of the *Everson* case and were therefore allowed to continue.

Until 1962, that is, when the Court, in a case known as *Engel v. Vitale*, declared that an officially sponsored prayer recited in public schools in New York was unconstitutional. The prayer read, in its entirety: "Almighty God, we acknowledge our dependence on Thee, and we beg Thy blessings upon us, our parents, our teachers, and our country." A year later, in a case originating in Pennsylvania, the Court found that the Lord's Prayer and Bible-reading showed the state's "official endorsement of Christian belief" and declared both unconstitutional.[51]

Following the school prayer cases, conservatives probed carefully the meaning of the framers when they proposed the First Amendment and found it had little to do with the Court's reading. The framers' concept of an established religion was, in essence, the situation that existed in many of the colonies and in Great Britain with the Church of England, an official church that occupied a privileged position with the state, was vested with certain powers denied to others, and was supported from the public treasury.[52] In 1775, nine colonies had such an arrangement, and the established church of Massachusetts was not abolished until 1833.[53] The framers did not in the least intend that the First Amendment ban all religious practices in public settings; indeed, laws requiring that those seeking public office believe in God existed long after adoption of the Bill of Rights.

Conservatives all but stumbled over examples of officially sanctioned exercises of faith that defied the Supreme Court's interpretation of the First Amendment. M. Stanton Evans, in his incisive 1994 book *The Theme Is Freedom*, asks how it is possible to reconcile the Supreme Court's reading of the First Amendment with the historical record. Evans states, "The First Amendment depicted by Black and other liberal jurists is a fabrication. The Court's alleged history is a complete misrepresentation of the record—a prime example of picking and choosing elements from the past to suit the ideological fashions of the present."[54] Erwin Griswold, dean of the Harvard Law School and LBJ's solicitor general, said, "We have a spiritual and cultural tradition of which we ought not to be deprived by judges carrying into effect . . . absolutist notions not expressed in the Constitution itself and surely never contemplated by those who put the constitutional provisions in effect. To say that they require that all trace of religion be kept out of any sort of public activity is sheer invention."[55] Billy Graham, Norman Vincent Peale, and Cardinal Spellman criticized the Court publicly, and many members of Congress denounced the ruling, calling for legislative reversal.

One of the unintended consequences of the school prayer cases was the development of a network of private Christian schools across the country. Parents and pastors joined to protect their children from the deepening secular bias in the public schools, where teachers and textbooks demeaned American history, traditional values, and Christianity, and dogmatically imposed the teaching of evolution and sex education. Thousands of alternative schools sprouted up and thrived; during the 1970s, new schools were rising at the rate of one per day (Jerry Falwell claimed it was every seven hours).[56] As tens of thousands of children made their way through these Christian schools and into colleges, both Christian and secular, they brought with them the tools to combat the reigning liberal establishment, and further swelled the ranks of the growing Christian right.[57]

Many public schools, however, defied the Court's rulings and continued to offer daily prayers and Bible distribution. Well into the 1990s, close to half of all public schools in the country continued these practices, often resulting in litigation by the ACLU and other secular groups.[58]

Restoration of legal prayer and Bible-reading continues to be a prominent item not only on the agenda of the Christian right, but among many mainline Christians as well. "There is no issue in American life in which the public will is so clear and the political establishment is so heedless," says theologian and conservative scholar Michael Novak. "The cultural and political elites have simply ignored the overwhelming support of the American people for voluntary school prayer—indeed for the role of religion and faith in the nation's life."[59] As recently as 2005, polls showed that 75 percent of all Americans thought that school prayer should be allowed in public schools. Its prohibition, Christian conservatives believe, leads to the moral breakdown of youth culture, rampant drug use, sexual promiscuity, high crime rates, the breakdown of authority, and the inability to differentiate between right and wrong.

School prayer was a potent political issue as well: In his 1964 presidential campaign, Barry Goldwater railed against the Supreme Court's exercises of "raw and naked power," and Richard Nixon castigated the Court in both his 1968 and 1972 campaigns—largely on the issue of "law and order," but on the prayer cases as well.[60] To the extent Goldwater or Nixon won evangelical votes, it was likely due to their stance on school prayer.

In both his 1976 and 1980 runs for the White House, Ronald Reagan called for a constitutional amendment to permit school prayer, but left it at that. Conservatives responded with a massive effort to force Reagan's hand—in 1982, the Leadership Institute, a Washington-based think tank, distributed over 40 million flyers supporting prayer in the schools, and busloads of students and parents rallied in front of the White House. Finally, in May 1982, with Jerry Falwell and other Christian leaders standing beside him, Reagan introduced a constitutional amendment to permit school prayer. After months of hearings, massive pressure from the Christian right, and a plea from Reagan, the Senate voted 56–44 in favor of the amendment, eleven votes short of the necessary two-thirds majority.

The Court revisited the prayer issue several times, most recently in 1992, when the question was whether brief mention of God could be included in graduation ceremonies. Despite argument by the Department of Justice that the Court should overturn its original prayer decision, the justices ruled 5–4 to ban such mentions of God. The decision further antagonized conservatives.

CRIME AND LAW ENFORCEMENT

Earl Warren felt the same way about criminals that he did about black children in segregated schools, about Communists and subversives, i.e., they deserved to be on an equal playing field, but this time with the criminal justice system. And as chief justice, he would personally see to it that the playing field was leveled. The result was an upheaval of the American criminal justice system, which conservatives used to their philosophical and political advantage for the remainder of the twentieth century.

Columnist Raymond Moley in 1931 called Warren "the most intelligent and politically independent district attorney in the United States."[61] He was known as a tough prosecutor who won some of his most difficult cases using exactly the tactics that he later found so abhorrent and declared illegal. But that was then. In the 1950s, Warren bought into the liberal notion that criminals were not really responsible for the crimes they committed, but the victims of social injustice of one sort or another. Solving the problem of crime in the 1950s and 1960s, he declared, "meant getting rid of the ghettos so that people with no schooling and no skills were no longer easy prey to all kinds of bad influence." The average criminal, he said, was being "put upon by the criminal justice system, stripped of humanity and dignity and opportunities for fair treatment."[62]

In three cases between 1959 and 1966, culminating in his famous opinion in *Miranda* v. *Arizona*, Warren rewrote the criminal procedure laws for the states.[63] He spelled out *whether* the defendant, while being interrogated by the police, was entitled to counsel and *when* he was entitled to counsel. If the police did not precisely follow the Supreme Court's rules in an arrest, the criminal would have to go free. The lengthy opinion was filled with a multitude of details about police techniques and procedure, matters that, until then, had always been determined by state and local officials.

Miranda, like *Brown* v. *Board of Education*, was almost devoid of legal reasoning. It reeked of language concerning the psychological imbalance between the police—comfortable, confident—and the poor criminal—trapped and scared. After *Miranda* came down, Warren explained that "the prosecutor under our system is not paid to convict people, but to protect the rights of the people in our community."[64] Although perhaps unconsciously so, it sounded as though Warren was interested in protecting the rights of the criminals rather than their victims. Which was, in fact, the result.

In his dissent in *Miranda*, Justice Byron White correctly predicted that "in some unknown number of cases the Court's rule will return a killer, a rapist or other criminal to the streets . . . to repeat his crime whenever it pleases him." FBI records showed that felonies increased by 89 percent between 1960 and 1967, nine times the population rate increase, and homicides were up 21 percent in the first nine months of 1968. A Gallup poll in March 1968 found that 63 percent of Americans considered the courts "too soft" on crime.[65] According to veteran criminal justice reporter Eugene Methvin, before *Miranda* "police solved more than 91 percent of murder cases, but [after *Miranda*] unsolved murders quadrupled. Robbery clearance rates dropped by more than a third. The proportion of violent crimes that went unsolved zoomed nearly 60 percent. By 1992 the activist restrictions on reasonable investigations was costing Americans more than 4,000 additional unsolved murders and 70,000 unsolved robberies every year."[66] Crime flourished.

Earl Warren's rewrite of criminal procedure spawned an industry of liberal public interest lawyers, public defenders, and criminologists, including the American Civil Liberties Union, which litigated and lobbied on behalf of criminal defendants. But it also set off a strong reaction from conservatives, galvanizing conservatives to use it as a powerful political force for the next twenty years. According to social critic Irwin Unger, "backlash Americans" (Reagan Democrats) "resented rich liberals, mostly WASPs, who defended the black militants, the minorities, and the troublemakers on spurious humanitarian or ideological grounds. . . . They demanded stricter laws and tougher punishments for criminals."[67]

Although there were many reasons besides the Warren Court's decisions for the increase in crime, conservatives used the rising crime rates to whipsaw liberals, who had little choice but to defend the Warren approach.

The criminal justice cases clarified the divide between left and right more than virtually any other issue. Liberalism, in the eyes of most rational people, seemed to have lost all sense of reality and decency. As crime surged and city dwellers huddled in their houses, as violent crimes dominated headlines day after day and civil order seemed a thing of the past, and as liberal judges continued to rule in favor of criminals rather than their victims, the conservative position, the reasonable position, resounded with people who had once been the backbone of the Democratic Party and postwar liberalism.

Many other Warren Court cases riled conservatives. Economic regulation, particularly that involving antitrust and labor relations, was strengthened, bringing the small and independent business community into alliance with conservatives. More prominently, the Court stretched the scope of the First Amendment beyond recognition in free speech cases. Although Warren took a strong view *against* the wholesale distribution of obscenity, his opinions opened the door to subsequent cases that would allow it, further stirring up Christian and social conservatives.

Liberals loved the Warren Court. It all but completed the destruction of federalism in the United States: Where the issue involved social problems and the choice was between the states and Washington,

Washington always won. Where the choice was between big government and small government, big government always won. The Warren Court merged Kennedy's high-sounding rhetoric with Johnson's arm-twisting ability to push things through the system, achieving what liberals wanted with none of the give-and-take and political constraints essential to the American democratic process.

Warren's legacy would be most evident in the expansion of what he termed "social justice." But perhaps an even greater legacy was his opening the floodgates of judicial activism and the lack of "judicial restraint." He elicited a conservative war cry heard thirty-five years after Warren's retirement, one that begat a new activism and a new area of conservative intellectual endeavor. Warren's notion of a "living Constitution," his idea that judges "must draw [the Constitution's] meaning from the evolving standards of decency that mark the progress of a maturing society,"[68] would allow, as Eugene Methvin put it, "every judge with an itch for political power to set himself up as a high priest free to impose his vision of 'evolving standards of decency' on the rest of America."[69] "Judicial restraint" became one of the most effective arrows in conservatism's political quiver.

ABORTION

No Supreme Court case in recent memory has had the political impact of *Roe v. Wade*, handed down in January 1973. By that time, Earl Warren was safely retired and writing his memoirs. But the Court continued to be laden with controversy. Toward the end of the Johnson administration, during the summer of 1968, Warren announced that he would retire once a new justice was confirmed, which was immediately interpreted as a way for Warren to influence who his successor would be. Warren finally retired in June 1969, his replacement to be named by his old political nemesis Richard Nixon.

Nixon, who had been in the White House for five years by the time *Roe* was decided, was a self-described "strict constructionist" on constitutional matters, had criticized Warren and his colleagues in both the 1968 and 1972 campaigns, and had promised to reshape the Supreme Court by appointing only "strict constructionists," especially on law and order issues. He had appointed appellate judges Warren Burger (in 1969, as the new chief justice to replace Warren) and Harry Blackmun (in 1970, after two southerners, G. Harold Carswell and Clement Haynesworth, were defeated in the Senate), and in 1971, Nixon appointed Lewis Powell, a prominent lawyer from Richmond, Virginia, who had served as president of the American Bar Association; and William Rehnquist, a Justice Department lawyer, to replace John Harlan and Hugo Black, respectively, thus satisfying, he thought, his conservative constituency.

Nixon did not really know much about any of his nominees except that they were well-connected Republicans who had no doubt told him that they were "strict constructionists." Unfortunately for Nixon, with the exception of Rehnquist, they were anything but. As mentioned, the Warren Court extended well beyond Warren's retirement—William Brennan, the brains behind the whole enterprise, stayed on the Court for twenty years after Warren's retirement, leading the remaining Warren judges, and Nixon's choices, to finish what Earl Warren had started.

Roe v. *Wade* was decided by a margin of 7–2, but only after it was reargued in order to accommodate Powell and Rehnquist, who were confirmed after the first argument. Chief Justice Burger had also delayed the case until after the 1972 election in order to protect Nixon, who was running for re-election against George McGovern, from having to deal with the abortion issue.

Harry Blackmun wrote the majority opinion, which was based largely on his personal preferences; Blackmun had served as general counsel to the Mayo Clinic in Minnesota, and Eisenhower had appointed him a federal judge in 1959. In his Senate hearings Strom Thurmond, a veteran conservative, had pronounced him a "strict constructionist," and he was unanimously confirmed. With only a breezy nod to the Constitution, his opinion in the *Roe* case included twelve pages on the history of abortion, twelve pages on the medical questions involved, and two short paragraphs on the Constitution. He concluded that the Fourteenth Amendment "is broad enough to encompass a woman's decision whether or not to terminate her pregnancy."[70] The effect was enormous: It voided laws restricting abortion, in one way or another, in virtually every state, and imposed rules permitting more abortions than in any other Western democracy.[71]

Catholic leaders were aghast: Terence Cardinal Cooke of New York called the decision "shocking and horrifying," and John Cardinal Krol of Philadelphia, president of the National Council of Catholic Bishops, thought it was "an unspeakable tragedy for this nation."[72] Politically, the case was a bombshell; after more than thirty years, abortion remains a wrenching and explosive force in America. "Few issues in American life," according to social commentator William Martin, "stir more passion or generate more high-profile political activism, and appear less amenable to satisfactory resolution than abortion."[73] For conservatives, the *Roe* decision had a massive political impact; it brought more people into the conservative movement, raised more money, and generated more political activism than virtually any other single issue in the history of the movement—even the prayer cases. Millions consider themselves conservatives because of their opposition to *Roe* v. *Wade*. For liberals, it had an equally massive impact, and preserving the right to abortion became their number-one cause.

Once again, the decision was not only incendiary on its merits. *Roe* v. *Wade* was judicial activism at its worst. The injury was intensified because the majority opinion was written by Blackmun, and joined by both Burger and Powell—all Nixon appointees. Only Rehnquist, Nixon's last appointee, dissented, joined by Justice Byron White, a Kennedy appointee.

There was no constitutional justification for the reasoning in *Roe*, and the majority knew it. The case has been described as including the most convoluted reasoning of almost any major Supreme Court case in history, and is as classic an example as exists of creative or activist constitutional jurisprudence. Until Justice Blackmun released the *Roe* opinion, the moral question concerning abortion had been decided by the state legislatures, complete with lobbying by proponents and opponents and accountability to the voters. After nearly two hundred years, making abortion a matter of constitutional law rather than part of the democratic process required some very fancy footwork. "Unfortunately," according to constitutional scholar Robert Bork, "in the entire opinion there is not one line of explanation, not one sentence that qualifies as legal argument. Nor has the Court in the sixteen years since ever provided the explanation lacking in 1973. It is unlikely that it ever will, because the right to abort, whatever one thinks of it, is not to be found in the Constitution."[74] Once again conservatives realized that the Court was giving itself license to ignore the Constitution whenever it wanted to, to ignore the concept of federalism whenever it wanted to, and in effect, do whatever it wanted regardless of the confines of the law.

The Supreme Court's abortion ruling troubled even people who approved of abortion. Supreme Court Justice Ruth Bader Ginsberg, who had previously served as general counsel of the ACLU and was an ardent supporter of abortion on demand, said at her confirmation hearing before the Senate Judiciary Committee in 1993 that *Roe* had been "wrongly decided," and has often expressed regret at the reasoning used in the case. "The *Roe* decision might have been less of a storm center," she said, had it "homed in more precisely on the women's-equality dimension of the issue. . . . It was heavy-handed judicial intervention [that] was difficult to justify and appears to have provoked, not resolved, conflict."[75] University of Chicago law professor and constitutional scholar Philip Kurland agreed:

> The most important recent decision that is without rational justification in constitutional terms is the abortion case. I have no quarrel with the result; I like it. Were I a legislator, I would vote for it. But the question whether abortion may be banned by the state in the first, second, or third trimesters of pregnancy is not a question that can be answered by the history or language of the Constitution and certainly does not fall within the expertise of the nine robed men in the marble palace. There would appear to be reason why the result was not justified by the opinion.[76]

Abortion was of marginal political importance before 1973; about the only organized opposition came from the Catholic Church. Mainstream Protestants may have been uncomfortable but not enough so to speak out, and evangelical Christians at the time were largely ambivalent on the issue. Jerry Falwell comments that "after *Roe* was decided, leaders of the Catholic Church had spoken courageously in opposition to the Court's decision, but the voices of my Protestant Christian brothers and sisters, especially the voices of fundamentalist leaders, remained silent."[77] But by 1980, evangelicals by the millions had changed their view, and made abortion their primary cause.

Following the *Roe* decision, roughly 1.6 million abortions were being performed per year across the country, and by 2004 approximately 40 million pregnancies had been terminated. The numbers were appalling; the right-to-life movement refers to the period as the new holocaust. But what many people did not realize was just who it was that was being aborted.[78] The *American Spectator* concluded, in a piece published in June 2004 by demographer Larry Eastland, that the women having abortions were more likely to be liberals than conservatives (by 30 percent), and more likely to be Democrats than Republicans. The implication, the *Spectator* concluded, could be devastating. "Liberals have been remarkably blind to the fact that every day the abortions they advocate dramatically decrease their power to do so. Imagine the number of followers that their abortion policies eliminate who, over the next several decades, would have emerged as the new liberal thinkers, voters, adherents, fundraisers, and workers for their cause."[79]

Politically, abortion continues to be as potent an issue as ever, and still motivates many people in Catholic and evangelical communities. "It is still a very important issue, even among our constituency," said Tony Perkins, head of the Family Research Council. "After thirty years, the passion for it, the commitment to it, has not diminished."[80]

The Supreme Court opened the door ever wider to judicial activism and to legislating from the bench, and throughout the 1970s the lower federal courts, many of whose judges were Kennedy-Johnson liberals, were only too happy to follow suit. The result was the judicial imposition of liberal ideology on the country, far more than either Congress or the executive branch could have conceived of.

The remedy, conservative legal scholars easily recognized, was to reapply the law and the Constitution as the legislature and the framers had intended. This required *legal* reasoning, not medical, or sociological, or psychological, or historical reasoning. And it required a return to a process that would become the watchword of conservative legal scholars. According to Robert Bork, originalism is the only approach that can make judicial review democratically legitimate, and simply means "that the judge must discern from the relevant materials—

debates at the Constitutional convention, the Federalist Papers and the Anti-Federalist Papers, newspaper accounts of the time, debates in the state ratifying conventions, and the like—the principles the ratifiers understood themselves to be enacting. The remainder of the task is to apply those principles to unforeseen circumstances, a task that law performs all the time. Any philosophy that does not confine judges to the original understanding inevitably makes the Constitution the plaything of willful judges."[81]

CONSERVATIVE PRESSURE FROM THE OUTSIDE

As conservatives watched what many Republican-appointed judges were doing, it became apparent that naming loyal Republican lawyers to the courts without understanding their philosophical principles was not only fruitless but dangerous. Many had no idea what the framers had in mind, and no understanding of the structure of the Constitution or how to interpret it. They relied solely on precedents set by the liberal judges who preceded them. Law schools still taught constitutional law, but students did not *read* the Constitution, they read Supreme Court cases *about* the Constitution. Originalism was a word without meaning to most lawyers, law professors, and judges, as was the concept of original intent. As for the *Federalist Papers*, they were mentioned occasionally, but rarely cited.

A few, however, did understand the basics. Once such, Raoul Berger, senior fellow at Harvard Law School, in 1977, published his classic book *Government by Judiciary: The Transformation of the Fourteenth Amendment*, which sounded the alarm about the federal court's encroachment on constitutional legislative authority. In the process, Professor Berger averred, federal judges had largely rewritten the Constitution in order to make it amenable to their own ideas. Berger was a liberal and had served in both the Roosevelt and Truman administrations, which, along with his reputation, made it difficult to ignore him. He was unapologetic that his "commitment to the Constitution rises paramount to every other consideration."[82]

Berger was not alone; Charles Rice, a law professor at Notre Dame Law School, John Baker, from LSU Law School, James McClellan, counsel to the Constitution Subcommittee of the Senate Judiciary Committee, and Antonin Scalia, who had taught at the University of Chicago Law School and was at the American Enterprise Institute in the late 1970s, are but a few who spoke out for originalism and expressed their concern for the lack of legal scholarship among the judges.

McClellan, who had taught political science and studied law, knew the Constitution backward and forward, and who had written abundantly on the framers and the Constitution, decided to educate judges about the Constitution and in 1982 launched the Center for Judicial Studies (CJS). CJS published a journal called *Benchmark* whose "Constitutional Commentaries" addressed particular constitutional issues. A complimentary subscription was sent to each and every federal judge in the country.

Jimmy Carter's presidency was yet another call to reform the judiciary. Although, fortunately, Carter had no Supreme Court appointments—the only twentieth-century president who did not—his district and appellate court nominees looked like ACLU choices (which in fact many were). Carter also nominated many more than his share of judges to fill vacancies that had been created by new legislation expanding the judiciary by 152 judges. (The bill was initially introduced in 1972, during Nixon's presidency, but the congressional Democrats stalled its passage until a Democrat occupied the White House). As a result, Carter, despite his single term, named over one-third of all sitting federal judges. As was the custom in those days, most were confirmed with only token opposition.

But opposition was rising, the most vociferous of which came when Carter named liberals Patricia Wald, who had served in the Carter Justice Department, and Congressman Abner Mikva of Illinois to the D.C. Circuit Court of Appeals. For almost the first time, conservative Republicans on the Senate floor rose in full voice, appalled at the prospect of yet more "activist" judges.

Paul Laxalt, Republican of Nevada, who subsequently served as chairman of Ronald Reagan's 1980 presidential campaign, spoke out against the nomination of Abner Mikva, who, he charged, would put his personal preferences before legal reasoning. Too often, Laxalt said, judicial decisions reflect individual beliefs of the federal judges dressed up in lawyers' language. Too often, the question posed by the courts is neither whether a lower court correctly applied the laws as passed by Congress or whether a particular policy is constitutionally permissible, but whether such policy corresponds to judicial notions of societal "oughts."

Laxalt reminded his colleagues of James Madison's warning that maintaining the sense in which the Constitution was approved and ratified was the only guarantee of a stable government. He was joined by thirty other senators, knowing they would not succeed, but determined to establish a record of opposition. And indeed, both Mikva and Wald were subsequently confirmed.[83]

Conservatives had to wait until 1981 and the inauguration of Ronald Reagan and a Republican Senate before a change could take place on the federal bench.

LAW AND ECONOMICS

Lawyers, judges, law professors, legal scholars—none knew much more, in the 1960s and 1970s, about economics than they did about the Constitution. Yet what they experienced every day—the matters handled, the issues taught, the cases decided—often had a great deal to do with the economy. So, too, for the legislators; they enacted laws with little heed to the economic consequences.

Aaron Director, one of the early free-market economists at the University of Chicago and a close associate (and brother-in-law) of Milton Friedman, began teaching economics at the law school in 1950. Director believed antitrust regulation was a hindrance to the free market and hurt consumers more than it protected them; more generally, he taught that laws should be construed not only in regard to justice, but for their overall economic consequences. Among his students was Robert Bork, whose 1978 book *The Anti-Trust Paradox* argued that the antitrust laws should largely be repealed, since the free market would provide all the regulation needed.[84]

Others agreed that economics should become part of a legal education; the *Journal of Law and Economics*, published from the University of Chicago, became a forum for a wide range of economic analysis as it applied to legal problems. The essential message was that the marketplace, if allowed to work without government interference, could regulate better than lawyers, judges, and legislators.

Such thinking began to spread beyond the confines of the south side of Chicago when the Olin and Scaife foundations, in the mid-1970s, started funding centers at top-flight law schools to publish journals and newsletters, hold conferences, provide fellowships, and otherwise instruct law students and faculty members about the free market.

By the late 1990s there were several dozen law and economics centers in law schools across the country. There were also several programs to educate federal judges on law and economics in week-long seminars taught by Nobel laureate economists, other judges, and top-notch law professors and economists. By the end of 2004, more than thirteen hundred judges had been trained.[85] Democrats repeatedly introduced legislation to bar judges from attending law and economics seminars, usually arguing that because corporations and foundations, such as Olin, were funding the seminars, judges would be biased in their favor. But such legislation has never passed, largely because of the popularity of the program among federal judges.

The impact of the law and economics movement on the legal profession has been nothing short of phenomenal. Anthony Kronman, dean of the Yale Law School, has called the movement the most powerful influence in the past twenty years of legal scholarship; the *Wall Street Journal* quoted Bruce Ackerman, professor of law at Columbia, as saying that law and economics was "the most important thing in legal education since the birth of the Harvard Law School."[86] And University of Massachusetts professor John Brigham, in his book *The Constitution of Interests*, wrote that "while law and economics is transforming the way American law is taught, practiced, and decided, the left has failed to respond. . . . Where the right has supplanted, the left has critiqued."[87]

Law and economics has also had considerable impact in the federal courts as judges began to use economic analysis in their review of antitrust cases, economic regulation, and even commercial litigation. Ronald Reagan appointed several conservative legal scholars to the courts of appeals who were well versed in economic analysis—Ralph Winter and Robert Bork from Yale and Richard Posner and Frank Estabrook from the University of Chicago, among others. According to Douglas Ginsberg, chief judge of the U. S. Court of Appeals for the District of

Columbia, and himself an advocate of law and economics, "Economic understanding has become much more generally accepted in the federal courts. . . . If a judge understands the economics [in a case involving economic regulation], he can understand more astutely whether the agency's work is acceptable."[88]

Law and economics was also important to conservatives, as it provided an intellectual discipline previously lacking. Just as the neoconservatives in the 1960s had brought an understanding of social science to the conservative movement, so the law and economics movement brought econometrics, and with it what had been an attitude became a science. The higher redoubts of the policy world had done their best to resist conservative impulses, but how could they put down a scholar, even a conservative scholar, armed with tools of the econometrician? "Conservatism," according to one law professor conversant in law and economics, "is an emotional response to the hypocrisy, banality, and moral indifference of liberalism."[89]

Conservative Public Interest Law

As the courts turned to the left, in the 1950s, and began to make sweeping changes in social policy, so-called public interest lawyers discovered that the courts were often more amenable to their arguments than were the legislatures and the Congress. Rather than simply wait until an appropriate case got into a courtroom, would it not be easier to find situations ripe for litigation, to control the subject matter before a court, and to direct which cases went to court in the first place? Doing so, lawyers realized, could allow them to help determine the outcome in a specific case, and the direction of the law generally. And so the public interest movement was born.

Through "public interest" organizations such as the American Civil Liberties Union, legal aid societies, the NAACP Legal Defense and Education Fund, the Sierra Club, and, with massive government funding, the Legal Services Corporation, liberals successfully changed the direction of the law and, accordingly, the direction of the country. As judges became more "activist," more willing to interpret the law for their own purposes rather than just to apply it, the public interest movement, working hand in hand with results-oriented judges, greatly increased the impact of the courts. The left had huge success with public interest law: Some of the most notorious cases in the country, including *Brown v. Board of Education*, the *Pentagon Papers* case, and *Roe* v. *Wade*, had been brought by public interest lawyers.

The liberal public interest bar had done more, however, than simply win influential cases. It had helped rewrite the procedural rules on who could get into court, what parties had standing to bring a lawsuit, where cases should be brought—finding, that is, a friendly judge—and how to bring similar cases in multiple jurisdictions in order to get a result suitable for an appeal to a sympathetic court. Public interest lawyers had also become very skillful fundraisers, extracting millions upon millions of dollars from the large liberal foundations and the federal and state governments. Congress, controlled by liberals during the 1960s and 1970s, helped as well by passing laws that provided for the award of attorneys' fees to lawyers bringing certain kinds of cases; in some cases, attorneys' fees could be awarded even where an attorney or public interest group had settled the case, or was not even successful, resulting in the transfer of large sums of money, usually taxpayer funds, filling the coffers of public interest firms.

Public interest law firms often testified before congressional committees, lobbied for and against legislation, and, during Democratic administrations, managed to be appointed to the federal bench and other high-level federal jobs where, from the inside, they could shepherd their pet projects through federal agencies. By 1989, public interest law had become big business: There were nearly 160 public interest law firms, employing nearly one thousand lawyers and spending over $120 million a year. Added to that was the $300-plus million appropriated by Congress for the Legal Services Corporation, much of which was spent on public interest activities.[90]

If liberals could use the law to their advantage, why, conservatives and libertarians began to ask, could they not "reverse-engineer" the process, and do the same? Using nonprofit organizations as their vehicle, conservatives started forming public interest law firms in the early 1970s, and within several years had built a respectable movement, albeit a far cry from the multimillion-dollar enterprise controlled by the left. Among the first was the National Right to Work Legal Defense Foundation, started in 1968, which brought lawsuits on behalf of employees to protect them from being forced to join unions, and class actions on behalf of workers abused, in one way or another, by labor unions. Since that time, the Defense Foundation has argued countless cases on behalf of hundreds of thousands of employees in class actions, and over twenty thousand individual workers. "NRWLDF has altered the legal landscape for employee protections against compulsory unionism," concluded the Heritage Foundation in 2004. In addition, the class-action victories it has won against unions have collected tens of millions of dollars, mostly in refunded union dues that were improperly assessed.[91]

Conservative and libertarian public interest lawyers have been particularly effective in litigating cases concerning property rights, the use of public lands, constitutional rights of free speech, and cases involving economic and religious liberty. School choice, which became a clarion call of the conservative movement in the 1990s, was largely a creature of the conservative public interest bar. Public interest lawyers have also filed *amicus curiae* briefs in a wide array of cases involving everything from criminal justice to environmental cases, often with positive results.

Reagan and the Courts

Ronald Reagan understood the federal courts well. As a westerner and a governor of California, he had learned that federal courts were usurping state power, that they were more concerned with the bureaucracy in Washington, the environmentalists, the regulators, and other special interests than with the average American citizen.

While governor, Reagan managed to name over six hundred judges. He set up judicial selection commissions in each county, which recommended judicial candidates on the basis of merit, and Reagan made the selection from the commissions' recommendations. "He earned a nationwide reputation," according to Ed Meese, who served as his legal affairs secretary in the governor's office, "for appointing the best, the most able judges."[92]

On entering the White House in 1981, Reagan immediately began to appoint highly regarded conservatives and libertarians to both the district courts and the circuit courts of appeals, most of whom were confirmed by the Republican Senate without much of a fight.[93] But unlike past Republican administrations, Reagan was not going to simply appoint well-connected lawyers and friends who wanted to be judges and hope for the best. The conservatives in the White House and the Justice Department knew that naming conservatives to the federal appellate courts was crucial to moving the courts to the right, and the Justice Department put in place the most comprehensive and thorough judicial recruitment and screening process in history to implement the process. The program's success became obvious when Reagan's appointees were subsequently nominated to the Supreme Court: Justices Antonin Scalia, Clarence Thomas, John Roberts, and Samuel Alito were all elevated from the Circuit Courts of Appeal; Judges Robert Bork and Douglas Ginsberg were nominated but not confirmed. All had been appointed by Reagan or George H. W. Bush.

To begin with, judicial selection was elevated to the top echelons of the administration. Within the first two weeks after the 1981 inaugural, regular meetings started to be held in the Roosevelt Room at the White House with the attorney general, the head of personnel, and the most senior staff present. "The second element," according to Ken Cribb, who helped to design the process, "was to put together an intellectual analysis to determine the actual views of the candidates instead of asking conclusive questions." Everything each candidate had ever written, each speech he had given publicly, each case he had written, if he was already a judge, was read and analyzed. Then, in interviews that often lasted for a full day or more, the candidate would be asked questions based on hypothetical fact situations, to which there was no obvious answer, to determine the thought process he or she would use and how he or she would rule in a factual case. "The conservative intellectual movement," added Cribb, "made this process possible. Bob Bork had written about it, Nino Scalia, who was still teaching at Chicago, understood it and had written about it, as had Raoul Berger from Harvard. It was an intellectual exercise, and it had never been used before."[94] After the nominee was chosen, Reagan personally called each one, telling him that "what he was trying to do was to restore fidelity to the written Constitution."[95]

Yet the process was far from foolproof, as two of Reagan's Supreme Court nominees—Justices O'Connor and Kennedy—have demonstrated. Reagan had promised, during the 1980 campaign, that he would name the first woman to the Supreme Court, and when the first opening occurred, with the retirement of Justice Potter Stewart, Reagan did exactly what Eisenhower, Nixon, or Ford, would have done—he named a politically well-connected lawyer and judge, Sandra Day O'Connor, without really knowing where she stood philosophically. In fact, O'Connor did vote with conservatives for much of her tenure on the Court, until the last five years or so, when she began to drift to the left. Anthony Kennedy, who became the "swing vote" between liberals and conservatives a dozen or so years after his appointment, surprised many people—but not all—by his shift to the left. Reagan named him in 1988 to the seat that Robert Bork had been nominated to fill. The Senate had been returned to the Democrats in the 1986 election, and the Reagan White House recognized it would thus be more difficult to get a conservative confirmed. Kennedy had been on the Ninth Circuit Court of Appeals in San Francisco, was well known personally to several top people in the administration, and according to former attorney general Edwin Meese, "Every case of his was scrutinized. There was probably as much data about him as anybody else when he was nominated."[96] Kennedy was the exception that proves the rule.

THE BORK NOMINATION

Justice Lewis Powell's announcement of his resignation in July 1987 threw Washington liberals into turmoil, knowing that Reagan's replacement would surely shift the balance of power on the Court. A year earlier, Reagan had nominated Antonin Scalia to the Court and elevated William Rehnquist to Chief Justice. Only a year before the 1988 presidential election, liberals thought it was time to put the brakes on Reagan. Robert Bork had been appointed to the D.C. Circuit five years earlier, was a true conservative intellectual, and was probably the best-qualified candidate who had ever been nominated to sit on the Supreme Court.

Reagan's announcement that he intended to nominate Bork set off a firestorm and one of the nastiest fights of the decade, a fight that forever would change the tenor of the nomination and confirmation of every subsequent conservative to the Court, and a fight that showed just how desperate liberals were to stay in power.

Teddy Kennedy set the stage for the battle in a statement on the Senate floor that left Bork's supporters speechless:

> Robert Bork's America is a land in which women would be forced into back-alley abortions, blacks would sit at segregated lunch-counters, rogue police could break down citizens' doors in midnight raids, children could not be taught about evolution.[97]

Kennedy wanted left-wing activist groups to bloody Bork before the hearings even started. As Judge Bork later wrote: "This was a calculated personal assault by a shrewd politician, an assault more violent than any against a judicial nominee in our country's history. As it turned out, Kennedy set the themes and the tone for the entire campaign."[98]

Bork was hated by liberals not only for ideological, but for political reasons as well. He had served as solicitor general of the United States—the third-highest-ranking job in the Justice Department—during the Nixon administration. During the Watergate investigation, in what would become known as the Saturday Night Massacre, Nixon had ordered that the special prosecutor, Archibald Cox, be fired, as Cox was trying to procure the tapes that would ultimately destroy Nixon's presidency. Cox had himself served as solicitor general in the Kennedy administration, was a professor at Harvard Law School, and was a liberal icon. Both Nixon's attorney general, Elliott Richardson, and his deputy attorney general, William Ruckelshaus, refused to fire Cox, resigning their positions in protest, and the job ultimately fell to the solicitor general—Bob Bork—who proceeded to fire Cox, as Nixon had requested.

It was ironic indeed that it fell to Ted Kennedy to be the ringleader in bringing down Robert Bork. Bork graduated at the top of his University of Chicago Law School class; Kennedy was expelled from Harvard for cheating. Bork enlisted in the Marine Corps before college, and re-entered as an officer between college and law school; Kennedy joined the army for four years after getting kicked out of Harvard, but his father saw that it was reduced to two years (Kennedy never rose above the rank of private). Bork taught law at Yale and served as solicitor general of the

United States; Kennedy had never held a job outside his elected jobs in Congress. Bork served with distinction on the U.S. Circuit Court of Appeals for the District of Columbia; the closest Kennedy ever came to a courtroom was under subpoena in 1970 for Mary Jo Kopechne's inquest. Bork had given countless speeches and written several serious books; Kennedy was so inarticulate when he was asked, on CBS by Roger Mudd in 1978, why he wanted to be president, he could not answer the question.

Judge Bork had been outspoken in his criticism of aberrational Supreme Court decisions for years. He had called the *Roe* v. *Wade* opinion "a serious and wholly unjustifiable usurpation of state legislative authority" and denounced most of the Court opinions involving civil rights, prayer in the schools, and reapportionment. He had called for the repeal of the antitrust laws and believed in free markets and the strict interpretation of the Constitution. But the chief danger was his mind: He was considered one of the brightest and most highly qualified nominees in years, and the American Bar Association had given him its highest rating, "exceptionally well qualified." Liberals knew that adding Bork to the Court would be more than just one more right-thinking judge; it would deal a devastating blow to their domination of it.

Bork may have been well qualified for the job, but he was a terrible witness for himself: too outspoken, too willing to say exactly what he thought, too willing to argue with the Democratic senators who wanted to see him go down in smoke. In response to a question from Republican senator Alan Simpson about why he wanted to be on the Court, Bork responded that, for him, being a justice would be "an intellectual feast." Not an insignificant problem was the fact that Republicans had lost control of the Senate in the 1986 election, with the Democrats holding a 55–45 majority. Any major embarrassment Democrats could foist onto Reagan would help them in the presidential race of 1988. And in the end, Democrats were successful; they defeated the nomination by a vote of 42–58.[99]

There were several lessons, both negative and positive, that conservatives took from this defeat. Why should articulate and intelligent lawyers or law professors state what they thought, why should they depart from the conventional wisdom, if it meant they could never be confirmed as judges? Was this any way to confirm judges? What did this process do to inspire the best lawyers to seek a judgeship? The campaign was anti-intellectualism at its worst. Liberals had always advocated appointing only the best people to the bench—graduates of the elite law schools, erudite and creative lawyers, experienced lower-court judges. Bork met all those criteria, and the Democrats' savaging of Bork did bother a good many liberals—they had abused their own standards for political purposes. Some argued that they had been honest and sincere in their attacks, but anybody with half a brain saw the hypocrisy in it all. As a result of the anti-Bork campaign, conservatives now knew that they needed to build an infrastructure to support their nominees the next time around, not be caught off-guard as with the Bork nomination. They needed media-savvy people ready to appear on the television shows, people ready to lobby the administration concerning whom to nominate in the first place and to lobby the Senate once nominations were made. They would also need the money to pay for it all.

"Borking" aside, Reagan reshaped the courts in a way not seen since the founding of the Republic, appointing nearly half of all sitting federal judges. Doing so was an essential part of his reform of the political landscape of the country. Reagan and his inner circle understood that the solution to the problem of a judiciary that had become, in effect, a legislature, and of a system that made what should have been democratic solutions, solutions reached by lawsuits, was to restore the constitutional rule of law. According to Reagan confidant and former attorney general Edwin Meese, "The conclusion that the President drew was obvious enough: if the problems we confronted had come about because of judges, then something had to be done about the judges. This was of key importance, in his view, not simply because of the individual issues involved, but because restoring the proper role of the judiciary was critical to our system of self-government."[100]

THE FEDERALIST SOCIETY

Until the 1980s, the law schools belonged to the liberals. Even more than the mainstay universities, the elite law schools—as one wag put it, the twenty-five that considered themselves in the top ten—were almost universally controlled by the left. Deans, faculty, scholars, everybody, with the exception of a law and economics devotee here and there, was a liberal. Not only was liberalism in control, but the law schools, like the rest of the law, had become politicized. Law had become the favored area of study among the radicals and idealists of the sixties and seventies, mostly because it was perceived as the best way to "change the world." "The forces that would break law to a tame instrument of a particular political thrust," wrote Robert Bork in *The Tempting of America*, " . . . have overrun a number of law schools, including a large majority of America's most prestigious, where the lawyers and judges of the future are being trained."[101]

The Constitution was virtually never taught in the law schools; the required course in constitutional law was based on what the Supreme Court said about the founding document. Natural law found no place in the law schools and was rarely even mentioned. Although the left was not wholly united in its legal philosophy, liberals generally believed that the Constitution was obsolete and needed revision, that it should be construed to provide a more liberal, socially permissive, and egalitarian world, and that federalism had outlived its usefulness. Some advocated writing new rights into the Constitution, such as the right to welfare, sexual freedom, and free medical care. The Constitution was, in short, an impediment to the liberals' ambitions for social reform—recall that Russell Kirk had called the Constitution the most successful conservative device in history—and the left was determined to emasculate it one way or another.

The most radical crowd in the law schools were the "Crits." As the antiwar and civil rights radicals began to congregate in the law classrooms, a school of thought known as Critical Legal Studies ("the Crits") emerged. CLS, a neo-Marxist movement, held that the law was oppressive and largely a tool of Corporate America, used by the rich to oppress the poor and downtrodden. The Crits who sought to destroy the system managed only to sound ludicrous (they never bothered to offer much of an alternative). Much of their rhetoric was disjointed and obtuse, a masterpiece of mumbo-jumbo. One of the CLS's most ardent members, Duncan Kennedy of the Harvard Law School, wrote that he opposed "illegitimate hierarchy, domination, and oppression," seeking instead "utopian speculation concerning an impossible Eden which aspires to a shared vision of a social harmony so complete as to obviate the need for any rules at all."[102]

Although the liberal faculty may have in large part owned the law schools, to their chagrin, not all students agreed with their teaching. A handful of conservative activists had already cut their teeth in the Goldwater campaign, Young Americans for Freedom, or the Young Republicans; had read *National Review*, *Human Events*, and *American Spectator*; and had graduated from ISI programs. Others unself-consciously believed in federalism and the rule of law. As they studied the legal system, they questioned not only their law professors, but the whole trend of the law since the Roosevelt administration. They had to look outside the law schools for their intellectual stimulation, or find sufficient resources in books and journals to keep their minds from being overcome by their leftist professors.

One of these was a serious young man who was alerted to the problem as a Princeton undergraduate, class of 1972, studying politics. In an article about him years later, the *Washington Post* reported that he had been inspired by the Goldwater campaign, stimulated by *National Review*, alarmed by the discord over the Vietnam War, and disenchanted with the liberal bias of college campuses. This Princeton student became a regular viewer of Bill Buckley's *Firing Line* and was excited when, in 1967, California governor Ronald Reagan cleaned up the floor with Bobby Kennedy in a televised debate. As he observed the Supreme Court's liberal activism under Chief Justice Earl Warren, he decided to study constitutional law. He was particularly impressed when he discovered the works of Yale Law School professor Alexander Bickel, one of academia's most outspoken critics of the Warren Court.[103] He decided that Yale would be the place for him, because he could study with Bickel, and entered with the class of 1975. Yale, according to the *Washington Post*, was a temple of legal liberalism. But when Professor Bickel became ill, the student discovered a professor named Robert Bork. A bit intimidated, he listened more than he spoke. Professor Bork remembered only one student—John Bolton, later named U.S. ambassador to the United Nations by George W. Bush—who expressed conservative views openly. "The rest," said Bork, "kept their heads down."[104] Sam Alito would not have been so lonely had he entered Yale Law School a dozen years later.

By 1982, despite the country's turn to the right and the election of Ronald Reagan, the law schools were more liberal than ever. But a small group of conservative law students from the University of Chicago and Yale believed that by banding together they might have the same sort of impact that conservative undergraduates had had twenty years earlier. "We had seen a lot of left-wing politics as undergraduates, but the politics of the law schools were worse," said Yale law student Steve Calabresi. "It felt like an island that was completely oblivious to what was happening around the rest of the country."[105]

Calabresi and two conservative friends from the University of Chicago Law School, David McIntosh and Lee Lieberman, formed a group that coordinated conservative activism in the law schools and gave fellow right-leaning law students the kind of support that Sam Alito never had. Ironically, all three were liberals when they entered college, and two were still liberals when they finished, but all soon found liberalism intellectually unrewarding and switched sides. The Federalist Society for Law and Public Policy Studies, they thought, would be an appropriate name to honor the Federalist Papers and the principles of the American founding. Soon they were in touch with Harvard law student Spencer Abraham, editor of an alternative conservative law review called the *Harvard Journal of Law and Public Policy*; Abraham was subsequently elected to the Senate from Michigan and, in 2001, became George W. Bush's secretary of energy. The four planned a conference on federalism, to be held on the Yale campus in April 1982, and invited like-minded students from a number of law schools. Nearly two hundred students showed up, many from distant campuses, and heard talks from a star-studded cast, including Robert Bork, Harvard professor Charles Fried—an anomaly at Harvard—Antonin Scalia, and Judge Ralph Winter.

The Federalist Society states its principles succinctly—government exists to preserve freedom, the separation of powers is central to the American form of government, the role of the judiciary is to say what the law is, not what the law should be. By the end of the 1990s chapters had been established in every accredited law school in the country, with over twenty-five thousand members. Hundreds of debates, lectures, and conferences were held each year. Its network of conservative and libertarian law students and lawyers (Federalist Society members are both conservative and libertarian, and like to distinguish between the two) was the most powerful force to arise in legal circles in decades. "If we had the infrastructure we have now when Bork was nominated," says Gene Meyer, president of the Federalist Society, "I believe he would have been confirmed."[106]

Most important, the Federalist Society has thrived on ideas. It has brought new ideas into the law schools and reintroduced ideas that the liberals would prefer to see abandoned, such as natural law and religious liberty, sovereignty and federalism. Many of those concepts would never be mentioned in law schools were it not for Federalist Society students. The Federalist Society did not discover the idea of originalism but, according to Gene Meyer, "It would not have flourished without us." By regularly sponsoring debates rather than one-sided lectures, the Federalist Society has spread its ideas to liberals as well as to conservatives, to noncommitted students as well as to believers.

According to Federalist Society lawyers, the Constitution is the best means of preserving the free society and the best way yet devised of governing human beings. "The reason we care about preserving the Constitution," says Gene Meyer, "is not because there is this wonderful document that they gave us, it is because those principles apply today every bit as much as when it was written, and that is the way to keep a society free."[107]

Liberals saw the handwriting on the wall. In current Senate confirmation hearings, one of the first questions likely to be asked of conservative federal judicial nominees is, "Are you now or have you ever been a member of the Federalist Society?" And, in more cases than liberals liked, the answer was "yes." These judicial nominees believed in restoring federalism and the separation of powers to the legal and political structure, and were proud of their affiliation with an organization that advocated these beliefs. As those who believed in constitutionalism began to populate the federal courts, as the conservative legal organizations began to have an impact, and as the law schools increasingly taught conservative principles, those on the right saw the beginnings of a return to "the least dangerous branch" as a way of restoring the rule of law.

If the Federalist Society was influential in the first twenty years of its existence, there was no telling what impact it would have in the future.

"I think [the Federalist Society] is going to have a tremendous impact over a long period of time," says retired *National Review* publisher Bill Rusher. "I don't think it has yet revolutionized the judiciary; I think the judiciary remains one of our biggest problems and I think the Federalist Society is one of our best instruments for solving it."[108]

As we will see in Chapter 14, Rusher's prediction would be realized in 2006.

CHAPTER TEN

Intellectual Developments, 1960 to the Present

As the conservative movement began to take shape, many sought to define what was conservative and what was not, and to direct the energies of the young movement to their particular brand of conservatism. As conservatives coalesced around Barry Goldwater and the right wing of the Republican Party, the intellectuals were drawn to Frank Meyer's fusionism. It was not enough to sit by idly and comment on politics; intellectuals wanted to see their ideas reflected in public policy. Conservative politicians likewise benefited from their counsel and contributed to the intellectuals' debates about conservatism through their platforms and policies. The participants in the surrounding debates changed, as the rising generation came of age and the founding generation faded into the past, but the principles remained the same. These debates about what truly constituted the movement subsided after conservatives gained control of the presidency in 1980 and both houses of Congress in 1994, and conservatives concentrated instead on the development, analysis, and execution of policy questions.

POLITICAL THEORISTS

Several academic political theorists contributed to these debates, some appearing regularly in conservative journals like *National Review* and others participating in movement politics. Still others were dedicated to solitary reflection and academic scholarship, addressing conferences of conservative intellectuals like the Philadelphia Society and writing prolifically.

One political theorist who had an immediate impact on the conservative movement was Willmoore Kendall, Bill Buckley's mentor at Yale and a senior editor at *National Review*. A child prodigy, Kendall graduated from the University of Oklahoma at the age of eighteen and won a Rhodes scholarship. He was a Trotskyite in his student days at Oxford, and like many of the literary giants of the era, went to Spain to support the Spanish Republic. But Kendall soon became disillusioned by the ruthless violence of the Communists: "He could tolerate the Communists' blowing up the plants of opposition newspapers. But when they deliberately killed opposition newsboys—this was too much."[1] Kendall applied his anti-Communism by working for the Army on psychological warfare. He moved progressively to the right and, by the 1950s, determined to become the philosopher of American conservatism.

Kendall admired the American political system, believing in the primacy of Congress and faulting liberals for elevating the presidency over it. The framers of the Constitution, Kendall argued, had intended congressional majorities to represent a national consensus of the many different communities within America—they believed that the judgment of the American people, in the aggregate and over time, would be right, as long as the nation remained religious and virtuous. Likewise, Kendall believed in the goodness and common sense of the American people and described himself as a down-home, "Appalachians to the Rockies patriot," or what today we might call a "red state" conservative.[2] In this sense, he understood the instinctive conservatism of the majority of Americans that emerged in the 1970s as the Reagan coalition.

The great difference between liberals and conservatives, in Kendall's view, was that conservatives believed civil society must rest on an unambiguous, non-negotiable consensus about its organizing principles or values. Once the question of fundamental values is closed, these values shape and give meaning to the life of the political community. Liberals, on the other hand, held that society must be "open," always subject to questioning and change—which Kendall argued could undermine the foundations of society itself. A prime example, to Kendall, of such a threat was Communism, which threatened the existence of everything

America stood for. In fact, Kendall once described himself as an "egg-head McCarthyite."

Like many a preacher's son, Kendall was colorful in practicing his vices. He fought bitterly with colleagues over personal and intellectual matters, drank heavily, and was a notorious womanizer. He was once caught *in flagrante delicto* with a secretary in the *National Review* offices after hours (the couch in question became known, around the *NR* offices, as the "Willmoore Kendall memorial couch"), and it was rumored that faculty wives at Yale, where he taught political science, were not beyond his reach. In the time they shared at Oxford in the 1960s, Jeffrey Hart relates that he struggled to keep up with Kendall's drinking, which was not even diminished by a seizure—his nitro pills took care of that.[3] His alcoholism drove Kendall to pettiness, which led to his fallings out with many friends. One was Bill Buckley, who wrote his former mentor in a parting blast:

> I have never had the power to prevent you from being the fool, and as my influence with you diminishes, and your deterioration accelerates, the chances that I could help you are slighter than ever. . . . [You] conclude that our current mendicancy is if not the result of our whorishness, at least a deserved result of it; and advise us that you feel about *NR* much as you would feel about an ex-wife of yours who had become a call-girl. . . . [But] our current mendicancy may or may not be the result of our whoring after Goldwater—one had to suppose that whoring is profitable—but is certainly in some measure the result of emoluments paid out over the years to nonperforming editors; and as to the reference you made to wives and call-girls, I can only welcome the news that you have finally learned to distinguish between the two.[4]

A massive store of amusing stories of Kendall's spectacular vices exists. But however amusing the stories, he sadly prevented himself from accomplishing as much as he might have. Kendall died at the early age of fifty-seven, leaving unfinished what was to be his major work on conservatism, though parts of it were published posthumously in 1971, under the title of *Willmoore Kendall Contra Mundum*. Though he is underappreciated today, so revered an authority as Leo Strauss told Kendall, "You [are] the best native theorist of your generation."[5]

No doubt Strauss's appreciation of Kendall was connected to Kendall's appreciation of Strauss. Reviewing Strauss's *Thoughts on Machiavelli*, Kendall claimed that "the Strauss revolution in the interpretation of modern political philosophy is the decisive interpretation since Machiavelli himself."[6] Strauss was born into a family of German Jews and was educated at Marburg, Hamburg, and Freiburg, studying under Edmund Husserl and Martin Heidegger. He had a promising career ahead of him in Germany, but observing the rise of the Nazis, Strauss fled to the United States, where he taught at the New School in New York and the University of Chicago before spending his last years at St. John's College in Annapolis, Maryland. It was during his time at Chicago that he left his mark on American conservatism.

Strauss believed that the inherent tension between philosophy and revelation, symbolized by the Greek philosophers on the one hand and the Bible on the other, was the impetus to the intellectual dynamism of the Western tradition. Though he wrote a popular work called *Natural Right and History*, Strauss thought that the tension between philosophers and the religious convictions or customs of the masses drove philosophers to write esoterically, concealing potentially subversive ideas from the unsophisticated followers of custom.[7] It was largely those ideas that provided ammunition for the many critics of his thought and those who wrongly equate it with neoconservatism.

Though not an active member of the conservative movement, Strauss had a great influence on conservatives because of his belief in the possibility of finding truth, his renewal of classical political philosophy, his criticism of modernity, his rejection of liberal positivism, and his call for political theorists to seek the best, rather than the most comfortable regime. He was an engaging teacher with a devoted following. When he died in 1973, Strauss's students memorialized him in the pages of *National Review*. Political theorist Werner Dannhauser called Strauss the greatest teacher of philosophy of his time. Harry Jaffa of Claremont McKenna College said, "For us who have had the privilege of knowing him as a teacher and as a friend, we can only say that he was the best, and the wisest, and the most just."[8]

By the time Strauss died, many of his students were influential political theorists in their own right. There were even different schools of "Straussianism": East Coast Straussians, led by Allan Bloom of the University of Chicago, and West Coast Straussians, led by Harry Jaffa at the Claremont Colleges in California. The East Coasters emphasized the difference between the elevated philosophical life and the lesser, nonphilosophical life, while the West Coasters focused more on American politics, in particular the founders and Abraham Lincoln, who, they believe, refounded and perfected the U.S. Constitution like a Platonic statesman. Jaffa and his disciples also believed that the Declaration of Independence articulates the self-evident truths of universal natural rights based on human equality.

Since Strauss has been cited as one of the several architects of the current invasion of Iraq, he has been subjected to many attacks in academia and the popular press. Writing in the *New Yorker*, Seymour Hersh revealed that Abram Shulsky, the director of the Pentagon Office of Special Plans, which reviewed the intelligence that claimed Iraq had WMDs, was "a scholarly expert in the works of political philosopher Leo Strauss." Days later William Pfaff, columnist for the left-leaning *International Herald Tribune* (even more left-leaning than its parent paper, the *New York Times*), helpfully explained for readers abroad the nuances of American politics: "The Republican Party . . . is a business party, anti-intellectual and to a considerable degree xenophobic. . . . The radical neoconservatives . . . want to remake the international order under effective U.S. hegemony. . . . The main intellectual influence on the neoconservatives has been the philosopher Leo Strauss."[9] Soon everyone on the left, and some on the right, was piling it on. But most were embarrassingly ignorant of Strauss and were simply looking for a convenient scapegoat; they were not much more sophisticated than the loudspeaker truck, observed by the author, on Constitution Avenue in front of the Department of Justice in Washington, blasting the news that the Bush administration had been captured by Leo Strauss!

The flurry of anti-Strauss books, connecting him to the rise of neoconservatism and American imperialism, has been met by a flurry of apologias by Strauss's followers.[10] While important neoconservatives like Irving Kristol and his son William have spoken highly of Strauss, it is a mistake to consider them Straussian in any programmatic way. Strauss wrote little to nothing about practical politics, immersing himself instead in scholarship.

Less controversial than Strauss was his contemporary Eric Voegelin.[11] Born in Cologne, Germany, Voegelin was raised and educated in Vienna, where he received his Ph.D. Having made a name for himself as an anti-Nazi intellectual, he was fired from his teaching position after the Germans annexed Austria in 1938, and fled to Switzerland. The Gestapo showed up at his apartment one morning to pick up his passport to prevent him from leaving the country; fortunately, the passport was at a police station, where it was needed to process his exit visa. Through a friend, Voegelin managed to collect the passport and exit visa before the Gestapo could catch up, and immediately caught a train to Geneva. Once in Geneva, he had trouble persuading the American vice consul to allow him to emigrate to the United States:

> He had grave suspicions about me. He explained that, since I was neither a Communist nor a Catholic nor a Jew, I therefore had no reason whatsoever not to be in favor of National Socialism and to be a National Socialist myself. Hence if I was in flight the only reason must be some criminal record.

Eventually he was allowed to leave.[12]

After moving through several different institutions, Voegelin finally found a full-time position at Louisiana State University, where he remained until 1958. He subsequently became director of the Institute for Political Science at the University of Munich, returning to the United States as a fellow at the Hoover Institution at Stanford from 1969 until his death in 1984.

Voegelin's greatest period of influence on the conservative movement was in the 1950s, when he produced his *New Science of Politics* (1952) and the first three volumes of *Order and History* (1956–57). In these works, Voegelin traced the contemporary crisis of the West with the belief of ideologues—whether Communists or Nazis—who tried to build utopian societies. This he claimed derived from a secularization of the Christian belief in the coming of the kingdom of God, bringing it down to this world, or as Voegelin put it, "Immanentizing the eschaton." Modern ideologues justified their pursuit of power by promising to use that power to eliminate inequality, poverty, or threats to racial purity. But to build the new order, they had to tear down obstacles to it, whether those obstacles were the property-owning middle class, the churches, or the Jews. In the process, they were ultimately driven to kill anyone who stood in their way.

Voegelin participated in conferences sponsored by the Philadelphia Society and the ISI and was published in conservative academic journals, but refused to identify himself explicitly with conservatism because of his opposition to political ideologies. He nevertheless inspired many devoted followers, mostly from the traditionalist wing of the conservative movement, including Russell Kirk, Gerhart Niemeyer, Ellis Sandoz, and Brent Bozell. (Bozell, in a demonstration of the movement's ability to mesh intellectualism with practical politics, railed against gnosticism in his renowned address to the 1962 YAF rally in Madison Square Garden, and made it a theme in his 1964 congressional campaign. It was surely the only occasion in which gnosticism was a topic of discussion in Madison Square Garden.) Later in the 1960s, YAF printed T-shirts as a rejoinder to their radical peers who pined for the Age of Aquarius: "Don't let them immanentize the eschaton."[13] Somehow, Voegelin's writings didn't translate easily into popular slogans.

Kendall, Strauss, and Voegelin all made a mark on the conservative movement, and conservative political theorists will build on the foundations they laid for years to come. At the time, Strauss was the most influential, if least understood. Voegelin has a small but dedicated following, several of whom are currently publishing a thirty-four-volume edition of his collected works. Because he burned so many bridges with friends, colleagues, and students, Kendall is the least appreciated of the three, even though he spoke most directly to a conservative American audience.

As they grew in number, conservative intellectuals gathered to found institutions in which they could discuss their ideas and hash out their differences. The most important was the Philadelphia Society, founded in 1964 and run for many years by conservative activist Don Lipset. The society, which has met continually since its founding, provides a forum for members of the movement—libertarians, traditionalists, anti-Communists, and eventually neoconservatives—to meet, exchange ideas, and debate the principles of conservatism. It became so important that, as Ken Cribb put it, by the early 1970s, "All conservatives of national stature knew each other by first name and handshake. There were about two hundred of us, basically the membership of the Philadelphia Society."[14] The Philadelphia Society continues to meet several times a year, often with several hundred conservative participants, and remains one of the central places where conservative ideas are exchanged and debated.

ECONOMISTS AND FINANCIAL WIZARDS

Conservative contributions to the field of economics did not stop with Nobel laureates Mises, Hayek, and Stigler. Far from it. New libertarian economists and financial wizards seemed to generate spontaneously, and by the mid-1960s there was a distinctly American "Chicago School" built upon the work of the émigrés who made up the "Austrian School."

Among classical liberal economists, Chicago School godfather Milton Friedman was especially adept at translating his economic ideas into popular public policy proposals. Friedman received his M.A. in economics at the University of Chicago and his Ph.D. from Columbia. In a course at Chicago, he was seated behind Rose Director, the younger sister of professor Aaron Director, whom he eventually married. Rose became his chief collaborator on many important works.[15]

Friedman gave a series of lectures at a Volker Fund summer institute and published them as *Capitalism and Freedom* in 1962 (though he could trace its origins back to his original participation in the Mont Pelerin Society). Although the book was completely ignored by the reviewers, ultimately over half a million copies were sold and it became among the most influential books of the decade. Like Hayek before him, Friedman argued that economic liberty is an indispensable precondition for political liberty, and he applied classical liberal principles to the problems of the 1960s, concluding, for example, that capitalism, far from hurting minorities, created new opportunities for them and showed that racial discrimination was economically disadvantageous.

Friedman called for the post office to be privatized, arguing that the government monopoly was inefficient. He thought that vouchers for students to attend private schools instead of public schools would increase choice, better meet particular student needs, and promote salutary competition. School choice became a Friedman hobbyhorse, and he and Rose established the Friedman Foundation to promote it. By the 1990s, school choice was adopted as an issue by Republican politicians, and choice was even implemented in select school districts in states like Wisconsin. But perhaps most audacious of all was Friedman's claim that the Great Depression was not caused by capitalism, but by government intervention in the economy, in the form of monetary mismanagement by the Federal Reserve Bank: "It exercised this responsibility so ineptly as to convert what otherwise would have been a moderate contraction into a major catastrophe."[16]

Capitalism and Freedom was an instant classic, and such a threat to liberal Keynesians that some "successfully lobbied to have it purged from their universities' libraries."[17] Conservatives viewed Friedman as the preeminent free marketeer.

Friedman was also successful in promoting policy changes based on his recommendations, which began with his correspondence with Barry Goldwater on economic policies in the early 1960s. During the 1964 campaign, Friedman published an op-ed piece in the *New York Times Magazine* explaining "The Goldwater View of Economics" to its detractors, and had the satisfaction of hearing his ideas broadcast to thousands at a Goldwater rally in Dodger Stadium.[18] Years later, as a member of Nixon's Commission on an All-Volunteer Armed Force, Friedman was instrumental in abolishing the draft, arguing that it was coercive and violated human freedom. Nixon, no doubt realizing that eliminating the draft would also eliminate the chief cause of demonstrations against the Vietnam War, had the draft abolished in 1973. Friedman was also an outspoken opponent of the Bretton Woods policy of fixed but adjustable exchange rates, and through his friend George Shultz, a former colleague at Chicago who became Treasury secretary, helped persuade Nixon to allow floating exchange rates. In 1981, President Reagan asked him to serve on his Economic Policy Advisory Board, where he contributed to the Reagan Revolution.

Friedman was awarded the Nobel Prize for Economics in 1976. He retired from Chicago a year later and relocated to San Francisco, where he became a senior fellow at the Hoover Institution at Stanford. He and Rose were approached by the Public Broadcasting Corporation (PBS) in the late 1970s about producing a television series on their ideas. The result was "Free to Choose," which became a book of the same name. "From our point of view," Friedman said, "it was one of the most exciting things we had ever done."[19] Friedman remained active until his death in 2006, publishing op-ed pieces and making public appearances in support of his favorite causes. "Rarely," observed the *New York Times*, "did anyone have such impact on both his own profession and on government."[20] The *Wall Street Journal* cited Friedman's tribute to Reagan that "'few people in human history have contributed more to the cause of human freedom,'" and rightly added, "The same can and long will be said of Milton Friedman."[21]

Notwithstanding the strides Friedman, Hayek, and other classical liberal economists had made, some conservatives felt that their arguments for capitalism were too utilitarian and lacked inspiration. George Gilder, for one, argued that the reason capitalism had failed to triumph over socialism by the late 1970s, even though socialism was by then widely regarded as a utopian failure, was that advocates for capitalism had failed to make a moral case to inspire followers. His book *Wealth and Poverty* called attention to the virtues that capitalism required successful entrepreneurs to cultivate. His moral argument boldly claimed that "the crucial rules of economic innovation and progress are faith, altruism, investment, competition, and bankruptcy, which are also the rules of capitalism. The reason capitalism succeeds is that its laws accord with the laws of the mind. It is capable of fulfilling human needs because it is founded on giving, which depends on sensitivity to the needs of others."[22] Irving Kristol worried that "a purely commercial code of ethics does not enable us to cope with those all too many instances when circumstances conspire to ruin us," but *National Review* stalwart John Chamberlain praised his characterization of entrepreneurship: "Gilder sings a hymn to the moral character of the enterpriser who brings such things as the silicon chip, conjured out of grains of sand, to economic fruition. The enterpriser, says Gilder, is a man of faith who believes in giving. . . . He is just a good man casting his bread upon the waters."[23]

Published shortly after Reagan's first inaugural, *Wealth and Poverty* became a bestseller and was hailed as "the intellectual manifesto of the Reagan years."[24] In contrast to the dour pessimism that plagued economists who grew up during the New Deal, Gilder, a former Rockefeller speechwriter, radiated a Reaganesque optimism about the future.

RESURGENT ANTI-COMMUNISM

Though anti-Communism was discredited in the eyes of many by the failure of the Vietnam War, true Cold Warriors did not give up the fight, and anti-Communism remained the linchpin of the conservative movement. Anti-Communists modified their rhetoric somewhat to emphasize national security instead of a crusade against an evil ideology, but their concerns remained the same. They were bitter about the triumph of détente, the cornerstone of the foreign policy of Nixon and his secretary of state, Henry Kissinger. Like Nixon, Kissinger was a figure with an ambivalent influence on the conservative movement. As the foremost proponent of realism in foreign policy, he was an enemy of soft-headed liberal idealism. Although he supported anti-Communist authoritarian regimes abroad—which his successors in the Carter administration refused to do—Kissinger also believed that a stable international order, balancing the power of the United States and the Soviet Union, should be the goal of U.S. foreign policy, instead of fighting Communism on ideological grounds and trying to roll back its influence. For this reason, many conservatives considered his foreign policy amoral and bankrupt.

The moral imperative of anti-Communism was highlighted in the mid-1970s by the emigration of dissident Soviet writer Alexander Solzhenitsyn to the United States. Solzhenitsyn had been a schoolteacher and devout Communist in his youth. During World War II, he served with distinction on the Eastern Front, but his criticism of Stalin in private correspondence landed him in the Gulag. Try as they might, the Soviets could not silence him, and his writings found their way to the West, where publishers were only too pleased to air them to the world. His story about life in Siberia, *One Day in the Life of Ivan Denisovich*, infuriated the Soviet regime, but was praised in the West. "The public acclaim by Solzhenitsyn of the kind of thing we were doing," said Bill Buckley, "was an enormous stroke in the ideological heavens and his

Gulag book simply broke the back of the intellectual pro-Communist left."[25] In 1970, he was awarded the Nobel Prize for Literature, but the Soviet government effectively forbade him to travel to Sweden to receive the award. Although a major embarrassment to Moscow, his fame throughout the outside world made it impossible for the KGB to kill him; when *The Gulag Archipelago* was published in the West (a microfilmed copy was smuggled out of the Soviet Union), the authorities shrewdly calculated that if they shipped him off to the United States, American liberals would silence him for them.

The Soviets' guess was right: Liberal intellectuals realized that Solzhenitsyn was as much a threat to their world as he was to Moscow's, and set out to destroy him. They viewed his Christian faith and criticisms of Western decadence, whether aimed at rock music or sexual "liberation," as downright reactionary. Mary McCarthy, who had joined other writers in condemning the Soviets' silencing of Solzhenitsyn in 1969, later wrote of his views of liberals: "He has it in for those people, just as he would have it in for you and me, if he could overhear us talking."[26] When several conservative senators suggested that President Gerald Ford meet with him at the White House, Ford refused, in the spirit of "détente," calling Solzhenitsyn a "goddam horse's ass."[27] The final straw came when he was invited to give the commencement address at Harvard in June 1978. In a speech that rocked liberalism to its core, and was a beacon of clarity to conservatives, Solzhenitsyn condemned the materialism, self-indulgence, moral cowardice, and misuse of liberty in the West, accusing the liberal elite of losing "civic courage" in the face of Communist evil. He accused the antiwar movement of betraying Asian nations, where, as a result, genocide and suffering had become a way of life. To those who called for détente, he warned, "Only moral criteria can help the West against Communism's well-planned world strategy. There are no other criteria."[28] In order to defeat the forces of evil, Solzhenitsyn followed Whittaker Chambers in recalling to his audience the Christian faith, the foundation of Western civilization.

The liberal establishment was stunned by Solzhenitsyn's words. In a hurried and harried defense, the *New York Times* editorialized that "Mr. Solzhenitsyn's world view seems to us far more dangerous than the easygoing spirit which he finds so exasperating. . . . Life in a society run by zealots like Mr. Solzhenitsyn is bound to be uncomfortable for those who do not share his vision or ascribe to his beliefs."[29] Henry Fairlie, in tandem, agreed in the *New Republic*: "To make the experience of Communist oppression seem ennobling, which is what Solzhenitsyn does, is surely an unforgivable misuse of suffering . . . the life of the prisoner has become the only one he can live, what was heard in Harvard Square was the voice of a man who no longer has an inkling of what it means to be free."[30] Conservatives were inspired. Michael Novak hailed it as "the most important religious document of our time . . . it was a ray of light for the entire race of men. He kept his eye upon the need to tell the truth, come what may."[31]

Solzhenitsyn wasn't the only man condemning détente. As described earlier, a group of liberal anti-Communist intellectuals had become disgusted with the Carter administration's inability to recognize the evils of Soviet Communism and had joined forces with various conservatives to form the Committee for the Present Danger. One prominent member was Georgetown University professor Jeane Kirkpatrick, who had been active in the presidential campaigns of Hubert Humphrey and Henry "Scoop" Jackson. Untypical, however, was the influence of her article "Dictatorships and Double Standards," a critique of Carter administration foreign policy published in *Commentary* in 1979. Kirkpatrick pointed out that Carter was willing to use American power on behalf of liberal causes he liked, but in his sniffy Puritanism, withdrew support from the authoritarian anti-Communist regimes of Iran and Nicaragua at crucial moments in their struggles against anti-American insurgents. By contrast, in the face of atrocities committed by the Communist governments of Vietnam and Cambodia, "The President continued to behave . . . not like a man who abhors autocrats but like one who abhors only right-wing autocrats."[32]

Kirkpatrick's essay was a powerful practical and moral case for American alliances with nondemocratic anti-Communist regimes. The urgency of the Communist threat was underlined one month after Kirkpatrick's essay appeared with the Soviet Union's invasion of Afghanistan.

Ronald Reagan read "Dictatorships and Double Standards" and fellow CPD member Richard V. Allen arranged an introduction, and soon Kirkpatrick was a foreign policy advisor to Reagan's 1980 presidential campaign. She became Reagan's UN ambassador in 1981, where she was an articulate, assertive spokeswoman for American national interests. (Allen, a former student of Eric Voegelin and long active in the ISI, became Reagan's first national security advisor.)

Besides the president himself, Kirkpatrick was the most effective spokesman for Reagan's foreign policy. Against the amoral realism of Kissinger's détente, she argued that American national interests and moral ends could be combined in foreign policy, rightly calling those who argued that the United States and the U.S.S.R. were equally oppressive, and therefore morally equivalent powers, the "blame America first" crowd.

Kirkpatrick brought several other conservative and neoconservative intellectuals with her to the UN mission, including AEI fellow Michael Novak as ambassador for human rights. Novak was another 1960s-era liberal who had moved steadily to the right during the 1970s and would have considerable influence on the conservative movement. Before beginning a career in academia and journalism, he had been a Roman Catholic seminarian, and he retained a greater interest in religion than did his fellow neoconservatives. Novak went further than Kirkpatrick in asserting the moral superiority of the American socioeconomic and political system, which he called "democratic capitalism." It wasn't just that Communism was evil, as earlier anti-Communists had said, or that America had a right to assert its national interests abroad, as Kirkpatrick insisted. Rather, Novak's 1982 *Spirit of Democratic Capitalism* argued the American system was morally superior to socialism (whether of the Soviet or Democratic Party variety). The proud descendant of Slovakian peasants who was raised in industrial Pennsylvania, Novak imbibed a deep appreciation for the opportunities democratic capitalism made available to hardworking men of talent, and believed that capitalism showed greater respect for human dignity than did socialism, which by definition limited freedom. Democratic capitalism even defeated socialism on its own terms: It created more wealth, which was distributed more equally, than any socialist system.[33] Like Kirkpatrick, Novak attacked the conceit of left-wing intellectuals who believed they could plan people's lives better than the people themselves.

Novak became a prolific critic of left-wing Catholicism, attacking, among other things, liberation theology—the Marxist strain of pseudo-Catholicism that had become the unofficial ideology of the Sandinistas in Nicaragua. In 1983 he blasted the Catholic bishops for releasing an unprecedented pastoral letter on nuclear policy, in which they appeared to abandon any pretense of a Cold War strategy. Together with Notre Dame philosopher Ralph McInerny, Novak launched a new journal called *Catholicism in Crisis* (later simply called *Crisis*) to criticize liberalizing trends in the Church in America. During the 1990s and into the twenty-first century, *Crisis* became instrumental in directing more socially conservative Catholics away from the liberal left and the Democratic Party and into the GOP.

Several conservative military strategists contributed to America's victory over Communism, but two merit special mention: Stefan Possony and Albert Wohlstetter. Possony, an Austrian émigré and expert on Soviet Communism, taught at Georgetown and was one of the first fellows at the Hoover Institution at Stanford. A longtime conservative stalwart and contributor to movement periodicals, his 1953 book *A Century of Conflict* explained the Soviet military strategy of using terror and revolution to subdue the enemy. To oppose such a policy, Possony advocated the development of weapons technologies so advanced as to overawe the Soviets or drive them to bankruptcy, a strategy that contributed to the development of the Strategic Defense Initiative, or "Star Wars." Wohlstetter, for his part, was trained in mathematical logic at Columbia University and deployed his intellectual firepower in nuclear strategy. He was a strong opponent of the strategies of the first strike and Mutual Assured Destruction, on the grounds that they were immoral, counterproductive, and of limited flexibility in the face of a Soviet threat. Instead, Wohlstetter called for employing a wide array of what amounted to imaginative strategic tricks to win the Cold War without ever firing a shot. He had a profound, though largely unnoticed, influence on policymakers in Washington, D.C., through his work for the Rand Corporation and later as a professor at the University of Chicago and UCLA. Among those he influenced were Senator Henry "Scoop" Jackson, *Wall Street Journal* editor Robert Bartley, Margaret Thatcher, Ronald Reagan, and future neoconservatives Richard Perle and Paul Wolfowitz.

CRITIQUING TRENDS IN HIGHER EDUCATION

As part of liberalism's lurch to radicalism during and following the Vietnam War, the left launched an attack on higher education, which reached its most insidious point by the late 1980s. Following in the foot-steps of their radical forebears, a group of students at Stanford began agitating to have the freshman Western Culture course abolished on the grounds that Western civilization was racist, sexist, and imperialist. Jesse Jackson led protesters, in front of the cameras, chanting "Hey-hey, ho-ho, Western Culture has got to go." Eventually the faculty voted to replace Western Culture with a multicultural potluck that included female and minority writers on the sole grounds that they were females or minorities. As the student newspaper put it: "We're tired of reading books by dead white guys" (which they probably hadn't).[34]

Into this riot of nonsense a shot was fired by University of Chicago political theorist Allan Bloom with *The Closing of the American Mind*. Despite—or perhaps because of—its misanthropic tone and its stinging rebukes to contemporary academic fads, Bloom's book, to the surprise of both author and publisher, became a huge bestseller—surely one of the most intellectually demanding works ever to earn that status.

Bloom was a student of Leo Strauss at Chicago and built a devoted student following of his own. He taught at Cornell in the 1960s and when it became a hotbed of radical activism moved, disgusted, to the University of Chicago, his alma mater, where he remained until his death in 1992. Bloom was a colorful, even flamboyant personality, lov-ingly memorialized by his friend Saul Bellow in the novel *Ravelstein*.

Socratic dialogue and the philosophical way of life, abandoned in most educational circles, were the essence of education, Bloom wrote in his renowned book. The substitution of mindless relativism for philo-sophical inquiry was impoverishing the lives of students, he argued, and contemporary higher education, as a result, was sowing the seeds of the destruction of democracy. According to Bloom, the threat to Western values came primarily from German philosophy in the relativism and historicism of Friedrich Nietzsche and Martin Heidegger, and its adop-tion in American culture made students numbly indifferent to truth. Their indifference was reinforced by popular culture:

> Picture a thirteen-year-old boy sitting in the living
> room of his family doing his math assignment while
> wearing his Walkman headphones or watching MTV.
> He enjoys the liberties hard won over centuries by

the alliance of philosophic genius and political hero-
ism, consecrated by the blood of martyrs; he is provided with comfort and leisure by the most productive economy ever known to mankind; science has
penetrated the secrets of nature in order to provide
him with the marvelous, lifelike electronic sound
and image reproduction he is enjoying. And in what
does progress culminate? A pubescent child whose
body throbs with orgasmic rhythms; whose feelings
are made articulate in hymns to the joys of onanism
or the killing of parents; whose ambition is to win
fame and wealth in imitating the drag queen who
makes the music.[35]

Reviewers were aghast. Typical was the *New York Times*, in which
Christopher Lehmann-Haupt wrote that "this book is going to make
a lot of people mad—feminists, scientists, black-power advocates and
champions of relevance. And indeed it is probably vulnerable to charges
of elitism, antiquarianism, exaggerated subjectivity and skewed general-
ization from the particular."[36]

More of a neocon than a traditionalist, Bloom stirred up the growing divide between the two camps. In a symposium in the conservative
journal *Modern Age*, his critics faulted Bloom's rationalism, his carica-
ture of modern German philosophy, and his Straussian coyness about
his own first principles. University of Michigan English professor Stephen Tonsor, a stalwart traditionalist, warned: "Those conservatives who
believe that Bloom is a fellow traveler should read his text carefully
once more. Bloom is a man of the Enlightenment sentimentalized by
Rousseau. He is an agnostic who lacks the courage of his convictions.
He may deplore the consequences of Nietzsche's thought but he also
knows that Nietzsche had the courage to think thought to its ultimate
conclusion, the thought with which Bloom has only toyed."[37] As with
many other issues, conservatives differed in their diagnoses of what was
wrong with higher education, and prescriptions for remedying them,
but they were unanimous in rejecting recent trends toward the vilification of the Western tradition and the abandonment of serious critical
thinking.

By the early 1990s, thanks in part to the efforts of conservatives like Bloom, William Bennett, Reagan's secretary of education, and journalists Charles Sykes and Roger Kimball, concern about the state of higher education was reaching critical mass. Even liberal standard-bearers in the print media, led by the *New York Times* and the *New York Review of Books*, were beginning to pay unflattering attention to the newly popular concept of "political correctness," a term used in the heyday of Uncle Joe Stalin and fellow travelers to describe one's faithful adherence to Marxist orthodoxy and the party line (used of course, with a characteristic Communist lack of irony). To 1990s leftists the term meant speech codes whose content would have been comical had those enforcing them not been so earnest. Fueling the flames of popular discontent with political correctness was Dinesh D'Souza's book *Illiberal Education*. D'Souza documented the ill effects of speech codes forbidding "insensitive" language, which the left used to stifle free inquiry. He found that multicultural curricula, in their zeal to replace the classics of the Western tradition, had substituted superficial works like *I, Rigoberta Menchu* on the grounds that they represented non-Western perspectives. He pointed out that racial preferences in college admissions policies, like those at Berkeley, which were intended to remedy racial discrimination, had the perverse effect of preferring unprepared blacks to capable Asians, and in the process making racial tensions worse.[38]

Illiberal Education was a muckraking exposé of the modern university and its abuses against free inquiry, common sense, and decency, and made these abuses widely known for the first time. D'Souza's critics hesitated to accuse him of espousing racist views because he was an immigrant from India—only whites could be racists. Surprisingly, *Illiberal Education* was warmly received by conservatives and independent-minded liberals alike. Eugene Genovese, one of the original masterminds behind the 1960s radicals' "long march through the institutions," wrote in the *New Republic*, "I fear that our conservative colleagues are today facing a new McCarthyism in some ways more effective and vicious than the old."[39]

D'Souza had been exposing the nonsensical in Ivy League college life since his days as an undergraduate at Dartmouth in the early 1980s, when he was editor-in-chief of the *Dartmouth Review*. The *Re-*

view was the conservative alternative newspaper on campus, advised by Dartmouth professor and *National Review* senior editor Jeffrey Hart, whose contributors took delight in tweaking the liberal sensibilities of the administration and faculty. The *Dartmouth Review* was only one, and perhaps the most notorious, of many conservative alternative college papers that sprang up during the 1980s. The Institute for Educational Affairs, a Manhattan-based outfit funded by the Olin Foundation, among others, had been subsidizing alternative conservative collegiate newspapers since the early 1980s, and founded the Collegiate Network to support such papers and protect their independence from university administrations. Later the Collegiate Network became part of the Intercollegiate Studies Institute, under whose management it has flourished and grown to include over one hundred campus newspapers, many of which have become a kind of farm team for the conservative media.

Another effort to subvert the liberal hegemony over higher education came from a man who had helped build it, David Horowitz. Editor of the New Left journal *Ramparts* in the late 1960s, he witnessed the left's callous indifference to human life at home and abroad, and was describing himself as a conservative by the late 1980s. Horowitz, a prolific and compelling writer, has devoted himself primarily to exposing left-wing ideological bias through the Center for the Study of Popular Culture, now called the David Horowitz Freedom Center. Among other things, he has called for an Academic Bill of Rights to eliminate ideological discrimination in higher education.

Although conservatives have made some inroads into the educational establishment, education, both secondary and higher, has remained a liberal stronghold—in the opinion of many, perhaps the last bastion of unadulterated liberalism in the country. But if conservatives made little headway in the established environment, they did what they always do—they made an end run around the power structure and began creating alternative institutions. Where universities were hostile to academic research of a conservative bent, conservatives developed think tanks. Where colleges abandoned traditional liberal arts curricula, conservatives carved out traditional programs within them or founded new liberal arts colleges. Where primary and secondary school education remained dominated by progressivism, conservatives promoted home schooling, charter schools, and vouchers for school choice.

CULTURAL CRITICISM

One campus newspaper that made it to the big time was R. Emmett Tyrrell, Jr.'s *The American Spectator*. Founded by Tyrrell at Indiana University in 1967, it was originally named *The Alternative*, and subsequently *An American Spectator* was added to the name in response to the regnant radical chic culture. After ten years Tyrrell decided to shorten the name to avoid unsolicited manuscripts from liberal oddballs. Tyrrell was part fun-loving jock, part intellectual contrarian. He had been on the renowned Indiana swim team, but was also fond of the comforts of the saloon. His "common sense, individualism, and cussedness" fueled *The American Spectator*'s affinity for the silent majority of sensible Americans.[40] Tyrrell was a student of American history and a devotee of H. L. Mencken and, like his mentor, mocked the subtle though perverse Puritanism of the day. Drinking, smoking, and eating red meat were celebrated in the pages of the *Spectator*. Praising martinis, Werner Dannhauser once wrote, "I put away my work, the daily drudgeries. Relaxing, I prepare my drink with loving care. Then I sit back and think of once and future deeds and speeches. . . . My friends and I are young again, alive with hope. Grace smiles on me as Mr. Death assumes a modest stance, and all the while martinis make the music for my memories."[41]

Though it operated out of a run-down farmhouse just off the Indiana University campus, *The American Spectator* was remarkable from the first issue for attracting many prominent cultural critics to its pages who disdained the New Left just as Tyrrell did. Tyrrell used his often rhetorical and mocking over-the-top prose to combat the left, ridiculing what he called the *Kultursmog* through a section called "The Continuing Crisis," which covered the absurdities of New Age culture and politics.

The *Spectator* was always a bit ahead of its times, and those it chose to include in the magazine often raised eyebrows among other conservatives. In 1969, Tyrrell published an interview with Irving Kristol, the coeditor, with Daniel Patrick Moynihan, of *The Public Interest*, and the reaction was derisive. M. Stanton Evans, who was then a sort of mentor to the magazine, questioned whether Kristol, who was supporting Hubert Humphrey for president, would ever be anything but a liberal. But the interview was the beginning of a long friendship with Kristol, during which *The American Spectator* became a bridge for a whole procession of liberals in their trek to the right, including Jeane Kirkpatrick, James Q. Wilson, Midge Decter, and Norman Podhoretz. Other stylish, thoughtful, and sometimes iconoclastic writers from beyond conservatism became a staple in the magazine, largely because they were so very literary—people like Lewis Lapham, who chastised Jimmy Carter, Sydney Hook on totalitarianism, and even Pat Moynihan, who never made it to conservatism, but who was serious about the movement. The magazine made a concerted effort to publish like-minded European writers, with frequent appearances by Malcolm Muggeridge, John O'Sullivan, and Peregrine Worthsthorne from the United Kingdom, Jean Francois Revel from France, and Italy's Luigi Barzini. Tyrrell finally gave up on the Midwest in the mid-eighties, moving the magazine to Washington, D.C., where it continues to thrive.

On a more rarefied plane, emerging from the remnant of people serious about high culture in New York City came the *New Criterion*, founded in 1982 by Hilton Kramer, the art critic for the *New York Times*. Kramer became increasingly fed up with the capitulation of the cultural establishment to the passing fads of the 1960s and the misuse of art in obeisance to left-wing politics. In a way, he was responding to the same trends as Tyrrell, but in a less popular, less political manner. He and the late *Commentary* music critic Samuel Lipman were joined by Roger Kimball, who became coeditor in 2005 after serving as managing editor for many years.

The leftist cultural establishment did not take kindly to Kramer's project. It was one thing to have him blasting liberals from his perch at the *New York Times*, but quite another to have a whole organ dedicated to propagating the views of like-minded critics. Before the first issue of the *New Criterion* was off the press, liberals were busily sharpening their knives. Leon Wieseltier, writing in the *New Republic*, put the magazine down as "philistinism with a twist—philistinism in the defense of modernism. The defense of modernism is a major objective of the neoconservative campaign in culture. .... It is status raised to an aesthetic principle, and meanness of spirit raised to a principle culture," thus accusing Kramer and company of bending art to the service of neoconservative politics.[42]

Kimball penned critical appreciations of the founding fathers of the movement such as Richard Weaver and James Burnham.[43] In its twenty-fifth anniversary issue, the *New Criterion*'s retrospective editorial noted that "recent cultural life is subject to some special deformations—above all, we think, an ongoing ambition to politicize culture and a concomitant effort to blur the distinction between high and low."[44] Kramer and Kimball promised to continue making discriminating criticism of contemporary trends and to recall the riches of the Western patrimony.

Despite the efforts of journals like the *New Criterion*, some thought conservatives paid insufficient attention to the transmission of Western culture. Surveying the wasteland of contemporary culture, Claes Ryn, political theorist and chairman of the National Humanities Institute, lamented that conservatives had invested too much thought, energy, and money on electoral politics over the last forty years. Ryn argued that what was needed was a revitalization of what Russell Kirk called the moral imagination, but unfortunately the "intellectual, aesthetic, and moral-spiritual renewal that might have transformed the universities, the arts, the media, publishing, entertainment, and the churches never came off. Without a major reorientation of American thought and sensibility, conservative politics was bound to fail."[45]

Political gains could not reverse the drift of contemporary culture, and electoral victory would not even be possible in the future if the people no longer understood the culture conservatives intended to conserve. In emphasizing the need for profound cultural renewal, Tyrrell, Kramer, and Ryn followed in the footsteps of Weaver, Kirk, and others in the immediate postwar conservative movement. While the foes changed, the cultural crisis of the West remained.

THE END OF THE COLD WAR

After barring East Germans from the West for almost thirty years, the Berlin Wall came tumbling down in November 1989. When the Soviet Union dissolved two years later, on Christmas Day 1991, the common enemy that united traditionalists, libertarians, anti-Communists, and neoconservatives was gone. Many predicted that the conservative movement would break apart also.

Tyrrell thought he was observing a conservative crackup, and wrote a book with that title. Like many others, he was concerned about conservatives' apparent inability to change American political culture. Conservatives, he thought, lacked panache, the flair for the dramatic that radicals used to change American culture in the 1960s. Without it, they would be lost: "Even as the liberal was brought down by too much imagination, the conservative was laid low by too little."[46]

Throughout the 1980s, there had been competition between different parts of the movement for the spoils of Reagan's victories. Each group wanted action, and each wanted government funding for its particular agenda. But all parties put their differences aside in order to rally behind Ronald Reagan. Once Reagan was out of office, however, and the Cold War was over, tensions flared up in a more serious way. Neoconservatives, who had been more effective than traditionalists in reaping the benefits of Reagan's ascendency, were viewed by many conservative veterans as interlopers who had wrongly deprived them of their just credit. Many thought these neocons were not really conservative, but were still social democrats at heart, pushed into the GOP by the radicalization of the Democratic Party.

Like many neoconservatives, Richard John Neuhaus, a Lutheran pastor and civil rights activist, moved rightward after becoming disillusioned with the left in the 1970s, and became head of the Rockford (Illinois) Institute's Center on Religion and Society. In addition to the center, Rockford backed the magazine *Chronicles*, edited by paleoconservative Thomas Fleming. Fleming was already on bad terms with Neuhaus because he openly disdained many of the 1960s protest causes dear to Neuhaus's heart. But when Fleming published articles that Neuhaus's friends Norman Podhoretz and Midge Decter thought were anti-Semitic, Neuhaus took their side against Fleming. The relationship between Fleming, Rockford, and Neuhaus steadily deteriorated, until both sides agreed to go their separate ways, and Neuhaus formed the Institute on Religion and Public Life in New York City and a monthly magazine he called *First Things*.

After parting company with Rockford and the paleoconservatives, Richard John Neuhaus thrived. He found a new spiritual home in the Catholic Church and was ordained to the priesthood (ironically, Tom Fleming had by then also converted). His institute and its journal, *First Things*, were highly successful. An ecumenical venture, *First Things* brought together Catholics, Protestants, and Jews to comment on a wide range of contemporary intellectual trends. It celebrated orthodoxy, but no particular religion; it published academics, but was accessible to a lay audience, making it the foremost conservative intellectual journal in America.

Neuhaus and some of his leading contributors were deeply concerned about the Supreme Court's rulings on abortion, euthanasia, and gay rights, and by its assertion of sovereignty over the whole American political system in order to give force to those rulings. Neuhaus organized a symposium reflecting on the problem, called "The End of Democracy? The Judicial Usurpation of Politics," which came out in the November 1996 issue of *First Things*.

The symposium raised the question of whether, given that the Supreme Court justices had twisted the Constitution and constitutional law willy-nilly to suit their policies, thus arrogating sovereignty over the decisions of the president and Congress, their authority was legitimate and ought to be obeyed. University of Tulsa philosophy professor Russell Hittinger, a conservative Catholic, said that the Court had explicitly staked its legitimacy on its 1992 *Planned Parenthood* v. *Casey* decision, in which it upheld abortion rights, demanding that it be obeyed in the name of the common good. Such assertions were illegitimate, and fundamentally undermined the ability of the American people to govern themselves. Retired federal judge and former Supreme Court nominee Robert Bork pointed out that "not one of these five decisions bears any resemblance to the actual Constitution . . . a majority of justices have decided to rule us without any warrant in law."[47]

It was the first time conservatives of such stature had questioned the legitimacy of trends in Supreme Court jurisprudence in terms so stark, and it was bound to cause controversy. Peter Berger, a close friend and collaborator of Neuhaus, resigned from the *First Things* board in protest, as did Walter Berns and Gertrude Himmelfarb. Neoconservative journalist David Brooks warned against conservatives' succumbing to "the anti-American temptation."[48]

Liberals looked on with what Himmelfarb aptly described as "undisguised *Schadenfreude*." But if—like many other intraconservative squabbles—it seemed that the heated debate that followed might portend the end of the conservative movement, it did not.

CRITIQUING THE WELFARE STATE

Conservatives began critiquing the welfare state at its very inception. But their warnings went unheeded, and twenty years after the implementation of the Great Society, its failures were there for all to see.

Sociologist Charles Murray analyzed its effects in his 1984 book *Losing Ground: American Social Policy, 1950–1980*. He found that most Great Society programs were not only expensive failures, but actually worsened the problems they were supposed to solve. As he put it, "The most troubling aspect of social policy toward the poor in late twentieth-century America is not how much it costs, but what it has bought."[49]

Murray showed that poverty rates for blacks and whites remained the same between 1968 and 1980, in spite of massive welfare payments. Moreover, welfare payments created monetary incentives for poor pregnant women not to get married. The result was that many—eventually most—did not, so their children were raised without fathers playing an active role in their lives. And these children were, naturally, more likely to get into trouble with the law. Hence the rising crime rates. Murray noted that more poor children were receiving an education after the Great Society than before, but the quality of that education had declined, even more among the disadvantaged than in the rest of the country, preventing the poor from catching up economically with the rest of the population. The persistence of the "underclass," as it became known, and the intractable nature of poverty showed how naive policy experts had been about poverty in the 1960s.

According to Murray, the biggest problem was that welfare policies were structured in such a manner as to encourage people to behave in ways that were socially destructive. He proposed the repeal of laws treating people differently on the basis of race and school vouchers to give poor students a chance to get a better education. Most controversially, he proposed:

> Scrapping the entire federal welfare and income-support structure for working-aged persons, including AFDC, Medicaid, Food Stamps, Unemployment Insurance, Worker's Compensation, subsidized housing, disability insurance, and the rest. It would leave the working-aged person with no recourse whatsoever except the job market, family members, friends, and public or private locally funded services. It is the Alexandrian solution: cut the knot, for there is no way to untie it.[50]

Murray said reform would come not when stingy budget hawks would cut welfare to save money, but when welfare advocates took an honest look at their work and realized they had failed.

Given Ronald Reagan's repeated calls for welfare reform, Murray's message attracted much criticism. He was called a Social Darwinist in the *Washington Post*, and condemned by the *New York Times* editorial page, which said his suggestions were dangerous, something "people in Washington have turned into a budgetary club against the poor."[51] Instead, the *Times* suggested the economic boom of the Reagan years justified funding new programs for the poor.

Another important book in this genre was Marvin Olasky's *The Tragedy of American Compassion*, published in 1992. Like many conservatives, Olasky had been a Communist in his youth, became disillusioned, and joined the ranks of the evangelical Christians in 1973. In his book, Olasky argued that private charities of the nineteenth century had been more successful and humane than the twentieth-century welfare state—private charities had stressed what he called affiliation, trying to help the poor by restoring broken family ties, whereas contemporary social policy emphasized personal autonomy. Private charities had tried to bond with those they cared for when they were truly on their own, whereas the welfare state was bureaucratic and impersonal. Private charities tried to discern who really needed help and who merely sought to live in indolence; the welfare state made no such distinctions. Most important, private charities succeeded because they were motivated by their faith in God, and suffered with those they cared for the way Christ suffered for humanity, not because helping the less fortunate made them feel better about themselves.[52]

In an attempt to get a feel for the contemporary charitable efforts to help the poor, Olasky had pretended to be homeless for a couple of days, frequenting downtown Washington churches catering to the homeless. He had received plenty of food and was offered clothing and shelter, but there was one thing he could not get: "A sweet young volunteer kept putting food down and asking me if I wanted more. Finally I asked, mumbling a bit, 'Could I have a Bible?' Puzzled, she tried to figure out what I had said. . . . When I responded, 'A Bible,' she said, politely but firmly, 'I'm sorry, we don't have any Bibles.'"[53] Even Christian charities, it seemed, had lost their proper sense of compassion.

Olasky's book built on the work of Murray (who wrote the preface), gave an equally accessible but more wide-ranging history of poverty relief in the United States, and proposed broader principles to guide reform. It also had a more immediate impact on policymakers. House Speaker Newt Gingrich read it on the recommendation of William Bennett, and drew public attention to Olasky's ideas. But liberals derided it, saying that "far from helping the poor . . . Olasky had provided a smokescreen for guiltlessly cutting back the welfare state."[54]

Situated as he was at the University of Texas at Austin, Olasky, a former speechwriter for Delaware governor Pierre du Pont, became an advisor to Texas governor George W. Bush. He wrote a manifesto for Bush's 2000 presidential campaign called *Compassionate Conservatism*, advocating government support for faith-based charities. But he has since distanced himself from the Office of Faith-Based Initiatives.

Through the efforts of men like Murray and Olasky, and other critics of the welfare state before them, conservatives had amassed an overwhelming body of evidence by the early 1990s to show that the Great Society not only was a failure, but had made social problems like endemic poverty worse. They gradually changed the climate and terms of the debate over welfare, paving the way for the reforms passed by the GOP Congress and signed by Bill Clinton in 1996.

STILL REDEEMING THE TIME

Conservative intellectuals have, unceasingly, continued to elaborate on their penetrating criticisms of liberal ideology and policy. As Russell Kirk said, quoting Burke, they continue to strive to "redeem the time." Academic political theorists put meaty tomes before the public. Economists dissected the flaws in socialism and pointed the way toward prosperity for all. Anti-Communists reminded Americans of the price of freedom and urged them to be a beacon of light to the world. Cultural critics celebrated the high culture of the West, and educators upheld the rigorous education needed to appreciate it. After years of falling on deaf ears, conservative warnings about the dangers of the welfare state began to be heard and resulted in policy changes. And in spite of the end of the Cold War, and their occasional philosophical differences, conservative intellectuals flourished: By 2006, they were more numerous, got more respect from their peers, and had more journals and publishing houses through which to spread their ideas than ever before.

CHAPTER ELEVEN

Ronald Reagan

The conservative movement came of age with Ronald Reagan. Reagan took the movement's ideas, communicated them to the American people in understandable terms, and applied them to practical politics. His political march moved the conservative cause from the fringes to the mainstream, from suspect ideology to respectable politics, shifting American politics from the left to center right. Within the movement he pulled anti-Communists, libertarians, economic conservatives, traditionalists, the Christian right, and even neoconservatives into a powerful coalition. Each had a place in his echelon, each was represented in his campaign for the presidency and subsequently in his administration, and the philosophy of each, fused into one, became the substance on which his presidency was based. Each part of the coalition brought something of value to the Reagan Revolution, each felt it had gained something in the doing—and yes, each felt a bit shortchanged that it did not get everything. This coalition not only provided Reagan with the tools he needed to get elected and reelected, but broadened the boundaries of the conservative movement. And it finally ended the monopoly held by the dominant political and philosophical force that conservatives had been fighting since 1945—the leftist, New Deal coalition.

The Reagan Revolution was not a revolution of politics but of ideas. As Reagan himself said in a 1981 speech, "Our victory . . . was not so much a victory for any one man or party as it was a victory for a set of principles—principles that were protected and nourished by a few unselfish Americans throughout many grim and heartbreaking defeats."[1]

Critics who like to point out that Reagan did not actually accomplish much, that his programs did not achieve what he had promised, fail to understand that Reagan ran for president in order to change the American people's concept of the role of government.

Beginning with his election as governor of California in 1966 by a million votes, just two years after Barry Goldwater *lost* California by a million votes; followed by his re-election, four years later, when he beat California superman Democrat Jesse Unruh by a half million votes; to his 1976 primary challenge against sitting president Ford, in which he came within a whisker of getting the nomination; to his ultimate landslide victory in 1980, beating incumbent Jimmy Carter with all but forty-nine electoral votes; and his re-election in 1984 by one of the largest margins in U.S. history, Ronald Reagan dominated conservative politics—indeed American politics—and demonstrated that a conservative politician, with a consistent conservative message, could be elected by landslide margins.

More important, with Ronald Reagan conservatives demonstrated that they could govern. Reagan was the first identifiable conservative to preside over a major state, and the first to be president. Until 1964 the conservative movement was a philosophical enterprise. With the Goldwater campaign it became a political enterprise. With the election of Ronald Reagan, the movement proved it was capable of governing.

Finally, Reagan took the negative edge off conservatism. He taught conservatives how to talk to and persuade voters, how to present issues and what to avoid. With his affable and sunny disposition, Reagan was able to persuade millions of people that conservatism was not something to be feared but a positive force that was good for them and for America. He showed people that conservatives were not just grumpy old men mulling over philosophical questions, but real, living Americans of all ages who had a rosy view of the future.

This chapter will look back to the 1940s when Ronald Reagan first stepped onto the political stage as president of the Screen Actors Guild to testify before the House Committee on Un-American Activities about Communist efforts to control Hollywood. It shows Reagan, the public speaker, columnist, and radio commentator, and how he educated millions of Americans on conservative principles and brought millions more into the conservative fold. And finally, we will see how he transformed the ideas and principles he had talked about for so many years into workable programs and policies.

The conservative movement reached its apex during Reagan's presidency, at least from a political perspective; it is unlikely that it will ever again have the combination of an articulate and polished politician and a committed philosophical conservative at its helm.

Reagan loved to remind liberals that he had cast his first vote in 1932 for Franklin Delano Roosevelt, and infuriated them by claiming that he, not modern American liberalism, was the legitimate heir to what Roosevelt had stood for in 1932. He remained a great fan of Roosevelt during the New Deal and a Democrat well into the 1950s, but as time went on he came to realize that much of what the New Deal had created was not the solution but the cause of the country's problems.

In his oft-repeated attacks on federal domestic policy, particularly welfare and aid to the poor, Reagan reminded his listeners about the damage that New Deal liberalism had done to the country, and echoed Roosevelt's 1935 warning:

> The lessons of history, confirmed by the evidence immediately before me, show conclusively that continued dependence upon relief induces a spiritual and moral disintegration fundamentally destructive to the national fiber. To dole out relief in this way is to administer a narcotic, a subtle destroyer of the human spirit. . . . It is in violation of the traditions of America.[2]

Reagan had also been a union man. Soon after arriving in Hollywood he joined the Screen Actors Guild (SAG) because, as he later explained, "Some of the studio bosses were abusing their power. Throughout my life, I guess, there's been one thing that's troubled me more than any other: the abuse of people and the theft of their democratic rights."[3] This idea was at the core of Reagan's philosophy not only concerning unions, but concerning big government, totalitarianism, whether fascism or Communism, and government regulators and bureaucrats. Reagan served on the board of directors and as president of the Screen Actors Guild during the 1940s and 1950s. His experience as a New Dealer and as a union official gave him enormous credibility in attacking liberal governmental policies and abuses. His Democratic union background also allowed him to appeal to the people who would become known as "Reagan Democrats," a significant part of his political base who contributed to Reagan's realignment of American politics.

ANTI-COMMUNIST

Reagan was introduced to Communism soon after World War II, when, as head of the Screen Actors Guild, he became enmeshed in attempts by Hollywood leftists to infiltrate the film industry. Although the Communists attempted to make their campaign look like a simple jurisdictional dispute among unions, of which there were many in Hollywood, Reagan recognized this as the ruse it was. Important matters were at stake. "Joseph Stalin," Reagan wrote in his autobiography, "had set out to make Hollywood an instrument of propaganda for his program of Soviet expansionism aimed at communizing the world."[4] Reagan quickly emerged as one of the most vocal opponents of any such attempts. So effective was he that Communists threatened to throw acid in his actor's face if he persisted, but he was undaunted, aided by the police, who armed him with a handgun and provided twenty-four-hour surveillance.

Reagan also cooperated with the FBI in its investigations of Communist infiltration of the industry. Since the FBI was despised and feared by leftists in Hollywood more than any other government agency, Reagan's willingness to work with it is indicative of his slide from left to right, at least concerning Communism. According to his FBI file, which was released in 1985, Reagan had been talking to the FBI since 1941—then about anti-Semites and Nazi sympathizers. His code name was "T-10."

In Washington, the House Committee on Un-American Activities began a series of hearings in 1947 to investigate Communist infiltration of the motion picture industry—hearings that ultimately resulted in a famous standoff between the committee and the "Hollywood Ten," a group of actors and screenwriters accused of being members of the Communist Party who refused to testify and subsequently were cited for contempt of Congress and blacklisted from the movie industry by a group of film executives. Among the first to testify at these hearings were "friendly" actors, such as Robert Montgomery, George Murphy (who in 1964 was elected to the United States Senate from California), and Ronald Reagan.

Although Reagan's testimony is not particularly noteworthy, that he did so at all, and the general position that he took, was noteworthy. Reagan, still a fervent New Deal Democrat, recognized that the American Communist Party was a subversive organization, led by the nose from Moscow to further its own totalitarian ideology. Reagan's testimony directly opposed the official policy of the Truman administration and of the Democratic Party, which naively believed, despite overpowering evidence, that Communism was "just another party," that the Soviet Union was a benign but unfriendly place that would eventually wither away, which in the meantime the West should "contain" with as little fuss as possible.

Reagan was one of the first nationally known Democrats to challenge "containment" and to advocate head-on confrontation with Communism. Throughout his political career, he never wavered in this belief; it was the foundation of his foreign policy as president.

In 1947, before the House committee, Reagan testified that:

> As a citizen I would hesitate, or not like, to see any political party outlawed on the basis of its political ideology. We have spent 170 years in this country on the basis that democracy is strong enough to stand up and fight against the inroads of any ideology. However, if it is proven that an organization is an agent of a power, a foreign power, or in any way not a legitimate political party, and I think the Government is capable of proving that, if the proof is there, then that is another matter.[5]

The next to testify, when Reagan was done, were a Russian émigré named Ayn Rand, film mogul Walt Disney, and actor Gary Cooper.

Ironically, one of the junior members of the committee was a newly elected congressman from California who, in his own right, would soon play a major role in America's battles against Communism. But in 1947, Richard Nixon was still practically unknown. Nixon had urged that Reagan testify before the committee, saying Reagan was "classified as a liberal and as such would not be accused of simply being a red-baiting reactionary."[6] It was also ironic that in 1950, Reagan would campaign for leftist Democrat Helen Gahagan Douglas in her run for the Senate against Nixon. Richard Nixon, never shy of name calling, stopped short of accusing Douglas of being a Communist, although he did describe her as being "pink right down to her underwear." Douglas responded by dubbing Nixon "Tricky Dick." (Helen Gahagan Douglas, a former actress and femme fatale, had simultaneous contact with no fewer than four future presidents. While Ronald Reagan campaigned for her against Richard Nixon in 1950 she was in the midst of an affair with Texas Congressman Lyndon B. Johnson. After Jack Kennedy, dispatched by his father to deliver a sizable contribution to Richard Nixon, was criticized for doing so, he apologized to Douglas, saying it was one of the stupidest things he had ever done.)

Reagan became Hollywood's best-known and most effective anti-Communist. Sterling Hayden, a second-rate Hollywood actor who had briefly been a member of the Communist Party, testified to the House Committee on Un-American Activities that the Communists' efforts to gain support from Hollywood film stars were never successful because of "a one-man battalion named Ronald Reagan."[7] Later in life Reagan often spoke of his days fighting Communists in Hollywood. What he learned by doing so made a deep impression on him and helped him understand the deadly threat the country faced. Reagan later wrote that he acquired "firsthand experience how Communists used lies, deceit, violence, or any other tactic that suited them to advance the cause of Soviet expansionism. I knew from the experience of hand-to-hand combat that America faced no more insidious or evil threat than that of Communism."[8]

Ronald Reagan was an outspoken anti-Communist throughout his political career. He talked about Communism in his campaigns, he wrote about it in his columns, he berated it in his radio broadcasts. In a radio talk in December 1976, he spoke of a five-year-old boy who fell into the Spree River in Berlin. The boy drowned because East German guards prevented West Berlin firemen from rescuing him. "Communism," said Reagan, "is neither an economic nor a political system—it is a form of insanity—a temporary aberration which will one day disappear from the earth because it is contrary to human nature. I wonder how much more misery it will create before it disappears."[9] In the late 1960s, Reagan and Paul Laxalt would often ride horses together in the Sierra Nevadas. "I didn't give a damn about the Russians," said Laxalt. "I was governor of the great state of Nevada and had other things on my mind. But you'd go on a ride with him, he'd be talking about the Cold War, he'd always be raising hell about those damned Russians."[10]

From the start, Reagan participated wholeheartedly in the anti-Communist movement. He spoke at rallies such as one in 1961 put on by the Christian Anti-Communism Crusade, and at numerous meetings and conventions organized by Young Americans for Freedom and similar groups, and was a regular speaker at annual Conservative Political Action Committee (CPAC) conferences. In 1979, he joined the neoconservative anti-Communist organization Committee on the Present Danger (CPD), which had an important impact on his 1980 campaign for president. Reagan shared the CPD view that the failure of the United States during the Carter administration to stay abreast of Soviet arms buildup had made the United States vulnerable to Soviet attack.

Reagan's anti-Communism was at the heart of his conservatism and a vital part of his entire political philosophy. He was, after all, an anti-Communist while still a New Deal liberal and long before he identified with domestic conservatives. For Reagan, America was "the shining city on the hill." God had reserved a special place for America and for Americans, and Reagan thought it was up to each one of us to preserve the freedoms that we had. Communism was freedom's exact opposite and a threat to the peace and freedom of the whole world. From his earliest political speeches to his last, he voiced this belief, often in almost the same words. Compare a speech he gave in 1952 to his Farewell Address when he left the White House in 1989:

From the 1952 speech:

> I, in my own mind, have thought of America as a place in the divine scheme of things that was set aside as a promised land. . . . I believe that God in shedding his grace on this country has always in this

divine scheme of things kept an eye on our land and guided it as a promised land for those people [who love freedom]. . . . The great ideological struggle we find ourselves engaged in today is not a new struggle. . . . It is simply the idea, the basis of this country and of our religion, the idea of the dignity of man, the idea that deep within the heart of each one of us is something so God-like and precious that no individual or group has the right to impose his or its will upon the people.[11]

And from his Farewell Address:

I've spoken of the shining city all my political life, but I don't know if I every quite communicated what I saw when I said it. But in my mind it was a tall, proud city built on rocks stronger than oceans, wind-swept, God-blessed, and teeming with people of all kinds living in harmony and peace; a city with free ports that hummed with commerce and creativity. And if there had to be city walls, the walls had doors and the doors were open to anyone with the will and the heart to get here. That is how I saw it, and see it still.[12]

In another sense, Reagan's anti-Communism, and in fact his entire political philosophy, was based on a strong sense of right and wrong. "This was a man," said Martin Anderson, "who had a very clear sense of what was right and what was wrong. And he saw things that bothered him and went after them. He did not do things for political reasons, he did them because they were right."[13] Edwin Meese agreed. "The first thing he said to the cabinet when he assembled us, on the twenty-first of January, was, 'I want all the decisions to be made on the basis of what is right, and not on what is politically advantageous.'"[14]

Reagan read and absorbed Whittaker Chambers's *Witness*, which pictured the struggle between East and West, between Communism and freedom, as a cosmic war of two mutually exclusive faiths.[15] He read columns of James Burnham and Frank Meyer in *National Review*, and devoured *Human Events*. When president, Reagan awarded the Medal of Freedom to Burnham and Chambers (posthumously). In Reagan's 1965 autobiography *Where's the Rest of Me?* Whittaker Chambers was the only conservative quoted or even cited; in one speech, Reagan credited Chambers with "beginning the counterrevolution of the intellectuals. . . . Chambers' story," Reagan continued, "represents a generation's disenchantment with statism and its return to eternal truths and fundamental values."[16] Asked by his aide Kenneth Cribb why he had chosen Chambers for the Medal of Freedom, Reagan replied, "Because one hundred years from now, people will have forgotten the details. But I wanted them to remember that Alger Hiss went to jail, and Whittaker Chambers was honored by his fellow citizens."[17]

I met with Reagan in 1992 in his office in Los Angeles when we published *Remembering Reagan* by Peter Hannaford. I had taken a copy of Whittaker Chambers's *Witness*, which we also published, to a gifted workman in Washington who had bound it in beautiful kid leather from El Salvador. I had it inscribed, in gold lettering, "For Ronald Reagan, the Greatest Cold Warrior." When I gave it to Reagan, he told me that Chambers had been particularly inspiring to him because of the way he had pondered the competition between this and that faith, between the question of God and man, and the great spiritual struggle between freedom and tyranny. He went on to tell me of his first meeting with Mikhail Gorbachev (his first meeting with a Soviet head of state) in Geneva in November 1985. He had arrived at the French ambassador's residence, where the summit would be held, a day early, and walking around the grounds found a beautifully appointed small stone chalet with a large fireplace. He instructed the Secret Service to build a roaring fire there the next morning. When Gorbachev arrived and they had exchanged greetings, Reagan invited Gorbachev to accompany him to the stone building, bringing no staff but his interpreter. "I started the conversation," Reagan told me, "by talking about our families, and how important families were to the peace of the world. Then I talked about faith, and my belief in God, and what a comfort my faith was to me as president in difficult times." Gorbachev was becoming engaged, Reagan said, warming up to this man whom he had viewed as a reckless movie actor–cowboy. Then, Reagan told me, he turned to Gorbachev and said they would be meeting and talking for the next few days in an attempt to negotiate an arms agreement. "In those talks," Reagan advised Gorbachev, "you have a choice. You can either negotiate with me in good faith, we can eliminate some of our nuclear weapons and we can make the world a safer place. Or," Reagan told him, "you can continue the arms race. But let me make it very clear that, if you do, that is a race that you cannot win." Gorbachev was stunned.

Although the Geneva summit produced no breakthrough agreements, Reagan firmly believed that his one-on-one conversation with Gorbachev radically changed their relationship and was the first step in the long process that ultimately brought the Soviet Union to an end.

MOVEMENT CONSERVATIVE

Although Reagan had been actively involved in California political circles and in anti-Communism in Hollywood, he was known nationally only as an actor. That all changed when, at the end of the Goldwater campaign, he made his famous "Time for Choosing" speech. It was on that day, October 27, 1964, that Reagan joined the conservative movement.

Reagan did not join the Republican Party until 1962. He campaigned for several Democratic candidates, including Truman for president in 1948, but also for Nixon in 1960. By 1964 the basic contours of his political and philosophical beliefs were well established, articles of faith.[18] Describing himself in the late 1940s as a "near hopeless hemophiliac liberal," by 1964 he was convinced that large domestic federal programs were more of a threat to individual freedom and personal achievement than beneficial. He believed through personal experience that high tax rates were harmful. He learned, as spokesman for General Electric (1954–62), that the proper role of government in the economy should be a limited one. Much later, in 1976, when asked what precipitated his move from left to right, he said it was "because I wrote my own speeches and did the research for them, I just woke up to the realization one day that I had been going out and helping to elect the people who had been causing the things I had been criticizing."[19]

But Reagan never considered himself part of the conservative movement. "He thought of himself as a conservative," said Ed Meese, "but he didn't think so much in organizational terms but more in philosophical terms. He considered himself part of a group of people who thought similarly on the leading political philosophical issues of the day."[20]

After Johnson had trounced Goldwater, Reagan recognized the damage Goldwater had done with the use of careless language, allowing Lyndon Johnson to tar him as an extremist. In order to appeal to average American voters, Reagan realized that conservative candidates must appeal to their positive rather than their negative side. In December 1964, in *National Review*, he cautioned Republicans to moderate their rhetoric, without, however, softening the conservative message. Democrats won, he said, because they were able to "portray us as advancing a kind of radical departure from the status quo." In order to win, wrote Reagan, "Our job beginning now is not so much to sell conservatism as to prove that our conservatism is in truth what a lot of people thought they were voting for when they fell for the corn-pone come-on. In short, it is time now for the soft sell to prove our radicalism was an optical illusion."[21]

Before long, conservatives were beginning to talk about Ronald Reagan as their next presidential candidate.

GOVERNOR

When Reagan ran for governor of California in 1966, trouncing incumbent Pat Brown, his election was the political high point of the decade for conservatives and launched Reagan as the leading conservative politician in the country. He had won a stunning victory, without compromising any principles in his campaign. Despite Democratic control of both houses of the California legislature, Reagan was able to get major welfare reform enacted and came close to getting a statewide referendum on spending control passed.

Reagan's two terms as governor gave a tremendous boost to conservatives nationwide. His pragmatism convinced them that he was not only their man on the issues, but a good politician. And though he was not always as much of a government-slasher as some would have liked, he never softened his rhetoric on Communism. He was the chief executive of the largest and, in many ways, the most radical state in the union, the state where the cultural revolution was born and matured, and in the very years that the cultural revolution was gripping the nation. In the belly of the beast, he said what he thought about student rebellion, about civil disorder and war protests, and about the "filthy speech move- ment" at the University of California; shortly after being elected, he had provided assistance to local law enforcement agencies and, at one point, called out the National Guard to restore order to California's campuses. "To Reagan," said his aide Ed Meese, "it was a public safety issue and an educational issue. The dissident students were interrupting the edu- cational mission of the universities."[22] Reagan had established his deci- siveness and demonstrated his refusal to bend to popular fads.

TEACHER

Within weeks of leaving the governor's office in January 1975, Reagan was on the "mashed potato circuit," as he called it, traveling from one end of the country to the other, making speeches and doing fundraisers for Republicans and generating over one hundred press stories a week. He spent the six years until he was inaugurated president in January 1981 as an active, perhaps *the* most active, conservative spokesman in the country.

Veteran conservative Richard Viguerie told me some years back that when he looks at a candidate for any office who claims to be a conserva- tive, he likes to ask whether the candidate "walks with conservatives." Does he talk like a conservative, show up at a rally, give a speech, and then leave, or does he participate, give advice and counsel in campaigns, endorse candidates, act like an active conservative? Reagan, says Vigue- rie, always walked with conservatives: "He was available to talk, he an- swered his phone or returned your call, he would show up anywhere he could to help with a political meeting, a fundraiser or a dinner speech." Reagan would take a week out of his schedule in October of each elec- tion year to tour the country, speaking on behalf of and endorsing can- didates. In 1974, Reagan campaigned for Utah senator Orrin Hatch, Illinois congressman Henry Hyde, and Ohio congressman Buz Lukens (who eventually wound up in prison), all of whom were running for the first time. He was a regular at Lincoln Day dinners across the country, and even before he joined the Republican Party, in 1962, Reagan would often be head of a Democrats for some Republican committee. But as far as who he would support, Reagan had no litmus test. "He did not seek out conservatives, or Republicans," said Nevada senator Paul Laxalt, Reagan's closest friend in Washington. "He just supported his guys. He was a team player. He was the Gipper. He knew, fundamentally, who he agreed with. There were not many philosophical discussions."[23]

In the fall of 1974, while Reagan was still governor, TV icon Walter Cronkite offered him a twice-weekly commentary on the *CBS Evening News*; big-time Eric Sevareid would have the alternate days. But Reagan turned Cronkite down, concerned that he would have no control over the proceedings.[24] "What Reagan wanted," according to his former aide and friend Martin Anderson, "was control of a large megaphone, one with which he could speak daily to potential voters on what they wanted to talk about."[25]

Reagan got that large megaphone in 1975 through a comprehensive media package that included a nationally syndicated newspaper column, radio show, and speaking engagements across America. Radio had been Reagan's first media outlet, his first job after college when he served as a radio announcer on WHO in Des Moines, Iowa, for Chicago Cubs games, and he knew its power. He could talk directly to people, he could expound on themes again and again, he could use his soothing and genial voice to persuade people of the truth of what he was saying, illustrating his points with anecdotes and humor. Reagan's listeners became an army of devoted followers and campaign workers, educated by him on the ideas and issues he held so dear. Perhaps even more important, the radio talks educated Ronald Reagan as he researched and wrote the scripts. His goal, according to an internal memorandum, was to "maintain influence in the Republican party; strengthen and consolidate leadership as *the* national conservative spokesman; and enhance his own foreign affairs credibility."[26]

Conservative talk radio had not yet gotten off the ground in 1975; in some respects, Ronald Reagan had the airwaves virtually to himself. It has been estimated that in the ensuing years Reagan's radio commentaries were heard by as many as 12 million Americans a week.[27]

According to Martin Anderson, who discovered Reagan's handwritten scripts and edited them for a book, "The broadcasts were much more widely listened to than people realize, and had a much greater benefit to Reagan than can be imagined. He was the Rush Limbaugh of the 1970s."[28] And for some unknown reason, Democrats did not bother to listen to the tapes before the 1980 campaign—if they had they would have understood Reagan much better and could have launched a more effective campaign against him.

Reagan's message was a breath of fresh air, a voice of sanity in an otherwise disjointed world. Jimmy Carter's presidency was full of gloom and doom, his Congress overwhelmingly liberal. Inflation was rampant, interest rates were skyrocketing, and unemployment was pervasive. The Soviet Union had invaded Afghanistan and was spreading its tentacles into Central America and Africa while Carter sat idly by. Government regulation was out of control, with new regulatory agencies and schemes seemingly springing out of nowhere. The few conservative voices were mostly small journals and periodicals and an occasional radio or television debate, but few reached any sort of national audience.

The themes of Reagan's radio talks dominated his 1980 campaign for the presidency. He spoke of the evils of Communism and the necessity of eradicating it short of nuclear war. He spoke often of the greatness of America, about the shining city on a hill and of the ordinary American people—those listening to his broadcasts. He spoke of the need to cut back government and he called for everyday Americans to regain control of their lives from the government and once again live the divine purpose of the country.

"Remember, during those Carter years," reflected Paul Laxalt, "there was serious discussion whether the presidency was too big for one man. Reagan filled that void in one hell of a hurry. They never talked that way again when he was president."[29]

Politician

Reagan was a good politician because he was not really a politician. He was a man of principle whose deeply held beliefs were the core of his political philosophy. Margaret Thatcher once said of him that he had only a few ideas, but they were big ideas, and they were good ideas. Others who were close to him recognized that he had small ideas as well, and knew all the details. He just kept them to himself. Reagan was also a master communicator who could explain complex ideas in simple terms. He did not lust for power but sought office to turn his ideas into policy.

When Reagan finished his second term as governor, in January 1975, the Republican Party was virtually moribund. Nixon had resigned in disgrace five months earlier, the Democrats held large majorities in both houses of Congress, and the Republican Party was practically broke. Worse, the party had no philosophical soul; any inroads conservatives had made during the Goldwater campaign ten years earlier had dwindled away. William Rusher, publisher of *National Review*, in 1975 published *The Making of a New Majority Party*, which called for the formation of a new, conservative party; the book was an instant success and sold over a quarter of a million copies.[30] At a conference cosponsored by Young Americans for Freedom and the American Conservative Union in February 1975, Reagan was introduced by New York senator Jim Buckley as "the Rembrandt of American Conservatism." To the wild cheers of the crowd, Reagan said, "Is it a third party we need? Or is it a new and revitalized second party, raising a banner of no pale pastels, but bold colors which make it unmistakably clear where we stand on all the issues troubling the people?"[31]

But the Democratic Party, although with more registered voters and elected politicians, was in no great shape either. Democrats were suffering from Vietnam and the radicalization of liberalism that followed it; the New Deal coalition was becoming ever more unreliable with blue-collar and Catholic voters moving to the right; and the party itself was inching inexorably toward the left.

Reagan left the governor's mansion in Sacramento with his reputation as a conservative intact, his political skills sharpened, and his leadership unquestioned. As Gerald Ford, who had replaced Nixon as president in August 1974, floundered about, conservatives urged Reagan to challenge him in the 1976 primaries and Reagan assented. In his autobiography Reagan wrote, "My theme on the campaign stump was familiar to anyone who had heard me speak over the years: It was time to scale back the size of the federal government, reduce taxes and government intrusion in our lives, balance the budget, and return to the people the freedoms usurped from them by the bureaucrats."[32] A major factor in Reagan's decision to run was Ford's submissiveness in his dealings with Soviet Communism. In a speech on Memorial Day in Atlantic City, Reagan made no bones about it: "The free world—indeed the entire non-Communist world—is crying out for strong American leadership, and we are not providing it."[33]

Although Reagan had the issues on his side and the backing of the conservative movement, Ford had the presidency, with all its power and its trappings. Ford beat Reagan in the New Hampshire primary by fewer than fifteen hundred votes and proceeded to beat him, albeit by slim margins, in Florida and Illinois as well. Pundits were beginning to ask Reagan when he was going to drop out, and his staff, largely unpaid as Reagan's money started to run out, threatened to quit. Elected Republicans were also asking him to bow out, raising Reagan's ire. "The governors and mayors orchestrated a campaign to run him out of the primary," Paul Laxalt told me, "and it really pissed him off. He didn't get mad very often, but he sure did that time."[34] Ford himself sent emissaries to Reagan, indirectly offering him the vice presidency if he would bow out of the race. But Reagan would have none of it, insisting that he would stay until the end.

In Florida, Reagan found the issue that would resound with conservatives and many others. Several years earlier Secretary of State Henry Kissinger had proposed withdrawing all American troops from Panama and transferring the canal to the Panamanians. Reagan thought this a singularly bad idea. It allowed him to criticize Kissinger unceasingly on a raft of other issues as well, accusing Kissinger of being the architect of America's retreat in the face of "Soviet imperialism" in Southeast Asia, the Middle East, and Africa. "When it comes to the Canal," thundered Reagan, "we bought it, we paid for it, it's ours, and we should tell Torrijos [Panama's head man] and company that we are going to keep it!" Again, over the Panama Canal, Reagan lost his temper, this time with Bill Brock, the chairman of the Republican National Committee, who had been raising vast sums of money on the issue by direct mail using Reagan's signature. Opponents of the treaty had put together a "truth squad" to tour the country. Reagan wanted the RNC to pay for it—with the money he had raised—but Bill Brock refused. Said Laxalt, "I was in my office, Reagan came in, saw that I was upset, and asked what the trouble was. And I said I'm pretty distressed with Bill Brock. He's a friend of mine but he stiffed us on the Panama Canal money. Reagan said, 'Give me that phone.' He put in a call to Brock and proceeded to chew his ass out. 'You think I raised all that money for you, and you aren't going to give some of it back?' Poor old Brock didn't get over that for a long time."[35]

To stay in the race, Reagan needed to win a big state, and North Carolina offered the best chance. North Carolina senator Jesse Helms, who greatly admired Reagan and had promised several years earlier to support him if he ever ran for president, took Reagan under his wing and provided him his incomparable team of political experts. In a move reminiscent of his 1964 Goldwater speech, Reagan bought thirty minutes of television time on virtually every station in the state, talking directly to North Carolina's voters. Four days later, he won the primary with 52 percent of the vote. Reagan went on to win primaries in Texas, Alabama, Georgia, Indiana, Arizona, and California, the last by a two-to-one margin. Reagan and Ford arrived at the convention in a virtual dead heat; Ford was ultimately nominated by 1,187 votes to Reagan's 1,070.

After his acceptance speech, Ford beckoned to Reagan to join him on the stage. "Does that mean I am supposed to go down there?" Reagan asked aide Michael Deaver. "It does, and you need to say something," Deaver responded. "What do I say?" asked Reagan. "Oh," said Deaver, "you'll think of something."[36] Reagan slowly made his way through the crowd to the podium. "Reagan had lost everything," said Martin Anderson. "He's crushed. He's wiped out. Nancy is probably ready to cry. And he doesn't have a speech and there's millions of people watching."[37] But Reagan, a far better speaker than Ford, made some brief and extemporaneous remarks that brought on the loudest and longest ovation of the convention. "We have got to quit talking to each other," said Reagan, "and about each other and go out and communicate to the world that we may be fewer in numbers than we have ever been, but we carry the message they are waiting for. There is no substitute for victory." It was the first speech of the 1980 campaign, and not unlike the 1964 Goldwater race, the loser turned out to be the winner.

Michael Reagan, who attended the convention with his father, told me that after it was clear that Ford would be nominated he asked his father if he was disappointed. "Not really," answered Reagan, "except that I had looked forward to sitting across a table from Leonid Brezh-nev, knowing that I was bargaining from a position of strength, and he from one of weakness. He would tell me all the things—the weapons systems, the ships, the missiles—all the things we would have to get rid of. And when he was finished, I would stand up, walk around the table, and whisper one word into his ear: 'Nyet!'"

At the end of the convention Reagan told his campaign workers that he would continue the fight he had started. He had well over $1 million left over from his campaign, a huge direct-mail list, and an unmatched ability to raise much, much more; daily access to the media; and a dedicated following. And most important, he had a stirring and popular message. Few presidential candidates in history could match that position.

THE WHITE HOUSE

It is all but universally agreed that Reagan brought a sense of optimism back into the public square. Indeed, in an interview in the *Washington Post* in 1981 Reagan said, "What I would really like to do is to go down in history as the president who made Americans believe in themselves again." Biographer Lou Cannon observed that "because of his ability to reflect and give voice to the aspirations of his fellow citizens, Reagan succeeded in reviving national confidence at a time when there was a great need for inspiration. This was his great contribution as president."[38]

When Reagan arrived at the White House in January 1981 he knew exactly what his priorities were. As he said after his two terms were over, "I had an agenda I wanted to get done. I came with a script."[39] Reagan knew the script, because he had written it himself over a lifetime of talking and writing about politics. First, cut taxes; second, deregulate business and the economy; third, terminate unnecessary and harmful government programs and cut the size of others; fourth, strengthen the military and win the Cold War. Finally, change the composition of the federal judiciary in order to address various social issues and alter the imbalance between state and federal power. Reagan's priorities were the same he had been speaking about since the 1960s, and his priorities were the policies of his administration. "Whatever he wanted the policy to be, was the policy," said Martin Anderson. "I cannot think of a single case where someone said, no, you're doing it the wrong way or doing the wrong thing. It just did not happen. It might have made some people upset, because they thought they were smarter than he was. . . . He made every major decision, no matter what anyone says."[40] Ed Meese agreed: "He knew what his mind was, and that was never in doubt."[41]

As president, Reagan often spoke at conservative banquets, rallies, and other meetings. He continued to read *National Review*, maintained a close relationship with Buckley and others in the movement, and never ceased to be helpful to conservatives running for office. He also continued to read *Human Events*, which, according to his friend Paul Laxalt, "struck just about the right chord for him." One day Laxalt made a reference to a piece he had read in *Human Events* and, according to Laxalt, "Reagan said he had not seen it. Well, the sons of bitches were hiding it from him and I called Jim Baker on it and he said, not me. Bullshit. I raised hell in just the right places, so he took Baker and Deaver out of the loop."[42]

COLD WARRIOR

Anti-Communism was at the heart of Reagan's conservatism. According to at least one observer, "His election was, in a real sense, the culmination of the long history of American anti-Communism."[43] From the time he first spoke out about Communism before the House Committee on Un-American Activities in 1947 Reagan believed the West should defeat it.

Reagan believed that, in any war, one side would eventually win and one side would eventually lose. The Cold War was no different. Containment, peaceful coexistence, détente, whatever it was called, simply prolonged the process of winning by propping up the enemy. Most of the "experts," academics, journalists, diplomats, bureaucrats, and politicians viewed détente as the only plausible strategy because the Soviet Union had become a permanent member of the international community.

The experts were, in Reagan's view, wrong. He was the president, not the so-called experts, and he would call the shots. U.S. foreign policy would be based on American ideals, democracy, and self-government. He believed that the United States had a special obligation to promote its ideals around the world. He did not want war with the Soviets, and never talked about conquering them. Nor was he opposed to negotiating; he would do so to try to weaken them. Reagan had spoken often of the economic disaster that accompanied Communism. Should the Communist leaders have to confront vigorous U.S. defenses, advanced American technology, a strong economy, and a stout stance against Soviet infringement, the U.S.S.R. would have to choose between retreat and crippling economic pressure.[44] "How long," Reagan asked, "can the Russians keep on being so belligerent and spending so much on the arms race when they can't even feed their own people?"[45] In essence, the new policy was based on the fact that there was no longer any "moral equivalence" between the United States and the U.S.S.R. On questions of morals and values, we were right, and they were wrong.

Reagan undertook a total reversal of U.S. foreign policy toward the Communist world; eleven years after his election, Soviet Communism crumbled.

Reagan outlined the new policy to the world in March 1983 in what would become the most celebrated speech of his presidency and perhaps of his entire career, known as the "Evil Empire Speech." Reagan summarized his views of Communism and how his administration would deal with it. To assure that there was no mistaking his intent, he spoke the phrase that would resound throughout the free world and creep behind the Iron Curtain:

> I urge you to beware the temptation of pride, the
> temptation of blithely declaring yourselves above it
> all and label both sides equally at fault, to ignore the
> facts of history and the aggressive impulses of an evil
> empire.

Reagan reminded his listeners that the struggle against Communism was not about weapons systems, bombs and rockets, but a spiritual one. It was a test, he said, of moral will and faith:

> Whittaker Chambers, the man whose own religious
> conversion made him a witness to one of the ter-
> rible traumas of our time, the Hiss-Chambers case,
> wrote that the crisis of the Western world exists to
> the degree in which the West is indifferent to God,
> the degree to which it collaborates in communism's
> attempt to make man stand alone without God. And
> then he said, for Marxism-Leninism is actually the
> second-oldest faith, first proclaimed in the Garden
> of Eden with the words of temptation, "Ye shall be
> as gods."

We would never give away freedom, he said, nor abandon our belief in God. "Let us pray for the salvation of all of those who live in that to-talitarian darkness," said Reagan, and "pray they will discover the joy of knowing God. But until they do, let us be aware that while they preach the supremacy of the state, declare its omnipotence over individual man, and predict its eventual domination of all peoples on the earth, they are the focus of evil in the modern world."[46]

Conservatives were elated. William F. Buckley, Jr., said that by call-ing the Soviet Union the Evil Empire, Reagan had provided the galva-nizing summation to Aleksandr Solzhenitsyn's *Gulag Archipelago*: "The countdown for Communism began then,"[47] he asserted. But liberals were predictably appalled. Liberal historian Henry Steele Commager found Reagan's religious references outrageous and told the *Washington Post*: "It was the worst presidential speech in American history, and I've read them all. No other presidential speech has ever so flagrantly allied the government with religion." Anthony Lewis, in the *New York Times*, sputtered that Reagan's review of moral equivalence was "primitive: that is the only word for it."

The real audience, of course, were the people enslaved behind the Iron Curtain. Reagan knew that his words would eventually reach them, and he wanted to give them hope, to assure them that the United States was on their side. If the Soviet Union was to fall, it would ultimately be felled by the Russian people. Reagan's hopes were not disappointed. Human rights activist Natan Sharansky was deep inside the Gulag, serv-ing a thirteen-year term on trumped-up charges of treason and spying for the United States. After he was released from the Gulag, Sharansky met with Ronald Reagan in the White House:

> I told him of the brilliant day when we learned about his Evil Empire speech from an article in *Pravda* or *Izvestia* that found its way into the prison. When I said that our whole block burst out into a kind of loud celebration and that the world was about to change, well, then the president, this great tall man, just lit up like a schoolboy. His face lit up and beamed. He jumped out of his seat like a shot and started waving his arms wildly and calling for everyone to come in to hear "this man's" story. It was really only then that I started to appreciate that it wasn't just in the Soviet Union that President Reagan must have suffered terrible abuse for this great speech, but that he must have been hurt at home too. It seemed as though our moment of joy was the moment of his own vindication. That the great punishment he had endured for this speech was worth it.[48]

Reagan made three other major addresses on Communism during his presidency, including his challenge to Mikhail Gorbachev, before the Brandenburg Gate in Berlin, "to tear down this wall." There was no doubt, at all, where Ronald Reagan stood.

Reagan was determined to break through liberal taboos. "For too long," Reagan later said, "our leaders were unable to describe the Soviet Union as it actually was. The keepers of our foreign-policy knowledge—in other words, most liberal foreign affairs scholars, the State Department, and various columnists—found it illiberal and provocative to be so honest."[49] He made the Evil Empire speech "with malice aforethought . . . the Soviet system over the years has purposely starved, murdered, and brutalized its own people. Millions were killed; it is all right there in the history books. It put other citizens it disagreed with into psychiatric hospitals, sometimes drugging them into oblivion. Is the system that allowed this not evil? Then why should we not say so?"[50]

Action followed talk. Several weeks after the Evil Empire speech,

Reagan sent troops to Grenada to oust the Cuban-backed Marxist government, thereby sending Moscow a message that such ventures would not go unnoticed by Washington. The CIA, under the leadership of fellow anti-Communist William J. Casey, was providing millions of dollars to the mujahideen in their battle against the Soviet invasion of Afghanistan, and aid was beginning to flow to the Contras in Nicaragua and to the anti-Communists in El Salvador. In March 1983, Reagan announced plans to build the Strategic Defense Initiative (SDI), a space-based antiballistic missile system designed to shoot down Soviet missiles as they approached the United States; and in October, against the advice of the pragmatists in the White House, and contrary to a huge propaganda and disinformation campaign launched by Moscow, with the approval of European allies, Reagan placed cruise and Pershing missiles in Western Europe.

What Reagan was doing was more than upsetting to the Kremlin. Russian leaders had dismissed Reagan's tough talk during his campaign as political posturing, sure that, once elected, he would do what every other president had done: proceed as before. But saying one thing and doing another was not Ronald Reagan's way, as the Kremlin soon learned. Early in Reagan's first term, PATCO, the air traffic controllers union, threatened to strike if they did not get a 100 percent pay raise. Reagan made it clear that he would fire everyone who struck, as a strike would be illegal and would paralyze the U.S. economy. They struck anyway, convinced Reagan was bluffing, at least partially because PATCO was the only union that had endorsed Reagan in the 1980 campaign. Reagan fired them, replacements were found, and airplanes continued to fly. Leaders in the Kremlin were stunned—this was not just any American president; this was somebody who actually did what he said he would do. George Shultz, who would later become secretary of state, remarked that firing the air traffic controllers was the most important foreign policy decision Reagan ever made. Later, Reagan's referring to the Soviet Union as an Evil Empire and suggesting that it was like a cancer that needed to be removed from the world body convinced the Soviets that this cowboy president was indeed starting World War III, fully prepared, if need be, to blow them off the face of the earth. That was, of course, the last thing Reagan wanted. He was no hawk, he did not want to "beat" the U.S.S.R. He just wanted to "end this thing."

The rest is, as they say, history. There will be debate over what brought the Cold War to an end, why the Soviet Union collapsed, until history stops unfolding. Liberals, peaceniks, and even some conservatives, particularly those who had no role in Reagan's activities, like to deny any credit to Reagan. Others attribute the entire victory to the foresight and tenacity of the Old Cowboy. The truth probably lies somewhere in between.

SUPPLY-SIDER

Economics, tax policy, and government spending was the next-most-important issue to Ronald Reagan. A strong economy would not only accelerate the fall of Communism, he believed, but was crucial so that the United States could take a strong stand in world affairs and be able to rebuild the military. And, besides, the American people deserved nothing less. Reagan never tired of saying that the American people were the most creative bunch ever assembled, and that if the government would just get out of the way, if it allowed the creative American people to have more of their money by reducing taxes, they could use their ingenuity to solve their problems far more efficiently than could the federal government. The coalition that Reagan put together to win the 1980 campaign was made up of just the people he had faith in, people who agreed with him about the size, intrusiveness, and expense of government. They knew what he had done as governor of California and believed he could get the country out of its late 1970s economic doldrums.

Reagan's position on government spending was strictly in line with classical conservative thinking. By the mid-1970s Reagan had become a true free-market advocate who believed that the economy would thrive if government were to spend less, tax less, and stay out of people's way. At the peak of his movie career he was in the 94 percent tax bracket, which was reason enough not to make another picture. Why, he asked, would anybody work hard when he could only keep 6 percent of his pay? Worse, when *he* did not work, many lower-paid people did not work either, so the effect of the exorbitant tax rate was to dampen the economy. Lower the marginal tax rate, and people would go back to work. "A few economists call this principle supply-side economics," Reagan wrote. "I just call it common sense."[51]

There was certainly much to be done. At the end of the Carter administration, the economy was in the worst recession since the 1930s. *Newsweek* summed it up in early January 1981: "When Ronald Reagan steps into the White House next week, he will inherit the most dangerous economic crisis since Franklin Roosevelt took office 48 years ago."[52] During 1980, inflation was at a record high of 13.5 percent, and mortgage interest rates had soared to 20 percent. Unemployment was the highest since 1940. Jimmy Carter's misery index—the sum of the inflation rate and unemployment—was 21.98; it had been 12.68 four years earlier. (When Reagan left office, in January 1989, the index was at 9.72.)[53]

Reagan was convinced that a large tax cut would bring several benefits. As he explained it, it really was not very complicated: "If you reduce tax rates and allow people to spend or save more of what they earn, they'll be more industrious; they'll have more incentive to work hard, and money they earn will add fuel to the great economic machine that energizes our national progress. The result: more prosperity for all and more revenue for government."[54]

It was common sense, yes, but it *was* also supply-side economics. Supply-side was one of the most potent new ideas to arise in a decade or more, and would become a keystone in Ronald Reagan's economic plan for the country. It was not really a new concept at all, but classical economics rediscovered by such as Milton Friedman, Art Laffer, and Martin Anderson, all of whom had counseled Reagan on economics and taxes for years, and made popular by a few editors and columnists, most prominently Bob Bartley of the *Wall Street Journal*. Very simply, the supply-side theory states that the more of one's income the government collects, the less that person works. If the tax rate is 100 percent, people will simply stop working, production will cease, and no revenue will be collected. If tax rates are zero percent, there are similarly no taxes to collect, there is no barrier to production, and production is thus maximized. Accordingly, there are always two tax rates that yield the same revenues—one for working less and paying a greater percentage in taxes, and one for working more and paying a smaller percentage.[55] The more extreme advocates believed that if taxes were cut deeply enough, tax revenues would actually increase. Other more moderate supply-siders thought that with tax cuts, tax revenues would stay neutral. But they all agreed that tax cuts were crucial to boosting a lagging economy.

Reagan was convinced that lower taxes would ultimately boost tax revenues, and thus reduce budget deficits. This, in turn, would relieve pressure on the demand for money, thereby lowering interest rates and prices and stimulating the economy. If he were wrong, and deficits actually increased, Reagan believed that it would at least put the brakes on Congress's insatiable appetite to spend additional funds. Most important, as an integral part of the "Reagan Revolution," his economic plan was designed to change the way the nation thought about economics and the marketplace.

I talked some time back about Reagan's economic program with Milton Friedman in his apartment on Nob Hill overlooking San Francisco Bay. He explained that:

> The crucial point about it is that a tax cut is seen as promoting the economy, not because it stimulates spending, but because it provides an incentive for investments and for more production. If you look at it from the point of view of deficit spending, a reduction in taxes is exactly equivalent to an increase in government spending. Under a supply-side approach, the tax reduction has exactly the opposite effect.

Friedman advised Reagan on another benefit of cutting taxes: reducing government revenue:

> My objective in cutting taxes is both to provide incentive for investment and also to reduce the revenue that the government gets.[56]

Reagan was something of an economic lonely warrior in 1981. The pragmatists on his senior staff—Chief of Staff James Baker, Assistant to the President Richard Darman, Budget Director David Stockman, and communications man David Gergen—were still living in the Keynesian world, thinking that tax cuts would bring bigger deficits, which would hurt the economy; most of the "experts" disagreed with him as well. But encouraged by Milton Friedman, Art Laffer, Martin Anderson, Ed Meese, and others, Reagan did not budge. Laffer recalls a meeting of the Economic Policy Advisory Board, a group of economists including Friedman, George Shultz, Alan Greenspan, Arthur Burns, and Laffer, when the matter of tax cuts versus tax increases was being discussed as part of a deal to get Congress to cut spending. Burns, the former head of the Federal Reserve, counseled Reagan: "My best advice to you, Mr. President, is that you should accept a revenue enhancer in order to get Congress to agree to these major cuts in spending."

Reagan responded: "You know, Arthur, I can't tell you how much I enjoy these Advisory Board meetings. But you know, I made a promise when I ran for office that I wouldn't raise taxes, and I intend to do all I can do to keep it. So every minute you spend in these meetings talking about tax increase is a minute I don't get the pleasure of discussing something I might actually do." Then Reagan leaned over to Burns and said: "Arthur, never mention a tax increase in my presence again. Is that clear?"[57]

Reagan was not about to be deterred by the economic experts, any more than he was by the foreign policy experts. Not unlike his reversal of foreign policy, his administration quickly implemented an economic plan that reflected what conservatives had urged for years, and what he had promised in the campaign. Dubbed "Reaganomics" by its critics, the plan was dramatic and had almost immediate impact. (Reagan took particular delight in pointing out that after the economy went through the roof in 1983 and 1984, "nobody calls it Reaganomics anymore.") Four primary elements were designed to reverse the high-inflation, slow-growth economic record of the 1970s: stabilize the value of the dollar and end runaway inflation through the use of strict monetary policy; institute a 25 percent across-the-board tax cut to spur savings, investment, work, and economic efficiency; cut domestic, nondefense spending and balance the budget; and make a strong attempt to roll back government regulation.

The first piece of business was the tax bill—the Economic Recovery Tax Act (ERTA), which was pushed through Congress in a record seven months. Reagan signed it in August 1981; the new law cut individual marginal tax rates by 25 percent across the board, eliminated indexing of tax rates, ending "bracket creep," and reformed various business-tax provisions. It was the largest tax cut in the history of the United States, and slashed revenue by $38 billion the first year, $91 billion the second year, and $139 billion the third.[58]

Reagan personally saw to it the tax bill got passed—he spent endless hours on the telephone and visiting with members of Congress, and spoke directly to the American people in radio broadcasts and on television, urging the public to back the tax cuts. Democratic leaders in Congress, who had always underestimated Reagan's abilities, could not believe the effect that his phone calls were having or how persuasive he could be on television. "I'm getting the shit whaled out of me," Tip O'Neill complained.[59] Majority Leader Jim Wright commented in his diary in June 1981, "I stand in awe . . . of [Reagan's] political skill. I am not sure that I have seen its equal."[60] Congress responded by overwhelmingly passing the bill. The *Washington Post* could not help but cite Reagan for "one of the most remarkable demonstrations of presidential leadership in modern history."

The impact of Reagan's tax cut was exactly what Reagan had predicted: According to economist and *Wall Street Journal* columnist Stephen Moore, "No event over the past quarter century has had a more profound impact on the U.S. economy and the prosperity of the 1980's and '90's than the Reagan tax cuts of 1981."[61] And tax revenues increased as well, as Reagan had predicted—between 1980 and 1990 federal tax collections doubled from $500 billion to $1 trillion. Tax rates went down but, as the supply-siders had predicted, revenue went up because of the prosperous economy that replaced the stagnant one Reagan had inherited.

But the immediate effect of the tax cuts, before the economy caught fire, was a reduction in revenue, and deficit projections started to rise. Non-supply-side conservatives, who hated deficits, and liberals, who hated the Reagan economic plan, ganged up to persuade Reagan to increase taxes to offset the deficits. Under mounting pressure, Reagan agreed to limited tax hikes in 1982, as part of a deal wherein Congress agreed to cut spending by two dollars for every dollar of tax increases, but the reduction in marginal rates remained. Reagan later explained the problem: "During the next three years, I was under almost constant pressure to abandon the economic program. Along the way, I made some compromises: to win congressional approval of additional spending cuts and show the financial community we were serious about reducing the deficit, I made a deal with the congressional Democrats in 1982, agreeing to support a limited loophole-closing tax increase to raise more than $98.3 billion over three years in return for their agreement to cut spending by $280 billion during the same period; later the Democrats reneged on their pledge and we never got those cuts."[62]

Reagan was happy to trade the deficits for the tax cuts. He knew the tax cuts would have the desired effect, and deficits would keep Congress from spending wildly—which is exactly what happened: The deficits ushered in a new era marked by profound fiscal restraint, as large and persistent deficits kept the lid on spending for the next fifteen years. But the tax code was still an abomination, full of loopholes and tax shelters, riddled with special exemptions and deductions, and virtually incomprehensible. Reagan had promised tax reform in his campaign, and meant it. In 1986, Reagan pushed through Congress the most comprehensive tax reform bill in history—a bill that had lawmakers, lobbyists, and journalists in Washington in an uproar for over two years. Among other things, the new law cut marginal tax rates and vastly simplified the tax code, eliminating many of the special provisions that lawmakers had included over many years. Passed by a Democratic House and a Republican Senate, the law was considered one of Reagan's most significant legislative accomplishments. Much of what was passed, however, to limit tax loopholes has, as the Tax Foundation said, "crept back into the system courtesy of politicians quick to give in to whatever lobby fills their pockets."[63] Much of the cut in rates was also reversed over the next ten years.

Reagan also knew that to stimulate the economy, he had to go beyond economics and renew the entrepreneurial spirit that had been so damaged during the Carter presidency. "The first thing Reagan did," explained Milton Friedman, "was to eliminate price controls on oil. That had as much to do with developing the entrepreneurial atmosphere as did the lower tax rates."[64]

Reaganomics was an unmitigated success, largely because of the 1981 reduction of marginal tax rates. The Dow Jones Industrial Average was at about 800 in 1981; twenty-five years later, it stood at 11,000, representing an increase in the value of American national wealth of some $25 trillion. Living standards have risen consistently ever since, and virtually all economic indicators are vastly higher. But more important is the change in attitude: the presumption that higher taxes solved economic problems has been reversed. Even today, after twenty-five years, top personal and corporate marginal tax rates are at 35 percent, compared with 70 percent for personal taxes and 48 percent for business taxes in 1981; taxes on dividends topped out at 70 percent in the late 1970s, and on capital gains at 50 percent; now both are at 15 percent. The tax-cutting attitude has spread beyond our shores as well; the average personal income tax rate in the industrialized world is now 43 percent, versus 76 percent in 1980. Most of the former Eastern Bloc countries, including Russia, have flat taxes with rates lower than those in the United States. As the *Wall Street Journal* points out, this decline in global tax rates has been the economic equivalent of the fall of the Berlin Wall.[65]

REVOLUTIONARY

Revolution: a fundamental change in political organization; especially: the overthrow or renunciation of one government or ruler and the substitution of another by the governed.

—Webster's New American Dictionary

Ronald Reagan was an unlikely revolutionary by the best of standards. How was it that a movie actor, one of the oldest elected presidents in history, a self-proclaimed outsider, a man educated at a small midwestern college that nobody had ever heard of, would become the president whose name was associated with a revolution? There was no Kennedy revolution, or Truman, or Johnson, or Nixon, or Clinton revolution. But there was a Reagan Revolution.

The Reagan Revolution was not a revolution of politics, or of policy, or of foreign policy, or of economics, even though Ronald Reagan assuredly changed policies in all of those areas, and dramatically changed the order of things. It was a revolution of ideas. It was a revolution because

Reagan adopted the ideas developed over the past fifty years by a small group of intellectuals and writers—ideas that, before he came along, were having a profound impact on American intellectual life. Reagan simply applied those ideas to politics, and by doing so gave them tremendous currency and demonstrated that they could work.

Reagan was a revolutionary not because he helped to win the Cold War, or because he pushed through a huge tax cut, or because he helped to deregulate business, or because he tried to cut the size of government. He was a revolutionary because he changed the way people thought about fundamental issues of governing, about economics, and about the social order. When he spoke of the Evil Empire people at first were aghast. But soon people began to say, you know, it *is* an Evil Empire, and no longer did they accept the U.S.S.R. as morally equivalent to the United States. When he first spoke of cutting taxes to stimulate the economy, people thought he was talking nonsense—"voodoo economics," as George H. W. Bush dubbed it. But after his tax cuts took off and the economy started to thrive, people recognized that cutting taxes stimulated the economy, and twenty years later, few could disagree.

Reagan was a revolutionary because—particularly in the midst of the post-Vietnam, post-Carter doldrums—he believed that the American people could handle their problems without the help of government; by the time he left the presidency, self-sufficiency had become the dominant attitude of the American people. During his first term, Reagan redefined foreign policy, abandoning the policies that had been in place since the early 1950s—détente, appeasement, and Mutually Assured Destruction—substituting a stronger defense, confrontation with the Soviet Union, and missile defense, the process that would end the Cold War. In a speech early in his administration at West Point, he quoted Sun Tzu to the effect that to subdue the enemy without firing a shot was the ultimate goal of war. He redefined the government's role in the economy, scrapping the policies that had prevailed since the Roosevelt administration, and instituting policies based on free markets, free trade, lower taxes, and less government. In 1984 the American people showed their approval by re-electing him by the largest electoral college margin of any president since Franklin Roosevelt.

Yet in another sense Ronald Reagan was not a revolutionary at all, merely the messenger who conveyed the ideas that had been developed by conservatives over the years. Ronald Reagan's ideas, the ideas behind the Reagan Revolution, were the ideas of men like Friedrich Hayek, Ludwig von Mises, Milton Friedman, Russell Kirk, Whittaker Chambers, and the others, the original conservative and libertarian thinkers. When Reagan was referred to as the Great Communicator, he used to say that he only communicated great ideas. It was those ideas, conservative ideas, which were revolutionary.

CHAPTER TWELVE

Conservatives and Free Enterprise

There is a great myth that big business and conservatism are closely aligned. The misconception is understandable—major corporations are creatures of capitalism and conservatives generally support the free market. But just as children do not always honor their mothers and fathers, businesses will abandon capitalist principles when they deem it to their advantage. The bigger the business, the more likely it is to do so. Big business routinely chases corporate welfare, seizes private property through the abuse of eminent domain, and lobbies for regulations to tie the hands of competitors. Corporate goliaths frequently endorse higher taxes and, in the various states, oppose tax-limitation measures.[1] Some of their greatest allies have not been conservatives, but liberal Republicans, with strong ties to Wall Street and Democrats. Big business generally likes big government—it likes economic regulation, it likes a complex tax code, and it likes an impenetrable bureaucracy. Businessmen are not interested in competition, but want monopolies, and big government—the biggest monopoly of all—is the easiest way to get one.

On the philanthropic front, businesses often give large contributions to groups that are hostile to the free market, as documented by the Capital Research Center, a conservative watchdog outfit, among others.[2] The late economist and libertarian Milton Friedman argued that businesses should have nothing at all to do with philanthropy—not because of the liberalism associated with corporate giving, but because it betrays shareholders. "One topic in the area of social responsibility that I feel duty-bound to touch on . . . has been the claim that business should contribute to the support of charitable activities and especially to universities," he wrote in *Capitalism and Freedom*. "Such giving by corporations is an inappropriate use of corporate funds in a free-enterprise society."[3]

Traditionally, conservatives have had to work hard to remind businesses that their freedom and prosperity depend upon a free-market system that must be protected against encroachments by government, and, sadly, by big business itself. This has been true since the earliest days of the conservative movement. Frank Chodorov, a libertarian writer who founded the Intercollegiate Studies Institute, refused to hold corporations in romantic esteem. He went so far as to accuse big business of leveraging government power in such a way as to fulfill the visions of Karl Marx.[4] Rallying to meet the threat, conservatives have created organizations such as the Foundation for Economic Education and publications such as the *Freeman*, allied themselves with upstart groups such as the National Federation of Independent Business and National Right to Work Committee, and promoted the procapitalist message of thinkers and activists such as Irving Kristol and William E. Simon. Ronald Reagan's ties to General Electric are a case study of an exception that proves the rule.

Notwithstanding the facts, liberals have done well in promoting the myth that the conservative movement is the handmaiden of big business. Ayn Rand, the libertarian philosopher, did not help matters when she declared big business "America's Persecuted Minority." An avowed atheist, she once proposed replacing the Cross of Christ with the dollar sign. (Her large and devoted following at one time included a young economist named Alan Greenspan). Rand's popular novels, *Atlas Shrugged* and *The Fountainhead*, roused great controversy among conservatives. Some, like Whittaker Chambers, decried her atheistic materialism; others, such as John Chamberlain, somewhat admired her views on capitalism as a sine qua non of freedom. Rand, who died in 1982, is perhaps most kindly understood as a staunch enemy of collectivism.

Whatever Rand's influence, liberals have not shrunk from portraying the conservative movement as a wholly owned subsidiary of big business. The day after the inauguration of President George W. Bush in 2001, *New York Times* columnist Paul Krugman dutifully voiced the refrain: "The new guys in town are knee-jerk conservatives; they . . . believe that what's good for business is always good for America."[5]

In the early 1930s, an outspoken capitalist warrior was Leonard E. Read. He was a top official in the western division of the U.S. Chamber of Commerce, was disenchanted with New Deal economics and became a born-again libertarian, focusing on free-market economics.[6] Read began to organize public-education campaigns to counter the forces of economic collectivism, and in 1946 established the Foundation for Economic Education (FEE) in an old mansion on the Hudson River. The organization's mission was to evangelize on behalf of free markets; before long both the Austrian free-market economists, Ludwig von Mises and Friedrich Hayek, were participating in its programs.

In 1954, FEE purchased the *Freeman*, which provided a crucial outlet for free-market writers, such as Frank Chodorov, who were shunned by the mainstream publications. Its readership was made up of small businessmen who were dismayed by the antibusiness trends of the New Deal and by the large corporations that embraced it. Together, FEE and the *Freeman* began to build a national constituency for conservative approaches to economic problems. Although Read insisted that he was a man of neither the right nor the left—he associated leftists with Communism and rightists with fascism—his organization and publication became an important part of the conservative movement that objected to economic intervention by the government.[7]

Read was not as alone as he imagined. He had allies in the mainstream business press, such as John Chamberlain, a senior editor of the *Freeman* who also wrote frequently for *Fortune*, which was part of Henry Luce's publishing empire. One of *Fortune*'s editors was John Davenport, scion of the family who had founded Yale University and a committed free marketeer. In a 1964 memo to Luce, Davenport outlined part of the *Fortune* philosophy: "The overwhelming part of the public business of America is done by private and business means if we include feeding, clothing, and housing the people. Most private activity is only possible as government . . . performs certain indispensable functions. But the key distinction is that not everything which is public is governmental."[8] Davenport also edited *Barron's*, wrote for *National Review*, and helped found the Mont Pelerin Society. Another journalist connected with both the *Freeman* and *Fortune* was Henry Hazlitt, who attacked Keynesian economics throughout his long life; his 1946 book *Economics in One Lesson* remains to this day a classic of conservative economic thinking.

After World War II, the *Wall Street Journal* became an increasingly powerful organ for conservative thought in its editorial pages, under the leadership first of Vermont Royster (1958–71) and then of Robert Bartley (1972–2001). Both won Pulitzer Prizes for their work, which sharpened supply-side concepts and called for tax cuts, and were aligned with the economic policies of the Reagan administration. If writers presented ideas, it took activists to implement them—and free enterprise had its share of these as well. In 1943, C. Wilson Harder quit his job at the U.S. Chamber of Commerce, fed up with how the organization was handling its small business members and their interests, and from his basement in San Mateo, California, started the National Federation of Small Business. It moved into more suitable quarters the next year and grew like a weed. A Washington, D.C., office opened its doors in 1947, and two years later, the group changed its name to the National Federation of Independent Business.

Harder was determined not to repeat the mistakes of the Chamber of Commerce—which often reflected the views of its own officials instead of its membership—and instead stayed in close contact with the NFIB's members to make sure their concerns were represented effectively. The organization eventually developed a system of polling to gauge members' opinions on various political issues through a newsletter called "The Mandate." Although its membership rolls were susceptible to the economy's ups and downs, the organization experienced steady growth and, by the end of the 1960s, it could boast 266,000 members. In 1977, the group's 500,000th member signed up. Its considerable influence came from the sense that it represented the authentic voice of America's small businesses. Conservatives could count on it as a firm ally in battles against governmental encroachment. When Bill Clinton pushed for a national health-care system, the U.S. Chamber of Commerce, which had endorsed Clinton's tax increases, met frequently with White House officials to see if a deal might be struck. The NFIB, on the other hand, rejected conciliatory gestures out of hand and staunchly refused to have anything to do with the proposal. It released a study showing that the Clinton plan would cost as many as 1.5 million jobs. Perhaps as a result, many businesses gave up their membership with the chamber and joined the NFIB. "We were getting creamed in the field by NFIB," complained one chamber official.[9]

About this time a new movement was emerging. It was not so much pro–small business as anti–big labor—or, more precisely, it was opposed to the compulsory unionism that was coming to dominate the American workplace. During the 1930s and early 1940s, as a result of the National Labor Relations Act (also known as the Wagner Act), unions had gained enormous clout, and their membership had boomed. In 1945, about 30 percent of nonagricultural workers were members of a union.

This was the high-water mark for big labor. But during World War II, when labor disputes threatened to undermine the war effort, public perception began to turn against the unions. An incident involving Montgomery Ward is revealing. In 1943, the retailer's union contract expired. Ward's chairman, Sewell Avery, give his employees a little more freedom. As it stood, their contract required that they pay union dues as a condition of working at Montgomery Ward. Avery, however, believed they should have a choice to join or not to join the union, which resulted in a standoff. Franklin Roosevelt ultimately stepped in—on the side of union bosses. He ordered Avery to capitulate, in the name of "labor peace" during wartime. When Avery refused, National Guardsman took over the company's Chicago headquarters and Avery, aged seventy, was forcibly removed from his office.[10]

Controversies such as this gave rise to the right-to-work movement—a name invented in 1941 by William B. Ruggles, an editor at the *Dallas Morning News*. In an editorial on Labor Day, he called for a constitutional amendment stating that: "No person shall be denied employment because of membership in or affiliation with a labor union or because of refusal to join or affiliate with a labor union." Over the next few years, a number of states passed right-to-work laws. The unions sued and, ultimately, the Supreme Court took up the case and ruled that states could have right-to-work laws if they so chose.[11]

The political battle eventually moved to Kansas, where a young engineer named Reed Larson became involved in the fight to adopt the right-to-work law. Initially, he experienced setbacks, including a gubernatorial veto, but in 1958 voters approved the measure and Kansas joined the ranks of right-to-work states. But similar initiatives in other states were defeated, and many believed the movement was dead.

It might have been, except that Larson moved to Washington, took charge of the financially strapped Right to Work Committee, and gave it new life. Many of Larson's accomplishments were defensive—he defeated federal measures to weaken right-to-work laws in the states as well as efforts to legalize "common situs" picketing, which means picketing an entire project to protest against a single subcontractor.

But, over the course of several decades, the Right to Work Committee went on the offensive as well. In 1960, about 23 percent of the population lived in right-to-work states; at last count, the figure was more than 38 percent. This increase was due partly to states' passing right-to-work laws—twenty-two currently have them—but mainly due to migration in the United States from the union-friendly Northeast and industrial Midwest to the South and the West.[12] The climate certainly helped, but so did Larson's activism: one study showed states with right-to-work laws attracting new businesses, creating more jobs, and expanding wages to a much greater extent than those states without them.[13] The Right to Work Committee ultimately became one of the most successful business-oriented organizations on the right and was a testament to what one individual—Reed Larson—could accomplish.

One of the opponents of right-to-work legislation, in its early days, was Ronald Reagan, still a Democrat, still a union leader, and fully committed to prounion issues. Labor leaders, including Reagan, correctly understood that these laws represented an enormous threat and opposed them vigorously.[14]

General Electric executive Lemuel Ricketts Boulware was looking around for a major personality to help his company improve relations with its workforce. In 1954, this search led him to Reagan—and to what may be the most important partnership between a corporation and a political figure in American history. "Looking back now I realize that it wasn't a bad apprenticeship for someone who'd someday enter public life," wrote Reagan in his autobiography, *An American Life*. "Those GE tours became almost a post-graduate course in political science for me."[15] Nancy Reagan viewed the affiliation as providential: "If you believe, as Ronnie does, that everything happens for a purpose, then certainly there was a hidden purpose in Ronnie's job for General Electric."[16]

Boulware was an unusual business executive—a committed anti-Communist and a financial supporter of several vital conservative institutions. An initial financier of the Intercollegiate Studies Institute, he was one of *National Review*'s first stockholders. In 1960, William F. Buckley, Jr., wrote to him about the health of his magazine and the conservative movement generally: "We aren't out of the woods, but when we are, boy, if it's the last thing I do, I'll build a statue with your name on it."[17]

Today, Boulware is probably best known as the father of "Boulwarism"—"a terrible word for a good idea," he called it.[18] The idea behind the word, invented by a journalist, merely maintains that corporations should present a vision directly to their employees and the communities in which they live, as opposed to dealing with them exclusively through their union leaders. Boulware believed that managers and workers should be partners united in the common cause of production and their shared interest in mutual prosperity, rather than adversaries who battled over the crumbs of a pie that never seemed to grow. Labor relations should be "thought out, not fought out," he once said.[19] Put another way, it was Boulware's way of dealing with GE's labor problems. The intensity of a 1946 strike had surprised and upset company leaders, who realized that they needed to improve the image of the company for its own workers.

Reagan's first involvement with the corporation came through his job as host of *General Electric Theater*, a television show, in 1954. It quickly turned into the top-rated program on Sunday evenings—and Reagan was suddenly one of GE's most prized employees. He was almost certainly its most famous, and the company took advantage of his fame by sending him to GE facilities, where he met the men and women who were ostensibly his colleagues. He shook hands in factories, ate meals in company cafeterias, and addressed assemblages of workers. The goal was to improve morale, from the top of GE's organizational chart to the bottom. Reagan also interacted with the communities that were home to GE plants, often speaking to civic groups on "the mashed potato circuit." According to biographer Lou Cannon, "Reagan was already a company man when he began his GE tours, but he was still a nominal Democrat who had been raised to be suspicious of Big Business. Over time, on tour for General Electric, these suspicions diminished and were replaced by distrust for Big Government."[20]

Reagan did not confine himself to discussing GE. After a speech to employees in Schenectady, New York, one listener asked Reagan what "the average guy" could do about federal budget deficits. Although Reagan, as president, would become a well-known deficit spender, he replied with clear advice: Every organization can pass resolutions asking an end to deficit spending. "Give the resolution to the press, send it to your congressman."[21] GE had no problem with such messages because they helped build team spirit inside the company and encouraged a better business climate around the country. But at the same time, Boulware was sensitive to accusations of partisanship. Although he was happy to distribute books by authors such as John T. Flynn, a harsh critic of the Roosevelt administration, he resisted the suggestion of Clarence Manion—dean of the Notre Dame law school, a talk-radio host, and an early backer of Barry Goldwater for president—that corporations buy and hand out copies of *The Conscience of a Conservative*. Boulware insisted that companies must be "lily white"—i.e., purely nonpartisan—and believed it would be "inappropriate" to place bulk orders for Goldwater's seminal book.

Reagan used his GE tours as an occasion for developing the themes that would animate his presidency. As with all of his speeches, Reagan wrote his own talks to corporate and civic groups—all of them variations of what would become known, famously among conservatives, as "The Speech." Reagan would deliver versions of it over and over, honing it to perfection over the years. This process culminated in 1964, when Reagan made his famous Goldwater speech—the performance that made him a political star who would soon run for governor of California and later for president. *Time* magazine journalist Hugh Sidey once commented that Reagan's second-term speeches in London and Moscow were the finest ever given by a president on foreign soil. He asked a White House speechwriter who had crafted these remarks. "Reagan," replied the speechwriter. "They were pretty much the speeches he had given when he worked for General Electric."[22]

As Reagan began to seek the presidency in the 1970s, conservatives frequently complained that big business was not doing enough to help them. After his election as president, he certainly did not draw heavily from the corporate world to fill his cabinet. Donald Regan, who served as Reagan's first Treasury secretary and then as White House chief of staff, came directly from Wall Street, where he once headed the New York Stock Exchange. Raymond J. Donovan, Reagan's first labor secretary, had a background in the construction industry, and his commerce secretaries also had business backgrounds. What is notable about these figures, however, is that conservatives both in and out of the administration did not regard them as close allies.

Conservatives' suspicions about big business were not new. In 1966, Young Americans for Freedom called upon its members to picket Volkswagen dealerships because the government of West Germany, a major shareholder in the company, approved the sale of a steel-rolling plant to China. "By the admission of the West German government, steel rolled from this plant could produce jeeps, trucks, helmets, and other military equipment, and perhaps even bomb encasements," warned Randal Cornell Teague, a southern regional representative for YAF, in a memo to state and chapter chairmen. "Obviously, this material would be used against American fighting men in South Vietnam."[23] Two years later, YAF launched a much more aggressive effort against IBM to protest its trade dealings involving technological equipment with Iron Curtain countries. YAF ran advertisements, sent press kits to members of the media, and ignited its network of activists. "The STOP-IBM campaign is becoming the most important single project in YAF's eight year history," wrote Teague.[24] In another memo, Teague claimed that "at least 62 groups in 24 states picketed and demonstrated against IBM's trade policies during the STOP-IBM Weekend," which coincided with the company's stockholders' meeting on April 29, 1968. YAF national chairman Alan McKay remarked at the gathering: "It is precisely because IBM possesses such (outstanding) stature and influence that we chose it for the focus of our campaign. By trading with the Communist nations, we save them from their own economic failures, thus perpetuating regimes that are repressive and form part of a system which, taken as a whole, poses the greatest threat to human freedom in our time."[25]

On the domestic front, big business worked against the interests of capitalism, lamented Irving Kristol. Kristol's rise to prominence as a leading thinker of the emerging neoconservative movement owed much to the wide readership of his monthly column in the *Wall Street Journal*. One of his most prominent articles, "Business and 'The New Class,'" appeared in 1975. "Businessmen are as human—and are as capable of self-deception—as anyone else," he wrote. Kristol noted that business leaders often complain about hostility toward free enterprise. Occasionally, they do more than talk, he went on: They take action. But their efforts, many of them in the arena of broad-based public education, are largely wasted . . . because they have chosen the wrong target. "From the very beginnings of capitalism, there has always existed a small group of men and women who disapproved of the pervasive influence of the free market on the civilization in which we live," wrote Kristol. These people were part of what Kristol dubbed the New Class: "We are talking about scientists, teachers and educational administrators, journalists and others in the communications industries, psychologists, social workers, those lawyers and doctors who make their careers in the expanding public sector, city planners, the staffs of the larger foundations, the upper levels of the government bureaucracy, etc." They are joined not only by their hostility to capitalism, but by the ironic fact that they are all products of it, he cautioned. Capitalism's prosperity makes their very livelihoods possible. Yet they are insulated from it, misperceive its workings, and hold it in contempt.[26]

One of Kristol's most devoted readers was William E. Simon, Treasury secretary in the Nixon and Ford administrations, who was profoundly affected by the notion that capitalism, in Kristol's words, "may yet turn out to be its own gravedigger." Simon became an instant crusader within the business community. In 1976, he gave a speech blasting the president of the Firestone Tire and Rubber Company for declaring that "the term 'free enterprise' is dead." Said Simon, "I shudder to think how many other business leaders share in that counsel of despair." He continued, "If they give up, who is left to uphold economic freedom?"[27] Simon implored corporate leaders to recognize the problem of subsidizing the universities in which their ideological foes held tenure. In a 1977 speech, delivered shortly after he left public office, Simon developed this theme:

> Most private funds—inevitably from business itself—flow ceaselessly to the very institutions which are philosophically committed to the destruction of capitalism. The great corporations of America sustain the major universities, with no regard for the content of their teachings. They sustain the major foundations which nurture the most destructive

> egalitarian trends. And with their advertising, they
> sustain the mass media, which today inevitably serve
> as a national megaphone for every egalitarian cru-
> sade. In the last analysis, American business is fi-
> nancing the destruction of both free enterprise and
> political freedom.[28]

Simon went on to fight these trends in his best-selling book *A Time for Truth* and as head of the John M. Olin Foundation, which, until spend-ing out its endowment in the early twenty-first century, devoted itself to preserving the free enterprise system. But big business never seems to have heeded this call—not when Kristol made it on the pages of the *Wall Street Journal*, and not when Simon made it in speeches and books. Most corporate leaders have never looked at the struggle to preserve free enterprise through long-term, principled lenses. Instead, they have approached politics as short-term pragmatists who are less interested in advancing future goals for the general good than in buying a seat for themselves at the politicians' table. Which is why their political spend-ing is so evenly divided between Democrats and Republicans. A 2002 report by the Center for Responsive Politics, a left-leaning watchdog group that tracks money in politics, makes this plain. It examined the giving patterns of the one hundred top political donors between 1989 and 2002—who gave more than $1 billion to candidates in federal elec-tions during those three years. Overall, Democrats collected about 60 percent of this massive pot.

Corporations and associations of businesses leaned, but only slightly, toward Republicans: 59 percent of their money went to the GOP. And within this category, many large companies actually preferred Demo-crats. Disney and AOL Time Warner, for instance, gave about two-thirds of their contributions to Democrats. Rather than principles, the biggest motivator for these companies seemed to be incumbency. Be-fore the GOP takeover of Congress in the 1994 elections, businesses on the whole were more likely to support Democrats than Republicans.[29]

So much for the best myth-making efforts of liberals who grumble that big business has bankrolled the conservative movement.

CHAPTER THIRTEEN

Religion and American Conservatism

The views of the Founding Fathers concerning the importance of religion for the proper ordering of society were fairly conventional. The Constitution made clear the new nation would not recognize an established church, but the Founders did not forget one of the most important lessons of the West going back to Constantine; namely, that without a divinely sanctioned morality a nation could not maintain the virtues necessary for a rightly ordered society.

The political philosophy that undergirded the importance of religion was republicanism, a combination of insights about the best way to prevent tyranny and preserve liberty. Republicanism was derived from Renaissance philosophers and seventeenth-century debates among British philosophers over the prerogatives of the monarchy and Parliament. The Founders' ideal of limited government stemmed directly from this republican outlook, and it held that unchecked power leads to political corruption and inevitably to the destruction of liberty, law, and natural rights. Republicanism of the Anglo-American variety sought to combine the best elements of popular influence, aristocratic tradition, and executive authority in a system of checks and balances.

According to M. Stanton Evans, in his authoritative book on the subject:

> American constitutional doctrine is the product of
> an immensely long development, unfolding over two
> millennia of Western thought and practice. It starts
> with the religious insight that there is a higher law
> above the state; finds backing for this structure in

the church, and thereafter in the feudal order; de-
duces from this a system of contractual statecraft,
representative bodies, and written guarantees of
freedom. . . . Taken as a whole, this history traces
a series of ever-narrowing and more definite limits
on the reach of secular power—which the American
Constitution is (or was) the ultimate expression.[1]

To George Washington there was no ambiguity at all: "Of all the
dispositions and habits which lead to political prosperity," said Washington, "religion and morality are indispensable supports." The link between religion and popular government undeniably was axiomatic for
the Founders. As Washington also wrote, "The rule, indeed, extends
with more or less force to every species of free government. Who that is
a sincere friend to it can look with indifference upon attempts to shake
the foundation of the fabric?"[2]

John Adams, Washington's successor as president, was no less em-
phatic about America's need for religion. Wrote Adams, "We have no
government armed with power capable of contending with human passions unbridled by morality and religion." "Our constitution," Adams
added, "was made only for a moral and religious people. It is wholly
inadequate to the government of any other."[3] Although the Founders'
beliefs about Christianity did not always conform to orthodox teaching,
in establishing the link between religion, political liberty, and limited
government they were expressing a conviction shared by even the most
devout and conventional Christians. Charles Carroll, a Roman Catholic
and signer of the Declaration of Independence, invoked the logic that
dominated the founding era. "Without morals a republic cannot sub-
sist any length of time," Carroll wrote.[4] Consequently, anyone who denounced the Christian religion was "undermining the solid foundation
of morals, the best security for the duration of free governments."[5]

POSTWAR CONSERVATIVES DEBATE RELIGION

The convictions of the Founding Fathers about religion and the good
society appealed greatly to the leaders of the conservative intellectual

movement that emerged during the 1950s. Conservative thinkers after World War II, including traditionalists, libertarians, and anti-Communists, certainly had many cultural and political instincts that differed from those of the founding generation of America. By 1950, the United States had changed since its founding; it had taken on responsibilities that the Founding Fathers could not have foreseen. Nevertheless, the links between virtue, religion, and ordered liberty were as important to the emerging conservative. Conservatives were alarmed not only by the advance of Communism, but also by the cultural crisis that afflicted the West. The concern was not simply with the proper relationship between the state and individual freedoms; it went to the very foundation of Western civilization. Traditionalist intellectuals such as the University of Chicago's Richard Weaver feared that the advances of science and the state's increasingly narrow range of interest in the physical conditions of human existence were responsible for a dangerous neglect of the spiritual and ethical impulses that had contributed to the West's vision of the world. "The denial of everything transcending experience," Weaver wrote, "means inevitably . . . the denial of truth"—and the triumph of relativism with man being "the measure of all things."[6]

Richard Weaver's book, *Ideas Have Consequences* (1948), considered by some to be one of the original sources of the conservative movement, put the case for religion in historical and philosophical terms. The West had come off its rails, according to Weaver, in the fourteenth century when William of Occam's nominalism undermined belief in universal truths. Well before the Enlightenment and the scientific revolution, various intellectuals in the West abandoned the notion that "there is a source of truth higher than, and independent of man."[7] For Weaver, the consequences were dire. The denial of anything transcending human experience meant an inevitable rejection of objective truth. Cut off from a transcendent vision of reality, human knowledge and wisdom were increasingly identified with knowledge of the natural world. In Weaver's historical account, science and rationalism drove the higher truths of Christianity into exile, leaving the West afloat, without transcendent realities.

Weaver's proposals for civilizational renewal, as his criticisms suggested, included a recovery of a metaphysical vision of human existence and the created order. He concluded his book with a call for piety, not necessarily of a Christian sort, but one consistent with his understanding of a transcendent vision. The first article of this piety was an attitude of reverence for nature, so that man would no longer simply be the measure of all things. The second was an acceptance of the "substance of other beings,"[8] which in turn would encourage chivalry and charity toward fellow men and women. Finally, Weaver's piety called for a reverence for the past—not as an "unfortunate inheritance" but as a source of wisdom and virtue.[9]

Like Weaver, Russell Kirk's argument for a "conservative mind" leaned heavily on the notion that the West's cultural and political achievements had depended on a recognition of the higher truths that Christianity had revealed. Kirk was adamant that conservatism was not "a fixed and immutable body of dogma," an assertion that prevented an easy correlation between conservative and Christian convictions. Even so, in his six canons of conservative thought, the first established the importance of religion:

> Belief that a divine intent rules society as well as conscience, forging an eternal chain of right and duty which links great and obscure, living and dead. Political problems, at bottom, are religious and moral problems. A narrow rationality, what Coleridge calls the Understanding, cannot of itself satisfy human needs. . . . Politics is the art of apprehending and applying Justice which is above nature.[10]

Kirk followed this positive description with several points wherein conservatism stood at odds with radicalism. He drew specifically on Christian teaching when he asserted that conservatism denies "the perfectibility of man and the illimitable progress of society."[11] Because conservatives hold that "humanity has a natural proclivity toward violence and sin," they invariably reject the variety of anti-Christian systems proposed to replace Christian ideas about human nature and the consequences of the Fall.

In a later book, *The Roots of American Order*, Kirk attempted to spell out the social consequences of Christianity for the United States. The coherence of America's political order, Kirk believed, came directly from a "Christian understanding of the human condition."[12] Most of the book was an effort to show just how deep the roots of America's political order were, extending from Great Britain and its traditions, back to Christendom, Jerusalem, and Athens. But Kirk by no means regarded the American Constitution as the culmination of the Judeo-Christian heritage; he cautioned that "Christianity prescribes no especial form of politics." Monarchy, autocracy, aristocracy, oligarchy, republicanism, democracy, and "even some of the twentieth-century totalist regimes" had coexisted with the Church. So no special affinity existed between Christianity, limited government, federalism, the separation of powers, and states' rights. Still, a religious people could not help but have their faith shape the moral order of their society and its political manifestation. Consequently, "Christian concepts of justice, charity, community, and duty may transform a society without any abrupt alteration of governmental framework. The worth of the person, the equality of all men before the judgment-seat of God, the limitations upon all earthly authority—such Christian convictions as these would shape the American Republic."[13]

Politicians did not hesitate to pit the atheism of the Soviet Union against the faith of the American people. This helped to push through a revision to the Pledge of Allegiance, at the urging of the Knights of Columbus in 1954, which added "under God" as well as a new phrase on United States' currency in 1957, "in God we trust." When "under God" was added to the pledge, President Eisenhower, reflecting the tenor of the times, said:

> In this way we are reaffirming the transcendence of
> religious faith in America's heritage and future; in
> this way we shall constantly strengthen those spiri-
> tual weapons which forever will be our country's
> most powerful resource in peace and war.

Whittaker Chambers went beyond these truisms to portray the antagonism between political liberty and Communism as a titanic struggle between God and man. In "The Letter to My Children" that opened *Witness,* Chambers explained that the crisis of Communism was essentially a crisis of faith. The roots of Communism went back, in his estimate, to the original sin of Adam and Eve—whether man would succumb to the temptation to "be as gods," or submit to the order and rule of God. Communism was the "great alternative faith," the effort to replace the mind and will of God with the intellect and ambition of man. Because the West, Chambers believed, was indifferent to God, thanks to secularization, he feared that the West could not survive. Indeed, because liberalism looked hollow in the face of so great a challenge, conservatism was the only possible response, for it yoked mankind's yearning for freedom to faith in God.

The American Catholic Church was at the forefront of the anti-Communist movement. In encyclicals from as early as the 1840s, the Church had, without equivocation, stated that Marxism and secularism were "the great enemy of Catholicism, the ultimate expression of modern man's revolt against God, the Church, and civilization."[14] Catholics also taught that because Marxists were atheists, and because they did not hesitate to annihilate their enemies, Catholics, and in fact all religious people, should expect to be persecuted and killed in any country ruled by Communists.

The country's most ardent, and best-known, Catholic anti-Communist was Edmund A. Walsh, the dean and founder of the School of Foreign Service at Georgetown University in Washington, D.C. Walsh was a student of Russian history and had been asked by the pope to go to Russia in the 1920s to run the Catholic Church's famine relief program and to oversee the interests of the Church. There he witnessed the political trials of priests and bishops, accused of conspiring to resist the regime, and the torture of others. Walsh became an outspoken and articulate anti-Communist, used his position at Georgetown to speak out constantly against the Communist menace, and led the movement to withhold diplomatic recognition of the Soviet Union—a movement that was successful until the election of FDR in 1932. Another prominent Catholic anti-Communist intellectual was Waldemar Gurian, a Russian-German émigré who taught political theory at the University of Notre Dame, founded the *Review of Politics,* and published several scholarly works before and after World War II warning of the Communist threat.

Wherever Communism had come to power it had persecuted and tortured Catholics. The Church, in response, launched a worldwide anti-Communist campaign that became the mainstay of the movement, educating both Catholics and non-Catholics about the evils of Communism and helping to organize anti-Communist organizations. Starting in 1930, the pope asked American Catholics to end each Mass with a prayer for the conversion of Russia and the fall of Communism.[15] As World War II erupted and FDR embraced the Soviet Union as an ally, the Catholic media never failed to remind its members of the persecution all religious sects were suffering under Communist rule. Catholics were particularly concerned about the future of Poland, and as peace was being negotiated in 1945, denounced the Yalta Peace Conference as "a sellout, a victory for Stalin, and a violation of the Atlantic Charter."[16] When Communists did seize power in Poland, despite Stalin's promise at Yalta, American Catholics denounced Roosevelt and the new Truman administration as appeasers and Communist sympathizers. Recognition of the Communist regime in Poland by Truman was viewed as a sword through the heart of worldwide Catholicism.

Catholics continued to raise the question of Communism whenever they could, often turning it into a political issue. James Buckley, brother of William F. Buckley, Jr., and future senator from New York, wrote an open letter to Catholics during the 1960 campaign. In it he stated that Kennedy's religion was the wrong Catholic issue; the real issue, he said, is "the Catholic opposition to Communism," and in that respect, "Kennedy has chosen to identify himself with that segment of American society which is either unwilling or unable to regard Communism as more than a childish bugaboo."

Catholic anti-Communism was further eroded with the election, in 1958, of Pope John XXIII, who encouraged Catholics to begin to conduct dialogue with Communists. His first major encyclical, *Mater et Magistra*, issued in July 1961, dealt mostly with conventional Catholic social policy, but also insisted that colonialism, not Communism, was the cause of the Third World's problems.[17] *National Review* responded to the encyclical with a stinging editorial, stating that "the most obtrusive social phenomena of the moment are surely the continuing and demonic successes of the Communists, and that the Pope had simply dispensed with the issue." *NR* went on to say that concerning the neglect of Communism, the document "would be seen by some as a venture in triviality coming at this particular moment in history," and jokingly concluded by saying that conservatives were telling each other "Mater

Si, Magistra No!,"[18] a play on Fidel Castro's response—Cuba Si, Yanqui No!—to the Kennedy administration's attempts to overthrow him.

Vatican II, which convened in spring 1962, concluded that Marxism had become a permanent force in global politics and that the Church would be better served by working within the existing world assisting in the problems of poverty rather than in trying to change the system. The result was a further erosion of the official Church's position on Communism. *National Review* devoted an entire issue to the matter in 1965, asking, on the cover, "What in the Name of God is Going On in the Catholic Church?" It included articles by Will Herberg, Thomas Molnar, and Brent Bozell, who warned that the crisis was intensified because Catholic malcontents took their norms not from the Church but from "mirrors arranged by Christianity's enemies."[19] Worldwide Catholic anti-Communism was revived in 1978 with the election of Pope John Paul II, whose career as a priest, bishop, and cardinal in Poland had been made fighting the Communists. Particularly important was the new pope's relationship with Ronald Reagan; as two lifelong anti-Communists—who had both survived assassins' bullets—they saw eye to eye on the Soviet Union and had the same view on nuclear weapons. They met at least seven times and, according to Reagan scholar Martin Anderson, had an active correspondence, which remains highly classified but includes some of the most interesting and important dialogue of the Reagan presidency.[20]

Even libertarian conservatives, those least likely to conceive of the contemporary crisis in philosophical terms, recognized the importance of religion to the West and the forms it had encouraged. The German free-market economist Wilhelm Roepke argued that Christianity provided the foundation for the West's idea of liberty. The ancients, both Christian and pagan, had spoken of human dignity and the absolute worth of the individual in ways that were crucial to recognizing the value of freedom and the danger of tyranny. But Christianity, according to Roepke, "was necessary to wrest man, as a child of God, from the grasp of the State."[21] The difference between ancient philosophy and Christianity on the nature of freedom lay precisely in the latter's respect for the person. While the ancients developed the idea of collective freedom that did not exclude "the total subjection of the individual," Christianity gave the West a conception of freedom that "guarantees the rights of the person, limits the action of the State, and comprehends the rights of the individual, the family, of the minority, of the opposition, of religious groups."[22] For Roepke, Christ's words, "Render unto Caesar the things which are Caesar's, but to God the things which are God's," expressed the fundamental truths of classical liberalism in its widest sense.[23] Roepke insisted that "the ethics of freedom can only be derived from the religious values embodied in the Judeo-Christian tradition."[24]

Friedrich Hayek, the author of *The Road to Serfdom,* which catalyzed American conservatism, fully recognized that the development of classical liberalism in the West was bound up with religion. Hayek, himself an agnostic, frequently asserted that to construct an absolute system of truth, as Christianity claimed to have done, was impossible, given the constraints of human existence. Even so, he understood that the idea of liberty as it developed in the West was bound up with Christian teaching about human fallibility and the distinction between state and church power. For instance, in his magisterial *The Constitution of Liberty* (1960), Hayek traced the origins of the modern conception of liberty and its dependence on the rule of law to medieval Christendom. That the "state cannot itself create or make law, and of course as little abolish or violate law, because this would mean . . . a rebellion against God who alone creates law" was a "profoundly important" backdrop for the modern West's understanding of freedom.[25]

The consensus on the value, if not the necessity, of faith among the various groups of post–World War II conservatives did not prevent tensions from arising. When Max Eastman, a contributor to *National Review,* resigned from the magazine in 1958 he cited as his reason his objections to the religious perspective inherent in its editorial policy. Eastman, like many postwar conservatives, had been a Marxist during the 1930s and harbored a tenacious suspicion of "ecclesiastical authoritarianism" and held that faith was at odds with human reason. But his decision also reflected a conviction that some of Christianity's teachings had important and even dangerous implications for politics.[26] Eastman's departure from *National Review* led William F. Buckley, Jr., to issue a handy resolution to the question of the relationship between conservatism and religion: "A conservative need not be religious, but a conservative cannot despise religion."[27] But this aphoristic response did not prevent libertarian and traditionalist conservatives from squaring off over the place of faith within American conservatism.

If conservatism lacked a consensus on the religious question, the input of political philosophers helped to keep the conversation going in a fruitful direction. When Kirk wrote with a sense of despondency that the immediate future of conservatism would be no more than "a series of leagues and coalitions of anti-collectivist elements against the collectivist tendency of the times," he seemed to be abandoning hope for a shared philosophical and religious basis.[28] But a revived interest in natural law and classical philosophy renewed the case of conservatism's need for religion.

Attention to natural law sprang from revived study of Edmund Burke. Kirk himself had hatched some of this interest with several of his books, but it was Peter J. Stanlis's study of Burke that fueled the great British statesman's usefulness to American conservatives. Stanlis, a professor of political science at Rockford College in Illinois, situated Burke in the philosophical and religious tradition of the West, running from Aristotle and Cicero down to Aquinas and Thomas Hooker. According to Stanlis, Burke conceived of natural law as a "divinely ordained imperative ethical norm" that "fixed forever" the "moral duties of civil society."[29] Stanlis was employing some of the insights of Leo Strauss on natural law; in an earlier book, Strauss had described Burke as "one of the most eloquent and profound defenders of Natural Law morality and politics in Western Civilization."[30] Many conservatives were encouraged by Strauss's criticism of modern political theory for its abandonment of the norms of ancient philosophers as well as the Christian tradition. This renewed attention to natural law led Will Herberg to opine that American legal and ethical thought was increasingly recognizing "the reality of something higher than positive law," and that particular something was the reality of a higher law stemming from the ancients and the Christian West "as the very cornerstone of their moral, social, and political philosophy."[31]

Further aid in tracing the close connection between conservatism and religion came from another European émigré scholar, Eric Voegelin. Like Strauss, Voegelin recognized that the wisdom of the ancients was superior to modern political theory, especially in their understanding of virtue, and a higher good than a simplistic freedom. Unlike Strauss, who often contrasted reason and revelation in ways that denied faith as an adequate basis for political philosophy, Voegelin drew more self-consciously on religious·truth. In his five-volume *Order and History*, Voegelin argued that the human community sought in various political theories was a reflection of an invisible and transcendent order. All of human history could be conceived as attempts to embody or enact this higher "order of being."[32] Although Voegelin was by no means a "movement" conservative, he did express the conservative concern for a comprehensive understanding of political order that looked beyond individual freedom to the ultimate ends for which men and women were created.

Despite the vitality of conservative thought during the 1950s, or perhaps because of it, there was a continuing tension between those who emphasized freedom over virtue and those who preferred virtue over freedom. Kirk and the rest of the traditionalists stood for order and consensus, morality and what they called "right reason," religion and virtue. Hayek and the rest of the libertarians and classical liberals believed above all in individual liberty, free markets, private property, and reason. Ironically, the man who healed the breach was the one who had originally pointed out the tension, namely, Frank Meyer, who continued to emphasize the importance of individual liberty but qualified freedom by arguing that it was the chief political end, even though virtue was the ultimate personal end. In the face of totalitarianism and Communism, political liberty was the ideal for Meyer. To try to use the state to achieve virtue would be to yield to the statist temptation. Nevertheless, to fail to distinguish between authoritarianism with its suppression of human freedom and the authority of God and transcendent truth was to be indifferent to the "organic moral order" out of which political liberty grew and even flourished.[33]

Meyer's fusionism produced a certain degree of agreement among America's libertarian and traditionalist wings. It identified two important strands of post–World War II conservatism and the place of religion in conservative thought. First, Meyer professed belief in an objective moral order and "immutable standards by which human conduct should be judged."[34] Second, he upheld the fundamental value of the human person and consequently opposed all attempts by the state to "enforce ideological patterns on human beings."[35] The sense of a common foe, whether specifically Communism or more generally government power, helped to make Meyer's proposal plausible. It meant that conservatism stood for, in the words of William Henry Chamberlain, a prominent conservative journalist and historian, "religion, patriotism, the integrity of the family and respect for private property as the four pillars of a sound and healthy society."[36] The dignity of the human person was the chief check upon the power of the state.[37] For all but a few conservatives, Christianity was the source of their beliefs. In the words of the economist Wilhelm Roepke, "The patrimony of Christian social philosophy" undergirded "all that is essential and enduring in liberalism."[38]

In 1949, Peter Viereck, noted poet and professor of history at Mount Holyoke College, published *Conservatism Revisited: The Revolt against Revolt*, one of the earliest books defining what the new conservatism should be. He called for a reaction to the "storm of totalitarianism" that had swept over Europe and the mindless materialism and moral relativism that was creeping across America. Communism and Nazism were utopian, and neither hesitated to liquidate anybody or any group that stood in its way. Liberalism, Viereck thought, held a naive belief in the basic goodness of man, which was inadequate to defend against the evil of tyranny. The alternative, according to Viereck, was a conservatism based on Christianity. Conservatism, he concluded, should be "the political secularization of the doctrine of original sin."[39]

The arguments about the significance of American conservatism did not simply emerge from the academics and intellectuals. In 1960, Senator Barry Goldwater of Arizona enunciated conservative convictions in his immensely popular book, *The Conscience of a Conservative*. Contrary to the prevalent idea that America's governing political theory was liberal, Goldwater asserted that "America is fundamentally a Conservative nation." In fact, "The preponderant judgment of the American people, especially the young people, is that the radical, or Liberal, approach has not worked and is not working. They yearn for a return to Conservative principles."[40] For Goldwater, those principles were fairly simple, having been "derived from the nature of man, and from the truths that God has revealed about His creation." As such, conservatism was a timeless outlook that was as out of date as "the Golden Rule, or the Ten

Commandments, or Aristotle's *Politics*."[41] In sum, the conservative "approach" was simply "an attempt to apply the wisdom and experience and the revealed truths of the past to the problems of today."[42]

A Pressing Need for a Return to Faith

The case for the importance of faith in American politics proved to be the seed of a conservative conviction that would bear much fruit. Indeed, the social upheavals witnessed during the 1960s only seemed to confirm the point that conservatives had been making about the importance of first principles and democracy's need for virtue. Most so-called middle Americans were concerned about passing on the inheritance of one generation to another. But the 1960s radicals provided a series of challenges that threatened the ability of both governmental and private institutions to preserve standards of social decency. Of particular concern were the feminist movement and the sexual revolution, both of which took direct aim at the conventions of middle-class family life and undermined the traditional role assumed by mothers in inculcating morality and responsibility in their children. Anti-America rhetoric included violent objection to the nation's involvement in the Vietnam War and its racial intolerance. The result of the 1960s discontent was to awaken middle Americans to the danger of a society bereft of religious faith and traditional morality.

In addition to the social upheavals protesting the new trinity—race, class, and gender—conservatives were troubled, as we saw in Chapter Nine, by direct assaults on American traditions being launched by the nation's courts. The U.S. Supreme Court's rulings that held that the historical practice of prayer and Bible reading at the beginning of the school day constituted an illegal establishment of religion convinced many Americans that a number of jurists were attempting to turn the republic into a secular state. Subsequent Supreme Court decisions about sexual mores were even more alarming; traditional religion and morality were, it seemed, under assault.

As a result, and as we have seen, evangelical Protestants emerged as important allies in the conservative movement. Although largely silent in the earlier debates among conservatives, various Protestants, previously politically inactive, realized that if the United States were to retain its Christian ethos, evangelicals could not sit by idly.

Jerry Falwell and Pat Robertson would eventually become the most visible conservative evangelical spokesmen, but a relatively obscure missionary, Francis Schaeffer, laid the intellectual groundwork for their subsequent activities and became known by some as the intellectual godfather of the religious right. Schaeffer spent most of his career explaining Christianity to the skeptical young. But in the mid-1970s, with his writings and his film on the legalization of abortion—which he considered to be the final evidence that secular thought had trampled on traditional convictions about the sacredness and dignity of human life—he alerted the religious right to the deeper philosophical and historical undercurrents that were threatening Western civilization.

Ronald Reagan served, in the words of George Nash, an "emblematic and ecumenical function" because of his ability to speak to the variety of concerns that brought conservatives together—as well as his ability to evoke religion, which he did in a way that reassured believers and disarmed skeptics. But according to Ed Meese, his closest advisor, Reagan was always careful "not to wear religion on his sleeve when he spoke, even though it entered, in one way or another, virtually every speech he made."[43] By speaking openly about the importance of faith in the character and destiny of the United States, Reagan was tapping a conviction that had been at the heart of conservatism since 1950.

The president's 1983 speech to the National Association of Evangelicals exemplified the place of religion in the resurgence of conservatism. It came on the heels of intense debates about a freeze on nuclear weapons and Reagan's decision to negotiate with the Soviets from a position of military strength. Even so, he conceded that as important as America's military strength was, "The struggle now going on for the world will never be decided by bombs or rockets, by armies or military might. The real crisis we face today is a spiritual one; at root, it is a test of moral will and faith." Reagan concluded that the West could survive "provided that its faith in God and the freedom He enjoins is as great as communism's faith in Man."[44]

A movement similar to the flight of nonpolitical Americans from the radicalization and secularization of the culture occurred, throughout the 1960s and 1970s, among mainline Protestant Christians and Catholics.

Many pastors and priests began to drift to the left, to become ever more secular, and to abandon their spirituality and faith for political advocacy and activism. Among mainline Protestant churches—those that had been, for much of American history, the mainstay of middle-class ethics, morality, and culture itself—secular liberalism, instead of faith in God, became the sacred doctrine. As the national churches accepted such absurdities as the political platforms of the National and the World Council of Churches, many of their members—people who were neither conservatives nor even political—felt disenfranchised and realized that in order to protect their way of life, they would need to become actively involved in political, philosophical, and cultural conservatism.

According to Irving Kristol, in the *Public Interest* in 1995, these Americans "looked at our high schools and saw that gay and lesbian organizations were free to distribute their literature to the students but that religious organizations were not. They saw condoms being distributed to adolescent teenagers while the Supreme Court forbade the posting of the Ten Commandments on the classroom wall. And so they rebelled and did the only thing left for them to do—they began to organize politically. In so doing, they may very well have initiated a sea-change in American politics and American life."[45] According to British historian Paul Johnson, the leftism and secularization that became such a powerful force in the churches set off a "great awakening" among the disenfranchised Christian rank and file that was, in its own right, a "new and non-elitist variety of ecumenicalism, a de facto unity that stretches across the sects and even into Catholicism." According to Johnson, such a popular ecumenicalism was based on the historical facts of Christian faith, which reasserted traditional moral values among Protestants, Catholics, and even nonpracticing Christians.[46]

Full Circle

American conservatism emerged after World War II with a profound sense that American culture, and the West more generally, faced a crisis of enormous proportions. Soviet Communism was not simply the political and ideological foe of liberal democracy, but offered a vision of human nature and the world that was not only fundamentally flawed, but pernicious. For the American political order to survive, a return to first principles was the order of the day. William F. Buckley, Jr.'s *God and Man at Yale,* published in 1951, articulated well the link between religious first principles and America's political ideals. Two attitudes were basic for the conservative, one having to do with "the role of man in the universe," the other with "the role of man in his society." "I had always been taught," he wrote, "and experience had fortified the teachings, that an active faith in God and a rigid adherence to Christian principles are the most powerful influences toward the good life." "I also believed," he added, "that free enterprise and limited government has served this country well and would probably continue to do so in the future."[47]

As basic and as simply stated as those convictions were for Buckley, they informed the conservative movement as they took shape in the writings of certain public intellectuals and became embodied in various institutions and political initiatives. Conservatives have never been of one mind about the particulars of religion or the precise relationship between faith and a free and ordered society. But without attention to such basic attitudes, American conservatism would have died on the vine.

CHAPTER FOURTEEN

We Are All Conservatives Now

As Ronald Reagan's administration began to wind down in the fall of 1988, conservatives had little to complain about. The movement had come a long way from those early, lonely days of the 1950s; it had not only matured, but had demonstrated its ability to provide a conservative administration with the necessary day-to-day personnel and outside support, and to hold its feet to the fire when things went astray. Politically, the movement could now assert itself as a national electoral force; in fact, few denied that conservatism had developed into one of the most potent political movements of the twentieth century.

Reagan had tested the principles of conservatism, and they worked. Supply-side economics had transformed the economy from the stagflation of the Carter years into a job- and wealth-creating engine, and the results were nothing short of astounding. A tough stance against Communism had helped to put the Soviet Union on the skids; it would be out of business within another couple of years. And most important, the conservative principles Reagan used had restored confidence in government by the American people, and had demonstrated that, in fact, Washington was governable.

Then there was the Reagan diaspora. The hundreds of conservative activists who had joined the Reagan administration on every level, from cabinet secretary to personal secretary, returned to the private sector, to foundations and think tanks, to the media or to university faculties, invigorated by their days of glory, even continuing the fight to move the country farther to the right. Others, either coming out of the administration or energized by the Reagan presidency, went into politics on their own, running for office on the local, state, and federal levels. By 1999, ten years after Reagan left office, hundreds of members of his administration had been elected to state or federal offices.

Nearly half of all federal judges, in 1988, were Reagan appointees, many outstanding scholars who would make their mark for years to come. "Federal judgeships at all levels," according to one Reagan scholar, "never had greater political symbolism or higher priority for a presidency" than under Reagan.[1] Reagan elevated William Rehnquist, the most conservative member of the Supreme Court, to chief justice and replaced him with Antonin Scalia; these two, with the addition of Clarence Thomas, whom George H. W. Bush appointed in 1991, formed the nucleus of conservative Supreme Court jurisprudence that extended well into the twenty-first century.

Conservatives were united, and rarely identified themselves by one of the factions that had existed in the 1960s and 1970s, or that would become all too prevalent ten years later. Economic conservatives, social issue conservatives, national security conservatives, even the Christian right and the neocons were not only all rowing the same boat, but were rowing in the same direction.

Although the conservative movement was well on its way to becoming institutionalized, it had, in a sense, suffered a setback during the Reagan presidency. "The movement went downhill a little in the 1980s," according to former Reagan aide T. Kenneth Cribb. "We needed six thousand appointees in the Reagan administration, and many conservatives who had been active in the states came to Washington to fill those jobs, leaving a gap of warriors at the local level."[2] But at the end of the administration, many returned home to rejuvenate the organizations they had left or to found new ones. A new infrastructure, funded by several large foundations—Bradley, Scaife, and Olin, primarily—was created, with many new faces and new ideas. Over the next decade old conservative organizations were expanding and new ones popping up to fill every niche and to take on every issue.

The congenial and persuasive Ronald Reagan had not only changed many people's minds, he had also realigned the political spectrum. There were the Reagan Democrats, who would provide the margin of victory to conservative Republican candidates over the coming years, as well as the neoconservatives—not so many people, but of considerable stature—who brought a new dimension. But the most phenomenal change was the growth and sophistication of the social conservatives, led by evangelical Christians, who had almost en masse joined the conservative movement and who, over the next twenty-five years, would become the Republican Party's largest voting bloc.

George H. W. Bush entered the White House in January 1989, to begin what many considered Reagan's third term. He carried the Reagan legacy with him and, as Texas congressman Dick Armey expressed it, with "more assets than any president in history. A thriving economy. A world awakening to new freedom. Socialist ideas in disgrace . . . seeing liberalism in its death throes."[3]

But Bush squandered his inheritance. Once sworn in, he asked for the resignation of every Reagan appointee, accepted most of them, and replaced them with vanilla Republicans loyal to the Bush family rather than to conservative principles. He spoke of "a kinder, gentler nation" than the one that had elected Reagan, vowed to be the environmental president, and adopted the State Department view of propping up the regime in Moscow rather than trying to accelerate the fall of Communism. His administration pushed through new, expansive federal programs, including a renewed and strengthened Clean Water Act and the Americans with Disabilities Act and, in a move that infuriated the right, he agreed to a tax increase after pledging, "Read my lips. No new taxes." Screamed the *New York Post* headline, "Read My Lips: I Lied!" John Fund, in the *American Spectator*, recounted that "President George H. W. Bush was asked at a news conference about his famous 'read my lips, no new taxes' campaign pledge. 'I haven't heard any "read my lips,"' said the reporter. To that the president responded, referring to the tax-eager Democrats, 'No, you haven't heard it, because I'm going to sit down and talk to them.' A massive tax hike ensued, followed by a recession and Bush's humiliating 37% showing in the 1992 election that he lost to Bill Clinton."[4]

But while Bill Clinton was beating Bush in 1992, other events were occurring behind the scenes that would have a profound impact on the conservative movement over the coming years. The first was launched by an articulate and angry old Reaganite who had cut his teeth in the Nixon White House and subsequently made a name for himself as a writer and commentator—Patrick J. Buchanan.

Bush, having squandered the Reagan legacy, did not deserve another four-year term, and Buchanan decided it was up to him to see that he didn't get it. "If the country wants to go in a liberal direction," Buchanan told the *Washington Post,* "if the country wants to go in the direction of [Democrats] George Mitchell and Tom Foley, it doesn't bother me as long as I've made the best case I can. What I can't stand are the backroom deals. They're all in on it, the insider game, the establishment game—this is what we're running against."[5]

Attacking Bush for spending and tax increases, for protecting "owls against loggers and feminists against the Virginia Military Institute," and a host of other issues, Buchanan launched a populist campaign aimed at working-class right-wingers, Catholics, and disenchanted Republicans. He called it a pitchfork rebellion, attacking homosexuals, multiculturalism, and abortion, arguing for a return to midwestern isolationism and protectionism, and advocating the "Reagan doctrine" in U.S. foreign policy. He touched off a battle between the so-called paleoconservatives, whose primary concern was the preservation of tradition, and the neocons, whom Buchanan viewed as nothing but leftists in disguise. Although he won no primaries, Buchanan did make a respectable showing in New Hampshire—enough to alert Bush to the attack on his right, and force him to start talking like a conservative.

Buchanan received significant support within the conservative movement, largely because conservatives felt no loyalty to George Bush. The American Conservative Union endorsed him, as did several notable political activists. "The ACU endorsement in itself wasn't terribly significant," wrote Fred Barnes in the *New Republic,* "but the fight over it was. That squabble was a preview," Barnes continued prophetically, "of fierce, acrimonious battles to come among conservatives."[6] Bush gave Buchanan, probably against his better judgment, a national platform at the Republican convention in Houston in August, where Buchanan, after throwing his support to Bush, gave the keynote address. After praising Ronald Reagan to the rafters, Buchanan took no prisoners:

> My friends, this election is about much more than
> who gets what. It is about who we are. It is about
> what we believe. It is about what we stand for as
> Americans. There is a religious war going on in our

> country for the soul of America. It is a cultural war,
> as critical to the kind of nation we will one day be as
> was the Cold War itself. And in that struggle for the
> soul of America, Clinton & Clinton are on the other
> side, and George Bush is on our side. And so, we
> have to come home, and stand beside him.[7]

If Buchanan had any impact, it was to accelerate the "culture wars," a banner that would be adopted by the paleoconservatives, the religious right, and segments of the rest of the conservative movement, and eventually encompass issues such as abortion, obscenity, the destruction of family values, immigration, and gay rights—all of which Buchanan accused Bill Clinton and his wife of advocating. Using his considerable skills as a writer, commentator, and organizer, Buchanan built a veritable industry around his cause. He ran in the primaries again in 1996 (this time actually winning the New Hampshire primary) and left again, after leaving the Republican Party altogether in 2000. Books on foreign policy, immigration and demographics, and the neoconservatives followed, as did a magazine called the *American Conservative*, giving him a "bully pulpit" of considerable scope.

The inauguration of Bill Clinton in January 1993 was a bitter pill for conservatives. After eight very satisfying years of Reagan and four very disappointing years of Bush, conservatives were not ready to relinquish the reins of power in Washington, particularly to a saxophone-playing, womanizing, non-inhaling pot-smoking, liberal baby-boomer.

But if conservatives detested Clinton, they also sharpened their teeth by fighting him. He galvanized the right to launch talk radio shows, conservative magazines and journals, and other newly developing, alternative media outlets. Conservatives learned how to use their power effectively to attack Clinton's initiatives, such as his campaign to allow gays into the military, and later to uncover Whitewater, Travelgate, Paula Jones, Monica Lewinsky, and the rest of the Clinton scandals. When, early in his administration, Clinton announced his plans to nationalize health insurance and to put first lady Hillary Rodham Clinton in charge of developing such a plan, conservatives launched a campaign that ultimately stopped the scheme dead in its tracks. "Hillarycare" came to be known as one of the greatest embarrassments of Clinton's presidency.

The high visibility of its downfall effectively stalled Clinton's legislative agenda.

As each Clinton initiative was beaten back—with opposition often led by the editorial page of the *Wall Street Journal*—conservatives took aim at the next one. It had been more than twelve years since conservatives had battled a liberal president, and now a new generation of young political activists began to learn what it meant to play defense rather than offense; needless to say, the Clinton administration was a veritable virgin forest of opportunities. Each battle won provided a surge of adrenaline throughout the movement. Not for nothing did Mrs. Clinton complain of a vast right-wing conspiracy.

Regnery Publishing, which had earned a reputation as the preeminent conservative book publisher, specialized, during the 1990s, in books on the Clinton administration, and as its president and publisher I led the charge. We published no fewer than nine "Clinton" *New York Times* bestsellers between 1993 and 2001, which spent a combined eighty-two weeks on the list and caused no little discomfort to the Clintons—and were at least partially responsible for my inclusion in Mrs. Clinton's vast right-wing conspiracy. The first, and the biggest of all Clinton books (and there were dozens and dozens published), was *Unlimited Access*. FBI Special Agent Gary Aldrich had been assigned to the White House to work on personnel clearances, among other things, and had access to everybody and everything. His exposé was a blockbuster, shot to the number-one spot on the *New York Times* bestseller list and stayed on the list for five months. Aldrich became a regular on every right-wing radio and television show in the country and appeared on most of the mainstream shows as well; George Stephanopolous, then a special assistant to the president, thought Aldrich was getting too much attention and called the networks and urged them not to put Aldrich on, resulting in even more publicity for Aldrich. Books followed on Clinton's days in Arkansas, on the Department of Justice, on Hillary Clinton, on the scandals, and on the impeachment. To cap it all off, *Final Days,* describing Clinton's hundreds of pardons, the theft of White House furniture, and the rest of the untidiness accompanying the Clintons' departure from 1600 Pennsylvania Avenue, was published shortly after Barbara Olson, the author, was killed at the Pentagon on September 11.

For conservatives, Bill Clinton was an effective substitute for the old

Soviet Union abroad and Chief Justice Earl Warren at home—he provided something to react to. Book after book exposing the latest Clinton fiasco emerged on the bestsellers lists, more than one talk-radio host made his or her reputation taking Clinton to task, the circulation of magazines such as *National Review* and the *American Spectator* skyrocketed, and a whole new generation of investigators, writers, journalists, and other muckrakers emerged from obscurity ready to pounce on Bill or Hillary at a moment's notice.

Conservatives drove Clinton from the left to the center. Clinton was forced to abandon campaign after campaign. The first two Clinton years focused the thinking of congressional conservatives, particularly those who had helped push legislation through Congress during the Reagan years, on the need to gain a majority in order to finish the Reagan Revolution. One of the instigators was a young, ambitious, and outspoken congressman from Georgia.

Newt Gingrich was first elected to the House of Representatives in 1978, and within hours of his election started explaining to anybody who would listen how he was going to change the balance of power in Washington, turning the House of Representatives into a branch "co-equal" with the White House—and of course scourging the Democratic majority and replacing it with Republicans—with himself in charge.

Gingrich remained a "back-bencher" until 1983, when he founded the Conservative Opportunity Society, a vehicle to take over Congress and overthrow the liberal welfare state. "We needed a positive vision of the future," said Gingrich. "We wanted to take the issues straight to the Democrats and offer better solutions to problems than they had."[8] He started making the rounds among conservative organizations and leaders in Washington, building his reputation as an aspiring and feisty conservative, never at a loss for words, never without a new idea or suggestion, and never failing to talk about how he was going to gain a Republican majority. He attacked the Democratic leadership, first Speaker of the House Tip O'Neill of Massachusetts and subsequently Jim Wright of Texas, whose resignation from Congress over Gingrich's ethics complaints against him finally put Newt on the map.

But his reputation among conservatives was truly earned when Republicans gained control of the House of Representatives in 1994. Gingrich and his Conservative Opportunity Society, with the help of a number of conservative activists, crafted a set of ten legislative proposals that they called the Contract for America; it became the campaign platform for virtually all Republicans challenging incumbent Democrats, and Republicans pledged all ten provisions would be brought to the House floor in the first one hundred days of the new Congress. It set forth legislation limiting the role of government, provided Republicans with a unified conservative voice, and ended with a challenge to voters: "If we break this contract, throw us out." It nationalized, for the first time in nearly eighty years, the congressional campaign, thereby putting Democrats on the defensive—and making it more difficult for them to run on local issues, and to provide pork to constituents. It also provided Republicans with a set of specific political programs, rather than relying on vague political rhetoric and promises. "The contract is the most important distillation of the conservative agenda since Barry Goldwater's *Conscience of a Conservative*," said Fred Barnes in the *American Spectator.*[9]

The 1994 election was the greatest conservative victory since Ronald Reagan's election in 1980, and, in the words of the *New York Times*, "a political upheaval of historic proportions."[10] Republicans—conservative Republicans—won fifty-two seats in the House of Representatives, gaining a majority for the first time since 1954. After eight years in the minority, Republicans also reclaimed their majority in the Senate. If that was not enough, Republicans gained a majority of governors, and hundreds of state legislators and lesser state and local officials. But more than voting for Gingrich and his crowd, voters were rejecting Clinton liberalism.

In sum, the 1994 election ended forty years of liberal domination of Congress, leaving only the executive branch in the hands of the left. "We designed the contract as the next wave of Reagan," said Gingrich. "We took ideas from him, we took speeches from him, we stood on his shoulders. Most of us had been active Reagan supporters. You can't understand what we did without understanding Reagan."[11] Many of the newly elected were part of the Reagan diaspora. "We were people who had come of age during Reagan's presidency," said David McIntosh, a member of the Class of 1994 and founder of the Federalist Society, who defeated an incumbent Democrat from Indiana. "Many of us propounded Reagan's philosophy. We were all startled when we got elected and came to Washington and realized there were seventy other people who had done the same thing. Without Reagan's inspiration, it would not have happened."[12]

The 1994 election also demonstrated that the conservative movement—the activists, the think tanks, the grassroots, and the communicators—could work together with political candidates, could develop a plan and a strategy together, and could then win together. All parts of the movement were enlisted to get the contract passed, and each was crucial to its success. Conservative talk radio, by then hugely powerful, played a big part. "Rush Limbaugh was personally incredibly helpful," said Gingrich. "Rush was, in some ways, at the peak of his first wave, he was fresh and exciting. He had a huge audience." At one point during a debate on the House floor over one of the contract's provisions, Gingrich stepped off the floor, called Limbaugh's studio, and asked him to request support from his listeners. "A Democratic member," said Gingrich, "I don't remember who it was, came up to me. He was stunned. He said, 'I don't know what you did, but would you please just tell them to quit?' His office was swamped, they couldn't do anything except answer phones."[13]

Conservatives were, for the first time in years, setting the agenda in Congress. All ten provisions of the contract were acted upon on the floor of the House, and nine actually passed. Several of the provisions eventually became law, some were watered down in negotiations with Democrats, a couple were vetoed by Bill Clinton, and parts of others were overturned by the courts. "Perhaps not since the start of the New Deal," wrote the *New York Times*, "to which many of the programs now under attack can trace their origins, has Congress moved with such speed on so many fronts."[14]

More important was the fact that many Democrats, stunned by the strength of conservative ideas, voted with the new conservative majority. Out of a total of 302 roll call votes on issues related to the Contract, conservatives prevailed on 299. The overall margin by which the items in the Contract were passed averaged about 70 percent, even though the Republicans held a puny twelve-seat margin over the Democrats, the smallest House majority margin in forty years.[15]

The Republican Congress, and its adherence to the Contract, was a check on the liberalism of the Clinton administration. This was amply demonstrated by the enactment of a broad welfare reform package, which eliminated one of liberalism's most cherished programs and substituted a system that conservatives had been proposing for years.

But Gingrich was a better revolutionary than a leader, and in the end, little changed. Although the Republican majority lasted for a dozen years, members of Congress, eaten up by their overwhelming desire to keep their jobs, and thinking they needed to move to the center to do so, abandoned their conservative principles. But that is another story for another time. Gingrich, in the end, was candid in admitting his mistakes.

> My colleagues and I failed on three levels: we failed to create a cadre of leaders who understood what we were doing, so they reverted to the norm when we left. We failed to create a third wave of reform after Reagan and the Contract, so we didn't have a package to keep moving forward. And we failed to generate a level of grassroots enthusiasm necessary to overwhelm Washington politics.[16]

While Buchanan and Gingrich were building their niches within the movement, the Christian right was gaining momentum and power. By the 2004 presidential election, over a quarter of all voters were evangelicals, and about 70 percent of those voted Republican, the largest Republican and conservative voting bloc.[17] But unlike the early days of the Christian Coalition and the Moral Majority, both of which were largely out of business by 2004, the new Christian right was working as much from the inside out as from the outside in: by 2004, several dozen members of Congress identified themselves as evangelical Christians, and several, including a number of cabinet members, were prominent in the George W. Bush administration. Christian right organizations, by that time, were sophisticated, well financed, and exercised considerable power. They were driven by the social issues—abortion, homosexuality, gay marriage, prayer in the schools, and permissiveness—and developed a powerful network to air their views and get what they wanted. Although some of their views are not shared by libertarians or economic conservatives, they have much more in common with other parts of the movement than many realize. Nearly half of small business owners, for example, claim to be evangelical Christians.[18]

The election of George W. Bush in 2000 was a mixed blessing for conservatives. Most supported him, some enthusiastically, others reluctantly, but to a man they wanted to be rid of the Clinton-Gore team, and Bush was the strongest candidate. Coming into office on the heels of a squeaker election that had finally been decided by the Supreme Court, Bush not only had virtually no mandate, but also had generated tremendous ill will from Democrats and the left. Nevertheless, he was the first Republican president in modern history to enter office with a Republican majority in both houses of Congress, and with a country that was considerably more conservative than the elections had indicated.

Bush was capable of making a superb conservative speech, and in small groups could pass himself off as another Ronald Reagan; indeed, he often reminded conservatives that he was following in Reagan's footsteps. At the fortieth anniversary celebration of the American Conservative Union in the summer of 2004, a gathering of over one thousand leading conservatives, Bush's self-defined list of his conservative credentials made Reagan look like a piker. But his talk was far more conservative than his action.

When the country went to war in the Middle East following the terrorist attacks of September 11, 2001, most conservatives supported Bush as an act of patriotism. But as the war in Iraq escalated and became viewed in the press as the neoconservatives' war, a rift between traditionalists and libertarians, on the one hand, and neoconservatives on the other shook the movement in a manner unlike anything since the 1970s. Many conservatives believed that the United States had no business involving itself in a war that was not in the national interest. The incursion into Iraq was nothing but Wilsonianism, they charged, and had been thrust on George Bush by a small group of neoconservative idealists.

As the second Bush presidency wore on, conservatives became increasingly disenchanted, mostly because the president had appealed to them by talking like a conservative while governing like a big-spending liberal. He was responsible for the largest increase in federal spending since Lyndon Johnson's Great Society, expanding government with more big programs: the No Child Left Behind Act, which forced the federal government into every school district in the country, and the Medicare prescription drug benefit, creating a budget-busting entitlement program. But their greatest complaint was Bush's failure to address the increasing problem of massive illegal immigration from Latin America.

There were some bright spots: his judicial appointments were largely conservatives—partly because of outside pressure, as we will see below—and by the end of 2006, he had appointed nearly a third of all federal judges. He had pushed five separate tax cuts through Congress, was strong on the social and pro-life issues, had made a concerted effort to at least partially privatize Social Security, and had withdrawn the country from the Kyoto environmental treaty. But his cabinet and sub-cabinet appointments were strangers to Reagan principles.

Both Nixon and Reagan had carried forty-nine states in their re-elections in 1972 and 1984. Bush, in 2004, carried thirty-one states in one of the closest presidential re-election races in history—running against a Massachusetts liberal with a voting record almost identical to Ted Kennedy's. Two years later, Republicans were badly pummeled, losing both houses of Congress and many state offices as well, and much of the blame went to George W. Bush.

But electoral politics aside, over the last years of the 1990s and into the new century, the conservative movement had grown by leaps and bounds. Its ranks had swollen with many people and enlarged institutions; it had developed new ideas and refined old ones; it had the ability to make things happen. In the process the various factions waxed and waned, often taking different directions, but always maintaining a sense of working for the same cause. In fact, the conservative movement had become institutionalized.

By the end of the twentieth century, conservatism had become part of the establishment; in another sense, conservatism *was* the establishment. Its institutions were part of the mainstream. Conservatives were in the center of the political spectrum—a Republican who was not a conservative was an oddity, and a Democrat was often judged not by how liberal he was, but by how conservative he was.

During the same period, the intellectual institutions of the right—the think tanks, the magazines and journals, the book publishers, the educators and professors and students in the colleges and universities—expanded exponentially. The National Committee for Responsive Philanthropy, a liberal group that keeps tabs on right-wing spending, estimated that conservative think tanks spent $1 billion during the 1990s.[19] (If all think tanks anywhere to the right of center are included, the number may be accurate.) The Heritage Foundation, launched in 1973, was by 2004 one of Washington's largest and most influential think tanks, with a budget of nearly $30 million, a serious endowment, and over two hundred employees and seventy-five scholars and experts of one sort or another. Its reports were accepted in Congress and elsewhere in the capital as authoritative and reasoned. It was often quoted and cited in everything from the establishment press to mainstream books, scholarly journals, and opinion journals, both left and right. About the same size as Heritage was the American Enterprise Institute, which had more of a neoconservative hue, the libertarian Cato Institute, and Stanford University's Hoover Institution. All issued a constant flow of papers and documents, held conferences, published their own books, held public and private lectures, and had a stable of fellows, many nationally known scholars. In many ways, they were more important than the universities. "The think tanks overshadow the universities," says Martin Anderson of the Hoover Institution. "You don't see anybody launching a presidential campaign by giving a lecture at Harvard or Yale. They go to Heritage, to AEI or to Hoover."[20]

If the left is still dominant anywhere in American public life it is in the universities, where a vast majority of faculty and administrative staff are decidedly left of center, left of the student body, and left of public opinion. But the right has its own forces, including The Intercollegiate Studies Institute, Young America's Foundation (the successor to the old Young Americans for Freedom), the Leadership Institute, The National Association of Scholars, and the Federalist Society.

Even the media, cemented in leftist dogma, was challenged. On Ronald Reagan's orders the Federal Communications Commission had in 1981 stopped enforcing the so-called fairness doctrine, which had required that any political discussion on radio or television be matched, minute for minute, by the opposing view. The result was the absence of virtually any political opinion commentary. Congress tried to re-enact it in 1987, but Reagan vetoed the bill. The result was a revolution in AM radio; by 2004 there were over four thousand talk-radio hosts broadcasting on fourteen hundred AM stations. All but a handful were conservatives. Rush Limbaugh, who started a national show in 1988, soon had an audience of over 15 million people a week and within a year or so was one of the most influential commentators in the country. Fox News, which took off in 1996, had, within eight years, a larger share of the television news market than any other cable channel. Delivering news under the headline of "fair and balanced," Fox provided an outlet to dozens of conservative commentators to an audience it estimates at over 80 million people. Coupled with hundreds of conservative "blogs," which informed millions of people each day, conservatives had, by the early part of the twenty first century, a responsible and muscular media presence.

Next to the "mainstream media"—the three major television broadcast networks, the big-city papers, the weekly news magazines, and the rest—what the conservatives have is still small. Small it may be, but its greatest impact is its ability to hold the mainstream media's feet to the fire. The blackout on conservative news and opinion is no more.[21]

Conservatives are, in a word, everywhere. "The Right," according to John Micklethwait and Adrian Wooldridge, both correspondents for the *Economist*, in their book *The Right Nation,* "clearly has ideological momentum on its side in much the same way that the Left had momentum in the 1960's."[22]

But a network of organizations and people, no matter how vast, is worthwhile only if it is effective, if it can produce something worth the time and money spent building and maintaining the movement. Conservatives demonstrated their effectiveness in the 1980s, and the movement has since grown and become far more sophisticated. But besides winning elections, what else could it do?

Well, it could do a great deal. One good example, like a good picture, can be more effective than all explanations. One effort—four efforts, actually, rolled into one—demonstrates the prowess, the strength, and the effectiveness of the conservative movement, demonstrates how its coordinate parts work together, and demonstrates the great implications of what it can do. Our picture is a period of seven months, in 2005, the results of which will be felt for decades to come.

Until George W. Bush nominated John Roberts in the fall of 2005, not a single serious Supreme Court fight had occurred since the confirmation of Clarence Thomas in September 1991. Clinton appointed

Ruth Bader Ginsberg in 1993, and Stephen Breyer a year later, but both sailed through the Senate with hardly a murmur of dissent. But when, on July 1, 2005, Sandra Day O'Connor announced that she would retire, and when Chief Justice William Rehnquist died soon thereafter, leaving two vacancies on the Court, the conservative movement moved into high gear.

Three weeks after Justice O'Connor announced her resignation, President Bush nominated John Roberts, a member of the U. S. Circuit Court of Appeals for the District of Columbia, who had served in Ronald Reagan's Justice Department, to fill the vacancy, and when William Rehnquist died two months later, Bush withdrew the pending Roberts nomination and renominated him to fill the chief justice slot, asking the Senate to accelerate the confirmation process so Roberts could be installed before the new Supreme Court term began in September. Roberts was confirmed by a vote of 78–22 at the end of September. Just several days later, the president nominated White House Counsel Harriet Miers to fill O'Connor's seat, and in less than a month, after furious opposition from conservatives, withdrew the nomination and instead nominated Samuel Alito, an appellate judge on the Third Circuit Court of Appeals, who had also served in the Reagan Justice Department. Alito was confirmed, after a threatened filibuster by Democrat John Kerry, by a vote of 58–42 in late January 2006.

Judicial appointments had been an issue in both the 2000 and the 2004 campaigns, and Bush had made it clear that he intended to appoint judges in the mold of Clarence Thomas and Antonin Scalia. "The call to rein in the federal judiciary became one of President Bush's best applause lines during the 2004 campaign," reported the *Wall Street Journal*. Few doubted that Bush's promise had played a significant part in his narrow victory over John Kerry and was vital in gaining him both the evangelical Christian and the Catholic vote.[23]

But the right was taking nothing for granted. Conservatives remembered George H. W. Bush's nomination of the vapid David Souter, in 1990, as well as Ronald Reagan's appointment of Anthony Kennedy, equally bland, several years earlier. They also knew that Bush's idea of a conservative judge, despite his campaign oratory, did not necessarily mean a judge in the mold of Scalia or Thomas. So from the first day of the new Bush administration, conservatives had brought pressure to bear, both within and outside the government, for judges who believed in the Constitution. At the request of Majority Leader Trent Lott, who did not want to have another Bork fight on his hands, several conservative lawyers put together a team of seasoned Washington hands who could compete on every aspect of the confirmation process with the left's sophisticated operation.

As early as 2002, a group of lawyers affiliated with the Federalist Society, from the big law firms in Washington and New York, and from various think tanks delved into the records of every potential nominee, reading every word written, every speech given, every legal opinion joined. Comprehensive, confidential internal memos were written on each possible candidate, assuring that the conservatives were better prepared than anyone else, including the Bush administration, about who these people were and what they believed. "We felt that we needed to duplicate everything that the administration was doing internally," said Leonard Leo, one of the organizers, "so that we'd have every bit of information that they had so when we were talking about prospective nominees, we could go toe to toe with them. We had people that would read every single thing that these people wrote so we knew, down to a tee, where they were on various issues."[24] These lawyers wanted candidates who would not try to rewrite the Constitution, who had impeccable credentials, and who were articulate, presentable, and smart. In the end, the group produced a list of four acceptable candidates for the Supreme Court: Samuel Alito, Michael Luettig, Michael McConnell, and John Roberts. All had served in the Reagan administration, all had clerked for Supreme Court justices, all were sitting federal appellate judges, all believed in the Constitution, and all were the products of the long-term strategy devised by conservatives in the Reagan administration to rein in the federal courts.

When it became apparent in November 2004 that Chief Justice Rehnquist was seriously ill, a small group of conservative leaders started to put together a battle plan.[25] A coalition of eighty-one conservative organizations was assembled, including grassroots organizations, think tanks activist groups, public relations specialists, and legal strategists from every part of the movement. Special organizations were set up, money was raised, advertising agencies engaged, and a full strategy was carefully devised. So that conservatives would not be caught off-guard, as when Robert Bork was named in 1987, media-savvy lawyers were recruited and given media training, prepared to make the case for confirmation before the left's battle could begin. "We needed to dispatch people to the green rooms while the president was still on TV announcing his candidate," said one of the media consultants, "so we could set the terms of the debate."[26]

Lawyers in charge of the project did not wait, however, for the nominee to be named. For months before the first vacancy occurred, conservative leaders met with members of the mainstream media, including liberals, most of whom had never experienced a Supreme Court nomination, telling them what was going on inside the White House and the Justice Department.

"We didn't even get into ideology," said one of the organizers. "We just said it's been ten years since a Supreme Court vacancy, none of you have seen this. We can tell you how you're going to have to shape your coverage. So we gave them a lot of logistical support and built a tremendous amount of goodwill."[27]

A group of four prominent conservatives, representing different parts of the movement, oversaw the venture and informed the Bush administration which candidates would be acceptable—and which would not. Known as "the four horsemen," the group included former attorney general Edwin Meese, former White House counsel C. Boyden Gray, Federalist Society executive vice president Leonard Leo, and evangelical Christian Jay Sekulow, head of the American Center for Law Justice. At the request of officials in the White House, the group drew up an inventory of their assets: the list of all organizations on board—all eighty-one of them—the money raised, consultants hired, media resources available, strategies, strengths, and weaknesses. The administration knew that the movement was a force to be reckoned with.

When the president announced that he would nominate John Roberts, and after Rehnquist's death when he announced that Samuel Alito was his choice, the conservatives flew into action on every front. In both cases, the campaigns were executed with nary a hitch. Hundreds, if not thousands, of conservatives, from every part of the movement, became involved. Senators heard from millions of citizens, urging them to vote for confirmation. Over $15 million was raised specifically for the campaign and spent on television advertising and other expenses. Dozens of well-informed lawyers appeared on hundreds of television and talk radio shows advocating confirmation. Electronic telephone banks were set up, sometimes launching hundreds of thousands of telephone calls in an evening urging people to contact members of the Senate who were on the edge on confirmation. Senators were supplied with questions for the hearings, and when something unexpected arose—as when memos written by Roberts while working in the Justice Department during the 1980s were released—lawyers were ready to appear on the talk shows, write op-ed pieces, and otherwise offset any negative propaganda coming from the left, and were able to give reasonable answers to the issues to the media.

The campaign was a complete success. The confirmation of the two new justices "is a Reagan personnel officer's dream come true," said Douglas Kmiec, who had worked in the Reagan Justice Department and went on to teach at the Pepperdine University Law School. "It is a graduation. These individuals have been in study and preparation for these roles all their professional lives."[28] Former attorney general Edwin Meese agreed. He said "Roberts and Alito were exactly the kind of people Ronald Reagan had been looking for. They were very bright, very committed to conservative principles and to the Constitution, and had a combination of deep philosophical roots and the intellect to both communicate their views and to be excellent judges."[29] The campaign also demonstrated how well the movement could work together as one when needed. It joined the best parts of the intellectual movement, through the vetting process, and the activists, who took what the lawyers had done and energized the country. It brought all branches together as well—economic conservatives, religious conservatives, traditionalists, neoconservatives, Catholics, and the rest.

The left, which had until then controlled the debate on Supreme Court nominations, was almost speechless, reduced to muttering that Roberts and Alito were "extremists" and outside the political mainstream. The cold fact was that the left had been outflanked by the right. According to Leonard Leo:

> We felt that the best way to proceed was to have
> a two-pronged communications strategy: One, the
> president has kept his promise, he's nominated a ju-

dicial conservative who will interpret the Constitution as it is written; secondly, the reason why the
left doesn't want this nominee is because they're
extreme in their views of what the Court should be
doing. So we turned the debate on the left and we
started caricaturing *them* as the extremists. And that
strategy worked. They played right into it. They just
dusted off the anti-Bork playbook. They felt that was
going to work but they hadn't factored in the enormous growth of the conservative movement between
1987 and the present and they hadn't factored in the
presence of alternative media. While we had good
relationships with ABC, CNN and the like, when
we were not penetrating there, we went to the alternative media and put pressure on mainstream media to do a slightly more balanced job. The left also
failed to take into account that we were now able to
raise a lot more money.[30]

If the performance in support of Roberts and Alito was well coordinated, the campaign against George W. Bush's nomination of Harriet
Miers was stunning. Miers was not on the conservatives' short list; she
was on nobody's list, in fact, except George Bush's. Miers was a former
president of the Texas Bar Association and without conservative credentials. Her appointment flew directly in the face of everything conservatives had been working toward for twenty years. She had no judicial
record, no written record to speak of, was unknown outside the White
House inner sanctum, and so far as anybody knew, had virtually no
opinion on issues such as judicial restraint, originalism, federalism, or
even the Constitution. Conservatives who had been working on judicial
appointments were stunned, and within hours a campaign was under
way to kill the Miers nomination.

The machinery that had been so carefully put together to help the
president get his nominees confirmed was turned upside down. Within
a week of the announcement half of the Republican members of the
Senate Judiciary Committee were expressing doubts that Miers should
be confirmed.[31] In response, having little to hang their hats on, White

House defenders of Miers assured conservatives that she would rule as they thought she should, that they should trust the president's judgment, and that Meiers was, in fact, a conservative. But the president's pleas went unheeded and changed nobody's minds. Instead, the backlash was intense, and it was apparent, from the first day, that Miers had little chance of joining the court.

Said Robert Bork in the *Wall Street Journal*:

> With a single stroke—the nomination of Harriet Miers—the president has damaged the prospects for reform of a left-leaning and imperialistic Supreme Court, taken the heart out of a rising generation of constitutional scholars, and widened the fissures within the conservative movement. That's not a bad day's work—for liberals.[32]

George Will in his syndicated column summed up the conservatives' complaint that Miers was unqualified:

> In their unseemly eagerness to assure Miers's conservative detractors that she will reach the "right" results, her advocates betray complete incomprehension of this: Thoughtful conservatives' highest aim is not to achieve this or that particular outcome concerning this or that controversy. Rather, their aim for the Supreme Court is to replace semi-legislative reasoning with genuine constitutional reasoning about the Constitution's meaning as derived from close consideration of its text and structure. Such conservatives understand that how you get to a result is as important as the result. Indeed, in an important sense, the path that the Supreme Court takes to the result often is the result.[33]

One conservative pundit after another joined in the criticism. Said *Washington Post* media critic Howard Kurtz, "Charles Krauthammer, David Frum, Bill Kristol, Laura Ingraham and their conservative colleagues didn't sink the Harriet Miers nomination on their own. But in the blink of a news cycle, they turned against their president, framed the debate and provided the passion that undermined her case."[34]

The campaign against the Miers nomination showed the conservative movement at its best and showed what power it had. It also showed something else: the movement had matured to such an extent that the campaign was truly spontaneous—it did not have to be orchestrated from the top down to be effective. Conservatives from every part of the movement arose, of their own volition, and all did their part to protect what they had built over many years. Principles superseded politics.

The conservative movement had used its resources to make a profound difference—a difference that would likely extend for years into the future. It was one of the few times in American history—perhaps the only time—when Supreme Court appointments had been so deeply influenced by the efforts of forces outside the government. Gone were the days when presidents appointed friends and colleagues to the highest judicial positions in the land, and gone were the days when the Senate would either rubber-stamp confirmations, or reject conservative candidates without a fight.

The resources the conservatives used were all of those things they had learned in over fifty years of building a movement. They combined substantive philosophical and intellectual endeavor with grassroots politics. They raised and spent money wisely for maximum impact. They developed a network of like-minded people whose skills complemented each other. They brought pressure on the right people in the executive branch, and in the congress. And above all, they had first-rate, well-trained, and experienced candidates who could withstand the rigors of a modern Supreme Court confirmation battle. Had the president had his way, there is little doubt that he would have nominated his friends and fellow Texans Alberto Gonzalez and Harriet Miers to the high court. Had either been confirmed, there is also little doubt that neither would have been more than a second-rate justice at best. Instead, conservatives had the resources to be able to virtually dictate that there would be no second-rate justices, but that only top-notch conservative candidates would be on the short list, and that when nominated, they would be confirmed. It was, in short, the merger of the conservative intellectual movement, of politically savvy conservative Washington insiders, and of hundreds of thousands of grassroots conservative activists who were able to make their voices heard. In John Roberts and Samuel Alito, the country got among the most qualified Supreme Court justices in history. "There is just no question that these two men are going to be leaders on this court by virtue of the power of their reasoning, the power of their intellects," according to Chuck Cooper, a Washington lawyer who often appears in the Supreme Court, and who served in the Reagan Justice Department. "They have the kinds of personal skills that will make them influential, in ways and at levels that complement the basic influence of the power their reasoning will exert. I doubt that these two men have half a dozen peers in the entire legal profession."[35]

It was particularly important to conservatives that their efforts were directed at preserving the Constitution. Roberts and Alito were both constitutionalists who would decide cases not on what they would have liked the Constitution to say, but what it actually does say. The Constitution was, after all, the very foundation of modern American conservatism.

In her book *Supreme Conflict,* ABC News reporter Jan Crawford Greenberg concludes that "Historians may judge [George W.] Bush as less than competent on many levels, but none will be able to write that he was unable to follow through on his campaign promises when it came to the Supreme Court. In pushing through John Roberts and Samuel Alito, George W. Bush did indeed give Americans Supreme Court justices closely aligned to Scalia and Thomas."[36] He only did so, however, because of the power and acumen of the conservative movement.

By the time the 2007 Supreme Court term ended, it was clear that the course the Supreme Court would take had been changed with its two new justices. Several cases, most decided by 5–4 majorities, and all dealing with issues that conservatives had long argued for, upheld restrictions on abortions, gave teachers the ability to control unruly students, abolished the use of affirmative action programs in high schools, and punched holes in the McCain-Feingold campaign finance law. As liberal Justice Stephen Breyer said in his dissent in the school desegregation case, one of the last cases decided in the term, "It is not often in the law that so few have so quickly changed so much."[37]

But the Roberts and Alito appointments changed more than just the outcome of a number of controversial cases. Conservatives had been as alarmed, from the beginning of Chief Justice Earl Warren's tenure in 1953, about the expanded role the courts were taking, and about the Supreme Court's willingness to become involved in areas traditionally reserved to the states and to the executive and legislative branches, as they were about the merits of the cases themselves. Now, in case after case, the court, led by Roberts, found that various questions had no business at all being decided in the judicial branch. Judicial activism, which had become conservatives' primary complaint about the liberalization of the courts, was being turned around. Roberts had long been an advocate of "judicial self-restraint," and had promised at his confirmation hearing that he would promote "a modest approach to judging, which is good for the legal system as a whole."[38] He added that he did not believe the courts should have a dominant role in solving society's problems, and was not putting that philosophy into practice. Constitutionalism was being returned to the courts. It was exactly what conservatives had been advocating for decades.

Over the next several years there will be many other opportunities for the newly constituted Supreme Court to have an impact—in cases involving school prayer and the separation of church and state, in cases involving racial preferences, in a host of federalism cases, criminal justice cases, and even those involving questions of national security.

Chief Justice John Roberts and Associate Justice Sam Alito are likely to be on the Supreme Court long after virtually everything else George W. Bush does will be forgotten. Their impact, over time, could rival that of Chief Justice Earl Warren and Associate Justice William Brennan, or could even be greater. Together with the relatively young Antonin Scalia and Clarence Thomas, the conservatives have a bloc on the Court almost unrivaled in history. As we saw earlier, the Supreme Court can have an enormous impact on American life. In deciding to focus their efforts in favor of the Constitution, the conservatives who orchestrated the campaign for Supreme Court justices may have been as effective as any group of conservatives preceding them. But they could not have done what they did without the resources of a movement that had been cobbled together over the past sixty years, and with assets in every part of American culture.

AFTERWORD

The passing of William F. Buckley, Jr, in late February 2008—just two weeks after the publication of the hardback edition of *Upstream*—marked the end of an era in modern American conservatism. Buckley was not only one of the founders of the movement, but one of the architects as well; maybe the most important architect. In many ways, he *was* the movement, at least the part of the movement that did not need to rely on the electorate to remain employed.

Buckley's emergence on the scene was one of the four incidents I drew upon, in Chapter Three, to mark the beginning of modern American conservatism. Together with the 1948 testimony of Whittaker Chambers before the House Un-American Activities Committee concerning the treasonous activities of Alger Hiss, the 1953 publication of Russell Kirk's *The Conservative Mind*, and the first meeting of the Mont Pelerin Society, in 1947, bringing together, for the first time, many of the world's free marketers, Buckley's publication of *God and Man at Yale* in early 1951 launched him as one of the most important public intellectuals of his time, while putting liberalism on notice that things would never be the same.

There from the outset, Buckley was a presence and a factor in virtually every phase of the movement. He had something to say about everything that happened, both inside the movement and in the political world, and what he had to say was more often than not the most prescient point about whatever the topic was. He brought countless people, and some of the best, into the movement. Some became the leaders, and many still remain involved. As his *National Review* pointed out in its editorial obituary, Buckley had a greater impact on the political life of this country—and a better one—than some of our presidents. Henry Kissinger, in his eulogy at the funeral Mass at St. Patrick's Cathedral in New York, said that Buckley inspired a political movement that changed American politics. His conservatism, asserted the former secretary of state, "was about the liberation of the human spirit, which is a deeper and more eternal undertaking than causes geared to political timetables. . . . [Bill Buckley] was truly touched by the grace of God."

Buckley was preceded in death by all of the other original conservatives—Barry Goldwater, Ronald Reagan, James Burnham, Frank Meyer, Russell Kirk, Milton Friedman, to name a few. As the last of those, his life can be seen as a capstone of the movement itself, spanning its beginnings, its growth, its heyday, and setting the stage for whatever will come next.

As conservatism moves into its mature years, as new generations join its forces, and as politicians who are more interested in expedience than principle claim allegiance to it, many of the ideas—the ideas on which it was formed—are often put aside in the hunt for votes. Although lip service continues to be paid to limited government, there are few places in the United States where government is limited, and government solutions for society's problems are generally the first thing to be proposed by Democrats and Republicans alike. So-called big government conservatism, a clear contradiction in terms, is raised on a nearly daily basis, usually as the justification for doing things for the good of the beleaguered portion of the populace in the name of humanitarianism. Such conservatives forget Ronald Reagan's admonition that government was not the solution but the problem—a principle that was a key element of his success. Fiscal responsibility, always high on the list of conservative virtues, is, in 2008, nothing but a warm and fuzzy memory from times past, before the George W. Bush administration. On another front, the traditional conservative notion of national security, which is called upon only to defend the best interests of the United States, strong but for use only on a limited basis and only when there is a clear exit strategy in place, is another fond remembrance of the Reagan years, a culprit made much worse by the most recent Republican administration's five-year-and-counting war in Iraq.

Traditional family values, one of the mainstays of the conservative movement from its earliest days, continue to be under assault. Evangelical Christians have, since the late 1970s, been the principal proponents of those values, and make up a considerable percentage of conservative activists and voters. But with the passing of leaders such as the Rev. Jerry Falwell and North Carolina's former senator Jesse Helms, and with dissatisfaction with many Republican elected officials, Evangelicals have started a shift to the center and, in some cases, even to the left, while calling on the federal government to impose their values on everybody else. Conservatives generally supported the election of George W. Bush in 2000, and his reelection in 2004. Many had worked hard in both campaigns; others were less enthusiastic, and a few even hostile. But as his second term drew to a close, few conservatives could find much good to say about the Bush administration, and even fewer felt that the support they had given the president in his campaigns had been repaid. In an interview with CBS in July 2006, William F. Buckley summed up the attitude many conservatives had about the president when he said, ". . . Mr. Bush faces a singular problem best defined, I think, as the absence of effective conservative ideology—with the result that he ended up being very extravagant in domestic spending, extremely tolerant of excesses by Congress. And in respect to foreign policy, incapable of bringing together such forces as apparently were necessary to conclude the Iraq challenge."

Similarly, conservatives were enthusiastic about the makeup of the 109th Congress. As it convened in January 2005, following George Bush's defeat of liberal Democrat John Kerry, Republicans held a ten-seat majority in the Senate and a thirty-seat majority in the House of Representatives—enough to assure passage of much of the Bush administration's agenda, and enough to stop virtually any Democrat initiative that did not have substantial Republican support. Even more satisfying was the fact that Republicans were generally solidly conservative—or so it seemed. But conservative majorities were more of a mirage than a reality, as Republicans repeatedly disgraced themselves in their willingness to ignore the most important elements of American constitutional government and give constituents and donors virtually anything they asked for. To conservative observers and critics, congressional Republicans increasingly appeared to be nothing more than the bankers to the Bush administration, giving the president whatever he wanted, questioning nothing, while allowing power to be shifted from the states to Washington and from Congress to the executive. Similarly, Republicans seemed too eager to make deals with congressional Democrats on such statist ideas as global warming, entitlement programs, and spending programs involving farm subsidies or mortgage bailouts.

After the disastrous congressional election of 2006, with the loss of both houses to Democrats, with Republicans in disrepute, and with many members of Congress who had been elected as conservative Republicans sent packing by their constituents, one had to wonder just what conservatives had to show for having such overwhelming control of the levers of government. What had this reputedly conservative administration, with the help of both houses of Congress in allegedly conservative hands, done that left conservatives so disgusted?

Let us take inventory:

- A war that, after five years of involvement, had cost nearly one trillion dollars, had resulted in the deaths of more than 4,000 American soldiers and injury to another 30,000, and which, in 2008 remained unresolved

- The disintegration of America's reputation around the world to the lowest point in a century

- Passage of the Medicare Prescription Benefit Act, estimated to add $8.7 trillion to Medicare's long-term unfunded liability, the largest increase in entitlement spending since the Great Society

- Increase in farm subsidies of some $500 billion with the passage of two bills, one supported by the Bush administration in 2002 providing $190 billion in farm subsidies over ten years, and the other, passed over the president's veto in 2008 with overwhelming Republican support, providing $307 billion in new subsidies. Said presidential aide Karl Rove after the first was passed, "it was a small price to pay for the reelection of a couple of Republican senators."

- Institutionalization of Republican pork-barrel spending, in the form of "earmarks," providing hundreds of millions of dollars to pet congressional projects largely for the purpose of buying reelection votes—spending that would have made even Lyndon Johnson blush

- Federalization of primary and secondary education with the passage of the Bush administration's so-called No Child Left Behind Act

- Growth of the federal budget by over one trillion dollars in eight years, and the introduction of a $3.1 trillion budget for 2009, the largest ever (nearly three times larger than the budget when Ronald Reagan took office in 1980, after taking inflation into account)

- A presidential race in which no true conservative was a viable candidate, and the nomination, in the late summer of 2008, of John McCain, a Republican who had been one of conservatives' least favorite public figures. And, on the Democratic side, the rise of a candidate farther to the left than any nominee since at least George McGovern, and probably since Franklin D. Roosevelt.

Liberals took glee in detailing the movement's shortcomings and predicting its imminent demise, claiming that George W. Bush was the most conservative president in modern history, that his presidency was a failure, as was Republicanism generally, and therefore the conservative movement was at an end. Said *The New Yorker*, always a reliable source on the state of conservatism, "the ascent of John McCain shows how little life is left in the movement that Goldwater began, Nixon brought into power, Ronald Reagan gave mass appeal, Newt Gingrich radicalized, Tom DeLay criminalized, and Bush allowed to break into pieces."

Several widely discussed books, published in 2007 and 2008, written by either disgruntled or concerned Republicans or neo-liberals, argued that traditional conservative solutions, which may have worked in the past, were no longer viable, and instead current-day problems, including health care, environmental issues, and the exodus of middle- and working-class voters from Republican ranks, called for bolder answers and new solutions embracing, rather than rejecting, big government. Conservatism, these books argued, needed to be modernized and made "relevant" to what was going on in the new century rather than offering classic and traditional solutions. And finally, political conservatives were told by the Republican leadership in Congress that to stay in office they needed to spend the taxpayers' money for constituents' pet projects, abandoning their principles along the way. When conservatives objected, they were punished by the Republican leadership for not playing the game.

It was not, in other words, an easy time to be a conservative, or an easy time for conservatives to stick to their guns.

Looking through the fog of all this, however, there were a good many bright spots. During the Republican primaries of 2008, Ronald Reagan continued to cast a long shadow, with each candidate claiming to be a Reagan conservative, and the Reagan years increasingly setting the tone for both presidential politics and presidential policies. But none of the 2008 candidates, no matter how much they tried to emulate Ronald Reagan, were able to pull together the old Reagan coalition of various strains of conservatives, moderate Republicans and Reagan Democrats—the coalition that had elected him and which had held together well enough to elect both Bushes, and to help Newt Gingrich take control of the House of Representatives in 1994. In fact, it is probably safe to say that each part of the conservative movement had its own candidate in the 2008 primaries: the libertarians had Ron Paul, economic conservatives had Mitt Romney, Evangelicals had Mike Huckabee, and national-security conservatives and the neocons had Rudy Giuliani. The old Reaganites had high hopes for Fred Thompson, but he fizzled out before he ever got started, and in the end, John McCain, who did not really represent any of the strands, who had been conservatives' hair shirt in the Senate, and who had never had much good to say about the movement, won the day. But even McCain, as soon as it became clear that he was the only one of many left standing and would get the nomination, immediately claimed to be a Reagan Republican, reminding voters that he held "his hero" Barry Goldwater's old Senate seat. He pledged, among other things, that he was a supply-sider and would veto any tax increase sent to him by the Congress, and promised that he would appoint judges only in the mold of Antonin Scalia and Clarence Thomas.

Meanwhile even old-line liberal scholars found more and more good things to say about conservative policies, about Ronald Reagan, and about the conservative movement generally. Sean Wilentz, a very partisan Democrat professor from Princeton, who had testified in favor of Bill Clinton in his impeachment hearings, published in May 2008 *The Age of Reagan*, a book arguing that conservatism has been the defining factor shaping American political history since the early 1970s, and arguing further that even Reagan's greatest admirers underestimate his accomplishments. Reagan, concluded Wilentz, was truly one of the great presidents, and the single most important political figure of his age.

If conservatives were dispirited by their political fortunes, their zeal for furthering their movement went on unabated. The activists, the think tanks, the magazines and journals, youth organizations, and the rest reflected the same sort of spirit and enthusiasm that conservatives had exhibited over the past several decades. Their attitude was simply that "we are in this for the long term, politics is an uncertain business subject to ups and downs, and if we lose, we'll regroup and be back the next time." How many times have I been asked, as I promoted *Upstream*, whether conservatives wouldn't be better off sitting out the Obama–McCain election, letting the Democrats win and disgrace themselves, and returning in four years to straighten out the mess? Conservatives were often reminded of the 1976 Carter–Ford election in which, after Reagan's loss to Ford at the Republican convention, many sat on the sidelines, and spent the next four years rebuilding their political apparatus to return with not only a conservative president in 1980, but with a Republican majority in the Senate as well. They were also reminded that when Reagan had left the governor's office in California in early 1975, the national Republican Party was broke, had no philosophical spine, and Democrats had large majorities in both houses of Congress, and the prospects of ever coming back to power seemed grim at best. What a difference five years in the wilderness could make.

Further, conservatives were encouraged by several monumental changes—one might even be so bold as to say structural changes. The federal courts, for one, were a bright spot, as the high-profile Roberts Supreme Court delivered opinions that confirmed that the battle conservatives had waged for the Bush appointees had been well worthwhile. Their delight was often confirmed by the agony apparent in liberals' commentary about the Neanderthals' now running the judiciary and the travesty of liberal justice being waged, not only in the marble palace across from the Capitol, but in many federal courthouses from one end of the country to the other. A large body of precedent was being established that once again gave the Constitution a reasonable basis for interpretation, and even more that the doctrine of originalism—the idea that the Constitution should be interpreted not by present-day standards, but by the debates and writings of the Founders at the time the Constitution was adopted and ratified—was becoming mainstream. Conservative judges could now not only be confirmed by the Senate, but their ideas and their scholarship had become respected and, when applied to cases before them, had become the basis for establishing the law of the land.

Supply-side economics was another bright spot, and was quickly becoming one of conservatism's lasting structural changes. Supply-siders relished the thought that nobody—not even Nancy Pelosi and Charlie Rangel—would likely ever propose raising top marginal rates to 70 percent again. For one thing, Democrats knew full well that if they did, they would suffer the same fate as Walter Mondale when he proposed a tax hike in his campaign against Ronald Reagan in 1984. And more important, even liberals could not refute the supply-siders' argument that increases in marginal rates will affect the economy—negatively. To be sure, liberals hate supply-side economics, but it is impossible to even have a discussion about taxes without making supply-side economics part of the debate.

The supply-side revolution, by 2008, had extended far beyond the shores of the United States, with tax cutting going on in many capitals and across the globe—everywhere, in fact, except in Washington. From countries in the old Soviet Bloc (including Russia) to the Baltic, Iceland, Hong Kong, Vietnam and even "old Europe"—France, Spain, and Germany, and even Sweden—many were cutting marginal tax rates, implementing the flat tax, and cutting corporate tax rates as a way of stimulating their economies. The worldwide explosion of wealth that had occurred over the past twenty years was, it was almost universally agreed, the product of free markets, free trade, the rule of law, and lower taxes—all things that Friedrich Hayek, Milton Friedman, and other free marketeers argued for since the 1940s.

The unanswered question, of course, is, What is next? Who are our new leaders? Where will the conservative movement be in five, or ten, or twenty-five years? A study of the history of the movement, which is what *Upstream* is, tells us that American conservatism has been around for a long time, that conservatives have always considered their battle to be a long-term undertaking, and that the fight is about much more than just politics. True conservative principles—things such as free markets, laissez-faire economics, limited government, a strong national defense, and traditional American values—do not change, are as valid now as they were in the middle of the twentieth century, and will still be as valid in fifty or one hundred years. Although politics and political victories are important, they are not the only thing, and as more than one has shown, a political loss can be, in the end, the road to subsequent victory. Adherence to principle is much more important, and compromising principles for the sake of a win here or there will mean, before long, that there are no principles left. As Barry Goldwater famously said nearly fifty years ago, "I would rather see the Republicans lose in 1960, fighting on principle, than I would care to see us win standing on grounds we know are wrong and on which we will ultimately destroy ourselves." If conservatives are to have any clout within the party whatever, as time goes on, Senator Goldwater's admonition is as true today as it was in 1960.

NOTES

CHAPTER 1: THE PASSING OF A CONSERVATIVE

1. Thomas E. Ricks and Charles Babington, "Republicans, Democrats Hail Reagan's Optimism," *Washington Post* (June 6, 2004).

2. Mary Leonard, "With Power of Personality, He Made His Mark," *Boston Globe* (June 10, 2004).

3. Alvin Felzenberg, "'There You Go Again': Liberal Historians and the *New York Times* Deny Reagan His Due," *Policy Review* (March–April 1997): 53.

4. Rene Sanchez, "A Nation and the World Pay Tribute to Reagan," *Washington Post* (June 7, 2004).

5. John M. Broder and Charlie Leduff, "100,000, One by One, Pay Tribute to a President," *New York Times* (June 9, 2004).

6. David Von Drehle, "A Day of Ritual and Remembrance," *Washington Post* (June 10, 2004).

7. For the full text of Mulroney's tribute, see *USA Today*, June 11, 2004.

8. For the full text of Thatcher's tribute, see www.cnn.com/2004/ALLPOLITICS/06/11/thatcher.transcript/.

9. For the full text of Bush's eulogy, see www.whitehouse.gov/news/releases/2004/06/20040611-2.html.

10. For the full text of Danforth's eulogy, see www.cathedral.org/cathedral/programs/reagan/jcdanforth.html.

11. Cited in Johanna Neumann, "Former President Reagan Dies at 93," *Los Angeles Times* (June 6, 2004).

12. Quoted in "Reagan: A Cold War Hawk Who Set the Stage for Peace," *Los Angeles Times* (June 6, 2004).

13. Ibid.

14. "Farewell to a President: Reagan's Inner Circle Setting Stage," *Los Angeles Times,* (June 9, 2004).

15. Bush eulogy, www.whitehouse.gov/news/releases/2004/06/20040611-2.html.

CHAPTER 2: IT WASN'T ALWAYS THAT WAY

1. Letter from Roger Sherman to John Adams, quoted in Ralph Rossum: *Federalism, the Supreme Court and the Seventeenth Amendment: The Irony of Constitutional Democracy* (Lanham, Maryland: Lexington Books, 2001), p. 105.

2. Woodrow Wilson, *The State* (Boston: D.C. Heath, 1889), p. 651. See also Ronald J. Pestritto, *Woodrow Wilson and the Roots of Modern Liberalism* (Lanham, Maryland: Rowman & Littlefield, 2005).

3. Kendrick A. Clements, *The Presidency of Woodrow Wilson* (Lawrence: University of Kansas Press, 1992), pp. 45–46.

4. Paul Johnson, *A History of the American People,* (New York: HarperCollins, 1997), p. 642.

5. Eugene Lyons, *Herbert Hoover: A Biography* (Garden City: Doubleday, 1964), pp. 154–155. See also Joan Hoff Wilson, *Herbert Hoover, Forgotten Progressive* (Boston: Little, Brown, 1975).

6. See David Fromkin, *A Peace to End All Peace: The Fall of the Ottoman Empire and the Making of the Modern Middle East* (New York: Henry Holt, 2001).

7. Unnamed historian quoted in Lyons, *Herbert Hoover,* p. 151.

8. Frank B. Freidel, *Franklin Roosevelt: The Apprenticeship* (Boston: Little, Brown, 1952), p. 135.

9. Ibid.

10. Sir Roy Forbes Harrod, *The Life of John Maynard Keynes* (New York: Harcourt, Brace, 1951), pp. 47–48.

11. Charles Beard, "A Five Year Plan for America," *Harper's Magazine* (December 1931). Beard and his wife famously became critics of the New Deal later in the 1930s.

12. Charles Abba, "Do You Still Believe in Laziness?" *Business Week* (June 24, 1931). See the discussion in Johnson, *History of the American People,* pp. 620–22.

13. Milton Friedman, *Capitalism and Freedom* (Chicago: University of Chicago Press, 1960).

14. Roosevelt, from speech of September 29, 1932, in Timothy Walsh and Dwight M. Miller, eds., *Herbert Hoover and Franklin D. Roosevelt: A Documentary History* (Westport, Conn.: Greenwood Press, 1998), pp. 54–55.

15. Walter Lippman, "The Permanent New Deal," *Yale Review* 24 (1935): 649–67.
16. Rexford G. Tugwell, *Roosevelt's Revolution: The First Year—A Personal Perspective* (New York: Macmillan, 1977), pp. xiii–xiv; see also Raymond Moley's comment to the effect that everything necessary for the New Deal was already in place when Roosevelt took office, in *Newsweek* (June 14, 1948).
17. Terry Teachout, *The Sceptic: A Life of H. L. Mencken* (New York: HarperCollins, 2002).
18. The House of Representatives also had eight Progressives and five members of the Farmer-Labor Party. The Senate had one Independent, one Progressive, and two members of the Farmer-Labor Party.
19. Whittaker Chambers, *Witness* (New York: Random House, 1952), p. 191.
20. Paul Hollander, *Political Pilgrims: Travels of Western Intellectuals to the Soviet Union, China, and Cuba, 1928–1978* (New York: Oxford University Press, 1981), 74–99; see also John Patrick Diggins, *The Rise and Fall of the American Left* (New York: W.W. Norton, 1992), pp. 146–54.
21. Quoted in Mona Charen, *Useful Idiots: How Liberals Got It Wrong in the Cold War and Still Blame America First* (Washington, D.C.: Regnery, 2003), p. 87.
22. Diggins, *American Left,* pp. 173–74.
23. Richard Gid Powers, *Not Without Honor: The History of American Anticommunism* (New York: Free Press, 1995), p. 188.
24. Harvey Klehr and John Earl Haynes, *The American Communist Movement: Storming Heaven Itself* (New York: Twayne Publishers, 1992), pp. 113–22.
25. Harry Hopkins, cited in George H. Nash, *The Conservative Intellectual Movement in America Since 1945* (Wilmington, Del.: ISI Books), pp. 1–2.
26. John W. Jeffries, "The 'New' New Deal: FDR and American Liberalism, 1937–1945," *Political Science Quarterly* 105 (Autumn 1990): 397–418.

Chapter 3: Intellectual Underpinnings

1. See Peter Viereck, *Conservatism Revisited: The Revolt Against Revolt, 1815–1949* (New York: Scribner, 1949) and Clinton Rossiter, *Conservatism in America* (New York: Knopf, 1955).
2. Quoted in Daniel Yergin, *Commanding Heights* (New York: Simon & Schuster, 1998), p. 14.

3. E. J. Dionne, Jr., *Why Americans Hate Politics* (New York: Simon & Schuster, 1991), p. 152.

4. Friedrich A. Hayek, *The Road to Serfdom* (Chicago: University of Chicago Press, 1944).

5. Henry Hazlitt, "An Economist's View of Planning," *New York Times Book Review* (September 24, 1944).

6. Carl J. Friedrich, "Review of *The Road to Serfdom*," *American Political Science Review* 39 (June 1945): 575–579.

7. Alvin Hansen, "The New Crusade Against Planning," *New Republic* (January 1, 1945).

8. Eric Roll, "Review of *The Road to Serfdom*," *American Economic Review* 35 (March 1945): 176–180.

9. Henry Hazlitt, "The Case for Capitalism," *Newsweek* (September 19, 1949).

10. Hans Sennholz, "Review of *Human Action*," *Freeman: Ideas on Liberty* (July 1966), 535–36.

11. F. A. Hayek, *Studies in Philosophy, Politics and Economics* (Chicago: University of Chicago Press, 1967), p. 149.

12. R. M. Hartwell, *A History of the Mont Pelerin Society* (Indianapolis: Liberty Fund, 1995), p. 213.

13. George Stigler, *Memoirs of an Unregulated Economist* (New York: Basic Books, 1985), Chapter 9. Cited in *Freeman* (June 1997).

14. Milton Friedman interview with author, July 12, 2005.

15. Hartwell, *History of the Mont Pelerin Society*, pp. 82–85, 222–224.

16. Milton Friedman interview with author, July 12, 2005.

17. Christian Parenti, "Winning the War of Ideas," *In These Times* (October 17, 2003). In an amusing ending, Parenti remarked, "Ultimately, progressives cannot and should not imitate all of Hayek's and the Mont Pelerin Society's methods. That world view and tactical repertoire is intensely elitist, in that it relied more on institutional hierarchy than popular education and mobilization."

18. See Richard Cockett, *Thinking the Unthinkable: Think-Tanks and the Economic Counter-Revolution, 1931–1983* (London: HarperCollins, 1995).

19. Prominent Mont Pelerin members who have held high-level policy positions include Chancellor Ludwig Erhard of West Germany, President Luigi Einaudi of Italy, Chairman Arthur F. Burns of the U.S. Federal Reserve Board, and President Václav Klaus of the Czech Republic. Eight Mont Pelerin members, including F. A. Hayek, Milton

Friedman, and George Stigler, won Nobel prizes in economics. See Hartwell, *History of the Mont Pelerin Society,* p. 45.

20. Author interview with Milton Friedman, July 12, 2005.

21. Cited in Richard Gid Powers, *Not Without Honor: The History of American Anticommunism* (New York: Free Press, 1995), p. 182.

22. Ibid, p. 183.

23. Ibid, p. 186.

24. X, "The Sources of Soviet Conduct," *Foreign Affairs* 25 (July 1947).

25. Historian John Lukacs was a notable exception to this criticism of Kennan. See Lukacs, "Review of George Kennan, *Memoirs 1925–1950* in *New Republic* (October 28, 1967).

26. Sidney Hook, *Out of Step* (New York: Harper & Row, 1987).

27. James Burnham, *The Struggle for the World* (New York: John Day, 1947). Burnham further developed his analysis in *The Coming Defeat of Communism* (New York: John Day, 1950).

28. Daniel Kelly, James Burnham and the Struggle for the World: A Life (Wilmington, Del.: ISI Books, 2002), pp. 131–32.

29. Roger Kimball, "The Power of James Burnham," *New Criterion* (September 2002).

30. The congressman was Richard Nixon. See Allen Weinstein, *Perjury: The Hiss-Chambers Case* (New York: Random House, 1997), p. 5.

31. HUAC Hearing, August 3, 1948, as quoted in G. Edward White, *Alger Hiss' Looking Glass Wars: The Covert Life of a Soviet Spy* (Oxford: Oxford University Press, 2004), pp. 53–54.

32. For the perjury indictment and conviction, see Weinstein, *Perjury,* pp. 266–67, 442.

33. George McGovern, "Nixon and Historical Memory," 34 *Perspectives* (1996), quoted in White, *Looking Glass Wars,* xvii. For Lake, see www .centerforse curitypolicy.org/index.jsp?section=papers&code=96-D_118.

34. See *Media Watch* (December 1996), at http://secure.mediaresearch .org/news/mediawatch/1996/mw19961201jca.htm. See also White, *Looking Glass Wars,* p. 231.

35. See the transcript of Lake's interview with Tim Russert on *Meet the Press* at www.centerforsecuritypolicy.org/index.jsp?section=papers& code=96-D_118.

36. Robert Novak, "Alger Hiss: Traitor or Fall Guy?" *Chicago Sun-Times* (November 21, 1996).

37. George Will, "Emblem of the Governing Class," *Washington Post* (November 21, 1996).

38. Whittaker Chambers, *Witness* (Washington, D.C.: Regnery, 1987), p. 7.

39. Ibid, p. 9.

40. For Kirk's biography, see James Person, *Russell Kirk: A Critical Biography of a Conservative Mind* (Lanham, Md.: Madison Books, 1999).

41. Russell, Kirk, *The Conservative Mind: From Burke to Santayana* (Chicago: Regnery, 1953), p. 7.

42. Ibid, p. 96.

43. Gordon Keith Chalmers, "Review of *The Conservative Mind,* by Russell Kirk," *New York Times Book Review* (May 16, 1953).

44. "Generation to Generation," *Time* (July 1953).

45. Clinton Rossiter, "Review of *The Conservative Mind,*" *The American Political Science Review* 47, (September 1953): 868–870.

46. *A Program for Conservatives* (Chicago: H. Regnery Co., 1954); *Academic Freedom* (Chicago: H. Regnery Co., 1955); *The American Cause* (Chicago: Regnery, 1957).

47. Henry Regnery, *Memoirs of a Dissident Publisher* (Chicago: Regnery, 1985), pp. 146–166.

48. Jonathan Schoenwald, *A Time for Choosing: The Rise of Modern American Conservatism* (Oxford: Oxford, 2001), pp. 20–21.

49. George H. Nash, "The Conservative Mind in America," *The Intercollegiate Review* 30 (Fall 1994), 27.

50. Richard M. Weaver, *Ideas Have Consequences* (Chicago: University of Chicago Press, 1948), p. 3–4.

51. Ibid, pp. 129–147.

52. See Frank Meyer, "Richard M. Weaver: An Appreciation," *Modern Age* 14 (Summer-Fall 1970): 243–48. See also Paul V. Murphy, *The Rebuke of History: The Southern Agrarians and American Conservative Thought* (Chapel Hill: University of North Carolina Press, 2001), pp. 170–171.

53. Ralph Eubanks, "Richard M. Weaver, Friend of Traditional Rhetoric: An Appreciation," in *Language Is Sermonic: Richard M. Weaver on the Nature of Rhetoric,* Richard L. Johannesen, Rennard Strickland, and Ralph T. Eubanks, eds. (Baton Rouge: Louisiana State University Press, 1970), p. 4. See also George Nash, "The Influence of *Ideas Have Consequences,*" in Ted J. Smith III, ed., *Steps Toward Restoration: The Consequences of Richard Weaver's Ideas* (Wilmington, Del.: ISI Books, 1998), pp. 81–124.

54. Robert A. Nisbet, *The Quest for Community: A Study in the Ethics of Order and Freedom* (New York: Oxford University Press, 1953).

55. David Brooks, "Robert Nisbet's Quest," *AEI Online* (January 1, 2000).

56. William F. Buckley, Jr., *God and Man at Yale: The Superstitions of "Academic Freedom"* (Washington, D.C.: Regnery Gateway, 1986), p. ix.

57. Ibid, p. liii.

58. Shelden Rodman and Frank Ashburn, "'Isms' and the University: Two Reviews of 'God and Man at Yale,'" *Saturday Review of Literature* (December 15, 1951).

59. William F. Buckley, Jr. letter to the chairman of the *Yale Daily News* (November 26, 1951).

60. McGeorge Bundy, "The Attack on Yale," *Atlantic Monthly* (November 1951).

61. Robert Hatch, "Enforcing Truth," *New Republic* (December 3, 1951).

62. William F. Buckley, Jr., "The Changes at Yale," *Atlantic Monthly* (December 1951).

Chapter 4: A Movement Takes Off

1. John Moser, "Principles Without Program: Robert A. Taft and American Foreign Policy," *Ohio History* 108 (1999), 177–192. Reprinted in the Ashbrook Center's *Dialogues,* at www.ashbrook.org/publicat/dialogue/moser.html.

2. Lee Edwards, *The Conservative Revolution: The Movement That Remade America* (New York: Free Press, 1999), p. 48. See also James T. Patterson, *Mr. Republican: A Biography of Robert A. Taft* (Boston: Houghton Mifflin, 1972).

3. See, e.g., William F. Buckley, Jr., "Reflections on Election Eve," *National Review* (November 3, 1956).

4. See Edwards, *Conservative Revolution,* pp. 60–66.

5. Russell Kirk and James McClellan, *The Political Principles of Robert A. Taft* (New York: Fleet Press Corporation, 1967).

6. On Knowland, see Gale Montgomery and James W. Johnson in collaboration with Paul G. Manolis, *One Step from the White House: The Rise and Fall of Senator William F. Knowland* (Berkeley: University of California Press, 1998).

7. Henry Hazlitt, *Economics in One Lesson: The Shortest and Surest Way to Understand Basic Economics* (New York: Three Rivers Press, 1988).

8. See Nash, *Conservative Intellectual Movement in America,* pp. 21–22.

9. Ibid, pp. 133–34.

10. Edwards, *Conservative Revolution,* p. 15.

11. William F. Buckley, Jr., Memorandum Re: A New Magazine, Henry Regnery Papers, Hoover Institution Library.

12. Ibid.

13. Author interview with William Rusher, July 12, 2005.

14. Lee Edwards, *Goldwater: The Man Who Made a Revolution* (Washington, D.C.: Regnery, 1995), p. 318.

15. William Rusher, *The Rise of the Right* (New York: William Morrow, 1984), p. 46.

16. Dwight MacDonald, "Scrambled Eggheads on the Right," *Commentary* (April 1956).

17. Jonathan M. Schoenwald, *A Time for Choosing: The Rise of American Conservatism* (New York: Oxford, 2001), p. 38.

18. Rusher, *Rise of the Right*, p. 73.

19. For a history of *National Review*, see Jeffrey Hart, *The Making of the American Conservative Mind: National Review and Its Times* (Wilmington, Del.: ISI Books, 2005).

20. Author interview with William F. Buckley, Jr., June 9, 2005.

21. Whittaker Chambers, "Big Sister Is Watching You," *National Review* (December 28, 1957).

22. L. Brent Bozell, "Freedom or Virtue?" *National Review* (September 1, 1962).

23. Frank Meyer, *In Defense of Freedom and Related Essays* (Indianapolis: Liberty Fund, 1996), p. 36.

24. Nash, *Conservative Intellectual Movement in America*, pp. 13–14.

25. Lee Edward, *Educating for Liberty: The First Half-Century of the Intercollegiate Studies Institute* (Washington: Regnery, 2003), p. 4.

26. Ibid, pp. 10–11.

27. Ibid, p. 15 n. 38.

28. Ibid, p. 27.

29. Arnold Forster and Benjamin R. Epstein, *Danger on the Right* (New York: Random House, 1964), p. 222.

30. Henry Regnery, *Memoirs of a Dissident Publisher* (New York: Harcourt Brace Jovanovich, 1979), p. 147.

31. Ibid, p. 15.

32. Cited in Donald T. Critchlow, *Phyllis Schlafly and Grassroots Conservatism: A Woman's Crusade* (Princeton: Princeton University Press, 2005), p. 70.

33. John Birch, after whom Welch named the organization, was a Baptist missionary working in China who was shot by Chinese Communist troops shortly after the end of World War II as ostensibly the first casualty of the Cold War.

34. For the history of the Birch Society, see Schoenwald, *A Time for Choosing,* pp. 62–99.

35. Ibid, p. 85 n. 69.

36. Perlstein, *Before the Storm,* p. 172.

37. Author interview with Paul Weyrich, September 14, 2006.

38. Author interview with William F. Buckley, Jr., June 9, 2005.

39. Schoenwald, *A Time for Choosing,* p. 32.

40. Author interview with Jon Utley, October 12, 2005.

41. William F. Buckley, Jr., *Miles Gone By: A Literary Autobiography* (Washington: Regnery, 2004), p. 467.

42. Cited in Rick Perlstein, *Before the Storm: Barry Goldwater and the Unmaking of the American Consensus* (New York: Hill & Wang, 2001), p. 19.

CHAPTER 5: POLITICAL THEORY BECOMES REAL POLITICS

1. William F. Buckley, Jr. and L. Brent Bozell, *McCarthy and His Enemies: The Record and Its Meaning* (Chicago: H. Regnery Co., 1954).

2. Barry M. Goldwater, *The Conscience of a Conservative* (Shepherdsville, Ky.: Victor, 1960), p. xxiii.

3. Reported Rick Perlstein, *Before the Storm: Barry Goldwater and the Unmaking of the American Consensus* (New York: Hill & Wang, 2001), p. 63.

4. Author interview with Paul Laxalt, October 24, 2006.

5. Perlstein, *Before the Storm,* p. 75.

6. Ibid, p. 76.

7. Barry Goldwater, *With No Apologies* (New York: Morrow, 1979), pp. 110–111.

8. Perlstein, *Before the Storm,* p. 92.

9. Stephen Shadegg, *Barry Goldwater: Freedom Is His Flight Plan* (New York: Fleet, 1962), p. 270.

10. M. Stanton Evans, *Revolt on the Campus* (Chicago: Regnery, 1961), pp. 74–86.

11. Ibid, p. 116.

12. Perlstein, *Before the Storm,* p. 108. For the history of YAF, see also Gregory L. Schneider, *Cadres for Conservatism: Young Americans for Freedom and the Rise of the Contemporary Right* (New York: New York University Press, 1999).

13. *Newsweek* (April 18, 1961).

14. *Time* (June 1961).

15. *U.S. News & World Report* (August 7, 1963).

16. Lee Edwards, *Goldwater: The Man Who Made a Revolution* (Washington, D.C.: Regnery, 1995), p. 153.

17. See *F. Clifton White, Suite 3505: The Story of the Draft Goldwater Movement* (New Rochelle, N.Y.: Arlington House, 1967).

18. The Gallup Poll: Public Opinion 1935–1971, reported in Michael W. Miles, *The Odyssey of the American Right,* (New York: Oxford University Press, 1980), p. 290.

19. Edwards, *Goldwater,* p. 185.

20. Miles, *Odyssey of the American Right,* p. 292.

21. Barry M. Goldwater with Jack Casserly, *Goldwater* (New York: Doubleday, 1988), pp. 153–154.

22. Edwards, *Goldwater,* p. 199.

23. Donald T. Critchlow, *Phyllis Schlafly and Grassroots Conservatism: A Woman's Crusade* (Princeton: Princeton University Press, 2005), p. 127.

24. Perlstein, *Before the Storm,* p. 391.

25. Ibid, p. 256.

26. *Washington Post* (May 29, 1998).

27. Perlstein, *Before the Storm,* pp. 436–38.

28. Cited in Lee Edwards, *The Conservative Revolution: The Movement That Remade America* (New York: Free Press, 1999), p. 130.

29. Ibid, p. 128.

30. Ibid, p. 136.

31. Perlstein, Before the Storm, pp. 473–75.

32. Richard Viguerie, *America's Right Turn: How Conservatives Used New and Alternative Media to Take Power* (Chicago: Bonus Books, 2004), p. 84.

33. Ibid, p. 84.

34. Ibid, pp. 98–100.

35. William Rusher, *The Rise of the Right* (New York: Morrow, 1984), p. 178.

36. Perlstein, *Before the Storm,* pp. 62, 458.

37. Ronald Reagan, *Speaking My Mind* (New York: Simon & Schuster, 1989), pp. 22–36.

38. *Conscience of a Conservative,* introduction by Patrick J. Buchanan (Washington, D.C.: Regnery, 1990).

39. Confidential Preliminary Report on the American Conservative Union, early 1965, American Conservative Union Papers, Hoover Institution.

40. *New York Times Magazine* (October 5, 2005).

41. "Spokesman for Conservatism," *Time* (July 10, 1964).

42. Jonathan Schoenwald, *A Time for Choosing: The Rise of Modern American Conservatism* (New York: Oxford University Press, 2001), p. 173.

43. Sam Tannenhaus, "The Buckley Effect," *New York Times Magazine* (October 5, 2005).

44. Ibid.

45. Ibid.

46. Ibid.

47. George Crocker, "A Dem under the Skin," *San Francisco Examiner* (November 14, 1965).

48. On the background to the Reagan's gubernatorial campaign, see Lou Cannon, *Governor Reagan: His Rise to Power* (New York: Public Affairs, 2003), pp. 129–145.

49. *National Review* (December 1, 1964).

50. Ibid, p. 135.

51. Ibid, p. 155.

52. Cannon, *Governor Reagan,* p. 154.

53. Ibid, p. 160.

54. Cited in Schoenwald, *A Time for Choosing,* p. 216 n. 77.

55. Ibid, p. 213.

Chapter 6: The Worst of Times

1. William J. Bennett, *Index of Leading Cultural Indicators* (New York: Simon & Schuster, 1994), p. 18.

2. Robert Dallek, *Lone Star Rising: Lyndon Johnson and His Times, 1908–1960* (New York: Oxford University Press, 1991), p. 555.

3. *Public Papers of the Presidents of the United States: Lyndon B. Johnson, 1963–64.* Volume I, entry 357, pp. 704–707. Washington, D.C.: Government Printing Office, 1965.

4. James Piereson, "Investing in Conservative Ideas," *Commentary* (May 2005).

5. Irwin Unger and Debi Unger, *Turning Point: 1968* (New York: Scribner, 1988), p. 31.

6. Thomas Sowell, "The Poverty Pimp's Poem," *Jewish World Review* (October 30, 1998).

7. Unger and Unger, *Turning Point,* p. 31.

8. James J. Kilpatrick, *The Sovereign States: Notes of a Citizen of Virginia* (Chicago: Regnery, 1957); Felix Morely, *Freedom and Federalism* (Chicago: Regnery, 1959); James Burnham, *Congress and the American Tradition* (Chicago: Regnery, 1959).

9. See Congressional Budget Office, *The Budget and Economic Outlook,*

Fiscal Years 2003–2012: A Report to the House and Senate Committees on the Budget (January 2002).

10. Congressional Budget Office, *The Budget and Economic Outlook, Fiscal Years 2005–2014: A Report to the House and Senate Committees on the Budget* (January 2004).

11. *Time* (November 16, 1962).

12. Jonathan Aitken, *Nixon: A Life* (Washington, D.C.: Regnery, 1993), p. 307.

13. Ibid, p. 308.

14. William Rusher, *Rise of the Right* (New York: Morrow, 1984), p. 194.

15. Ibid.

16. Aitken, *Nixon,* p. 322.

17. Author interview with Patrick Buchanan, December 5, 2006.

18. John Judis, *William F. Buckley, Jr.: Patron Saint of the Conservatives* (New York: Simon & Schuster, 1988), p. 280.

19. Letter from William Rusher to the author, September 26, 2006.

20. Lou Cannon, *Governor Reagan: His Rise to Power* (New York: Public Affairs, 2003), p. 260.

21. Ibid, p. 259.

22. See also Irwin Unger, *The Movement: A History of the New Left, 1959–1972* (New York: Dodd, Mead, 1974), pp. 136–37.

23. Barry Goldwater with Jack Casserly, *Goldwater* (New York: Doubleday, 1988), p. 222.

24. Norman Podhoretz, *Breaking Ranks: A Political Memoir* (London: Weidenfeld & Nicholson, 1979), p. 181.

25. H. W. Brand, *The Strange Death of American Liberalism* (New Haven: Yale University Press, 2001), p. 95–97.

26. John Kenneth Galbraith, "An Agenda for American Liberals," *Commentary* (June 1966), p. 30.

27. William Bennett, speaking at a conference on the Conservative Movement at Princeton University on December 4, 2005.

28. Unger and Unger, *Turning Point,* pp. 127–28.

29. Thomas W. Pauken, *The Thirty Years War: The Politics of the Sixties Generation* (Ottawa, Ill.: Jameson Books, 1995), pp. 52.

30. Rebecca Klatch, *A Generation Divided: The New Left, the New Right, and the 1960s* (Berkeley: University of California Press, 1999), pp. 331–334. Klatch underestimates the endurance of YAF, but is otherwise on target.

31. Schoenwald, *Time for Choosing,* p. 251.

32. Author interview with Paul Laxalt, October 24, 2006.

33. Richard Nixon, "What Has Happened to America?" *Reader's Digest* (October 1967).

34. Edwin Diamond and Steven Bates, *The Spot: The Rise of Political Advertising on Television* (Cambridge, Mass.: MIT Press, 1992), p. 161.

35. Steven F. Hayward, *The Age of Reagan: The Fall of the Old Liberal Order, 1964–1980* (Roseville, Calif.: Prima, 2001), p. 212.

36. Schoenwald, *A Time for Choosing,* p. 254.

37. Lance Morrow, "Naysayer to the Nattering Nabobs," *Time* (September 30, 1996).

38. Hayward, *Age of Reagan,* p. 257.

39. Rowland Evans and Robert Novak, *Nixon in the White House: The Frustration of Power* (New York: Random House, 1971), p. 372.

40. Melvin Small, *The Presidency of Richard Nixon* (Lawrence: University of Kansas Press, 1999), p. 204. For a reappraisal of Nixon as a progressive, see Joan Hoff, *Nixon Reconsidered* (New York: Basic Books, 1994), who notes that the programs Nixon blasted on the campaign trail flourished under his tenure.

41. Author interview with Milton Friedman, July 12, 2005.

42. William F. Buckley, Jr., *Inveighing We Will Go* (New York: G.P. Putnam's Sons), p. 89; see also Hayward, *Age of Reagan,* pp. 277–88.

43. Author interview with Patrick Buchanan, December 5, 2006.

44. Edwards, *Conservative Revolution,* pp. 170–72.

45. *Human Events* (July 19, 1971).

46. Cited in Kevin Smant, *Principles and Heresies: Frank S. Meyer and the Shaping of the American Conservative Movement* (Wilmington, Del.: ISI Books, 2002), p. 321.

47. Peter W. Schramm, "John M. Ashbrook," in John A. Garraty and Mark C. Carnes, eds., *American National Biography, Volume I* (Oxford University Press, 1999).

48. Jules Witcover, *The Party of the People: A History of the Democrats* (New York: Random House, 2003), pp. 570–74.

49. Theodore White, *The Making of the President 1972* (New York: Athanaeum, 1973); "The Hitler Analogy," *Time* (August 29, 1972).

50. Paul Johnson, *A History of the American People* (New York: HarperCollins, 1998), p. 896.

51. *National Review* (February 16, 1973).

52. "More Sad Than Bad," *Time* (October 30, 1972.)

53. Hayward, *Age of Reagan,* p. 385.

54. Author interview with Patrick Buchanan, December 12, 2006.

CHAPTER 7: THE NEOCONS, THE NEW RIGHT, AND THE GRASSROOTS

1. Fred Barnes, "Big Government Conservatism," *Weekly Standard* (August 18, 2003).

2. James Neuchterlein, "Neoconservatism Redux," *First Things* (October 1996).

3. John B. Judis, "Trotskyism to Anachronism: The Neoconservative Revolution," *Foreign Affairs* 73 (July-August, 1995): 126.

4. Irving Kristol, *Neoconservatism: The Autobiography of an Idea* (New York: Free Press, 1995), p. 233.

5. Irving Kristol, "Forty Good Years," *The Public Interest* (Spring 2005).

6. Daniel P. Moynihan, "The Professors and the Poor," *Commentary* (August 1968).

7. Herbert Stein, *Presidential Economics: The Making of Economic Policy from Roosevelt to Reagan and Beyond* (New York: Simon & Schuster, 1984), p. 139.

8. Author interview with Midge Decter, October 6, 2006.

9. Edward C. Banfield, *The Unheavenly City: The Nature and Future of Our Urban Crisis* (Boston: Little, Brown, 1970). See also Charles Kesler, "Edward C. Banfield, RIP," *National Review* (November 8, 1999).

10. James Q. Wilson, "The Independent Mind of Edward Banfield," *Public Interest* (January 2003).

11. Author interview with William F. Buckley, Jr., June 23, 2005.

12. Author interview with Ben Wattenberg, October 2, 2006.

13. Nathan Glazer, "Neoconservatives From the Start," *Public Interest* (Spring 2005).

14. Murray Friedman, *The Neoconservative Revolution: Jewish Intellectuals and the Shaping of Public Policy* (New York: Cambridge University Press, 2005), p. 116.

15. Ibid, p. 121.

16. Ibid, p. 127.

17. Judis, "Trotskyism to Anachronism."

18. Friedman, *Neoconservative Revolution*, p. 141.

19. He was also the brother of Walt Whitman Rostow, one of Johnson's Vietnam War architects. Their names, and that of their third brother Ralph Waldo Emerson Rostow, have always been a subject of fascination. The Rostow brothers were the children of a couple of ardent and active socialist Russian immigrants who named their children after three prominent American socialists.

20. Midge Decter, "Breaking Away," *Hoover Digest* (January 2002).

21. Author interview with Midge Decter, October 6, 2006.

22. Letter to the author from Peter Stanlis, September 18, 2006.

23. John J. Miller, *A Gift of Freedom: How the John M. Olin Foundation Changed America* (San Francisco: Encounter Books, 2006), p. 110.

24. Stefan Halper and Jonathan Clarke, *America Alone: The Neoconservatives and the Global Order* (Cambridge: Cambridge University Press, 2004), p. 47.

25. "The David I Knew," *Wall Street Journal* (May 9, 1986).

26. Irving Kristol, "The Neoconservative Persuasion," *Weekly Standard* (August 25, 2003).

27. Rich Lowry, "Big Government Falls Flat" *National Review* (February 21, 2006).

28. Patrick J. Buchanan, *Where the Right Went Wrong: How Neoconservatives Subverted the Reagan Revolution and Hijacked the Bush Presidency* (New York: Thomas Dunne, 2004).

29. Irving Kristol, "The Neoconservative Persuasion," *Weekly Standard* (August 25, 2003).

30. Author interview with Richard Viguerie, March 23, 2006.

31. Author interview with Paul Weyrich, September 14, 2006.

32. Ibid.

33. Author interview with Richard Viguerie, March 23, 2006.

34. Ibid.

35. Paul Gottfried, *The Conservative Movement* (New York: Twayne, 1993), p. 79.

36. Author interview with Paul Weyrich, September 14, 2006.

37. Author interview with Pat Buchanan, December 5, 2006.

38. Lee Edwards, *The Conservative Revolution: The Movement That Remade America* (New York: Free Press, 1999), pp. 183–187.

39. *Newsweek* (October 25, 1976).

40. Sarah Diamond, *Not by Politics Alone: The Enduring Influence of the Christian Right* (New York: Guildford Press, 1998), p. 62.

41. See Donald Critchlow, *Phyllis Schlafly and Grassroots Conservatism: A Woman's Crusade* (Princeton: Princeton University Press, 2005), pp. 214–16.

42. Quoted in Michael Cromartie, *Religious Conservatives in American Politics 1980–2000: An Assessment* (Witherspoon Lecture, Family Research Council, April 16, 2001).

43. Jerry Falwell, *Falwell: An Autobiography* (Lynchburg, Va.: Liberty House Publishers, 1997), p. 358.

44. Quoted in William C. Martin, *With God on Our Side: The Rise of the Religious Right in America* (New York: Broadway Books, 1996), p. 193.

45. Ibid.

46. Ibid, 194–97.

47. Diamond, *Not by Politics Alone,* p. 65 n. 26.

48. Author interview with Richard Viguerie, March 23, 2006.

49. Author interview with Paul Weyrich, September 14, 2006.

50. Dinesh D'Souza, *Fallwell, Before the Millennium: A Critical Biography* (Chicago: Regnery, 1983), p. 60.

51. Cromartie, *Religious Conservatives.*

52. Falwell, *Autobiography,* p. 389.

53. Ibid.

54. D'Souza, *Falwell,* 143–44; "Rev. Jerry Falwell, Leader of Moral Majority, Dies at 73," *Boston Globe* (May 16, 2007).

55. D'Souza, *Falwell,* p. 141.

56. Diamond, *Not by Politics Alone,* p. 67.

57. Ibid, p. 68.

58. "Palast Investigates . . . Pat Robertson," *London Observer* (May 23, 1999).

59. Dinesh D'Souza, "Pat Robertson's World," *American Spectator* (November 1986).

60. William P. Martin, *The Best Liberal Quotes Ever: Why the Left Is Right* (Naperville, Ill.: Sourcebooks, 2004), p. 247.

61. Martin, *With God on Our Side,* p. 339.

62. Author interview with Donald Hodel March 14, 2006.

63. Author interview with Tony Perkins, December 6, 2006.

64. Ibid.

65. Author interview with Midge Decter, October 6, 2006.

66. Author interview with Donald Hodel, March 14, 2006.

67. Ibid, pp. 80–83.

68. Ibid, pp. 109–36.

69. Ibid, pp. 137–62.

70. Ibid, pp. 213–15.

71. Phyllis Schlafly, "What's Wrong with 'Equal Rights' for Women?" *The Phyllis Schlafly Report* (February 1972); quoted in Critchlow, *Phyllis Schlafly,* p. 218.

72. Author interview with Phyllis Schlafly, November 10, 2005.

73. Critchlow, *Phyllis Schlafly,* p. 220.

74. Ibid, p. 377, n. 22.

75. Ibid, p. 226.

76. Ibid, p. 227.

77. Ibid.

78. Author interview with Phyllis Schlafly, November 10, 2005.

79. Critchlow, *Phyllis Schlafly*, p. 214.
80. Sylvia Ann Hewlett, *A Lesser Life: The Myth of Women's Liberation in America* (New York, 1986), p. 211, quoted in Steven Hayward, *The Age of Reagan: The Fall of the Old Liberal Order, 1964–1980* (Roseville, CA: 2001), p. 310.
81. Author interview with Paul Weyrich, September 14, 2006.

Chapter 8: The Bargain of a Lifetime

1. James Piereson, "Investing in Conservative Ideas," *Commentary* (May 2005).
2. Don Graham, "Constitutional Amendment," *Texas Monthly* (October 2000).
3. Lee Edwards, *Educating for Liberty: The First Half-Century of the Intercollegiate Studies Institute* (Wilmington, Del.: ISI Books, 2003), pp. 50, 116.
4. Gregory L. Schneider, *Cadres for Conservatism: Young Americans for Freedom and the Contemporary Right* (New York: New York University Press, 1999), p. 225, n. 63.
5. John von Kannon interview with the author, September 20, 2006.
6. H. C. Cornuelle, *Mr. Anonymous, The Story of William Volker* (Caldwell, Ida.: Caxton Printers, 1951), p. 87.
7. Ibid, p. 202.
8. John Blundell, "Waging the War of Ideas—Why There Are No Substitutes," (Washington, D.C.: Heritage Lecture #254, June 1990).
9. Author interview with John Rasien, September 28, 2006.
10. Author interview with Milton Friedman, July 12, 2005.
11. Martin Davis, "Measuring Success in Generations," *Philanthropy Magazine* (May/June 2004).
12. Ibid.
13. Lee Edwards, "Earhart Foundation," in Bruce Frohnen, Jeremy Beer, and Jeffrey O. Nelson, eds., *American Conservatism: An Encyclopedia* (Wilmington, Del.: ISI Books, 2005), p. 248.
14. Dolores Proubasta, "Henry Salvatori," Society of Exploration Geophysicists, Virtual Geoscience Center (February 9, 2006), www.mssu.edu/seg-vm/bio_henry_salvatori.html.
15. Ibid.
16. *Society of Exploration Geophysicists Bulletin,* Missouri Southern State University, October 2006.
17. John Gizzi, "After Henry Salvatori: California's 'Most Generous' Conservative Philanthropists," *Foundation Watch* (October 1998).

18. William F. Buckley, Jr. "Henry Salvatori, RIP," *National Review* (August 11, 1997).

19. "Scaife: Funding Father of the Right," *Washington Post* (May 2, 1999).

20. Ibid.

21. Sarah Scaife Foundations, 2004 Annual Reports, www.scaife.com/.

22. Ryan Lizza, "Silent Partner: The Man Behind the Anti-Trade Revolt," *New Republic* (January 10, 2000).

23. *Textile Workers v. Darlington Co.* 380 US 263 (1965).

24. Author interview with John von Kannon, September 20, 2006.

25. Lizza, "Silent Partner."

26. Ibid.

27. "Milliken: A Man Worth Listening To," Free Congress Foundation (September 25, 2001).

28. Author interview with Patrick Buchanan, December 6, 2006.

29. Donald Critchlow, *Phyllis Schlafly and Grassroots Conservatism: A Woman's Crusade* (Princeton, N.J.: Princeton University Press, 2005), p. 52.

30. John Miller, *The Gift of Freedom: How the John M. Olin Foundation Changed America* (San Francisco: Encounter Books, 2006), p. 32.

31. Ibid.

32. Ibid, p. 4.

33. Ibid, p. 39.

34. Ibid, p. 63.

35. John Gurda, *The Bradley Legacy: Lynde and Harry Bradley, Their Company, and Their Foundation* (Milwaukee: Lynde and Harry Bradley Foundation, 1992), p. 140.

36. John Miller, *Strategic Investment in Ideas: How Two Foundations Reshaped America* (Washington D.C.: Philanthropy Roundtable, 2003), p. 36.

37. Author interview with John von Kannon, September 20, 2006.

38. Miller, *Strategic Investment in Ideas*, 35–58.

39. Ibid.

40. Piereson, "Investing in Conservative Ideas," 47.

41. Heather MacDonald, "The Billions of Dollars That Made Things Worse," *City Journal* (Autumn 1996).

42. See Ford Foundation Annual Report, 2005, at www.fordfound.org/publications/recent_articles/ar2005_presence.cfm.

43. Piereson, "Investing in Conservative Ideas," 50.

44. Andrew Rich, "The War of Ideas: Why Mainstream and Liberal Foun-

dations and the Think Tanks They Support Are Losing the War of Ideas in American Politics," *Stanford Social Innovation Review* (Spring 2005).

45. Piereson, "Investing in Conservative Ideas."

46. Rich, "War of Ideas," 20.

47. David Callahan, "Liberal Policy's Weak Foundations," *Nation* (November 13, 1995).

48. The National Committee for Responsive Philanthropy, *Axis of Ideology: Conservative Foundations and Public Policy* (March 2004).

49. Ibid.

50. *Buying a Movement: Right Wing Foundations and American Politics* (Washington, D.C.: People for the American Way, 1996).

51. William F. Buckley, Jr., "Marvin Liebman, RIP," *National Review* (April 12, 1997).

52. Author interview with Richard Viguerie, March 23, 2006.

53. Viguerie interview on C-SPAN Booknotes, September 5, 2004, transcript at www.booknotes.org/Transcript/?ProgramID=1796.

54. Ibid.

55. Ibid.

56. Rick Perlstein: *Before the Storm: Barry Goldwater and the Unmaking of the American Consensus* (New York: Hill and Wang, 2001), p. 475.

57. Author interview with Donald Hodel, March 14, 2006.

58. Richard Viguerie interview on C-SPAN Booknotes, September 5, 2004.

59. Author interview with John von Kannon interview with the author, September 20, 2006.

60. Stacey Koon with Robert Dietz, *Presumed Guilty: The Tragedy of the Rodney King Affair* (Washington, D.C.: Regnery Gateway, 1992).

61. *Koon v. United States* 518 US 81 (1996).

CHAPTER 9: THE LAW, THE COURTS, AND THE CONSTITUTION

1. Russell Kirk, *The Conservative Mind: From Burke to Santayana* (Chicago: H. Regnery Co., 1953), p. 96.

2. Ibid, p. 96.

3. Frank Meyer, "Conservatism and Republican Candidates," *National Review* (December 12, 1967).

4. Clarence Thomas, ISI Dinner for Western Civilization, Wilmington, Delaware, May 4, 2006.

5. Russell Kirk, *The Conservative Mind: From Burke to Santayana* (Chicago: H. Regnery Co., 1953), p. 81.

6. George Nash, *The Conservative Intellectual Movement in America Since 1945* (Wilmington, Del.: ISI Books, 1996), p. 198.

7. Frank Meyer, "Conservatism," in Robert Goldwin, ed., *Left, Right and Center* (Chicago: Rand McNally, 1965), p. 4.

8. Franklin D. Roosevelt, *Rendezvous with Destiny,* J.B.S. Hardman, ed. (New York: Dryden, 1944), p. 255.

9. Richard Epstein, *How Progressives Rewrote the Constitution* (Washington, D.C.: Cato Institute Press, 2006), p. 2.

10. Russell Kirk, *The American Cause* (Chicago: H. Regnery Co., 1957), p. 86.

11. Barry M. Goldwater, *The Conscience of a Conservative,* (Shepherdsville, Ky.: Victor, 1960), p. 18.

12. Felix Morely, "American Conservatism Today," *National Review* (March 24, 1964).

13. G. Edward White, *Earl Warren: A Public Life* (New York: Oxford University Press, 1982), p. 67.

14. Ibid, p. 69.

15. Ibid, p. 71.

16. Ibid.

17. Leo Katcher, *Earl Warren: A Political Biography* (New York: McGraw-Hill, 1967), p. 150.

18. Earl Warren, *The Memoirs of Earl Warren* (Garden City, N.Y.: Doubleday, 1977), p. 122.

19. White, *Earl Warren,* p. 138; Peter Irons, *A People's History of the Supreme Court* (New York: Penguin, 2000), p. 393.

20. *Tinker v. Des Moines Independent Community School District* 393 U.S. 503 (1969).

21. Philip B. Kurland, "Government by Judiciary," *Modern Age* 20 (Fall 1976): 361.

22. L. Brent Bozell, *The Warren Revolution: Reflections on the Consensus Society* (New Rochelle, N.Y.: Arlington House, 1966).

23. William F. Harvey, "An Appointment to the Supreme Court," *Chronicles Magazine* (June 2005).

24. Stephen J. Markman and Alfred S. Regnery, "The Mind of Justice Brennan," *National Review* (May 18, 1984).

25. Ibid.

26. Ibid.

27. Ibid.

28. White, *Earl Warren,* p. 162.

29. Cited in Bernard Schwartz, *A History of the Supreme Court* (New York: Oxford University Press, 1993), p. 288.

30. Ibid, p. 286.
31. White, *Earl Warren,* p. 171.
32. Rehnquist's memo acknowledged that this "is an unpopular and un-humanitarian position for which I have been excoriated by 'liberal' colleagues." But in its key passage, Rehnquist insisted that "one hundred and fifty years of attempts on the part of this court to protect minority rights of any kind—whether those of business, slaveholders, or Jehovah's Witnesses—have all met the same fate. One by one the cases establishing such rights have been sloughed off, and crept silently to rest. If the present court is unable to profit by this example, it must be prepared to see its work fade in time, too, as embodying only the sentiments of a transient majority of nine men." William Rehnquist, "A Random Thought on the Segregation Cases," U.S. Senate, Committee on the Judiciary, Hearings, *Nomination of Justice William Hubbs Rehnquist to Be Chief Justice of the United States,* 99th Congress, 2nd Session (July 29–31, and August 1, 1986).
33. Charles W. Ogletree, Jr., *All Deliberate Speed* (New York: Norton, 2004), p. 3.
34. James Jackson Kilpatrick, *The Lasting South* (Chicago: Regnery, 1957), p. 202.
35. Ibid.
36. *Watkins v. United States,* 354 US 178 (1957).
37. *Yates v. United States* 354 US 298 (1957); Sweezy v. New Hampshire, 354 US 234 (1957).
38. *National Review* (June 29, 1957).
39. See, e.g., Stephen B. Presser, *Recapturing the Constitution: Race, Religion, and Abortion Reconsidered* (Washington, D.C.: Regnery, 1994).
40. David Lawrence, "Treason's Biggest Victory," *U.S. News & World Report* (June 28, 1957), 150–152.
41. Jonathan Schoenwald, *A Time for Choosing: The Rise of Modern Conservatism* (Oxford: Oxford University Press), p. 40.
42. *National Review* (June 29, 1957).
43. White, *Earl Warren,* p. 238.
44. Ibid, p. 239.
45. Bozell, *Warren Revolution,* p. 110.
46. Baker v. Carr 369 US 186 (1962).
47. Author interview with Paul Laxalt, October 24, 2006.
48. Baker v. Carr 369 US 186 (1962).
49. William Martin, *With God on Our Side: The Rise of the Religious Right in America* (New York: Broadway Books, 1996), p. 77.

50. *Everson v. the Board of Education of Ewing Township, New Jersey* 330 U.S. 1 (1947).

51. *Engel v. Vitale* 370 US 421 (1962).

52. M. Stanton Evans, *The Theme Is Freedom: Religion, Politics, and the American Tradition* (Washington, D.C.: Regnery, 1994), p. 275.

53. Ibid, p. 278.

54. Ibid, p. 281.

55. Quoted in *Reader's Digest* (September 1979), p. 89.

56. Martin, *With God on Our Side,* p. 169.

57. Ibid, p. 169.

58. Irons, *People's History,* p. 412.

59. Quoted in *Reader's Digest* (November 1992).

60. Lucas Powe, Jr., *The Warren Court in American Politics* (Cambridge: Harvard University Press, 2000), p. 495.

61. *Oakland Tribune* (September 20, 1931).

62. Quoted in White, *Earl Warren,* p. 265.

63. *Miranda v. Arizona* 384 US 436 (1966).

64. Quoted in White, *Earl Warren,* p. 271.

65. Irwin Unger and Debi Unger, *Turning Point, 1968* (New York: Scribner, 1988), p. 345.

66. Eugene Methvin, "Up from Activism: A New Court?" *American Spectator* (May 2006).

67. Unger and Unger, *Turning Point,* p. 347.

68. Methvin, "Up from Activism."

69. Ibid.

70. *Roe v. Wade* 410 US 113 (1973).

71. Mary Ann Glendon, *Abortion and Divorce in Western Law: American Failures, European Challenges* (Cambridge: Harvard University Press, 1987), p. 337.

72. Quoted in Irons, *People's History,* p. 449.

73. Martin, *With God on Our Side,* p. 193.

74. Robert Bork, *The Tempting of America: The Political Seduction of the Law* (New York: Free Press, 1990), p. 112.

75. *New York Times* (June 16, 1993).

76. Kurland, "Government by Judiciary," 366.

77. Jerry Falwell, *Falwell: An Autobiography* (Lynchburg, Va.: Liberty House, 1997), p. 358.

78. Paul Johnson, *A History of the American People* (New York: Harper-Perennial, 1999), p. 964.

79. Larry L. Eastland, "The Empty Cradle Will Rock," *American Spectator* (June 2004).

80. Author interview with Tony Perkins, December 6, 2006.

81. Robert Bork, "Slouching Toward Miers," *Wall Street Journal* (October 19, 2005).

82. Raoul Berger, *Government by Judiciary: The Transformation of the Fourteenth Amendment* (Cambridge: Harvard University Press, 1977).

83. As a matter of full disclosure, I was Paul Laxalt's counsel on the Senate Judiciary Committee at the time, and covered his judicial nomination duties for him. I convinced him to take on these nomination fights, wrote his speeches for him, and generally assisted him in all matters involving them. Mikva was confirmed by a vote of 58–31, and Wald by a margin of 77–21.

84. Robert Bork, *The Anti-Trust Paradox: A Policy at War with Itself* (New York: Basic Books, 1978). See John Miller, *Gift of Freedom: How the John M. Olin Foundation Changed America* (San Francisco: Encounter, 2005), 64. Richard Posner, another Director student, was appointed to the Circuit Court of Appeals by President Reagan, and become one of the essential advocates of law and economics; and Henry Manne, yet another student, taught in a number of law schools and successfully promoted the idea that teaching economics should be an essential part of legal education.

85. Miller, *Gift of Freedom,* p. 69.

86. Quoted in Ibid, p. 70.

87. Quoted in Ibid, p. 81.

88. Author interview with Judge Douglas Ginsberg, January 19, 2007.

89. Author interview, November 20, 2006. The interviewee prefers to remain anonymous.

90. Lee Edwards, *Bringing Justice to the People* (Washington, D.C.: Heritage Books, 2004).

91. Ibid, p. 160.

92. Author interview with Edwin Meese, January 4, 2007.

93. Among the Federal Appellate Judges that Reagan named who were either subsequently nominated to the Supreme Court, who would be notable conservatives, were Antonin Scalia, Clarence Thomas, Ralph Winter, James Buckley, Robert Bork, Kenneth Starr, Richard Posner, and Douglas Ginsberg.

94. Author interview with T. Kenneth Cribb, December 6, 2006.

95. Ibid.

96. Author interview with Edwin Meese, January 4, 2007.

97. Bork, *Tempting*, p. 268.

98. Ibid.

99. Lee Edwards, Conservative Revolution: *The Movement That Changed America* (New York: Free Press, 1999), pp. 236–38.

100. Edwin Meese, *With Reagan: The Inside Story* (Washington, D.C.: Regnery Gateway, 1992), p. 316.

101. Bork, *Tempting*, p. 3.

102. Randall Kennedy, "Form and Substance in Private Law Adjudication," 95 *Harvard Law Review* 1685, 1746 (1976).

103. Dale Russakoff and Jo Becker, "A Search for Order, An Answer in the Law," *Washington Post* (January 8, 2006).

104. Ibid.

105. Quoted in Miller, *Gift of Freedom*, p. 88.

106. Author interview with Gene Meyer interview, May 24, 2006.

107. Ibid.

108. Author interview with William Rusher, July 12, 2005.

CHAPTER 10: INTELLECTUAL DEVELOPMENTS, 1960 TO THE PRESENT

1. George Nash, *The Conservative Intellectual Movement Since 1945* (Wilmington, Del.: ISI Books, 1996), pp. 211–212. Emphasis in original.

2. Willmoore Kendall and George Carey, *Basic Symbols of the American Political Tradition* (Baton Rouge: Louisiana State University Press), p. 154; Willmoore Kendall, *Willmoore Kendall Contra Mundum* (New Rochelle, N.Y.: Arlington House, 1971), 306; see the discussion in Nash, *Conservative Intellectual Movement*, pp. 224–26. For an appreciation of Kendall's contribution to American conservatism, see John A. Murley and John Alvis, eds., *Willmoore Kendall: Maverick of American Conservatives* (Lanham, Md.: Lexington Books, 2002).

3. See Jeffrey Hart, *The Making of the American Conservative Mind: National Review and Its Times* (Wilmington, Del.: ISI Books, 2005), pp. 39–40, 161–170.

4. William F. Buckley, Jr., to Willmoore Kendall, February 13, 1964. Letter in author's possession.

5. Murley and Alvis, *Willmoore Kendall,* p. 237.

6. Kendall, *Contra Mundum,* p. 454.

7. Leo Strauss, *Natural Right and History* (Chicago: University of Chicago Press, 1953).

8. Harry V. Jaffa, "The Achievement of Leo Strauss," *National Review* (December 7, 1973).

9. Seymour M. Hersh, "Selective Intelligence," *New Yorker* (May 12, 2003); William Pfaff, "The Long Reach of Leo Strauss," *International Herald Tribune* (May 15, 2003).

10. See, inter alia, Peter Berkowitz, "What Hath Strauss Wrought?" *Weekly Standard* (June 6, 2003); Thomas Pangle, *Leo Strauss: An Introduction to His Thought and Legacy* (Baltimore: Johns Hopkins University Press, 2006); Catherine and Michael Zuckert, *The Truth about Leo Strauss* (Chicago: University of Chicago Press, 2006).

11. For a comparison of Strauss and Voegelin, see Ted V. McAllister, *Revolt against Modernity: Leo Strauss, Eric Voegelin, and the Search for a Post-Liberal Order* (Lawrence, Kan.: University of Kansas Press, 1995).

12. Eric Voegelin, *Autobiographical Reflections* (Baton Rouge: Louisiana State University Press, 1989), pp. 42–44.

13. On Bozell, see Rick Perlstein, *Before the Storm: Barry Goldwater and the Unmaking of the American Consensus* (New York: Hill and Wang, 2001), p. 164; on YAF, see McAllister, *Revolt against Modernity*, p. 262.

14. Author interview with T. Kenneth Cribb, December 6, 2006.

15. See Milton and Rose D. Friedman, *Two Lucky People: Memoirs* (Chicago: University of Chicago Press, 1998).

16. Milton Friedman, *Capitalism and Freedom* (Chicago: University of Chicago Press, 1962), p. 38.

17. Perlstein, *Before the Storm*, p. 421.

18. Milton Friedman, "The Goldwater View of Economics," *New York Times Magazine* (October 11, 1964); on Friedman at Dodger Stadium, see Perlstein, *Before the Storm*, pp. 422–23.

19. Author interview with Milton Friedman, July 12, 2005.

20. Holcomb B. Noble, "Milton Friedman, Free Markets Theorist, Dies at 94," *New York Times* (November 16, 2006).

21. "Capitalism and Friedman: The Man Who Made Free Markets Popular Again," *Wall Street Journal* (November 17, 2006).

22. George Gilder, *Wealth and Poverty* (New York: Basic Books, 1981), p. 265.

23. Irving Kristol, "A New Look at Capitalism," *National Review* (April 17, 1981); John Chamberlain, "Unleashing the Entrepreneur," *National Review* (April 17, 1981).

24. See J. David Hoeveler, *Watch on the Right: Conservative Intellectuals in the Reagan Era* (Madison: University of Wisconsin Press, 1991), pp. 111–112.

25. Author interview with William F. Buckley, Jr., June 9, 2005.

26. Quoted in Edward D. Ericson, Jr. and Daniel J. Mahoney, eds., *The*

Solzhenitsyn Reader: New and Essential Writings, 1947–2005 (Wilmington: ISI Books, 2006), p. xxii.

27. Editors' introduction, Ibid, pp. xxii–xxvi.

28. Ibid, pp. 562–575.

29. *New York Times* (June 13, 1978). See also Joseph Pierce, *Solzhenitsyn: A Soul in Exile* (Grand Rapids: Baker Books, 2001), pp. 235–36.

30. Henry Fairlie, "Solzhenitsyn's Mental Prison: Mother Russia's Prodigal Son," *New Republic* (July 29, 1978).

31. Michael Novak, *On Cultivating Liberty* (Lanham, Md.: Rowman & Littlefield, 1999), p. 227.

32. Jeanne Kirkpatrick, "Dictatorships and Double Standards," *Commentary* (November 1979).

33. Michael Novak, *The Spirit of Democratic Capitalism* (New York: Simon & Schuster, 1982).

34. William J. Bennett, *The De-Valuing of America: The Fight for Our Culture and Our Children* (New York: Summit Books, 1992), pp. 169–74.

35. Allan Bloom, *The Closing of the American Mind: How Higher Education Has Failed Democracy and Impoverished the Souls of Today's Students* (New York: Simon & Schuster, 1987), pp. 74–75.

36. Christopher Lehmann-Haupt, "Books of the Times," *New York Times* (March 23, 1987).

37. Stephen Tonsor, "überstudiert in Chicago," *Modern Age* 32 (Winter 1988): 58.

38. Dinesh D'Souza, *Illiberal Education* (New York: Free Press, 1991).

39. Eugene Genovese, "Heresy, Yes—Sensitivity, No," *New Republic* (April 15, 1991).

40. J. David Hoeveler, *Watch on the Right: Conservative Intellectuals in the Reagan Era* (Madison: University of Wisconsin Press, 1991), pp. 207–32.

41. Werner Dannhauser, "The Metaphysical Martini," *American Spectator* (November 1981).

42. Leon Wieseltier, "Matthew Arnold and the Cold War," *New Republic* (December 27, 1982).

43. Roger Kimball, "The Power of James Burnham," *New Criterion* (September 2002); "The Consequences of Richard Weaver," *New Criterion* (September 2006).

44. *New Criterion* (September 2006).

45. Claes Ryn, "What's Left? What's Right?" *American Conservative* (August 28, 2006).

46. R. Emmett Tyrrell, Jr., *The Conservative Crack-Up* (New York: Simon & Schuster, 1992).

47. Bork, "Our Judicial Oligarchy," in Mitchell S. Muncy and Richard John Neuhaus, eds., *The End of Democracy? The Judicial Usurpation of Politics* (Dallas: Spence, 1997), p. 14.

48. These responses are helpfully collected in Muncy and Neuhaus, eds., *The End of Democracy.*

49. Charles Murray, *Losing Ground: American Social Policy, 1950–1980* (New York: Basic Books, 1994), p. 9.

50. Murray, *Losing Ground*, pp. 227–228.

51. *New York Times* (February 3, 1985).

52. Marvin Olasky, *The Tragedy of American Compassion* (Washington, D.C.: Regnery, 1992), pp. 99–115.

53. Olasky, *Tragedy*, p. 209.

54. *New York Times Magazine* (September 12, 1999).

Chapter 11: Ronald Reagan

1. Ronald Reagan, *Speaking My Mind* (New York: Simon & Schuster, 1989), pp. 93–101.

2. Cited in Steven Hayward, *The Age of Reagan: The Fall of the Old Liberal Order, 1964–1980* (Roseville, Calif.: Forum/Prima, 2001), p. 452.

3. Ronald Reagan, *An American Life* (New York: Simon & Schuster, 1990), p. 90.

4. Ibid, p. 110.

5. House Committee on Un-American Activities, *Hearings Regarding the Communist Infiltration of the Motion Picture Industry*, 80th Congress, 1st Session, October 23–24, 1947 (Washington: Government Printing Office, 1947).

6. For HUAC in the late 1940s, see Lee Edwards, *The Conservative Revolution: The Movement That Remade America* (New York: Free Press, 1999), pp. 30–33.

7. Reagan, *An American Life*, p. 114.

8. Ibid, p. 115.

9. Kieron Skinner, Annelise Anderson, and Martin Anderson, eds., *Reagan in His Own Hand: The Writings of Ronald Reagan That Reveal His Revolutionary Vision for America* (New York: Free Press, 2001), p. 12.

10. Author interview with Paul Laxalt, October 24, 2006.

11. "America the Beautiful," William Woods College, commencement address, Fulton, Missouri, May 3, 1952.

12. Reagan, *Speaking My Mind,* pp. 409–418.

13. Author interview with Martin Anderson, October 16, 2006.

14. Author interview with Edwin Meese, January 4, 2007.

15. See Ted V. McAllister, "Reagan and the Transformation of American Conservatism," in W. Eliot Brownlee and Hugh Davis Graham, eds., *The Reagan Presidency, Pragmatic Conservatism and Its Legacies* (Lawrence, Kan.: University of Kansas Press, 2003), p. 43.

16. John B. Judis, "The Two Faces of Whittaker Chambers," in Patrick A Swann, ed., *Alger Hiss, Whittaker Chambers, and the Schism in the American Soul* (Wilmington, Del.: ISI Books, 2003), p. 236.

17. Author interview with T. Kenneth Cribb, August 9, 2006.

18. McAllister, "Reagan and the Transformation of American Conservatism," p. 51.

19. Jules Whitcover and Richard Cohen, "Where Is the Rest of Ronald Reagan?" *Esquire* (March 1976).

20. Author interview with Edwin Meese, January 4, 2007.

21. "The Republican Party and the Conservative Movement," *National Review* (December 1, 1964).

22. Author interview with Edwin Meese, January 4, 2007.

23. Author interview with Paul Laxalt, October 24, 2006.

24. Kiron K. Skinner, Annelise Anderson, and Martin Anderson, eds., *Reagan's Path to Victory: The Shaping of Ronad Reagan's Vision: Selected Writings* (New York: Free Press, 2004), p. xiii.

25. Author interview with Martin Anderson, October 16, 2006.

26. Skinner, Anderson, and Anderson, *Path to Victory,* p. xiv.

27. Ibid.

28. Author interview with Martin Anderson, October 16, 2006.

29. Author interview with Paul Laxalt, October 24, 2006.

30. William A. Rusher, *The Making of the New Majority Party* (New York: Sheed & Ward, 1975).

31. Bob Colacello, *Ronnie and Nancy: Their Path to the White House, 1911–1980* (New York: Warner Books, 2004), p. 439.

32. Reagan, *An American Life,* p. 201.

33. Colacello, *Ronnie and Nancy,* p. 440.

34. Author interview with Paul Laxalt, October 24, 2006.

35. Ibid.

36. Author interview with Martin Anderson, October 16, 2006.

37. Ibid.

38. Lou Cannon, *President Reagan: The Role of a Lifetime* (New York: Public Affairs, 2000), p. 837.

39. Ibid, p. 771.
40. Author interview with Martin Anderson interview, October 16, 2006.
41. Author interview with Edwin Meese, January 4, 2007.
42. Author interview with Paul Laxalt, October 24, 2006.
43. Richard Gid Powers, *Not Without Honor: The History of American Anticommunism* (New York: Free Press, 1995), p. 390.
44. Edwin Meese, *With Reagan: The Inside Story* (Washington, D.C.: Regnery Gateway, 1992), p. 167.
45. Reagan, *An American Life,* p. 559.
46. Reagan, *Speaking My Mind,* pp. 168–80.
47. William F. Buckley, Jr., "Remarks at the *National Review* 35th Anniversary Dinner," *National Review* (November 5, 1990).
48. Interview with Natan Sharansky, *Weekly Standard* (June 21, 2004).
49. Reagan, *Speaking My Mind,* p. 179.
50. Ibid, p. 169.
51. Reagan, *An American Life,* p. 231.
52. Harry Anderson et al., "The U.S. Economy in Crisis," *Newsweek* (January 19, 1981).
53. See www.miseryindex.us/indexbymonth.asp.
54. Reagan, *An American Life,* p. 232.
55. Jude Wanniski, *The Way the World Works* (Chicago: Regnery Publishing, 1978), p. 97.
56. Author interview with Milton Friedman, July 12, 2005.
57. Peter Robinson, *How Ronald Reagan Changed My Life* (New York: Regan Books, 2003), p. 55.
58. For an overview of Reagan's tax policy, see W. Elliot Brownlee and C. Eugene Steuerle, "Taxation," in Brownlee and Graham, eds., *Reagan Presidency,* pp. 155–181.
59. Dinesh D'Souza, *Ronald Reagan: How an Ordinary Man Became an Extraordinary Leader* (New York: The Free Press, 1997), p. 89.
60. Quoted in James T. Patterson, "Afterword: Legacies of the Reagan Years," in Brownlee and Graham, eds., *Reagan Presidency,* p. 362.
61. Stephen Moore, "Reagan Changed the World," *National Review Online* (August 17, 2001).
62. Reagan, *An American Life,* pp. 314–315.
63. Gerald Prante, "Tax Reform: What Has Changed Since 1986?" *Tax Foundation Commentary* (October 10, 2006).
64. Author interview with Milton Friedman, July 12, 2005.
65. "Reagonomics at 25," *Wall Street Journal* (August 12–13, 2006).

CHAPTER 12: CONSERVATIVES AND FREE ENTERPRISE

1. Timothy P. Carney, *The Big Ripoff: How Big Business and Big Government Steal Your Money* (Hoboken, N.J.: John Wiley & Sons, 2006).
2. See the CRC website, www.capitalresearch.org/.
3. Milton Friedman, *Capitalism and Freedom* (Chicago: University of Chicago Press, 1962), p. 135. See also Henry Manne, "Milton Friedman Was Right," *Wall Street Journal* (November 24, 2006).
4. Aaron Steelman, "Frank Chodorov: Champion of Liberty," *Freeman* (December 1996).
5. Paul Krugman, "Jerking the Other Knee," *New York Times* (January 21, 2001).
6. Mary Sennholz, "Leonard Read, the Founder and Builder," *Freeman* (May 1996).
7. Nash, *Conservative Intellectual Movement,* pp. 27–28. See also Leonard E. Read, "Neither Left Nor Right," *Freeman* (January 1956).
8. John Davenport memorandum, November 4, 1964, Davenport Papers, Hoover Institution.
9. Tom Richman, "The Biggest Kid on the Block," *Inc.* (June 1982), 57; John Judis, "Abandoned Surgery," *American Prospect* (March 21, 1995); Jack Faris, "Challenging the Regulators," *My Business* (April/May 2003); "The History of NFIB," NFIB brochure, March 2005.
10. George C. Leef, *Free Choice for Workers: A History of the Right to Work Movement* (Ottawa, Ill.: Jameson Books, 2005), pp. 27–28.
11. Ibid, p. 29.
12. Richard Vedder, "Right to Work Movement," in Bruce Frohnen, Jeremy Beer, and Jeffrey Nelson, eds., *American Conservatism: An Encyclopedia* (Wilmington, Del.: ISI Books, 2006), pp. 736–37.
13. Leef, *Free Choice for Workers,* p. 205.
14. Thomas W. Evans, *The Education of Ronald Reagan: The General Electric Years and the Untold Story of His Conversion to Conservatism* (New York: Columbia University Press, 2006), p. 4.
15. Ronald Reagan, *American Life* (New York: Simon & Schuster, 1990), p. 129.
16. Nancy Reagan with William Novak, *My Turn: The Memoirs of Nancy Reagan* (New York: Random House, 1989), p. 128.
17. Evans, *Education of Ronald Reagan,* p. 106.
18. Ibid, p. 38.
19. Joan Cook, "Lemuel Ricketts Boulware, 95: Headed Labor Relations for G.E.," *New York Times* (November 8, 1990).

20. Lou Cannon, *Governor Reagan: His Rise to Power* (New York: Public Affairs, 2003), p. 109.
21. Evans, *Education of Ronald Reagan,* p. 96.
22. Ibid, p. 201.
23. Randall Teague memorandum, April 22, 1966, YAF Papers, Hoover Institution.
24. Ibid.
25. Alan McKay memorandum, May 2, 1968, YAF Papers, Hoover Institution.
26. Irving Kristol, "Business and The New Class," *Wall Street Journal* (May 19, 1975).
27. John Miller, *The Gift of Freedom: How the John M. Olin Foundation Changed America* (San Francisco: Encounter Books, 2006), p. 51.
28. Ibid, p. 57.
29. Center for Responsive Politics, "Blue Chip Investors: The Top 100 Donors to Federal Elections, 1989–2002," October 2002, www.open secrets.org/pubs/toporgs/index.asp.

CHAPTER 13: RELIGION AND AMERICAN CONSERVATISM
1. M. Stanton Evans, *The Theme Is Freedom* (Washington, D.C.: Regnery, 1994), p. 312.
2. Saul Padover, ed., *The Washington Papers* (New York: Harper, 1955), pp. 318–19.
3. Evans, *The Theme Is Freedom,* p. 317.
4. Bernard Steiner, *The Life and Correspondence of James McHenry* (Cleveland: Burrows Brothers, 1907), p. 475.
5. Richard Weaver, *Ideas Have Consequences* (Chicago: University of Chicago Press, 1948), p. 4.
6. Ibid, pp. 2–3.
7. Ibid, p. 113.
8. Ibid, p. 175.
9. Ibid, p. 182.
10. Russell Kirk, *The Conservative Mind: From Burke to Eliot* (New York: Avon, 1968), p. 17.
11. Ibid, p. 19.
12. Russell Kirk, *The Roots of American Order* (Wilmington, Del.: ISI Books, 2003), p. 174.
13. Ibid, p. 175.
14. David J. O'Brien, *American Catholics and Social Reform: The New Deal Years* (Oxford: Oxford University Press, 1968), pp. 81–82.

15. Richard Gid Powers, *Not Without Honor: The History of American Anticommunism* (New York: Free Press, 1995), p. 110.
16. Ibid, pp. 175–76.
17. See Patrick Allitt, *Catholic Intellectuals and Conservative Politics in America, 1950–1985* (Ithaca: Cornell University Press, 1993), p. 92.
18. Ibid, p. 94; Judis, p. 186.
19. L. Brent Bozell, "Who Is Accommodating to What?" *National Review* (May 4, 1965).
20. Author interview with Martin Anderson, October 16, 2007.
21. Wilhelm Roepke, "Liberalism and Christianity," *Modern Age* 1 (Fall 1957): 129.
22. Ibid.
23. Ibid.
24. Quoted in Erik von Kuehnelt-Leddihn, "Letter from the Continent," *National Review* (April 4, 1956).
25. Friedrich A. Hayek, *The Constitution of Liberty* (Chicago: University of Chicago Press, 1960), p. 163.
26. Max Eastman, "Am I Conservative?" *National Review* (January 28, 1964).
27. Jeffrey Hart, *The Making of the American Conservative Mind: National Review and Its Times* (Wilmington, Del.: ISI Books, 2005), p. 151.
28. Russell Kirk, "The Seventh Congress of Freedom," *National Review* (May 3, 1958).
29. Peter Stanlis, *Edmund Burke and the Natural Law* (Ann Arbor, Mich.: University of Michigan Press, 1958), p. 54.
30. Ibid, p. xi.
31. See Will Herberg, "Conservatives, Liberals, and the Natural Law, I," *National Review* (June 5, 1962); Herberg, "Conservatives, Liberals, and the Natural Law, II," *National Review* (June 19, 1962).
32. Eric Voegelin, *Order and History, Vol. 2: The World of the Polis* (Baton Rouge: Louisiana State University Press, 1957), p. 2.
33. See Frank Meyer, "Freedom, Tradition, Conservatism," *Modern Age* 4 (Fall 1960): 355–363.
34. Frank S. Meyer, ed., *What Is Conservatism?* (New York: Holt, Rinehart, and Winston, 1964), pp. 229–32.
35. Ibid.
36. William Henry Chamberlain, "Conservatism in Evolution," *Modern Age* 7 (Summer 1963): 254.
37. Wilhelm Roepke, "Liberalism and Christianity," *Commonweal* (July 18, 1947).

38. Wilhelm Roepke, "Liberalism and Christianity," *Modern Age* 1 (Fall 1957): 134.
39. Peter Viereck, *Conservatism Revisited: The Revolt Against Revolt, 1815–1949* (New York: C. Scribner, 1949), pp. 28, 30.
40. Barry Goldwater, *The Conscience of a Conservative* (Shepherdsville, Ky.: Victor, 1960), p. 3.
41. Ibid, p. 5.
42. Ibid.
43. Author interview with Edwin Meese, January 4, 2007.
44. For the text of the speech, see www.ronaldreagan.com/sp_6.html.
45. Irving Kristol, "American Conservatism, 1945–1995," *Public Interest* (Fall 1995).
46. Paul Johnson, "An Almost Chosen People," *First Things* (June/July 2006).
47. William F. Buckley, Jr., *God and Man at Yale: The Superstitions of "Academic Freedom"* (Chicago: H. Regnery Co., 1951), p. xiii.

CHAPTER 14: WE ARE ALL CONSERVATIVES NOW

1. David M. O'Brien, "Federal Judgeships in Retrospect" in W. Eliot Brownlee and Hugh Davis Graham, eds., *The Reagan Presidency, Pragmatic Conservatism and Its Legacies* (Lawrence, Kan.: University of Kansas Press, 2003), p. 327.
2. Author interview with T. Kenneth Cribb, December 6, 2006.
3. Quoted in Daniel J. Balz and Ronald Brownstein, *Storming the Gates: Protest Politics and the Republican Revival* (Boston: Little, Brown, 1996), p. 131.
4. John Fund, "A Tax by Any Other Name," *American Spectator* (February 2007).
5. "The Iron Fist of Pat Buchanan," *Washington Post* (February 5, 1992).
6. Fred Barnes, "Heir Apparent," *New Republic* (March 30, 1992).
7. See www.buchanan.org/pa-92–0817-rnc.html.
8. Author interview with Newt Gingrich, December 8, 2006.
9. Fred Barnes, "Contract Hit!" *American Spectator* (January 1995).
10. *New York Times* (November 10, 1994).
11. Author interview with Newt Gingrich, December 8, 2006.
12. Author interview with David MacIntosh, September 6, 2006.
13. Author interview with Newt Gingrich, December 8, 2006.
14. Quoted in Jeffrey Gaynor, "The Contract with America: Implementing New Ideas in the U.S.," *Heritage Lecture #549*, Heritage Foundation, October 12, 1995.

15. Ibid.
16. Author interview with Newt Gingrich, December 8, 2006.
17. *New York Times* (November 9, 2006).
18. Balz and Brownstein, *Storming the Gates,* p. 163.
19. Cited in John Micklethwait and Adrian Wooldridge, *The Right Nation: Conservative Power in America* (New York: Penguin Books, 2004), p. 113.
20. Author interview with Martin Anderson, October 16, 2006.
21. Richard A. Viguerie and David Franke, *America's Right Turn: How Conservatives Used New and Alternative Media to Take Power* (Chicago: Bonus Books, 2004), p. 189.
22. Micklethwait and Wooldridge, *Right Nation,* p. 380.
23. "In Judge Battles, Mr. Sekulow Plays a Delicate Role," *Wall Street Journal* (May 17, 2005).
24. Author interview with Leonard Leo, December 28, 2006.
25. "In Alito, GOP Reaps Harvest That Was Planted in 1982," *New York Times* (January 30, 2006).
26. Author interview with Leonard Leo, December 28, 2006.
27. Ibid.
28. "In Alito, GOP Reaps Harvest That Was Planted in 1982," *New York Times* (January 30, 2006).
29. Author interview with Edwin Meese, January 4, 2007.
30. Author interview with Leonard Leo, December 28, 2006.
31. *Washington Times* (October 11, 2005).
32. Robert Bork, "Slouching Toward Miers," *Wall Street Journal* (October 19, 2005).
33. George Will, "Defending the Indefensible," *Washington Post* (October 23, 2005).
34. Howard Kurtz, "Conservative Pundits Packed a Real Punch," *Washington Post* (October 28, 2005).
35. Author interview with Charles Cooper, April 17, 2007.
36. Jan Crawford Greenberg, *Supreme Conflict: The Inside Story for the Control of the United States Supreme Court,* (New York: Penguin, 2007), p. 314.
37. Quoted in *The Washington Post* (July 4, 2007).
38. Quoted in *The Wall Street Journal* (July 2, 2007).

BIBLIOGRAPHY

Aitken, Jonathan. *Nixon: A Life*. Washington, D.C.: Regnery Gateway, Inc., 1993.

Allitt, Patrick. *Catholic Intellectuals and Conservative Politics in America, 1950–1985*. Ithaca, N.Y.: Cornell University Press, 1993.

Anderson, Martin. *Revolution: The Reagan Legacy*. Stanford: Hoover Institution Press, 1990.

Andrew III, John A. *The Other Side of the Sixties: Young Americans for Freedom and the Rise of Conservative Politics*. New Brunswick: Rutgers University Press, 1997.

Balz, Daniel J. and Brownstein, Ronald. *Storming the Gates: Protest Politics and the Republican Revival*. Boston: Little, Brown, 1996.

Banfield, Edward C. *The Unheavenly City: The Nature and Future of Our Urban Crisis*. Boston: Little, Brown, 1970.

Barnes, Fred. "Big Government Conservatism." *Weekly Standard* (August 18, 2003).

Bartley, Robert L. *The Seven Fat Years: And How to Do It Again*. New York: Free Press, 1992.

Bennett, William J. *The De-Valuing of America: The Fight for Our Culture and Our Children*. New York: Summit Books, 1992.

———. *Index of Leading Cultural Indicators*. New York: Simon & Schuster, 1994.

Berger, Raoul. *Government by Judiciary: The Transformation of the Fourteenth Amendment*. Indianapolis: Liberty Fund, 1997.

Bloom, Allan. *The Closing of the American Mind: How Higher Education Has Failed Democracy and Impoverished the Souls of Today's Students*. New York: Simon & Schuster, 1987.

Bork, Robert. *The Tempting of America: The Political Seduction of the Law*. New York: Free Press, 1990.

Bozell, L. Brent. "Freedom or Virtue?" *National Review* (September 1, 1962).

———. *The Warren Revolution: Reflections on the Consensus Society.* New Rochelle, N.Y.: Arlington House, 1966.

Brand, H. W. *The Strange Death of American Liberalism.* New Haven: Yale University Press, 2001.

Brown, Ruth Murray. *"For a Christian America": A History of the Religious Right.* Amherst, N.Y.: Prometheus Books, 2002.

Brownlee, W. Elliot, and Graham, Hugh Davis. *The Reagan Presidency: Pragmatic Conservatism and Its Legacies.* Lawrence, Kan.: University Press of Kansas, 2003.

Buchanan, Patrick J. *Where the Right Went Wrong: How Neoconservatives Subverted the Reagan Revolution and Hijacked the Bush Presidency.* New York: Thomas Dunne Books, 2004.

Buckley, Jr., William F. *God and Man at Yale: The Superstitions of Academic Freedom.* Chicago: Regnery, 1951.

———. "Henry Salvatori, RIP." *National Review* (August 11, 1997).

———. *Inveighing We Will Go.* New York: G.P. Putnam's Sons, 1972.

———. "Marvin Liebman, RIP." *National Review* (April 12, 1997).

———. *Miles Gone By: A Literary Autobiography.* Washington, D.C.: Regnery, 2004.

———. "The Question of Robert Welch." *National Review* (February 13, 1962).

———. *The Unmaking of a Mayor.* New York: Viking Press, 1966.

———. *Up from Liberalism.* New Rochelle, N.Y.: Arlington House, 1968.

Buckley, Jr., William F., and Bozell, L. Brent, *McCarthy and His Enemies: The Record and Its Meaning.* Chicago: Regnery, 1954.

Burnham, James, *The Coming Defeat of Communism.* New York: John Day, 1950.

———. *Congress and the American Tradition.* Chicago: H. Regnery Co., 1959.

———. *The Struggle for the World.* New York: John Day, 1947.

———. *The Suicide of the West: An Essay on the Meaning and Destiny of Liberalism.* New Rochelle, N.Y.: Arlington House, 1964.

Callahan, David. "Liberal Policy's Weak Foundations." *Nation* (November 13, 1995).

Cannon, Lou. *Governor Reagan: His Rise to Power.* New York: Public Affairs, 2003.

———. *President Reagan: The Role of a Lifetime.* New York: Simon & Schuster, 1991.

Carney, Timothy P. *The Big Ripoff: How Big Business and Big Government Steal Your Money.* Hoboken, N.J.: John Wiley & Sons, 2006.

Chamberlain, John *A Life with the Printed Word.* Washington, D.C.: Regnery Gateway, 1982.

Chambers, Whittaker. *Witness.* New York: Random House, 1952.

———. "Big Sister Is Watching You." *National Review* (December 28, 1957).

Cockett, Richard. *Thinking the Unthinkable: Think-Tanks and the Economic Counter-Revolution, 1931–1983.* London: HarperCollins, 1995.

Colacello, Bob. *Ronnie and Nancy: Their Path to the White House, 1911 to 1980.* New York: Warner Books, 2004.

Collier, Peter, and Horowitz, David. *Destructive Generation: Second Thoughts about the Sixties.* New York: Free Press, 1996.

Cornuelle, H.C. *Mr. Anonymous, The Story of William Volker.* Caldwell, Idaho: Caxton Printers, 1951.

Critchlow, Donald T. *Phyllis Schlafly and Grassroots Conservatism: A Woman's Crusade.* Princeton: Princeton University Press, 2005.

Davis, Martin. "Measuring Success in Generations." *Philanthropy Magazine* (May/June 2004).

Decter, Midge. "Breaking Away." *Hoover Digest* (January 2002).

Diamond, Sarah. *Not by Politics Alone: The Enduring Influence of the Christian Right.* New York: Guildford Press, 1998.

———. *Spiritual Warfare: The Politics of the Christian Right.* Boston: South End Press, 1989.

Diggins, John Patrick. *The Rise and Fall of the American Left.* New York: W. W. Norton, 1992.

———. *Up from Communism: Conservative Odysseys in American Intellectual History.* New York: Harper & Row, 1975.

D'Souza, Dinesh. *Falwell, Before the Millennium: A Critical Biography.* Chicago: Regnery, 1983.

———. "Pat Robertson's World." *American Spectator* (November 1986).

Dunn, Charles, and Woodard, J. David. *American Conservatism from Burke to Bush: An Introduction.* Lanham, Md.: Madison Books, 1991.

East, John P. *The American Conservative Movement: The Philosophical Founders.* Chicago: Regnery Books, 1986.

Edwards, Lee. *Bringing Justice to the People.* Washington, D.C.: Heritage Foundation, 2004.

———. *The Conservative Revolution: The Movement that Remade America.* New York: Free Press, 1999.

———. *Educating for Liberty.* Washington, D.C.: Regnery, 2003.

————. *Goldwater: The Man Who Made a Revolution*. Washington, D.C.: Regnery, 1995.

————. *Missionary for Freedom: The Life and Times of Walter Judd*. New York: Paragon House, 1990.

Epstein, Richard. *How Progressives Rewrote the Constitution*. Washington, D.C.: Cato Institute Press, 2006.

Ericson, Jr., Edward D. and Mahoney, Daniel J., eds. *The Solzhenitsyn Reader: New and Essential Writings, 1947–2005*. Wilmington: ISI Books, 2006.

Evans, M. Stanton. *The Future of Conservatism*. New York: Holt, Rinehart and Winston, 1968.

————. *The Revolt on the Campus*. Chicago: Regnery, 1961.

————. *The Theme Is Freedom: Religion, Politics, and the American Tradition*. Washington, D.C.: Regnery, 1994.

Evans, Rowland and Novak, Robert. *Nixon in the White House: The Frustration of Power*. New York: Random House, 1971.

Evans, Thomas W. *The Education of Ronald Reagan: The General Electric Years and the Untold Story of His Conversion to Conservatism*. New York: Columbia University Press, 2006.

Falwell, Jerry. *Falwell: An Autobiography*. Lynchburg, VA: Liberty House Publishers, 1997.

Forster, Arnold, and Epstein, Benjamin R. *Danger on the Right*. New York: Random House, 1964.

Friedman, Milton. *Capitalism and Freedom*. Chicago: University of Chicago Press, 1960.

Friedman, Milton, and Friedman, Rose. *Two Lucky People: Memoirs*. Chicago: University of Chicago Press, 1998.

Friedman, Murray. *The Neoconservative Revolution: Jewish Intellectuals and the Shaping of Public Policy*. New York: Cambridge University Press, 2005.

Frohnen, Bruce, Beer, Jeremy, and Nelson, Jeffrey O., eds. *American Conservatism: An Encyclopedia*. Wilmington: ISI Books, 2005.

Galbraith, John Kenneth. "An Agenda for American Liberals." *Commentary* (June 1966).

Gilder, George. *Wealth and Poverty*. New York: Basic Books, 1981.

Glazer, Nathan. "Neoconservatives From the Start." *Public Interest* (Spring 2005).

Goldwater, Barry M. *The Conscience of a Conservative*. New York: McFadden Books, 1960.

————. *With No Apologies*. New York: Morrow, 1979.

Goldwater, Barry M., with Casserly, Jack, *Goldwater*. New York: Doubleday, 1988.

Gottfried, Paul. *The Conservative Movement*. New York: Twayne Publishers, 1993.

Green, John C., Rozell, Mark J., and Wilcox, Clyde, eds. *The Christian Right in American Politics: Marching to the Millennium*. Washington, D.C.: Georgetown University Press, 2003.

Greenburg, Jan Crawford. *Supreme Conflict: The Inside Story for the Struggle for Control of the United States Supreme Court*. New York: Penguin, 2007.

Gurda, John. *The Bradley Legacy: Lynde and Harry Bradley, Their Company, and Their Foundation*. Milwaukee: Lynde and Harry Bradley Foundation, 1992.

Hall, Kermit L., ed. *The Oxford Companion to the Supreme Court of the United States*. New York: Oxford University Press, 1992.

Halper, Stefan A. and Clark, Jonathan. *America Alone: The Neoconservatives and the Global Order*. Cambridge: Cambridge University Press, 2004.

Hart, Jeffrey. *The American Dissent: A Decade of Modern Conservatism*. Garden City, N.Y.: Doubleday, 1966.

———. *The Making of the American Conservative Mind: National Review and Its Times*. Wilmington: ISI Books, 2005.

Hartwell, R.M. *A History of the Mont Pelerin Society*. Indianapolis: Liberty Fund, 1995.

Hazlitt, Henry. *Economics in One Lesson: The Shortest and Surest Way to Understand Basic Economics*. New York: Three Rivers Press, 1988.

Hayek, Friedrich A. *The Constitution of Liberty*. Chicago: University of Chicago Press, 1960.

———. *The Road to Serfdom*. Chicago: University of Chicago Press, 1944.

———. *Studies in Philosophy, Politics and Economics*. Chicago: University of Chicago Press, 1967.

Hayward, Steven F. *The Age of Reagan: The Fall of the Old Liberal Order, 1964–1980*. Roseville, Calif.: Prima, 2001.

Hodgson, Godfrey. *The World Turned Right Side Up*. Boston: Houghton Mifflin, 1996.

Hoeveler, J. David. *New Humanism: A Critique of Modern America, 1900–1940*. Charlottesville: University of Virginia Press, 1977.

———. *Watch on the Right: Conservative Intellectuals in the Reagan Era*. Madison: University of Wisconsin Press, 1991.

Hollander, Paul. *Political Pilgrims: Travels of Western Intellectuals to the Soviet Union, China, and Cuba, 1928–1978*. New York: Oxford University Press, 1981.

Johnson, Paul. *A History of the American People.* New York: HarperCollins, 1997.

Judis, John B. "Trotskyism to Anachronism: The Neoconservative Revolution." *Foreign Affairs* 73 (July–August, 1995).

———. *William F. Buckley, Jr.: Patron Saint of the Conservatives.* New York: Simon & Schuster, 1988.

Katcher, Leo. *Earl Warren: A Political Biography.* New York: McGraw-Hill, 1967.

Kelly, Daniel. *James Burnham and the Struggle for the World: A Life.* Wilmington, Del.: ISI Books, 2002.

Kendall, Willmoore, and Carey, George. *Basic Symbols of the American Political Tradition.* Baton Rouge, La.: Louisiana State University Press, 1970.

———. *Willmoore Kendall Contra Mundum.* New Rochelle, N.Y.: Arlington House, 1971.

Kilpatrick, James J. *The Lasting South.* Chicago: Regnery, 1957.

———. *The Sovereign States: Notes of a Citizen of Virginia.* Chicago: H. Regnery Co., 1957.

Kimball, Roger. "The Power of James Burnham." *New Criterion* (September 2002).

Kirk, Russell. *Academic Freedom.* Chicago: H. Regnery Co., 1955.

———. *The American Cause.* Chicago: H. Regnery Co., 1957.

———. *The Conservative Mind: From Burke to Santayana.* Chicago: Regnery, 1953.

———. *Program for Conservatives.* Chicago: H. Regnery Co., 1954.

———. *The Roots of American Order.* Wilmington, Del.: ISI Books, 2003.

Kirk, Russell, and McClellan, James. *The Political Principles of Robert A. Taft.* Chicago: Wilcox and Follett, 1952.

Kirkpatrick, Jeane. "Dictatorships and Double Standards." *Commentary* (November 1979).

Klatch, Rebecca. *A Generation Divided: The New Left, the New Right, and the 1960s.* Berkeley, Calif.: University of California Press, 1999.

Klehr, Harvey, and Haynes, John Earl. *The American Communist Movement: Storming Heaven Itself.* New York: Twayne Publishers, 1992.

Koon, Stacey, with Dietz, Robert. *Presumed Guilty: The Tragedy of the Rodney King Affair.* Washington, D.C.: Regnery Gateway, 1992.

Kristol, Irving. "Forty Good Years." *The Public Interest* (Spring 2005).

———. *Neoconservatism: The Autobiography of an Idea.* New York: Free Press, 1995.

———. "The Neoconservative Persuasion." *Weekly Standard* (August 25, 2003).

Leef, George C. *Free Choice for Workers: A History of the Right To Work Movement.* Ottawa, Ill.: Jameson Books, 2005.

Liebman, Marvin. *Coming Out Conservative.* San Francisco: Chronicle Books, 1992.

Lowry, Rich. "Big Government Falls Flat." *National Review* (February 21, 2006).

Lyons, Eugene. *Herbert Hoover: A Biography.* Garden City: Doubleday, 1964.

MacDonald, Heather. "The Billions of Dollars that Made Things Worse." *City Journal* (Autumn 1996).

Martin, William C. *With God on Our Side: The Rise of the Religious Right in America.* New York: Broadway Books, 1996.

McAllister, Ted V. *Revolt against Modernity: Leo Strauss, Eric Voegelin, and the Search for a Post-Liberal Order.* Lawrence, Kan.: University of Kansas Press, 1995.

McDonald, W. Wesley. *Russell Kirk and the Age of Ideology.* Columbia, Mo.: University of Missouri Press, 2004.

McGuigan, Patrick B., and Weyrich, Dawn M. *Ninth Justice: The Fight for Bork.* Washington, D.C.: Free Congress Foundation, 1990.

McNamara, Patrick. *A Catholic Cold War: Edmund J. Walsh, S.J., and the Politics of American Anticommunism.* New York: Fordham University Press, 2005.

Meese, Edwin. *With Reagan: The Inside Story.* Washington, D.C.: Regnery Gateway, 1992.

Methvin, Eugene. "Up from Activism." *American Spectator* (May 2006).

Meyer, Frank. "Conservatism and Republican Candidates." *National Review* (December 12, 1967).

———. *In Defense of Freedom and Related Essays.* Indianapolis: Liberty Fund, 1996.

———. "Freedom, Tradition, Conservatism." *Modern Age* 4 (Fall 1960): 355–363.

———. "Richard M. Weaver: An Appreciation." *Modern Age* 14 (Summer-Fall 1970): 243–48.

Micklethwait, John and Wooldridge, Adrian. *The Right Nation: Conservative Power in America.* New York: Penguin Press, 2004.

Miles, Michael W. *The Odyssey of the American Right.* New York: Oxford University Press, 1980.

Miller, John J. *A Gift of Freedom: How the John M. Olin Foundation Changed America*. San Francisco: Encounter Books, 2006.

———. *Strategic Investment in Ideas: How Two Foundations Reshaped America*. Washington, D.C.: Philanthropy Roundtable, 2003.

Morley, Felix. *Freedom and Federalism*. Chicago: H. Regnery Co., 1959.

———. "American Conservatism Today." *National Review* (March 24, 1964).

Moynihan, Daniel P. "The Professors and the Poor." *Commentary* (August 1968).

Muncy, Mitchell S., and Richard John Neuhaus, eds., *The End of Democracy? The Judicial Usurpation of Politics*. Dallas: Spence, 1997.

Murphy, Paul V. *The Rebuke of History: The Southern Agrarians and American Conservative Thought*. Chapel Hill, N.C.: University of North Carolina Press, 2001.

Murray, Charles. *Losing Ground: American Social Policy, 1950–1980*. New York: Basic Books, 1994.

Nash, George. *The Conservative Intellectual Movement in America Since 1945*. Wilmington, Del.: ISI Books, 1997.

Neuchterlein, James. "Neoconservatism Redux." *First Things* (October 1996).

Niels-Bjerre-Poulsen. *Right Face: Organizing the American Conservative Movement, 1945–1965*. Copenhagen: Museum Tusculanum Press, 2002.

Nisbet, Robert A. *Conservatism: Dream and Reality*. Minneapolis: University of Minnesota Press, 1986.

———. *The Quest for Community: A Study in the Ethics of Order and Freedom*. New York: Oxford University Press, 1953.

Novak, Michael. *The Spirit of Democratic Capitalism*. New York: Simon & Schuster, 1982.

O'Brien, David M. *Storm Center: The Supreme Court in American Politics*. New York: W.W. Norton, 1986.

Olasky, Marvin. *Compassionate Conservatism: What It Is, What It Does, and How It Can Transform America*. New York: Free Press, 2000.

———. *The Tragedy of American Compassion*. Washington, D.C.: Regnery, 1992.

Patterson, James T. *Mr. Republican: A Biography of Robert A. Taft*. Boston: Houghton Mifflin, 1972.

Pauken, Thomas W. *The Thirty Years War: The Politics of the Sixties Generation*. Ottawa, IL: Jameson Books, 1995.

Perlstein, Rick. *Before the Storm: Barry Goldwater and the Unmaking of the American Consensus.* New York: Hill and Wang, 2001.

Person, James. *Russell Kirk: A Critical Biography of a Conservative Mind.* Lanham, Md.: Madison Books, 1999.

Pestritto, Ronald J. *Woodrow Wilson and the Roots of Modern Liberalism.* Lanham, Md.: Rowman & Littlefield, 2005.

Phillips, Kevin. *The Emerging Republican Majority.* New Rochelle, N.Y.: Arlington House, 1969.

Piereson, James. "Investing in Conservative Ideas." *Commentary* (May 2005).

Podhoretz, Norman. *Breaking Ranks: A Political Memoir.* London: Weidenfeld & Nicholson, 1979.

Powe, Jr., Lucas. *The Warren Court in American Politics.* Cambridge: Harvard University Press, 2000.

Powers, Richard Gid. *Not Without Honor: The History of American Anti-communism.* New York: Free Press, 1995.

Presser, Stephen B. *Recapturing the Constitution: Race, Religion, and Abortion Reconsidered.* Washington, D.C.: Regnery, 1994.

Reagan, Ronald. *An American Life.* New York: Simon & Schuster, 1990.

———. *Speaking My Mind.* New York: Simon & Schuster, 1989.

Regnery, Henry. *Creative Chicago: From the Chap-Book to the University.* Evanston: Chicago Historical Bookworks, 1993.

———. *A Few Reasonable Words: Selected Writings.* Wilmington, Del.: ISI, 1996.

———. *Memoirs of a Dissident Publisher.* Chicago: Regnery Books, 1985.

———. *A Perfect Sowing: Reflections of a Bookman,* Jeffrey Nelson, ed. Wilmington, Del.: ISI Books, 1999.

———. *William H. Regnery and His Family.* Three Oaks, Mich.: Henry Regnery, 1981.

Rich, Adam. "The War of Ideas: Why Mainstream and Liberal Foundations and the Think Tanks They Support Are Losing the War of Ideas in American Politics." *Stanford Social Innovation Review* (Spring 2005).

Robinson, Peter. *How Ronald Reagan Changed My Life.* New York: Regan Books, 2003.

Roepke, Wilhelm. "Liberalism and Christianity." *Modern Age* 1 (Fall 1957).

———. *Economics of the Free Society.* Chicago: Henry Regnery Company, 1963.

Rossiter, Clinton L. *Conservatism in America: The Thankless Persuasion.* New York: Knopf, 1962.

Rossum, Ralph. *Antonin Scalia's Jurisprudence: Text and Tradition.* Lawrence: University of Kansas Press, 2006.

————. *Federalism, the Supreme Court and the Seventeenth Amendment: The Irony of Constitutional Democracy.* Lanham, Md.: Lexington Books, 2001.

Rusher, William. *The Making of the New Majority Party.* New York: Sheed & Ward, 1975.

————. *The Rise of the Right.* New York: Morrow, 1984.

Shadegg, Stephen. *Barry Goldwater: Freedom Is His Flight Plan.* New York: Fleet, 1962.

Schlafly, Phyllis. *A Choice Not an Echo.* Alton, IL: Pere Marquette Press, 1964.

Schneider, Gregory L. *Cadres for Conservatism: Young Americans for Freedom and the Rise of the Contemporary Right.* New York: NYU Press, 1999.

Schoenwald, Jonathan M. *A Time for Choosing: The Rise of Modern American Conservatism.* Oxford: Oxford, 2001.

Schwartz, Bernard. *A History of the Supreme Court.* New York: Oxford University Press, 1993.

Skinner, Kieron Anderson, Annelise and Anderson, Martin, eds., *Reagan: A Life in Letters.* New York: Free Press, 2003.

————. *Reagan in His Own Hand: The Writings of Ronald Reagan That Reveal His Revolutionary Vision for America.* New York: Free Press, 2001.

————. *Reagan's Path to Victory: The Shaping of Ronald Reagan's Vision: Selected Writings.* New York: Free Press, 2004.

Smant, Kevin J. *Principles and Heresies: Frank S. Meyer and the Shaping of the American Conservative Movement.* Wilmington, Del.: ISI Books, 2002.

Sowell, Thomas. "The Poverty Pimp's Poem." *Jewish World Review* (October 30, 1998).

Stanlis, Peter. *Edmund Burke and the Natural Law.* Ann Arbor, Mich.: University of Michigan Press, 1958.

Starbuck, Dane. *The Goodriches: An American Family.* Indianapolis: Liberty Fund, 2001.

Stein, Herbert. *Presidential Economics: The Making of Economic Policy from Roosevelt to Reagan and Beyond.* New York: Simon & Schuster, 1984.

Stigler, George. *Memoirs of an Unregulated Economist*. New York: Basic Books, 1985.

Strauss, Leo. *Natural Right and History*. Chicago: University of Chicago Press, 1953

Swan, Patrick A., ed. *Alger Hiss, Whittaker Chambers, and the Schism in the American Soul*. Wilmington, Del.: ISI Books, 2002.

Tanenhaus, Sam. "The Buckley Effect." *New York Times Magazine* (October 5, 2005).

———. *Whittaker Chambers: A Biography*. New York: Random House, 1997.

Tyrrell, Jr., R. Emmett. *The Conservative Crack-Up*. New York: Simon & Schuster, 1992.

Unger Irwin, and Unger, Debi. *Turning Point: 1968*. New York: Scribner, 1988.

Viereck, Peter. *Conservatism Revisited: The Revolt Against Revolt, 1815–1949*. New York: Scribner, 1949.

Viguerie, Richard, and Franke, David. *America's Right Turn: How Conservatives Used New and Alternative Media to Take Power*. Chicago: Bonus Books, 2004.

———. *Conservatives Betrayed: How George W. Bush and Other Big Government Republicans Hijacked the Conservative Cause*. Los Angeles: Bonus Books, 2006.

———. and Allen, Steven J. *Lip Service: George Bush's Thirty Year Battle with Conservatives*. Chantilly, VA: CP Books, 1992.

———. *The New Right: We're Ready to Lead*. Washington, D.C.: Viguerie, 1980.

Voegelin, Eric. *Autobiographical Reflections*. Baton Rouge: Louisiana State University Press, 1989.

———. *The New Science of Politics*. Chicago, University of Chicago Press, 1952.

———. *Order and History, Vol. 2: The World of the Polis*. Baton Rouge: Louisiana State University Press, 1957.

Wanniski, Jude. *The Way the World Works*. Chicago: Regnery Publishing, 1978.

Weaver, Richard M. *Ideas Have Consequences*. Chicago: University of Chicago Press, 1948.

Weinstein, Allan. *Perjury: The Hiss-Chambers Case*. New York: Random House, 1997.

Witcover, Jules. *The Party of the People: A History of the Democrats*. New York: Random House, 2003.

White, F. Clifton, with Gill, William J. *Suite 3505: The Story of the Draft Goldwater Movement.* New Rochelle, N.Y.: Arlington House, 1967.

White, G. Edward *Alger Hiss' Looking Glass Wars: The Covert Life of a Soviet Spy.* Oxford: Oxford University Press, 2004.

———. *Earl Warren: A Public Life.* New York: Oxford University Press, 1982.

Yergin, Daniel. *The Commanding Heights: The Battle between Government and the Marketplace that Is Remaking the Modern World.* New York: Simon & Schuster, 1998.

PERSONAL INTERVIEWS BY THE AUTHOR

Anderson, Martin, The Hoover Institution, Stanford University, Palo Alto, California, July 14, 2005 and October 16, 2006

Bork, Robert, McLean, Virginia, February 25, 2007

Buchanan, Patrick J., McLean, Virginia, December 5, 2006

Buckley, William F., Jr., Stamford, Connecticut, June 9, 2005 and New York City, June 23, 2005

Codevilla, Angelo, Plymouth, California, July 17, 2005

Cooper, Chuck, Washington, D.C., April 17, 2007

Cribb, T. Kenneth, Washington, D.C., December 6, 2006

Decter, Midge, New York City, October 6, 2006

Eberle, Bruce, Vienna, Virginia, February 14, 2006

Friedman, Milton, San Francisco, California, July 12, 2005

Gingrich, Newt, Washington, D.C., December 6, 2006

Ginsberg, Judge Douglas, Washington, D.C., January 19, 2007

Goeglein, Tim, Washington, D.C., January 16, 2006

Hodel, Donald, Washington, D.C., March 14, 2006

Kannon, John von, Washington, D.C. April 12, 2006

Keene, David, Washington, D.C., June 10, 2007

Laxalt, Paul, Washington, D.C., October 24, 2006

Leo, Leonard, Washington, D.C., December 28, 2006

McIntosh, David, Washington, D.C. September 6, 2006

Meese, Edwin, Washington, D.C. January 4, 2007

Meyer, Eugene, Washington, D.C., May 24, 2006

Pence, Michael, Washington, D.C., December 6, 2006

Perkins, Tony, Washington, D.C., December 6, 2006

Robinson, Ron, Herndon, Virginia, November 30, 2006

Rusher, William, San Francisco, California, July 12, 2005

Schlafly, Phyllis, Washington, D.C., November 10, 2005

Viguerie, Richard, Manassas, Virginia, March 23, 2006

INDEX